SHADOW OVER THE ATLANTIC

OSPREY
PUBLISHING

Aside, of course, from the veterans of *Fernaufklärungsgruppe* 5, four individuals played a key role in the gestation of the story that follows. In this regard, I would like to mention Hellmut Hetz, Bob Hanes and Eddie J. Creek who, many years ago, brought to my attention the work of Oskar H. Schmidt, without which, this book would never have been written.

Shadow over the Atlantic is dedicated to those four gentlemen.

SHADOW

OVER THE

ATLANTIC

The Luftwaffe and the U-boats: 1943–45

ROBERT FORSYTH

First published in Great Britain in 2017 by Osprey Publishing,
PO Box 883, Oxford, OX1 9PL, UK
1385 Broadway, 5th Floor, New York, NY 10018, USA
E-mail: info@ospreypublishing.com

OSPREY PUBLISHING, PART OF BLOOMSBURY PUBLISHING PLC

OSPREY is a trademark of Osprey Publishing, a division of Bloomsbury Publishing Plc.

ISBN: 978 1 4728 2045 7
PDF ISBN: 978 1 4728 2046 4
ePub ISBN: 978 1 4728 2047 1

Index by Zoe Ross
Cartography by Bounford.com
Profile and badge artwork (plate section, pp. 38–40) by Jim Laurier
Typeset in Adobe Garamond Pro and Bodoni
Originated by PDQ Digital Media, Bungay, Suffolk
Printed in China through World Print Ltd.

17 18 19 20 21   10 9 8 7 6 5 4 3 2 1

Osprey Publishing supports the Woodland Trust, the UK's leading woodland conservation charity. Between 2014 and 2018 our donations are being spent on their Centenary Woods project in the UK.

To find out more about our authors and books visit **www.ospreypublishing.com**. Here you will find extracts, author interviews, details of forthcoming events and the option to sign up for our newsletter.

Front cover: An in-flight view of Ju 290A-5 Wk-Nr 0170 KR+LA (EN Archive) (also on Title page); below, an Allied shipping vessel is attacked by a German U-boat. (Topfoto.co.uk)
The following images within the plate section were kindly supplied by the Hetz family:
Officers of 3.(F)/Aufkl.Gr.10 (p. 3); Hptm Fischer, Maj Augustin, Oblt Schmidt (all p. 9); Officers and NCOs of 1.Staffel (p.10); Senior NCOs of FAGr 5, Villa in Mont de Marsan (both p. 11); Lt Wessel, Officers of the *Gruppenstab* (both p. 13); Officers and NCOs of the *Stabskompanie* (p. 14); NCOs of 1./FAGr 5 (p. 17); Hptm Nather, Hptm Bergen and Oblt Heindorff (both p. 19); Hptm Eckl (p. 24); Hptm Fischer and Oblt Abel (p.26); Officers of 1./FAGr 5, *Gruppe* football team (both p.29); Camouflaged vehicles (p.33); Vehicle of FAGr 5 with MG 151 (p.34); FAGr 5 trailer, Three officers of FAGr 5 (both p.35).

CONTENTS

INTRODUCTION AND ACKNOWLEDGEMENTS

'I've got something for you.'

So announced my good friend, Eddie Creek, upon his return from a holiday in the United States. It was 13 years ago. Eddie was visiting our office at the time and, with a wry smile, dropped onto my desk a slender, softcover volume in an untitled, wine red cover.

I raised an eyebrow and glanced at him quizzically before picking it up and flicking through it. There were 145 pages and they were covered in typewritten German text. There was the occasional, pencilled annotation in the margin. It looked like a typed draft or a manuscript.

I went to the first page where there was a title: *Fernaufklärungsgruppe 5 Atlantik – Eine Aufzeichnung von Oskar H. Schmidt.*

To say my jaw dropped or my heart missed a beat would be untrue, but my eyes did widen a little in surprise. I seem to recall that I simply looked at Eddie and murmered '*How…?*'

It was a rare history of a little-known but most interesting Luftwaffe unit – one that I knew had flown Junkers Ju 290s from western France in 1943/44 on long-range reconnaissance and convoy-shadowing operations in support of the U-boats. As far as I was aware, in the English language at least, there was very little known about its activities. But here was an account written by the former chief of the *Stabskompanie* of the *Gruppe* based partly on his memory and the memories of his former comrades, partly on private records and partly on official reports.

It transpired that, while in America, Eddie had visited his good friend and fellow aviation enthusiast, Bob Hanes. Bob, in turn, had known the late

Hellmut Hetz, a former pilot in 1./*Fernaufklärungsgruppe* 5 (FAGr 5), well from when they had both worked for Eastern Airlines. Bob recalls:

> I met Hellmut when I was working for Eastern Airlines in Houston, Texas. He was the Chief Check-Out Pilot for Eastern Airlines at JFK Airport. We spent a number of evenings talking about his experiences flying in the Luftwaffe, as he had flown so many different types of aircraft, including the Ju 88, Ju 188 and the Ju 290. He was also a test pilot on the Me 262 and went operational on the Ar 234 towards the end of the war. He used to kid that he was one of the first American war brides, as he had married an American in Germany after the war. He was a real gentleman and a hell of a pilot. I had told Hellmut that I was very interested in the Ju 290, as I had never read too much about the aircraft, and his wife, Romaine, was kind enough to send this package to me after his death.

Although this intriguing piece of Luftwaffe history subsequently fell into my hands, and I could see its significance, I was also aware from information on the Internet that a book project on FAGr 5 was, apparently, already under way in Germany, though there were no details. So I put the Schmidt volume on my shelf – where it would remain for a long time – and waited eagerly for the book's publication.

The following year, 2004, and with no further news, I decided to write to Oskar H. Schmidt telling him I had a copy of his work and asking whether it would be possible to meet him in Germany to discuss the possibility of my writing a history of FAGr 5. *Herr* Schmidt replied:

> In the confusion of the last days of the war, together with my friend and *Kommandeur*, Hermann Fischer, I left some cases containing important documents (logbooks and war diaries) with a farmer in central Germany. We believed they would be safe there. But with the division of Germany, this area – the DDR (German Democratic Republic) – fell under Soviet control. It was only after the reunification of Germany that I was able to get in contact with the farmer's surviving children. However, I was informed that the cases were taken off by the Russians and have never been seen since.

As such, *Herr* Schmidt regretted that he was unable to help further but wished me 'all the best for your further investigations and much success.'

Over the coming years, as I visited archives in the UK and Germany to undertake research on other writing projects, I would use any spare time I had to locate information, no matter how inconsequential, on the history of

FAGr 5. I also mentioned to a few fellow aviation researchers that I was interested in the unit. Very gradually, I began to build up a file of documentary information and, with the aid of Schmidt's work, a more complete picture of the unit's activities began to emerge.

Beyond Oskar H. Schmidt's account, the most detailed coverage of FAGr 5's history can be found in Karl Kössler's and Günther Ott's excellent 1993 book *Die großen Dessauer: Junkers Ju 89, Ju 90, Ju 290, Ju 390* (Aviatic Verlag). To this day, this book forms an essential and unrivalled study of the Ju 290 and the units with which it served. It proved a key aid to my research. These authors had access to many surviving logbooks of former FAGr 5 aircrew.

A more recently available and invaluable resource, which shines light on the operations of the *Gruppe*, are the HW 13 files held at the UK National Archives, comprising records of the Government Code and Cypher School. These files contain a detailed summary of British radio intercepts and intelligence on Luftwaffe operations over the Bay of Biscay and the Atlantic. To this can be added various British Air Ministry translations of German reports, British interrogation reports and, assisting with 'the view from the other side', RAF combat reports and diaries. In Germany, the Bundesarchiv-Militärarchiv yielded a fascinating report compiled by the *Kommandeur* of FAGr 5 on his unit's activities in late 1943.

After absorbing all the information I had amassed and read, I was left with an impression of 'heroic failure'; the crews of FAGr 5 had a thankless, tiring and, unlike their fighter pilot comrades, an inglorioius task. They would spend many hours in their big Ju 290s, flying over endless stretches of grey sea, more often than not in dreadful weather, using technology that was often faulty, to try to locate enemy convoys, which against the vastness of the ocean, really did equate to needles in haystacks. They had to undertake these missions often in a lone aircraft against the prospect of ever-increasing enemy air opposition. And crucially, despite continual demands from Grossadmiral Karl Dönitz for air reconnaissance support for his U-boats, they did it with woefully inadequate numbers of aircraft. Yet, to execute such missions required very skilled pilots, highly trained navigators and radio operators, and sharp-eyed gunners, all with plenty of stamina.

Ultimately, however, FAGr 5 was unable to render sufficient assistance to the U-boats, but that was no fault of its crews. To the contrary, they proved themselves equal to their task time and again.

Meanwhile, several years passed, but still no book on the *Gruppe* appeared from anywhere else. Then, in early 2015, I received an offer to publish the story and so, after 12 years of inaction, it became a case of *carpe diem*.

In writing this book, I must acknowledge, first and foremost, Oskar H. Schmidt, upon whose endeavours, together with those of his comrades, it is largely based. However, during my research and preparation I received assistance from several colleagues and fellow researchers and in this regard I would like to express my foremost thanks to 'my Old Texas Friend', Bob Hanes, and to Eddie J. Creek, for introducing me to Oskar Schmidt's history of the *Gruppe*. My thanks also to Nick Beale for kindly contributing the fruits of his research into the little-known 4./FAGr 5; his chapter on this *Staffel* serves to enhance and complete the story. At the time of writing, Nick runs a fascinating and extensive website at www.ghostbombers.com which shines a light on many aspects of Luftwaffe history that may otherwise lie undiscovered. It is thoroughly recommended.

Eddie J. Creek, Dave Wadman, J. Richard Smith, Edgar Brooks, Andrew Arthy, Chris Goss, Martin Pegg, Steven Coates, Andy Thomas, Adam Thompson, Edwin 'Ted' Oliver, Juan Carlos Salgado Rodríguez, Gordon Williamson, Jochen Mahnke, Dr. James H. Kitchens III, Dennis Davison and Ian Burgham have all kindly helped with documents, photographs, opinions and general goodwill over the years, for which I am most grateful.

Dr. Konrad Knirim was good enough to allow me to reproduce the recollections of Hellmut Nagel. For those wishing to learn more about Luftwaffe navigational methods and timekeeping, Dr. Knirim is a leading authority on historic military watches and clocks. He is the author of the highly acclaimed *Militäruhren: 150 Jahre Zeitmessung beim deutschen Militär* (2002) and *British Military Timepieces* (2009). He runs a detailed website on military timepieces at www.knirim.de.

I would also like to acknowledge my editor, Tony Holmes, as well as Marcus Cowper, Kate Moore and Gemma Gardner at Osprey Publishing for their belief and support in this project.

My thanks too must go to Sally-Kate – as always. Her love and support have been immeasurable.

Robert Forsyth
November 2016

AUTHOR'S NOTE

TIMES AND TIMING

All times in this book are as taken from original documents. However, the interpretation and understanding of the complexities of UK and Continental European time variations can be challenging, to say the least.

I can only recommend the late Roy Conyers Nesbit's illuminating overview in *RAF Records in the PRO*[1] from which I take the liberty of quoting an extract:

> ... the times of take-off and landing of aircraft based in the UK can vary from local time to Greenwich Mean Time (GMT), and ... it is sometimes difficult to distinguish which were entered in the records. Generally times were recorded in local time, but where they were taken from navigators' logs in Squadrons based in the UK, they were usually in GMT.
>
> During the war, local time varied from GMT to British Summer Time (BST, 1 hour in advance of GMT) to British Double Summer Time (BDST, 2 hours in advance of GMT). An example of this difference in times is:

GMT	BST	BDST
14.00 hrs =	*15.00 hrs =*	*16.00 hrs*

Local time in the UK varied as follows:

From	02.00 hrs Sunday	15 Aug 1943	BST
	02.00 hrs Sunday	2 Apr 1944	BDST
	02.00 hrs Sunday	17 Sep 1944	BST
	02.00 hrs Monday	2 Apr 1945	BDST

On the other hand, the Germans used Central European Time (CET, 1 hour in advance of GMT) and German Summer Time (GST, 2 hours in advance of GMT), so that for example:

GMT	CET	GST
14.00 hrs =	15.00 hrs =	16.00 hrs

Local time in Germany varied as follows:

From	02.00 hrs Monday	4 Oct 1943	CET
	02.00 hrs Monday	3 Apr 1944	GST
	02.00 hrs Monday	2 Oct 1944	CET
	02.00 hrs Monday	2 Apr 1945	GST

LUFTWAFFE NAVIGATIONAL LOCATION SYSTEM

Readers in this book will notice that many German navigational fix/position references follow a four-digit suffix after the line of longitude. For example '25° West 4546': this four-digit number was a reference to a map grid system comprised of larger ('*Großtrapez*'), medium ('*Mitteltrapez*') and small ('*Kleintrapez*') positional squares based on the *Gradnetzmeldeverfahren* ('grid method'). The size of a *Großtrapeze* was approximately 70 x 111 kilometres, while a *Mitteltrapez* had an area of approximately 35 x 28 kilometres and the *Kleintrapez* of approximately 9 x 11 kilometres. Each *Mitteltrapez* was, in turn, sub-divided into 8 numbered squares, and the *Kleintrapez* into numbered 9 squares, with the square reference numbers running sequentially in columns, from top to bottom, left to right as one looked at the map.

The above example of '25° West 4546' refers to a position in the Atlantic in '*Großtrapez*' 45 and then '*Mitteltrapez*' 4 (of 8 squares) and '*Kleintrapez*' 6 (of 9 squares).

Those readers wishing to know more details are recommended to consult the following websites available at the time of writing:

- The Luftwaffe Map Reference System (Gradnetzmeldeverfahren) by Andreas Brekken at:
  www.stormbirds.com/eagles/research/gradnetz/gradnetz.html
- Info for LUMA [Luftwaffe Grid Map Converter] at:
  http://www.gyges.dk/LUMA%20Guide%20v2007%2005.pdf

GLOSSARY

Abwehr	German Military Intelligence Service
Aufklärungsgruppe	Reconnaissance Group (flying)
B-Dienst (*Beobachtungsdienst*)	Interception and recording, decoding and analysis section of *Marinenachrichtendienst* (Naval Intelligence Service)
Befehlshaber der Unterseeboote (BdU)	Commander of Submarines
Bildoffizier	Photographic Officer
Deutsche Kreuz (DK)	German Cross
Deutsche Kreuz in Gold (DKG)	German Cross in Gold
Ehrenpokal	Honour Goblet awarded to Luftwaffe aircrews for 'For Special Achievement in the Air War'
Einsatzkommando	Operational Detachment
Erprobungsstelle	Test Centre
(F)/Aufkl.Gr	Long-Range Reconnaissance Group
Fernaufklärungsgruppe (FAGr)	Long-Range Reconnaissance Group
Fernerkunder	Long-range reconnaissance aircraft
Ferngerichtete Drehringlafetten (FDL)	remotely controlled gun mounts
Fliegerführer	Air Commander (usually a regional or functional tactical appointment)
Fliegerverbindungsoffizier (*Flivo*)	Air Liaison Officer
FuG (*Funk-Gerät*)	Radio set/apparatus/equipment
General der Aufklärungsflieger	Commanding General of the

14

	Reconnaissance Arm
Generalluftzeugmeister	Inspector-General of the Luftwaffe
Gross Registered Tonnage (GRT)	The volume of space on a ship available for cargo
Gruppe	Luftwaffe 'group' (usually comprising three or four *Staffeln*)
Gruppenstab	Group Staff
Hiwi (*Hilfswilliger*)	Foreign volunteer worker
Hydraulische Drehringlafetten (HDL)	hydraulically operated gun mounts
Instep	RAF term for patrol intended to shield Coastal Command units from enemy fighter attack while on operations in the Bay of Biscay
Kampfgeschwader (KG)	Bomber Wing
Kampfgeschwader zur besonderen Verwendung (KGr.z.b.V)	Battle Wing for Special Purposes
Koluft (*Kommandeur der Luftwaffe bei einem Armeeoberkommando*)	Luftwaffe Commander assigned to an Army command
Kommando der Erprobungsstellen (KdE)	Commander of Luftwaffe Test Centres
Kriegsmarine	German Navy
Küstenfernaufklärungsstaffel	Long-Range Coastal Reconnaissance Squadron
Küstenfliegergruppe (Kü.Fl.Gr.)	Coastal Air Group
Lufttransportstaffel (LTS)	Air Transport Squadron
Luftwaffenführungsstab	Luftwaffe Command Staff
MAC	Merchant Aircraft Carrier
Nachrichtenoffizier	Signals Officer
Oberkommando der Luftwaffe (Ob.d.L. later OKL)	High Command of the Luftwaffe
Oberkommando der Wehrmacht (OKW)	Supreme Command of the Armed Forces
Offizier zur besonderen Verwendung (Offz.z.b.V.)	Officer assigned for special duties
Organisation Todt	Nazi civil and military engineering group
Pulk	Slang given to a formation of enemy aircraft

Reichsluftministerium (RLM)	Reich Air Ministry
Reichsverkehrsministerium (RVM)	State Transport Ministry
Ritterkreuz	Knight's Cross
Schwan (or *Schwan-See*)	FuG 302 C 'Swan'/'Swan Lake' droppable radio buoy
Seeaufklärungsgruppe (SAGr)	Maritime Reconnaissance Group
Seekriegsleitung (SKL)	Maritime Warfare Command
Spiess	A title given to the Senior Sergeant or NCO of a unit
Stabskompanie	Staff Company
Technisches Amt	Technical Office
Unterseebootsflottille	U-boat flotilla
Verbandsführerschule	Unit Leaders' School
VLR	Very Long Range
Wetterwarte Atlantik	Atlantic Weather Station

CONVOY PREFIXES

HX	Halifax–UK
KMS	UK–North Africa–Port Said (Slow)
MKS	Mediterranean–North Africa–UK (Slow)
ON	UK–North America
ONS	UK–North America
OS	UK–West Africa
SC	Halifax–UK (Slow)
SL	Sierra Leone–UK

FERNAUFKLÄRUNGSGRUPPE 5 /
Ju 290 AND Ar 234 RANGES AND BASES: 1943–1945.

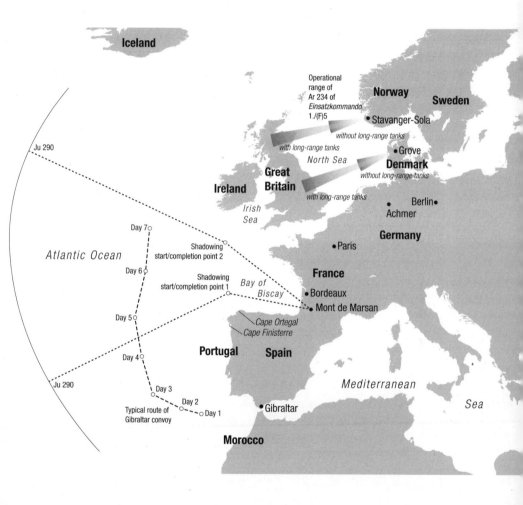

CHAPTER ONE

DARK WATERS

The Luftwaffe can raise not only the diminishing number of ships sunk by U-boats, but can strike a decisive blow against British sea power by paralysing her supplies. The Luftwaffe would fulfil its true purpose if so used.

'The Operational Use of the Luftwaffe in the War at Sea 1939–1943', Luftwaffe 8.*Abteilung* Historical Report, January 1944

In January 1944, in a report on the operational use of the German Air Force in the war at sea, an officer of the Luftwaffe historical research section wrote:

The Luftwaffe is particularly mobile. It is the Luftwaffe that as a rule locates a convoy and directs U-boats to it. It is the Luftwaffe that seeks out aircraft carriers in order to sink them first. It is the Luftwaffe that fights the U-boats' worst enemy, the fighter, and destroys enemy shipping unaided. But the engagements of the Luftwaffe are only of short duration. If an attack is unsuccessful, then the U-boats are at an advantage because they can lurk along the convoy route for a long period and make another attack later. The U-boat can also summon the Luftwaffe to make surprise attacks. If contact with the enemy is lost, it can again call on the Luftwaffe to carry out reconnaissance so that this may be restored. Both services accordingly help each other as well as possible. From this it is understood that the commands of the Luftwaffe and the U-boats must be closely connected.[1]

Some 30 years before, Imperial Germany was quick to recognize the tactical value of cooperation between the first U-boats and early military aeroplanes. A photograph from World War I shows a military seaplane resting on the surface of the water, while its observer stands on one of the aircraft's floats, clutching the leading edge of the wing to steady himself, as he passes the commander of a surfaced U-boat what is described as an 'important report.'[2]

Following the end of the war in 1918, Germany, despite being a vanquished naval power, never let go of its belief in the submarine as an effective weapon, and as the Weimar Republic gave way to the Nazi era and the process of rearmament, there were those who worked hard to drive forward a renewed U-boat construction programme. The man upon whose shoulders this task was chiefly placed was Karl Dönitz. The son of an optical engineer for Karl Zeiss at Jena, he had joined the *Kaiserliche Marine* (Imperial Navy) in 1910, receiving a commission three years later. His first years in the Navy were spent on board the cruiser *Breslau*, mostly in the Mediterranean.

Between 1916 and 1918 Dönitz served in the U-boat arm, but was captured after the sinking of his boat off Malta at the end of the war. In 1919 he joined the *Reichsmarine*, the small navy allowed Germany under the terms of the Treaty of Versailles. During the 1930s, he embraced National Socialism, and in 1935 was appointed by Generaladmiral Erich Raeder to (re)build the U-boat fleet.[3]

Dönitz held firmly to two principles; that in order to use U-boats effectively against enemy shipping in what he believed would be 'convoy' warfare, large numbers or 'packs' of boats would need to be deployed. This 'pack' philosophy envisaged groups of U-boats smashing through a convoy's defences, the convoy having first been located, with the boats assembled in the optimum position to launch a simultaneous attack. However, a prerequisite for this was the need for the best possible reconnaissance, preferably from the air. Indeed, as early as 1937, Dönitz recognized that air reconnaissance would, in fact, be *vital* to the efficacy of submarine warfare, especially since the U-boat in itself had little reconnaissance capability: 'it must act in cooperation with a branch of the armed forces more suited to reconnaissance duties. And for these, the best instrument is the aeroplane.'[4]

However, this requirement was at odds with fundamental Luftwaffe doctrine; in the years immediately before the outbreak of war in 1939, senior German military planners had envisaged and prepared for a 'strategic' deployment of the Luftwaffe in a war on land, mounted against enemies who were seen as potential threats to the 'security of the Reich'. Indeed, in January 1944, a Luftwaffe historical report noted that 'there had never been any doubt of the possibility and necessity of using the bulk of the Luftwaffe in full force for strategic purposes on land.'

Consequently, in technical terms, priority was placed on the development of aircraft suited for war over land against land forces. As such, aircraft and equipment intended for use in direct cooperation with the other branches of the armed services received lesser attention. The 'weaker' development was for cooperation with the Navy, for example, the stronger would be the strategic (land) force, which would benefit from better development and training. In such an environment the Kriegsmarine could expect support only from coastal reconnaissance in the Baltic and the North Sea, although it was also the intention to form air units for the aircraft carrier, *Graf Zeppelin*, then under construction.[5]

For some 20 years, the German Navy and Army had competed to build their own, autonomous air arms. German naval aviation had undergone a foundational and acrimonious change between 1935 and 1939, when General Hermann Göring, as commander of the new Luftwaffe, had grasped effective control of the *Luftwaffenkommando-See*, the small naval air arm operated by the Kriegsmarine, and in doing so responsibility for aerial reconnaissance and the air support of naval units when in contact with an enemy. This left tensions simmering between the Luftwaffe and the Kriegsmarine and, in reality, neither force could field significant assets under the prevailing infrastructure. Then, in 1937 a conference was held to agree the respective zones of operation for the air force and naval air units. The Kriegsmarine retained control only of those units deemed to be an extension of the fleet as well as some coastal aviation.[6]

In command of this revised air organization was the *Oberbefehlshaber der Luftwaffe – Führer der Seeluftstreitkräfte* (Commander of Naval Units on the Staff of the *Ob.d.L.*). In March 1939, this was redesignated as the *General der Luftwaffe beim Oberbefehlshaber der Marine* (Luftwaffe General to the Commander in Chief of the Navy) who reported directly to Göring (and who acted as the main liaison with the Kriegsmarine).[7] Under this arrangement, the Luftwaffe controlled the shadowing and reporting of enemy convoys and their locations, and all other shipping at sea and in coastal waters.

Joint air and naval exercises in the mid- to late 1930s conducted in the North Sea and the Baltic, involving reconnaissance aircraft, had shown that cooperation *was* possible, and the potential for Atlantic reconnaissance was also examined. During a major wargame manoeuvre in the winter of 1938/39, which included officers from the staff of the *General der Luftwaffe beim Oberbefehlshaber der Marine*, daily reconnaissance sorties had been despatched boldly across the North Sea and the Shetlands, to fly around the coasts of Britain and Ireland, returning over France.[8] By all accounts they were successful.

New aircraft deemed to be suitable for long-range maritime reconnaissance had been expected to become available during the late 1930s, but it was always an uphill struggle because Generalmajor Ernst Udet, the extrovert World War I fighter ace in charge of the Luftwaffe *Technisches Amt* (Technical Office), was an advocate of small, fast aircraft. Both he and General der Flieger Erhard Milch, the Secretary of State for Aviation, shared an aversion to long-range military aircraft because of their cost and the drain they placed on metal and other vital raw materials. Indeed, Göring had scrapped the four-engined Dornier Do 19 long-range bomber in April 1937, while the prototype Junkers Ju 89 was converted to become the Ju 90 transport (see Chapter Two).

When, however, in August 1938, a four-engined Focke-Wulf Fw 200 Condor airliner landed in New York on its record-breaking, non-stop propaganda flight across the Atlantic, for a while at least, a delighted Udet forgot his aversion to four-engined, long-range aircraft.

Whatever the motives of either side in the unsettled arrangement between the Luftwaffe and the Kriegsmarine, over the following years, and as the war progressed, the relationship that developed was never easy, a situation that was reflected in the very processes of 'cooperation'. Offensive operations against the British Home Fleet in October 1939 highlighted major shortcomings in the ability of Luftwaffe crews to fly in bad weather over the sea, resulting in a lack of reconnaissance, 'shadowing' and attack. On another occasion in the same month, in an operation off the east coast of England, a tactical plan failed between new Ju 88 Luftwaffe bombers and He 115 floatplanes of a naval *Küstenfliegergruppe* (coastal air group), resulting in the loss of four of the latter aircraft with damage to another. But worse was to come in February 1940, when Luftwaffe bombers erroneously sank two German destroyers engaged in an operation against British fishing vessels off Dogger Bank. Not surprisingly, Grossadmiral Raeder, Commander-in-Chief of the Kriegsmarine, was livid.[9]

The main long-range reconnaissance aircraft used by the Luftwaffe for maritime work at this time was the tandem-engined Dornier Do 18 flying boat, which equipped the small number of *Küstenfernaufklärungsstaffeln* (long-range coastal reconnaissance squadrons) of the *Küstenfliegergruppen* (coastal air groups). The Do 18 had originally been developed as a trans-ocean mailplane for Lufthansa in 1934, and four years later one example had achieved a seaplane record for flying non-stop in a straight line for 8800 km between England and Brazil. However, according to German opinion, it offered no real comparison to contemporary British aircraft and, aside from reconnaissance, even in terms of offensive capability, it had a restricted payload with no provision for carrying torpedoes or mines. At the end of October 1939, the Kriegsmarine admitted that the 56 Do 18s then available to it had achieved a total patrol range of 500,000 km, or just over 150 km per day. Furthermore, ten of the flying boats had been lost, with replacements arriving at a rate of only three per month. In an ominous portent of things to come, Admiral Alfred Saalwächter, commander of *Marinegruppe West*, noted that no increase in the supply of such aircraft could be expected.[10]

In 1939, Konteadmiral Dönitz held discussions with Major Edgar Petersen, a Luftwaffe staff officer who had also commanded the *Fernaufklärungsstaffel Ob.d.L.* Petersen was an advocate of long-distance and night flying and served as an adviser on the staff of Generalleutnant Hans Geisler, the commander of X. *Fliegerkorps* and one-time *Führer der Marineluftstreitkräfte*. In September 1939, Petersen had suggested to Geisler that existing Fw 200s could and should be converted for long-range reconnaissance purposes.[11] He believed that the Focke-Wulf would be able to fly from Germany, across France to the main U-boat operational area to the west of the English Channel, and back. The problem was that the first *Gruppe* of Fw 200s would not commence (bombing) operations until the spring of 1940.

By June 1940 the invasion of France had given the Germans airfields on the Atlantic coast and the U-Boat Staff Officer in the Naval Staff Operations Division was enthused:

> ...the possibility arises of air reconnaissance of the enemy convoy routes and disposition in the area south and south-west of Ireland and perhaps even in the remoter areas to the west and north. The task of the aircraft will be to intercept enemy convoys and other valuable ships, shadow them and, even if contact should be lost, regain it on the following morning.

At the same time, Dönitz was requested to produce his plans for direct cooperation between *Befehlshaber der Unterseeboote* (BdU) and the Naval Air Commander, and to ascertain from Göring what his intentions were in terms of rendering support for Atlantic reconnaissance. The reality was that for most of 1940, the only aircraft available for such a task were those of Kü.Fl. Gr.406 (Do 18s) and 506 (He 115s) and such 'cooperation' that there was, was invariably hit and miss.[12]

When, in January 1941, the Fw 200 Condor bombers of 1./KG 40 based at Bordeaux-Mérignac were placed under the operational control of the BdU, things were still hit and miss. There was only a small number of aircraft available and they suffered from technical problems. On two early attempts to locate convoys in January 1941, the Condors lost contact, and generally the U-boats had to maintain their own reconnaissance.[13] When the U-boats were moved north, from west of the North Channel, to track diverted convoys, their zone of operations stretched as far as the coast of Iceland, a point which the Fw 200s struggled to reach. The main issue however, was that there were too few aircraft, and when a shadower was observed, the British simply diverted their ships. As Günter Hessler describes:

> With a view to keeping air shadowers unobserved, they were ordered on 3rd March not to bomb the convoys. Flag Officer U-boats took this step reluctantly, being aware of the tonic effect of successful air attacks on aircrews engaged in long and wearying reconnaissance. But the large Condors found unobserved shadowing impossible, and on 31st March, general freedom of bomber attack on all targets was restored.[14]

From March 1941, leadership of Luftwaffe maritime reconnaissance over the North Sea between 52° and 58° North remained the responsibility of the *Führer der Seeluftstreitkräfte*, while north of this parallel it was in the hands of the *Fliegerführer Nord* (Air Commander North). The English Channel and the area west of the Scilly Isles and Ushant (Ouessant) was the jurisdiction of the recently formed *Fliegerführer Atlantik* (Air Commander Atlantic).[15] Indeed, this latter tactical command had been established by order of the *Führer* – probably as a result of pressure from Dönitz and others – and was subordinated to *Luftflotte* 3. Its first commander was the highly decorated anti-shipping specialist Oberstleutnant Martin Harlinghausen, whose brief was to work closely with the BdU in operations against enemy supply shipping in the Atlantic which, effectively, meant the convoy routes to and from Britain and the Mediterranean and the US East Coast, as well as those passing over the eastern, southern and western coasts of the British Isles.[16]

But from the autumn of 1940, the air-naval chain of communication proved cumbersome and slow to function. Response to the sighting of enemy shipping by the Condors of KG 40, which added, inherently, the role of reconnaissance to their anti-shipping operations, meant that a report on the sighting of enemy shipping was first transmitted to the *Geschwader* base at Bordeaux-Mérignac. It was then passed to the headquarters of the tactical command, IV. *Fliegerkorps* at Dinard. The *Korps* then transferred the information to *Luftflotte* 3 in Paris, which then relayed it to *Marinegruppe West* and finally to the BdU at Sengwarden near Wilhelmshaven (later Paris). This procedure frequently took a day to complete, resulting in missed opportunities and a devaluation of KG 40's 'raw' reconnaissance intelligence.[17]

That year, the Navy requested that a flying unit be formed for the *specific* task of carrying out long-range maritime reconnaissance and rendering support for the U-boats and surface ships, rather than just a *Gruppe* that was also committed to offensive missions. From the second half of 1941, Dönitz began to beat the drum again and again: any lack of success against convoys was attributable fairly and squarely to a lack of boats and a lack of 'eyes' in the air.[18] Until these 'eyes' became widely available, the U-boat itself would continue to be the main instrument of reconnaissance, but even in good visibility the best range of vision from a U-boat was some 30 km.

In mid-1941, as the strength of I./KG 40 increased and the U-boats had returned to more easterly waters, BdU hoped for at least two to three Condors to be made available daily for reconnaissance (still in addition to the primary bombing operations of the *Gruppe*). But at just this point, control of the *Gruppe* had been removed from the BdU and assigned to *Fliegerführer Atlantik*, where Harlinghausen did his best to ensure smooth cooperation – something in itself that suspicious minds within U-boat command believed was a measure by Göring to illustrate how KG 40's assignment to BdU was not an acceptable state of affairs.[20]

In the period 15 March to 31 October 1941, Luftwaffe reconnaissance reported 56 convoys and shadowed many of them for several days at a time, thus enabling the U-boats to close in for attack. As a result of this all too brief period of close cooperation with Luftwaffe reconnaissance, the U-boats claimed to have sunk '74 merchant vessels totalling 390,000 tons, one aircraft carrier and one destroyer'. Unless this is a chronologically inaccurate reference to HMS *Audacity* (the escort carrier sunk by a U-boat on 21 December 1941 having been shadowed by Fw 200s), this is not correct. In the period 13 March to 31 December 1942, the bomber force of the *Fliegerführer Atlantik* claimed to have accounted for 161 vessels totalling 903,000 Gross Registered Tonnage (GRT) sunk, seven vessels probably sunk, totalling 31,000 GRT and 113 vessels damaged totalling 590,000 GRT.[21]

However, the inescapable fact was that from the summer of 1941, by far the bulk of the Luftwaffe was committed to the east for the invasion of the Soviet Union – a land campaign. This meant that Luftwaffe commands in the West found it increasingly difficult to carry out the tasks allotted to them, including that of maritime reconnaissance, anti-shipping and minelaying operations.[22] Such duties became ever more peripheral.

By late 1941, the convoys were receiving regular destroyer escort as well as cover from aircraft and thus the task of the U-boats became ever harder. Subsequently, the main point of U-boat effort was moved west, farther out into the Atlantic, targeting the eastbound Atlantic convoys, well beyond the range of the relatively few Fw 200s that there were. The plan was that by the late autumn of 1941, operations were to be conducted exclusively in North American waters, which provided favourable attack conditions along with plentiful targets.[23] As the Luftwaffe historical branch noted, 'in the middle of December 1941 cooperation with the C.-in.C. U-boats in the joint campaign against enemy shipping in the eastern Atlantic came practically to a standstill.'[24]

By late 1941 to early 1942 as a result of an increase in the defensive armament carried by enemy shipping, the low-level, lateral attacks mounted by the Fw 200s of KG 40, which had proved so successful earlier, had become increasingly unsustainable, initially against convoys, but soon even against single vessels. Nevertheless, though their efforts were muted to some extent, and some aircraft were moved away from France, the Condors were still able to perform occasional valuable reconnaissance for the U-boats so that they could be directed towards targets.[25]

Aside from the Fw 200s, the only aircraft of any range available to the *Fliegerführer Atlantik* were the Ju 88s of Kü.Fl.Gr.106, which could be deployed only against convoys off the eastern coast of Britain. Even these operations eventually passed to the control of IX. *Fliegerkorps*, and, between July 1940 and December 1943, the bomber units of that *Korps* claimed 42 vessels sunk totalling 167,000 GRT, 38 vessels of 171,000 GRT probably sunk and 118 vessels damaged, totalling 439,000 GRT.[26]

The *Fliegerführer Atlantik* was then confined to operations off the south and western coasts of England, but in May 1942 BdU again requested assistance to provide cover for U-boats as they transited in and out of the Bay of Biscay and to repulse enemy anti-submarine aircraft. For the rest of 1942 and early 1943 this became the main function of the *Fliegerführer Atlantik* and its small number of twin-engined fighter *Gruppen*.[27]

The historian John Terraine asserts that the U-boats 'were at the very height of their powers in the Atlantic' in May and June 1942, and this despite appalling weather, which saw gales and dense fogs in mid-summer.[28] But Dönitz was aware that, increasingly, the boats were being captained by untested commanders and raw crews amidst steadily more challenging conditions.

The bad sentiment between the Kriegsmarine and the Luftwaffe continued to fester in early June 1942 when, after the RAF had managed successfully to reconnoitre German naval ship positions off Norway, conversely, the Luftwaffe proved incapable of performing any level of acceptable 'counter-reconnaissance'. Raeder's staff mocked the latter for its apparent inability to conduct even the 'fundamental requirements of any sort of naval warfare.'[29]

Out at sea at this time, one of Dönitz's tactics was to endeavour to locate a convoy before it entered the 'Greenland air gap' and to attack it as it was crossing those 'unprotected' waters. As the convoy re-emerged from the gap, so the U-boats would then withdraw. Another tactic, which was deployed in October 1942, was to position two 'packs' of boats on the departure side of the air gap and to lie in wait.[30] Yet the need for 'eyes' was becoming ever more urgent. On 13 July 1942, 970 km west of Ireland, the wolfpack of nine boats led by inexperienced captains located a convoy, but then lost it. For three days, they searched – fruitlessly.[31]

By mid-1943, U-boats would attempt to move ahead of a convoy in order to attack while submerged if they were unable to do so on the surface. They would also try to exploit the disruption caused by a first attack, with one boat often following another from the same direction two or three kilometres behind.[32] A Luftwaffe report from April 1944 described in detail how U-boats formed for reconnaissance, and the weaknesses arising from such tactics:

The best formation for reconnaissance is the 'Reconnaissance Line Abreast' formation, in which the largest possible number of U-boats is, with a necessary sacrifice of formation in depth, placed next to each other with their areas of vision overlapping. In this way it is possible to cover comparatively large sea areas. It is occasionally possible, however, that a convoy can slip through this reconnaissance strip [patrol line] at night. To avoid this, the whole strip moves to and fro so that, in all probability, it will sight the convoy moving along its estimated route by day. This means that at night the strip must move on the estimated course of the convoy at a speed designed at all costs to keep it ahead of the convoy.

Paradoxically, most U-boat commanders preferred to attack at night, despite the threat posed by radar and enemy methods of illumination.[33] The report continued:

This strip formation may sound very advantageous in theory; in practice, however, gaps will appear in individual strips through inaccurate navigation. In bad visibility, fog, rain or storm, the situation may become even worse. It is thus possible for a convoy to slip through the line or discovering its presence in the vicinity, to avoid it all together by a wide detour. It is not difficult to realize how small an area a strip of 25 U-boats can cover compared with the area in which convoys move. Clearly it is possible for a convoy to avoid interception, even without taking advantage of poor visibility.

> Our policy in U-boat warfare is only to attack a convoy where a large number of craft is available for the assault, the aim being to destroy the core of the enemy, i.e., the valuable merchant vessels, by penetrating the escort forces in a simultaneously launched mass attack with the largest possible number of U-boats.

However, in order to put theory into practice, it was recognized that such a concentration of U-boats could be assembled only by 'flawless *shadowing*' of a potential target. But shadowing from the sea brought its own difficulties; convoys invariably adopted counter-measures – zigzagging their courses at regular intervals of between three and 15 minutes by up to 20°, so that the fixing of a mean course was extremely difficult. In addition a convoy would endeavour to shake off a shadower by wider alterations of course, usually at dusk. In hours of daylight, a surface shadower had to remain just within sight to be able to observe the convoy and yet remain undetected. If it was spotted, the convoy escort would make all effort to force the U-boat to dive, where submerged, it became much slower than the target.

The Luftwaffe believed that, 'the disadvantages suffered by the U-boat of low eye-level, short-range of vision and lack of mobility do not apply in the air … The Luftwaffe is in a position to cover the wide spaces of the Atlantic and to survey all shipping movements. The task of air reconnaissance is therefore to find a target, report it, shadow it and direct the U-boats to it … By means of coordination it will be possible to create the most favourable conditions for the attack, and without serious losses, to inflict the heaviest damage on the enemy.'[34]

Certainly by the early autumn of 1942, Dönitz was expressing his envy of the Allies' long-range reconnaissance aircraft. 'In the Atlantic,' he wrote, 'the enemy's daily reconnaissance forces us to dispose U-boats far out in the centre of the ocean … There are also some aircraft of particularly long range which are used as convoy escorts. They have been met 1300 km from British bases.'[35]

However, the early autumn of 1942 was a difficult time for the British; many convoys were slow and these always suffered greater losses, usually of some 30 per cent, than the faster ones. There was an urgent need for more escorts, particularly destroyers, of which there was a grave shortage.[36] This shortage, as well as a lack of available fuel, meant that the convoys had to maintain the shortest route across the Atlantic (the Great Circle). This worked in the favour of the U-boats.[37]

In October 1942, the Germans had 196 boats operational.[38] Between August and December 1942, 54 U-boats were lost, of which 26 succumbed to attack by aircraft.[39] It was a grim business. When a boat was depth-charged, the effect was often total, as one account described: 'Over the place of the explosion, gathering slowly from the depths beneath, was a nasty, oily litter of timber, clothing, pocket books, cigarettes, food packages and bits of human flesh which immediately attracted the attention of the wheeling gulls.'[40]

That autumn the weather turned for the worse. U-boats, merchantmen and their escorts struggled with it, the U-boats seeking relief from the endless buffeting and crashing of the waves by diving below the angry surface. In these conditions, the contribution of long-range aircraft from either side would have been folly. Yet, despite the weather, of six attempts to attack convoys in October, although two failed, in three of them, the U-boats accounted for the sinking of 30 merchant ships.

At the beginning of 1943, the Allies recognized that the battle in the Atlantic would become a 'deadly, ruthless series of fights, in which no mercy would be expected and little shown.'[41] They had good cause to think this; in 1942 the U-boats had sunk 1,160 ships totalling 6,266,215 tons in all waters.[42] The weather would also continue to show no mercy: winds howled at up to 250 km/h, bringing, as one U-boat man remembered, 'driving snow, sleet, hail and frozen spray. It cut our faces like a razor, and threatened to tear away our eye masks; only the steel belts around our waists secured us to boat and life.'[43]

The bad weather in the early new year saw the number of vessels sunk by U-boats reduce to 37, totalling 203,123 tons. Yet the Luftwaffe believed that it was not weather that was responsible for the decline, but rather that the unfavourably positioned reconnaissance patrol lines of U-boats were simply unable to prevent no fewer than seven convoys from 'slipping through the net'. According to Luftwaffe analysts, this was an 'outstanding example of the effect of inadequate reconnaissance reports on the figures of enemy shipping losses. It is evident that considerable damage might have been inflicted on enemy shipping if, with the aid of air reconnaissance, it had been possible to concentrate all U-boats in that area, and thus to make the fullest use of our whole U-boat strength.'[44] For the Luftwaffe, this was a curious comment; it is nothing short of an admission of failure to respond to naval requirements.

As an example, the *Falke* pack of 14 U-boats had been formed in January south-east of Greenland to strike at North and Outbound North (Slow) convoys, and from where it formed a line stretching beyond the range of Allied aircraft based on Iceland. The conditions were atrocious and one boat, a new Type IXC40, *U-167*, was battered by thunderous seas which damaged its bridge, threw a crew member overboard, injured the commander and forced the boat to abort and return to France. Also in the *Falke* group was the new Type VII, *U-632*. This boat was spotted on the surface by a British-crewed B-17, which dropped depth charges from 80 ft and damaged it. Despite this, the *Falke* pack searched fruitlessly for days for a westbound convoy. In the end it achieved nothing. In Berlin, Konteadmiral Eberhard Godt, Chief of BdU Operations, commented in his war diary that U-boats were 'totally unsuitable' for finding convoys. Such a task required many U-boats and many wasted days searching. What was needed was long-range search and shadowing aircraft: 'If we had aircraft the war would be very different.'[45]

Dönitz succeeded Raeder as Commander-in-Chief of the Kriegsmarine at the end of January 1943 and was promoted to Grossadmiral, but he also remained in command of the BdU with his HQ brought from France to the Hotel am Steinplatz at Charlottenberg in Berlin. He told his staff: 'The sea war is the U-boat war.'[46]

On 26 February 1943, Dönitz travelled to the *Führerhauptquartier Werwolf* at Vinnytsia in the Ukraine. There, he and Hitler pored over large maps, studying what distant areas could be covered by various types of long-range aircraft. Hitler had been informed by Göring that the construction of such aircraft would be given priority, but he remained sceptical over the prior 'illusory' promises of the Reichsmarschall. Dönitz explained to the *Führer* that no enemy shipping had been sunk over a 14-day period that month, because 'nothing was sighted'. Whilst this may have been attributable to weather and poor visibility, or possibly the enemy's actions in locating the U-boats, Dönitz cited the primary cause as being the complete absence of Luftwaffe reconnaissance.[47]

Indeed the Luftwaffe admitted that in late 1942 to early 1943, 'the absence of air reconnaissance was the sole reason why the full force of our U-boats could not be brought to bear on a sighted target, and why they often returned to base after an abortive trip still fully armed with torpedoes; and this at a time when the loss of every single freighter was keenly felt by the enemy.'[48]

On 5 March 1943, the *Reichsluftministerium* (RLM – the Reich Air Ministry) had held a conference in Berlin on transatlantic and long-range aircraft. It was attended by Oberst Karl-Henning von Barsewisch, the *General der Aufklärungsflieger,* and Oberstleutnant Theodor Rowehl, the commander of the *Versuschsstelle für Höhenflug* (Test Station for High-Altitude Aviation). Von Barsewisch remarked:

> It seems from what was said in the talk with Dönitz [and Hitler] that the U-boat war stands or falls by reconnaissance aircraft. This has been explained to the *Führer*, he has approved it and the Reichsmarschall has promised to fulfil the request. Undoubtedly, we must have a reconnaissance aircraft which can match the demands for mid-Atlantic cover.[49]

In von Barsewisch's view, Dönitz and the *Seekriegsleitung* (SKL – Maritime Warfare Command) regarded the four-engined Messerschmitt Me 264 (see

Chapter Fourteen), and later, the proposed Ta 400 from Focke-Wulf, as more preferable aircraft with which to conduct long-range maritime reconnaissance missions than the existing Bv 222 flying boat. His opinion had probably been influenced by the failure of refuelling trials with the Bv 222 involving U-boat tankers. Dönitz's problem was that the Ta 400 was not expected to appear before 1946, and thus for the foreseeable future, the Kriegsmarine would have to rely on the Junkers Ju 290 and possibly Ju 390, and Heinkel He 177 bomber to provide interim maritime reconnaissance capability.[50] Yet it would not be until 3 May that the SKL noted that the Luftwaffe had finally decided to 'plan for a long-range reconnaissance aircraft suitable for Atlantic missions.' Generalfeldmarschall Milch and Generaloberst Hans Jeschonnek, the Chief of the Luftwaffe General Staff, were agreed that the Me 264 was unlikely to make its operational debut before 1944 or even 1945, and a number of technical experts were instructed to explore urgently the possibility of fitting auxiliary tanks to the Me 264 to increase range still further.

By March 1943, the U-boat arm had just about reached the strength which Dönitz had hoped it would back in 1939.[51] That month it sank 108 ships of 627,377 tons giving the Grossadmiral some reason for cheer.[52] Also, between 1 March and 22 April 1943, the Luftwaffe managed to maintain daily reconnaissance operations over a sea area from 38° to 49° North and 10° to 20° West, often involving six aircraft, which observed approximately four million tons of merchant shipping and warships totalling about 300,000 tons, and during which period convoys moved within the effective range of German long-range bombers for at least four to five days. During these six weeks, according to a report of January 1944, the irony was that the Luftwaffe was unable to mount a concentrated attack against enemy merchant shipping because of the 'predominance of reconnaissance operations for *Marinegruppe West*.'[53]

That spring, the Luftwaffe noted, 'the enemy provided his convoys from Britain to Gibraltar with air cover in addition to moving them further and further out of range of the Fw 200. New location equipment and methods made U-boat operations more difficult.'[54]

Indeed, for the Germans, a worrying new dimension now made its debut over the Atlantic in the form of American-built B-24 Liberator Very Long Range (VLR) anti-submarine aircraft. To patrol the Atlantic, RAF Coastal Command had initially operated a mix of single- and twin-engined biplanes and monoplanes including Avro Ansons, Lockheed Hudsons, Vickers Vildebeests, Saro Londons and Supermarine Stranraers. These were augmented by the Short Sunderland and Consolidated Catalina flying boat and, later, Vickers Wellingtons, Handley Page Halifaxes, Armstrong Whitworth Whitneys and Boeing Fortress Is. But on 17 March 1943, a

Liberator flew for nearly nine hours from its base in Northern Ireland to reach a convoy. On its way, it had attacked a U-boat, forcing it to remain submerged for most of that day. The aircraft then attacked another boat with similar effect. When it returned to base, it had been in the air for 18 hr 20 min.[55] The Liberators would soon be joined by radar-equipped Wellingtons and Halifaxes. John Terraine succinctly describes the effects of the appearance of aircraft as being 'especially nerve-racking for [U-boat] crews returning from hard actions in mid-Atlantic, perhaps with damage or injured men aboard. This pressure on morale, at times when it would normally be expected to ease, is a factor in the battle that is not to be ignored.'[56]

The Allies were now able to extend their air cover from flying boats and land-based bombers to just about any point in the Atlantic north of 45° North, though this scope faltered when it came to the sea north of the Azores, and so Dönitz next ordered his boats to move farther west into that area.[57] But it was a game of cat and mouse; of 174 scheduled North Atlantic convoys, 105 were rerouted so that they were not sighted by the U-boats.[58] However, the British had recognized in April 1943 that the wolfpacks could no longer be evaded by simply rerouting convoys; as Winston Churchill has recorded, 'The issue had to be fought out by combined sea and air forces round the convoys themselves.'[59] This meant air–sea cooperation.

The escort groups had been strengthened, and were operating on a more sophisticated basis, as well as benefitting from more escort carriers, which brought, in addition to VLR aircraft, naval fighters. The Atlantic air 'gap' was closing and this meant nowhere was safe for U-boats to attack without the threat of attack from aircraft. Fifteen U-boats had been lost in March and 15 more in April, and morale among the crews was beginning to suffer, yet by the end of April there were 193 boats in the West, and more boats than ever before were operating on the North Atlantic convoy routes.[60]

But in May, Dönitz had come to realize just how great Allied sea and air dominance was, as 41 boats were lost in that month. He decided to pull his boats out of the North Atlantic 'using the utmost caution' to an area south-west of the Azores. 'We had lost the Battle of the Atlantic,' he wrote.

On 31 May 1943, Dönitz had a meeting with Hitler at the Berghof at which the *Führer* agreed fully with the Admiral's contention that even by that stage of the war, it was not too late to start building long-range aircraft suitable for cooperation with the U-boats. Dönitz further put forward the case for more specialist U-boat cooperation training with the Luftwaffe. He reasoned that naval aviation crews should spend four to five months at sea, be trained in celestial navigation, drift computation, convoy-shadowing tactics, detection-finding signalling, liaison with other aircraft at long-range and other forms of communication. Such training should take place alongside U-boat crews, with the training flotilla in the Baltic Sea. According to the record of the meeting, Dönitz stressed the following:

> A situation must not arise where cooperation in the Atlantic between U-boats and the Luftwaffe breaks down because certain mistakes are made which actually have nothing to do with the fundamentally sound principle of cooperation. Such errors might lead to the false generalization that cooperation is useless. The *Führer* agrees fully with the views expressed and stresses once more the tasks, prospects and possibilities which our own air force would have in the Atlantic. He then closes with the words: 'It seems that long-range bombers should be sent into the Atlantic area.'[61]

In the spring of 1943, at a critical stage in the U-boats' Atlantic campaign, a decision was taken – as a first step towards building a dedicated long-range maritime reconnaissance force – to form a new specialist unit in the form of *Seeaufklärungsgruppe* (SAGr) 129, equipped with the Blohm & Voss Bv 138 and huge Bv 222 flying boats. The tri-motor Bv 138 had a range of 4300 km, but early examples suffered from a poor serviceability rate, particularly associated with its engines and with the hull and floats during bad weather. Although these problems were eventually solved, and the aircraft enjoyed a reputation for toughness and versatility, as the war progressed, the Bv 138 was really capable only of undertaking coastal patrols and anti-submarine work because of its lack of speed and relatively short radius of action.[62] The six-engined Bv 222 became the largest flying boat to see operations during World War II. Conceived originally to fly passengers from Berlin to New York, the prototype had first flown in 1940 and in Luftwaffe use it was given the name '*Wiking*'. Fitted with FuG 200 radar and formidable armament, from late 1942 it was decided to utilize the very few Bv 222 prototypes that were available as a long-range maritime reconnaissance aircraft. The aircraft had a ferry range of 6100 km and an endurance of 28 hr at 245 km/h at sea level.

To this end, a first *Staffel*, 1./SAGr 129, was formed on 13 July at Biscarosse on the French Atlantic coast from the *Aufklärungsstaffel See* 222 and elements of 3./Kü.Fl.Gr.406. It was envisaged that further *Seeaufklärungsgruppen* would be established during 1943.[63]

Hitler again met with Admiral Dönitz at the *Wolfsschanze*, his headquarters in the mosquito-ridden forests of East Prussia, on 8 July 1943. Once more a discussion took place on naval aviation during which Hitler reassured Dönitz that all effort was being made to speed up manufacture of the Me 264, which would be used 'later' to work in conjunction with the U-boats. Hitler further promised that he would do everything in his power to deliver the aircraft and avoid false hopes. Dönitz respectfully expressed 'his conviction that efficient reconnaissance in the Atlantic will always be needed even after the new submarines are at our disposal.'[64]

A typical Atlantic convoy would have to cross 3,000 miles of ocean within 19–20 days running westbound, and within 15–18 days heading eastbound. In May 1940, convoys usually comprised 46 vessels, a figure that stayed fairly constant until 1943, when the optimum number increased.[65] In terms of the general composition of Allied convoys, for the period July–October 1943, the Luftwaffe recorded the following information:

Troop convoys usually consisted of 5 to 20 large passenger vessels or large freighters suitable for use as troop-transports. Supply convoys generally comprised 20 to 25 freighters. Both types of convoy, and tankers in particular, are extremely important objectives and their destruction has a lasting effect on the enemy war effort.

The strength of the escorting force varies widely and is provided according to the value and importance of the convoy. A temporary shortage of warships has also probably enforced restricted employment of escort vessels. For example, a convoy of 14 troop-transports was escorted by 1 auxiliary cruiser, 1 depot ship, 3 auxiliary aircraft carriers, 2 destroyers and 6 small escort vessels. The composition of escorts for freighter convoys varies a great deal, ranging between 5 and 18 warships for every 45 freighters. So far no aircraft carriers have been reported acting as escorts and even a cruiser is rarely seen.

The US–Britain convoys move from the large ports of the American East Coast along the Great Circle to the northern entrance of the Irish Sea. If U-boats attack, or even if they are located, the convoys take evasive action by moving below the coast of Greenland and Ireland. According to statistical data, which extends over a sufficiently long period, one troop-transport convoy runs at the same time interval on this double route every sixth or seventh day and one freighter convoy every thirteenth day. Convoys from the US to Britain generally comprise 35 vessels escorted by a varying number of destroyers and corvettes, and frequently by cruisers as well according to the value of the cargo.[66]

One historian describes the battle in the Atlantic from the Allied perspective as being no more than an 'acceptable running skirmish' by the autumn of 1943.[67] On the German side, September saw a decline in U-boat losses to just nine submarines, but the tonnage sunk amounted to only 156,419 tons of which just 43,775 tons were achieved in the Atlantic.[68]

By late 1943, the *Oberkommando der Luftwaffe* (OKL) and the Kriegsmarine concluded that the recipe for success in cooperation in convoy warfare lay in the Luftwaffe carrying out four fundamental tasks:

1. The location of convoys by long-range reconnaissance.
2. The mounting of aerial torpedo attacks against enemy aircraft carriers, if present, and which were anticipated as accompanying 'all convoys in future'.
3. The jamming of enemy radio and radar, and hence the effectiveness of convoy defence.
4. The sinking of as many enemy ships in the convoy as quickly as possible.

If these four measures were carried out effectively, then it would be the mission of the U-boats to attack and completely destroy a scattered and defenceless convoy.

It was recognized, however, that significant success could only be achieved if the U-boat and air forces summoned by shadowing aircraft to attack convoys were able to deal crippling blows in *combined* attacks.[69] The problem, however, was, in the opinion of some senior German naval officers, that Göring simply did not understand how air power could contribute positively to the war at sea.[70] Not only that, but the *Fliegerführer Atlantik*, Generalleutnant Ulrich Kessler, had become dismayed over the low priority given to his command, probably a result of Göring's indifference. 'Before taking up my command, I was informed that *Fliegerführer Atlantik* was to be built up to at least division strength,' Kessler wrote to Jeschonnek on 5 September 1943. 'Nothing of the kind has taken place. On the contrary, my strength has been steadily reduced.'[71]

In an assessment of the 'strategic air situation in the Atlantic 1943/44' the Luftwaffe noted that, 'There is no longer a gap in the Atlantic. The enemy can cover the whole of the North Atlantic from Bermuda, Newfoundland, Iceland, the British Isles, Gibraltar and the Azores.'[72]

In a somewhat optimistic tone, a Luftwaffe report declared in January 1944 that, 'German U-boats from French and Norwegian bases have created a serious threat to enemy sea routes. The Luftwaffe is also advancing further and further into the Atlantic.'[73] But the same report contained the following warning:

There have never yet been any miracles in a war ... Military miracles arise only from intense preparation and the use of adequate, first-rate forces at a favourable moment, at the same time having nullified possible enemy counter-measures. The air war over the Atlantic, which may be further intensified in the future, must also be considered in this light. However, a sudden change in the supply battle against Britain and America cannot be expected immediately. Success will rather be achieved only after a lengthy period of operations by numerically and technically adequate forces. This must be clearly understood.

However, it is all the more necessary to adhere to the primary strategy in the West, namely the widest possible employment of the Luftwaffe in cooperation with U-boats against Anglo-American supply lines. Plans should be made and put into operation on a long-term basis irrespective of any theories and obstacles which can only weaken in every possible way any decision which may be made.[74]

In very early 1943, following instructions from the Ob.d.L., the *General der Aufklärungsflieger*, Oberst Karl-Henning von Barsewisch, ordered the establishment of a *Fernaufklärungsgruppe* to be equipped with 'four-engined aircraft' for reconnaissance over the Atlantic specifically to assist the U-boats. It was intended to use the Junkers Ju 290 to fulfil this role.[75]

CHAPTER TWO

JUNKERS' COLOSSUS: THE Ju 290

It really was a giant piece of hardware...

Hans-Werner Lerche, Rechlin test pilot

BUILDING A GIANT

As with several of Germany's multi-engined aeroplanes of World War II, the concept of the Junkers Ju 290 lay in the design of a commercial transport aircraft intended for the German state airline, Deutsche Lufthansa.

During the second half of the 1930s, Nazi Germany became very 'air minded', creating and developing an ever-expanding infrastructure of state-sponsored flying schools and aero-clubs, as well as encouraging aircraft and aircraft engine manufacturers and aero-industry companies to increase production on an unprecedented scale. The Nazis also attached considerable importance to the development of commercial aviation. The previous decade, despite the restrictions of the Treaty of Versailles and with limited resources,

Germany's civilian air fleet grew to a size comparable to French and British operators. Simultaneously, there was a rigorous expansion in airline traffic from 7,733 passengers and 35.57 tons of freight in 1922 to 120,000 passengers and 607 tons in 1925.

By February 1923 various amalgamations of small German airlines left just two major operators – Junkers-Luftverkehr and Deutscher Aero Lloyd, which operated airline services around Continental Europe, with further routes to Scandinavia, London, Budapest, Switzerland and Italy. Junkers-Luftverkehr was part of a multi-faceted business based at Dessau on the River Elbe, north of Leipzig, originally established by Professor Hugo Junkers in 1895. An ill-fated venture with the Soviet government during the early 1920s, however, had almost resulted in complete financial disaster for the firm. Suffering from the military restrictions enforced by Versailles and fearful of the severe economic consequences of war repatriation payments sought by Britain and France, Germany was eager to cooperate in any bi-lateral ventures with the Soviet Union in order to allow continued, if not covert, development of its aircraft industry. By signing the Treaty of Rapello, the Soviet Union had declared itself willing to place airfields, aircraft manufacturing facilities and labour at Germany's disposal in return for German technical knowledge and training.

The potential for large-scale manufacturing of aircraft in the Soviet Union free of Allied intervention was irresistible. In November 1922, encouraged and supported by the German government to the tune of 100 million Reichsmarks, Junkers signed a contract with the Soviet government to build airframes and engines designed by his company for use by the Soviet Air Force at the former Russo-Baltic factory at Fili, near Moscow. Professor Junkers was well aware that a lucrative market still existed for military aircraft as well as civil, and that, wherever possible, every commercial type should be built with potential military conversion in mind.

By 1923, Junkers was producing significant numbers of its trademark, all-metal aircraft, some of which had performed long-range flights as far afield as China, as well as making record-breaking endurance flights. By late 1925, the three-engined Junkers G 24 monoplane was operated by most of the leading central European airlines, and it offered their passengers increased comfort in the form of leather armchairs, overhead luggage nets, a toilet, a complimentary route map and a cabin boy attendant. For the business traveller, typewriters and radio telephones were available on request. Meanwhile, Junkers engine works manufactured petrol aero engines.

However, key figures in the *Reichsverkehrsministerium* (RVM – the State Transport Ministry) wanted to emulate the British example of Imperial Airways, a single, leading, domestic and international 'flag carrier'. Despite objections from Professor Junkers, the owner of Junkers-Luftverkehr, the men from the ministry were determined and conspired to achieve their ambitions by nefarious means and heavy-handedness: Junkers was threatened with the withdrawal of government subsidies and attempts were made to lean on the banks to end lines of credit to Junkers' businesses unless they accepted a merger between the two airlines. Under heavy pressure, Junkers conceded.

A cornerstone of German civil aviation – indeed, very much a 'beacon to the world' – *Deutsche Lufthansa Aktiengesellschaft* (DLH) was formed in Berlin in January 1926 as a result of the merger. Over the following years, through a process of strong, even ruthless management and innovation, DLH expanded its fleet and network. Its senior executives, especially its operations director, Erhard Milch, understood that the customer was king. As early as 1928, stewards were introduced to serve drinks and snacks on some flights, and reclining seats were added to at least one of its biplane types. Strangely, however, as the airline achieved greater efficiency, the superior levels of passenger comfort it provided sometimes worked against it and there were complaints from customers if their aircraft arrived early at their destination.

In 1932, DLH commenced using what would become the ubiquitous and highly successful Junkers Ju 52/3m tri-motor, all-metal airliner on its key international routes. Ironically, however, within three years of its introduction, Hugo Junkers would be dead, hounded to his grave by a highly orchestrated process of investigation – spearheaded largely by Milch – into apparent financial misconduct and irregularities within his various businesses. On 3 April 1935, the Junkers companies were nationalized and effectively placed under control of the RLM under the direction of Heinrich Koppenberg, who had been appointed by Milch.

From Berlin, where the vast Tempelhof airport with its extended runways and passenger halls, restaurant, administration, hangar and servicing areas – known as the *Luftkreuz Europas* (Europe's air crossroads) – represented the state of the art in air travel and design, DLH's aircraft flew progressively across an expanding domestic route network that included Königsberg, Leipzig-Halle, Rhein-Main, München, Hamburg, Köln, Dresden, Stuttgart, Düsseldorf and Essen, while the aircraft of many other nations gave Tempelhof a distinctly international atmosphere. The carriage of airmail, for example, increased dramatically from 748 tons in 1934 to 1,408 tons in 1935. At Leipzig-Halle, passenger numbers grew from 65,230 in the financial year 1933, to 75,000 in 1935, to 266,378 in 1936. In 1936 Rhein-Main airport handled 58,010 passengers and 796 tons of mail along with 801 tons of freight on 5,270 flights, while the following year, these volumes increased to 70,910 passengers and 7,090 flights respectively, along with 1,452 tons of mail and 966 tons of freight.

Deutsche Lufthansa had also expanded its overseas operations, forging global links with operators as far afield as Brazil and China. The airlines of other nations witnessed the growth of DLH with considerable envy.

But such volumes and expansion demanded new aircraft, capable of carrying greater numbers of passengers and heavier payloads for longer distances. Thus it was that during the mid-1930s, the senior management of DLH turned to the still fledgling Luftwaffe, monitoring the development of military aircraft designs that could be adapted into the commercial transport role. Once again, inspiration came from Junkers.

The all-metal, twin-engined Junkers Ju 86 was powered by a range of engines including the Junkers Jumo 205 Diesel, which unfortunately proved terribly unreliable – the aircraft became known to its crews by the unhappy moniker of 'The Flying Coffee Grinder'. In April 1937, no fewer than 18 Ju 86s were lost in crashes, mainly due to lubrication problems resulting in overheated engines, seized pistons and bearings, as well as broken gear wheels and connecting rods. One Luftwaffe bomber commander recalled:

> We operated the Ju 86 A-1 as a medium bomber with Junkers diesel engines and, later, BMW radial engines, with a crew of four – pilot, navigator, radio-operator/bomb-aimer and gunner. The Jumo Diesels gave us a lot of headaches and we suffered frequently from broken pistons, poor manufacture and high levels of repair and unserviceability. In reality, we always saw the Ju 86 as a stopgap for the Heinkel He 111.[1]

Phased out as a bomber in favour of aircraft such as the He 111, the Ju 86 soldiered on as a reconnaissance aircraft in limited numbers until mid-1944. But in the 1930s many, if not most, senior officers in the Luftwaffe remained convinced that the way to win a war in the air was by the use of heavy/four-engined bombers, capable of delivering heavy offensive loads at long range. They believed that Germany's main enemy in the future would be the Soviet Union. Therefore, any war would involve industrial targets deep within the Soviet Union, perhaps even east of the Ural Mountains; hence the concept of an ultra-long-range bomber, or 'Ural Bomber', was born. Encouraged by Oberstleutnant Wilhelm Wimmer, then head of the *Technisches Amt* of the RLM, who was considered to have 'the best technical mind in the Luftwaffe', Generalmajor Walther Wever, the first Chief of Staff of the Luftwaffe, had ordered a specification to be issued to Junkers and Dornier for an aircraft of this type. It was a specification that was well in advance of the plans of most of the world's air forces and it would stretch the resources of the still very young post-war German aircraft industry to its limits – demanding the carrying of a heavy bombload over a great distance with the benefit of speed and good defensive armament. This was despite the fact that German engine technology was still some years away from producing equipment that could give such aircraft the necessary range and reliability at an affordable cost.

In the spring of 1935, Wimmer accompanied the Reichs Minister for Aviation, Generaloberst Hermann Göring, to Dessau for an inspection trip. In a vast hangar, Göring was shown a mock-up of the Ju 89. Aghast, he turned to Wimmer and asked 'What on earth is that?' Wimmer replied that it was the Ural Bomber, assuming the Minister had been previously advised. But an apparently angered Göring proclaimed, 'Any major project such as this can only be decided by me personally.'[2] Nevertheless, by May 1935, the development of such a heavy bomber had become the top priority of the Luftwaffe, and by late November 1935, its development programme included two new prototypes, the Dornier Do 19 and the Junkers Ju 89. But less than two months later, on 6 January 1936, three prototype Ju 89s were listed, with a fourth assigned as a transport for DLH, with a target date for a pre-production series of March 1938.[3]

Junkers subsequently produced one prototype of its big, all-metal, four-engined Ju 89 *Grossverkehrsflugzeug* (large transport) by 1936. Structurally similar to the Ju 86 and designed by Junkers chief designer, Diplom-Ingenieur Ernst Zindel, the unarmed Ju 89 V1, powered by four 1,075 hp Jumo 211A 12-cylinder liquid-cooled engines, made its first flight two months after the competing Dornier Do 19 on 11 April 1937 with company test pilot Peter Hesselbach at the controls. Similar in size to the British Short Stirling bomber, the aircraft had a monocoque fuselage and boasted a wingspan of 35.02 m and a wing area of 184 m^2. It weighed 17,000 kg empty and had a take-off weight of around 23,000 kg. Further tests showed that the aircraft had a maximum speed of 390 km/h, but the installation of armament, planned as a 7.9 mm MG 15 machine gun in the nose and a 20 mm MG FF cannon in a dorsal and ventral turret, would have reduced such a performance considerably. The V1 was followed in July 1937 by the V2, fitted with 960 hp DB 600A engines. The aircraft could reach 390 km/h at maximum speed and could carry a bombload of 1600 kg, slightly heavier than the Dornier, over a marginally greater range, together with a crew of nine, including five gunners operating a similar armament to that carried by the Do 19. But both aircraft types were underpowered for their size and weight, and comparatively, neither could match the performance of the new American B-17 Flying Fortress.

Some initial, sub-assembly work had commenced on a third prototype, the V3, which was to have carried mock-ups of the two fuselage turrets, when the entire development programme was scrapped on 29 April 1937.

One catalyst for this had been Wever's death in an air crash in June 1936, after which Göring had reversed the Ural Bomber building programme in favour of the construction of smaller, faster twin-engined aircraft, such as the He 111 and the planned Ju 88. Apparently, the commander of the Luftwaffe had been swayed to act when he was advised of the heavy fuel consumption of the Do 19 and Ju 89 and that three twin-engined aircraft could be built for every two four-engined machines. Furthermore, engines of a sufficient power needed to optimize the performance of such aircraft were still lacking.

The loss of the Luftwaffe was to be Lufthansa's gain. The airline had already shown some interest in the Ju 89 and as such, Junkers sought permission from the RLM to assign the major components of the V3, namely the wings and tail assembly, to the production of a new, private-venture, wide-bodied, commercial aircraft for DLH. The RLM agreed to Junkers' request on the condition that new engines would be fitted to any new machines. The fuselage would be a completely new design.

The emerging aircraft was to be the Junkers Ju 90.

'*DER GROSSE DESSAUER*'

The four-engined, all-metal, low-wing Ju 90 was a design that Ernst Zindel had first created in April 1936, before the inaugural flight of the Ju 89 V1 had even taken place. Zindel envisaged a large four-engined aircraft to be termed as a *Transozeanflugzeug* (pan-oceanic aircraft) or *Schweretransport* (heavy transport).[4] Certainly, and in comparative terms, at the time of its release, the first prototype of the Ju 90 was the largest aircraft in Germany; its wingspan of 35.27 m was greater than that of the Do 19, and at 26.45 m it was a metre longer than that aircraft.

Construction of the aircraft took place at the Junkers works at Dessau where the wings, undercarriage and tail unit intended for the Ju 89 V3 were mated to the more streamlined fuselage of the Ju 90, although the aircraft did retain the Ju 89's rectangular cross-section and rounded top. Aside from the Junkers double-wing type control surfaces, which had a corrugated covering, the rest of the aircraft was formed of smooth, flush-riveted Duralumin. The wings were built around five tubular girder spars covered with a smooth stressed skin. The leading edge was quite markedly swept, the trailing edge almost straight.

Initially, the first prototype, the Ju 90 V1, would be powered by the 960 hp DB 600 engines intended for the Ju 89 V3, although ultimately, it was intended to fit the type with 1,550 hp BMW 139 radials, which were then undergoing development.

For further design work, Zindel handed the Ju 90 over to Diplom-Ingenieur Heinz Kraft, who had worked in the Junkers construction office since 1935, having joined the firm from Rohrbach.[5] Kraft would oversee the design of the Ju 90 and Ju 290 from the firm's design office in Prague.

The first prototype of the Junkers Ju 90, the V1 Wk-Nr 4913 D-AALU, made its inaugural flight piloted by Hesselbach on 28 August 1937. However, after just a few months' trials, D-AALU, named *Der Grosse Dessauer* after the Junkers plant at Dessau, broke up in flight and crashed just north-east of Libbesdorf, a village near the factory, after conducting flutter tests on 7 February 1938. Debris from the rudder, doors and engines were scattered around the village.[6]

The V2, Wk-Nr 4914 D-AIVI *Preussen*, first took to the skies on 2 December 1937, powered by four 830 hp BMW 132H radials. Six months later, the aircraft was being used for tests by DLH.

It was, undeniably, an impressive aircraft, elegant for its size. Passengers were accommodated four-abreast in facing rows on either side of a central aisle, in a roomy cabin measuring 2.83 m across internally, which was augmented by two toilets, a cloakroom and a mail compartment aft, while a food storage area, baggage hold and another cloakroom were located forward. The passenger seats could be converted into berths for night travel. Further baggage holds were located between the two wing spars and at the extreme aft of the fuselage.

The aircraft were powered variously by four 830 hp BMW 132H radials (as in the V2 and V3), 1,340 hp Jumo 211 Fs (the V4), 1,200 hp Pratt & Whitney SC3-G Twin Wasps (Wk-Nr 0002 and 0004) or 1,560 hp BMW 801As (on the V7 and V8).

From July 1938, two Ju 90s, starting with the V3 Wk-Nr 4915 D-AURE *Bayern*, were deployed on a trial basis on DLH's Berlin–Vienna route, but just four months later, on 21 November 1938, while undergoing tropical flight tests for the airline, the V2 crashed at Bathurst in The Gambia, as a result of engine failure, killing 12 of the 15 people on board.

Fortunately, however, despite this inauspicious start to testing, a short run of ten Ju 90 A-1 (Z-2) production machines was planned, with DLH placing an order for eight. Interest also came from South African Airways for the remaining two (as the Ju 90 Z-3 with Twin Wasp engines), but this did not progress, and the outbreak of World War II prevented further civil use of the type.

Despite the Ju 90's deployment as a civil transport, as early as March 1937, there were those in the *Technisches Amt* of the RLM that believed their aircraft should be used only in a limited military role.[7] Yet, the Ju 90 prototypes saw both civil and military service, with the V3 used briefly as a transport by 4./KGr.z.b.V.107 during the Norwegian campaign in April 1940, after which it was returned to DLH. Likewise, in 1943, the Ju 90 V4 Wk-Nr 4916 D-ADLH *Schwabenland* served with the *viermotorige-Transportstaffel*, a specialist four-engined transport unit which operated under the direct control of the Luftwaffe High Command and which would eventually count several Ju 90A-1s on its strength. The V5 Wk-Nr 4917 D-ANBS, which first flew on 5 December 1939 and was the first aircraft to be fitted with new, oval tail fins, and V6 Wk-Nr 4918 D-AOKD were built as military prototypes. The rectangular windows of the earlier prototypes were replaced by round, 'porthole'-style windows. The latter aircraft was fitted with the innovative *Transporterklappe*, known more usually as the '*Trapoklappe*', a hydraulically operated ventral loading ramp which would enable military vehicles and guns to be driven directly into the fuselage, as well as allowing the dropping of large quantities of supplies by parachute. When lowered, the *Trapoklappe* raised the angle of the rear fuselage to a level position, allowing vehicles sufficient clearance to embark, and when closed, the ramp was pneumatically sealed. One of the ramp's most practical features was that it had access steps faired centrally along its length with treaded edges to assist vehicles with adhesion during loading and unloading.

The Ju 90 V7 Wk-Nr 4919 D-APFH featured a considerably modifed, narrower, wing design, with a straight inner section leading edge, while the fuselage was lengthened by 1.98 m immediately aft of the rear spar attachment point, increasing overall length from 26.45 m to 28.5 m. The span of the new wing was 42 m, compared with preceding aircraft, which had spans of 35.27 m. The extended fuselage eliminated a yawing problem, as did the introduction of a tail assembly with horizontal stabilizers with marked dihedral. The V8 Wk-Nr 4920 D-AQJA also had the longer fuselage and was fitted with defensive armament, introducing a small gondola beneath the port side of the fuselage nose which housed two 20 mm MG 151 cannon, as well as a rearward-firing 13 mm MG 131 machine gun at the extreme aft point of the aircraft.

Importantly, however, in 1940 it was decided to exploit the design of the Ju 90 further, in order to create a large military aircraft able to undertake long-range transport and reconnaissance operations. But it was not until 11 February 1941 that the *Technisches Amt* instructed provisionally that the Ju 90 V11 Wk-Nr 900011 D-AFHG *Oldenburg* was to be assigned for this purpose, although this was not fully confirmed until October of that year. Given an increased span of 42 m, new, more angular and taller tail fins and rudders, and a return to rectangular fuselage windows, the aircraft was also a little longer than the Ju 90, measuring 28.68 m in length.

Junkers also fitted the aircraft with the *Trapoklappe*. Powered by four 1,560 hp BMW 801A engines, it emerged as the new Ju 290 V1 Wk-Nr 29000001 BD+TX.

'A GIANT PIECE OF HARDWARE'

The Ju 290 V1 commenced flight-testing at Dessau on 16 July 1942 with Junkers test pilot Flugkapitän Hans-Joachim Pancherz at the controls along with flight engineer, Diplom-Ingenieur Rolf Geyling.

Like the Ju 90, it was one of the largest land aircraft in the German inventory (the Blohm & Voss BV 222 flying boat was larger), its fuselage marginally longer than the Messerschmitt Me 323 six-engined transport and its span almost 10 m greater than the four-engined Focke-Wulf Fw 200 Condor. It had a very roomy cockpit and a cavernous freight area, and although a ventral gondola was fitted, the forward dorsal turret was omitted and the aircraft carried no defensive armament. Internally, the copious, metal-walled stowage area measured 16.3 m in length and was 2.75 m wide and 2 m high.

Diplom-Ingenieur Kraft maintained overall control of the development programme, and within three months of the V1 flying, the Ju 290 V3 Wk-Nr 290110152 SB+QB was rolled out, Pancherz piloting it on its inaugural flight on 16 October; the V2 Wk-Nr 290110151 CE+YZ followed on 2 December. This latter aircraft had been converted from the Ju 90 V13, which had been slated for civil use by DLH; indeed, as late as 16 September 1942, German production plans still showed the aircraft as a 'model for DLH use'.[8]

Meanwhile, the V1 concluded its flight-testing without any major problems on 22 November, and shortly thereafter the aircraft was flown to Lecce in southern Italy by Junkers works pilots Flugkapitäne Eduard Dautzenberg and Walter Hänig, along with Geyling, for operational trials in the Mediterranean environment.[9] This was most probably in timely recognition of the fact that large-capacity transport was becoming an urgent requirement in the North African theatre.

Although the prototypes were manufactured at Dessau, Junkers decided that ensuing series production would be transferred to its Bernburg plant, where assembly facilities had been steadily developed.[10] Meanwhile, the V2 and V3 served to become the first machines in the new A-1 transporter series, powered by 1,600 hp BMW 801L radial engines.

Within the first three months of 1943 four more Ju 290A-1s were produced, representing the entire sub-series, the first machine being built from the V4, the remaining three as newly built A-1s. Again all the airframes (with the exception of one, which was assigned to destruction testing at the Letov factory at Letnany in occupied Czechoslovakia) were test-flown without any major problems by Pancherz. These aircraft were assigned, officially at least, a crew of eight and were fitted with an HDL (*Hydraulische Drehringlafette* – hydraulically operated gun mount) 151 gun turret (15 mm MG 151 cannon) in the B1 *Stand* (forward dorsal), a single MG 151 mounted into the ventral gondola C1 *Stand* (forward ventral) and C2 *Stand* (aft ventral), and a further MG 151 at the H *Stand* (tail). A single such weapon could also be installed on FDL (*Ferngerichtete Drehringlafetten* – remotely controlled mounts) on each side of the fuselage.

Aircrew found the Ju 290 a comfortable aircraft to fly; it offered a straightforward take-off, it was stable in the air, and the slotted ailerons needed only the lightest of control. Although there was little risk of stall, changes in power or speed required immediate trimming, which was managed by a three-axis electric trimmer, a slide on the control wheel and an override trimmer, which could be operated by the flight engineer. In the spacious cockpit, dual controls were available, with a console located between the pilot and co-pilot, but one weak point was the restricted view when on the ground.[11] Flieger-Stabsingenieur Hans-Werner Lerche was a test pilot at the *Erprobungsstelle* Rechlin in April 1943; he described the Ju 290 as a 'flying delicacy':

> My first flight in this precious 'ship' was in the Ju 290 CE+YZ [an A-1 from the second prototype]. Later, I flew the Ju 290s SB+QG [an A-2] and SB+QB. Although I had already flown the larger Messerschmitt Me 323, the giant powered cargo glider with six Gnome-Rhône engines, the Ju 290 was a 'real' aeroplane. And, considering its large size, it was exceptionally pleasant to fly.
>
> I remember well a particularly interesting flight in a Ju 290 when we had to evaluate the FuG 101 precision radio altimeter. At long last there was a task that made a pilot's heart beat faster! Just imagine: officially permitted low-level flying with such a huge 'steamer'! It was simply fascinating. As it was impossible to do this over land, even over the largest fields, I flew the required measuring run over Lake Müritz. Of course, one had to be terribly careful because the pilot's seat was fairly high up in the Ju 290 cockpit and it would not have been the first time that someone had tickled the waves with the propeller tips. But I really enjoyed this low-level flight.
>
> Later on I also had the opportunity to ferry a newly completed Junkers Ju 290 from the factory at Dessau to Rechlin. It really was a giant piece of hardware with its 42 m span and enormous fuselage. On overland flights I

could really enjoy the excellent view from the Ju 290 cockpit. Despite its size the aircraft was pleasant to fly, but on landing one always had to remember that the height of the pilot's eye level on touching down was more than 6 m above the ground. The qualities and performance of the Ju 290 transport, reconnaissance and bomber variants exceeded those of the Focke-Wulf Fw 200 Condor quite considerably, especially as regards armament and maximum range – which, in the case of the Ju 290, was some 6000 km.[12]

The Ju 290 first saw operational service under some of the most demanding conditions imaginable – especially for a still largely untried aircraft. At the end of December 1942, along with a *Staffel* of Ju 90s and some Fw 200s from I. and IV./KG 40, the Ju 290 V1 and A-1s were assigned to take part in the attempt to keep the German 6.*Armee* – surrounded by Soviet forces amidst the frozen ruins of Stalingrad – supplied by air. The aircraft were allocated to the mixed-type heavy transport *Gruppe*, KGr.z.b.V.200, based at Berlin-Staaken under the command of Major Hans-Jürgen Willers, a very experienced pilot who had previously flown He 111s with KG 4, KG 54 and KG 40. The first two Ju 290s to depart for Russia were the V1 BD+TX and the A-1 Wk-Nr 290110152 SB+QB. Following an interim stop at Wiener-Neustadt, the V1 landed at Stalino on 28 December. It made its first run to Pitomnik airfield, inside the Stalingrad pocket, in dense fog and with a strong risk of icing, on 10 January. But the mission was without incident. For its part, Wk-Nr 0152 suffered engine problems and was forced to return to Dessau, from where it took off once again on 6 January, staging via Warsaw, Kiev and Poltava, reaching Stalino at 1023 hrs on the 12th.

However, as Flugkapitän Walter Hänig attempted to take off from Pitomnik on the return from his second supply flight in the early hours of 13 January, the Ju 290 V1 crashed. Hänig, along with his Junkers flight engineer, Flieger-Oberingenieur Robert Stiefel, and three of his Luftwaffe crew members, together with 40 of the 75 wounded Wehrmacht troops on board, were killed. It was a grim beginning for the Ju 290.

Despite their valuable load capacities, and the obvious advantages of the *Trapoklappe* loading system over the more makeshift capabilities of the Fw 200, the big aircraft proved an easy target for Soviet fighters. Wk-Nr 0152's flight to the pocket on the 13th would be its only one. The aircraft was piloted by the very experienced Major Hugo Wiskandt, who had joined Junkers in 1925, but who served later as *Staffelkapitän* of 1./KGr.z.b.V.172. He was accompanied by Flugkapitän Hesselbach as co-pilot and navigator, and Diplom-Ingenieur Geyling. The aircraft took off from Stalino in refreshingly clear winter skies, en route for Pitomnik, accompanied by an

Fw 200. But a short while into their flight the German aircraft were attacked by a formation of five Soviet fighters. The Ju 290A-1 received multiple hits, but was able to make it to Pitomnik, where an inspection revealed that the aircraft's fuel feed system had been damaged. After some hasty and temporary repairs, the aircraft took off again to return to Stalino, but with a restricted load of only some ten badly wounded soldiers. At Stalino, a full count showed that the Junkers had been hit no fewer than 123 times. Under such circumstances, no further operations were considered possible, and so on 17 January, it undertook a 5½-hour direct flight back to Rangsdorf in Germany. From there it flew to Tempelhof for major repair work, and not long afterwards it would be assigned another, equally dangerous task.[13]

The Ju 290A-1 returned to the Eastern Front, where it remained until early February 1943, but worsening conditions on the ground combined with the appalling sub-zero conditions meant that it became all but impossible to continue making any meaningful flights. Eventually, Stalingrad and 6.*Armee* were lost, with 91,000 survivors passing into Soviet captivity.

By the spring of 1943, the Axis war effort in North Africa had become increasingly precarious. During the final months of the previous year, the Germans had pulled back towards Tunisia pursued by the British Eighth Army, and the Allies had landed in North-West Africa in Operation *Torch*, opening up a second front. It was therefore decided to establish a bridgehead at Tunis.

The Luftwaffe was at full stretch assisting Rommel in attacking the enemy invasion front and convoys off the North-West African coast and ports, in engaging the enemy air forces in the Algiers area and in maintaining and protecting the air routes between Italy, Sicily, Tripoli and Gabes/Tunis along which transports flew.[14] Transport missions were flown daily to the Tunis bridgehead, flying in replacement troops, aviation fuel, air-to-ground and Flak ordnance, anti-tank munitions and general supplies, while on the return flights Ju 52/3ms and a handful of Me 323s airlifted out wounded personnel and empty fuel drums. Then in late December 1942, several of the Mediterranean-based transport *Gruppen* were ordered to relocate urgently to Russia to assist with the crisis at Stalingrad, leaving a force of 200 Ju 52/3ms to maintain supply flights to German forces in Tunisia, along with 15 Me 323s and a force of *Regia Aeronautica* SM.81s and SM.82s. On 18 January 1943, however, the Luftwaffe suffered a blow at Tunis when no fewer than 23 Ju 52/3ms were destroyed on the ground during an Allied air raid. Tripoli was taken by Montgomery five days later. From February 1943 onwards, it was no longer a question of stemming the tide, but how long the inevitable could be held off. Yet the transports continued to fly determinedly despite increasing numbers of Allied fighters. Rommel left North Africa in early March, never to return, and in May the two armies comprising *Heeresgruppe Afrika* under Generaloberst Hans-Jürgen von Arnim disintegrated into isolated pools of resistance.

In order to shore up the Luftwaffe transport effort, at least two Ju 290A-1s – Wk-Nr 290110152 SB+QB, which had been repaired after suffering the aforementioned heavy damage during the Stalingrad airlift, and the newly delivered Wk-Nr 290110154 SB+QD – were handed over to *Lufttransportstaffel* (LTS) 290. LTS 290 had been established at Tempelhof in January 1943 as a specialist four-engined transport unit, which operated under the direct control of the OKL. Known initially as the *Transporterstaffel Berlin-Tempelhof* under Hauptmann d.R. Hans Haumann, who had previously flown Ju52/3ms with KGr.z.b.V.107, command was passed after only a short time to Hauptmann Heinz Braun, a former Fw 200 pilot with 7./KG 40 who had suffered wounds while attacking enemy shipping in the Atlantic in 1940.[15] The *Staffel* also numbered most of the available Ju 90s, the Ju 252 V5 and an unarmed Fw 200, as well as an armed C-5, and a small number of Italian Piaggio P.108 bombers. It would deploy its aircraft from Grosseto, some 150 km north of Rome on the Italian west coast, on transport missions to supply German forces in North Africa.

The Ju 290s, with their comparatively vast payloads, may have been a welcome sight to the men of *Heeresgruppe Afrika*, but their abilities were severely put to the test. Conditions in Tunisia were far from ideal: large aircraft such as the Ju 290 could really only be effective in conditions of air supremacy, with adequately prepared landing grounds and local military stability, none of which was the case in the Tunis area.[16]

On 7 April 1943, the Ju 290 Wk-Nr 0152, piloted once more by Major Wiskandt, suffered 50 per cent damage when it crash-landed at Megrine, just outside Tunis, and the aircraft was subsequently abandoned. Three weeks later on 1 May, Ju 290A-1 Wk-Nr 0154, re-coded as J4+AH and flown by Hauptmann Kurt Vogel, endured similar damage at Sidi Ahmed, south-west of Bizerta, and was also abandoned; it had been delivered by Junkers only in February.

Simultaneous to the Ju 290's deployment to Russia and North Africa was the request in the spring of 1943 from Oberst Karl-Henning von Barsewisch, the *General der Aufklärungsflieger*, for 12 Ju 290s to be built as long-range reconnaissance machines. However, this idea was quashed by the *Technisches Amt* in March 1943 on the basis that at that stage of the war, what was more urgently needed was fighters, particularly Fw 190s, to defend the skies over the Reich and the occupied territories, and to deal with the increasing threat from the Allied strategic air forces in the West as well as the ever-strengthening Soviet Air Forces in the East. Furthermore, it was the view of those in the

Technical Office that a suggestion to increase the number of Ju 290s in 1944 from 86 machines to 174 could be carried out only at the expense of Fw 190 production. Even a proposal to convert four Ju 290 transports as reconnaissance aircraft was rejected.

However, in effect, the Ju 290 owed its survival to Grossadmiral Dönitz. As has been related in Chapter One, as the *Befehlshaber der Unterseeboote*, Hitler favoured Dönitz and trusted his judgement, and, with enemy convoys in the Atlantic now operating beyond the range of the Fw 200, Dönitz had made a strong case to the *Führer* for the urgent need for increased longer-range air reconnaissance to contribute to the steadily worsening state of the U-boat war.[17] As Ju 290 historians Karl Kössler and Günther Ott note, this 'obviously had its effect'.[18] The decision to halt further work on the Ju 290 was reversed.

Thus, as early as March 1943, the aircraft development department at the *Technisches Amt* issued an order to Junkers to produce no fewer than 30 *Umrüstsätze* (conversion kits) with which to convert Ju 290A-1 transporters into long-range reconnaissance aircraft, or *Fernerkunder*. Furthermore, with immediate effect, three transporters that were already under construction – Wk-Nrs 0157, 0158 and 0159 – were to be changed on the assembly line to a preliminary reconnaissance variant, the A-2, while all subsequent aircraft from Wk-Nr 0160 would be built as the new long-range reconnaissance Ju 290A-3. This machine was intended to initially supplement, and ultimately to replace, the more limited range and slower Fw 200 in the long-range maritime reconnaissance role. Indeed, in a study of April 1944, one senior Luftwaffe staff officer commented on the value of seizing the Azores and French possessions in West Africa in order to obtain bases for the offensive against enemy shipping: 'From these bases,' he wrote, 'Ju 290s could reach almost to the American coast and enemy convoy traffic would be under the constant observation of the Luftwaffe for the greater part of its crossing. The immediate result would have been a great increase in sinkings.'[20]

Hans-Joachim Pancherz undertook the first flights in the three Ju 290 A-2s, coded SB+QG (0157), SB+QH (0158) and SB+QI (0159), in May and June 1943. Powered by BMW 801Ls, the aircraft were fitted with additional radio equipment and FuG 200 *Hohentwiel* air-to-surface vessel search radar for sea reconnaissance work, with extra armament in the form of a second, electric-hydraullically operated HDL 151 dorsal turret. The ensuing five-aircraft Ju 290A-3 series, all test-flown by Eduard Dautzenberg, was similar to the A-2, but was installed with more powerful 1,700 hp BMW 801Ds together with a Focke-Wulf Fw 20 reduced-drag, lower-profile aft dorsal gun turret and improved gondola design. Additionally, both the A-2 and A-3 carried a single MG 151 in the tail operated by a prone gunner, accessible from inside the fuselage. This 'tail' turret had a traverse of 60°, with an elevation of 45° above and 60° below the horizontal. In the case of the A-3, provision was made to mount manually operated MG 131s in left and right waist positions, which could be easily removed and stowed in the fuselage when not in use. The A-3 also featured additional armour for the pilots' area, weapons stands and engines, and carried FuG 10 and FuG 16Z VHF transceivers, FuG 200 radar (see Chapter Five), and a rubber dinghy contained in purpose-built fuselage accommodation.[21]

As far as Dönitz and the Kriegsmarine were concerned, these aircraft were needed out in the Atlantic and could not come quickly enough. With progress now under way, the next requirement was for experienced and capable crews to fly them.

CHAPTER THREE

EYES OVER THE EASTERN FRONT

The reconnaissance observer (long-range) needs to be primarily trained in navigation, instrument flying, high-altitude flying, and in aerial photography. His employment is essential in aerial warfare...

Generaloberst Oswald Lutz, *Zusammenarbeit zwischen Panzertruppe und Luftwaffe* (Cooperation between armoured troups and the Luftwaffe), 12 September 1936

As crucial to the overall German war effort on the Eastern Front as the Luftwaffe's fighter, dive-bomber, bomber and ground-attack operations were, those conducted by the long-range air reconnaissance units were of equally vital importance.

One such unit was the 3.(F) *Staffel* of *Aufklärungsgruppe* 10 ('F' was for *Fern* – long-range). In November 1942, 3.(F)/Aufkl.Gr.10 was based at Tazinskaya in southern Russia, some 250 km south-west of Stalingrad and equipped mainly with the Junkers Ju 88D-1, as well as some D-2s and D-5s – the reconnaissance variant of the Luftwaffe's new twin-engined *Schnellbomber*. On paper, the unit formed part of FAGr 4 based at Mariupol, but in practice it operated semi-autonomously in support of 4.*Panzerarmee* in its operations in the Don bend. This was a difficult time for German forces on the Eastern Front. By mid-November, the German line in the southern sector stretched from Voronezh at its northernmost point to Elista and Essentuki in the south, curving back to Novorossisk on the Black Sea – a vast area of conquest won by the Wehrmacht in just six months. In the centre of this line was the city of Stalingrad on the River Volga, most of which 6.*Armee* had taken in fierce fighting in October. Indeed, by mid-November, General Alfred Jodl, Chief of the Wehrmacht Operations Staff at the *Oberkommando der Wehrmacht* (OKW – Supreme Command of the Armed Forces), believed the city to be 'practically conquered'. Some 6.5 km of the Volga bank had been secured and the Soviets pushed back to the fortified riverbank with the enemy command sliced in two.[1] However, on the morning of 19 November, as Hitler and his generals were distracted by the Allied landings in Tunisia, the Soviet South-Western and Don fronts, followed the next day by the Stalingrad Front, launched Operation *Uranus*, a fierce counter-offensive involving more than one million men, 13,500 guns and mortars, and 100 rocket batteries, designed to lock and trap 6.*Armee* within the bomb- and shell-shattered ruins of Stalingrad. To those with sufficient precognition, the appalling spectre of the sudden loss of Stalingrad and the prospect of the entrapment of an entire army was looming.

Tasked with providing vital short- and long-range reconnaissance over this sector were the four *Staffeln* of *Aufklärungsgruppe* 10 '*Tannenberg*'. The *Gruppe* had been awarded the honour title in commemoration of the battle of Tannenberg in August 1914, which saw a great victory for German forces over the Russians. The 3.(F)/Aufkl.Gr.10, under the command of Major Horst Klinger, had been formed in November 1938 from elements of 3./Aufkl.Gr.11 at Neuhausen in East Prussia and equipped initally with Dornier Do 17Fs – a field-modified reconnaissance variant of the slim, twin-engined Do 17E bomber, powered by twin 750 hp BMW VI 7.3D inline engines. In addition to a pair of cameras, the F-1 could carry a 4,500-kg bomb load and had increased fuel capacity.

By 1942, like many Luftwaffe flying units, it had experienced a 'busy' war thus far. The unit first saw operations during the campaign in Poland in 1939, in which it fell under the control of a *Koluft* (*Kommandeur der Luftwaffe bei einem Armeeoberkommando* – Luftwaffe Commander assigned to an Army command), a senior Luftwaffe officer, usually of the rank of Generalmajor or Oberst, who was attached to the staff of an Army command and who exercised direct command over all air units assigned to that command – usually short-range reconnaissance, signals and Flak formations.

He would be responsible for keeping the army informed of the results of reconnaissance operations in his sector.[2] In this case 3.(F)/Aufkl.Gr.10 took its orders from Generalmajor Victor Krocker, the *Koluft Heeresgruppe Nord*, and operated as a reconnaissance unit for *General der Artillerie* Georg von Küchler's 3.*Armee*. The *Staffel* was transferred to Oberbruch-Süd in February 1940 in readiness for operations in the West. From Oberbruch its new, improved Do 17Ms and Ps, fitted respectively with Bramo 323A-1 and BMW 132 radial engines, flew missions over the Netherlands and later over the English Channel monitoring shipping and British coastal fortifications. During the German assault in the West in May, operating under the direction of the *Koluft* 6, Oberst Günther Lohmann, they provided reconnaissance support for the amoured formations of *Panzergruppe Kleist* as they thrust through Belgium and northern France, before moving successively in June to fields at Savy, Saint-Mard, La Fortelle, Vimeroy, Orleans, and La Nieppe in the Pas de Calais, from where observation missions were again flown over the Channel for German coastal artillery until May 1941.

That month the *Staffel* was transferred to Jüterbog-Damm in eastern Germany where, under the command of Hauptmann Bruno Rainer, it prepared for its part in Operation *Barbarossa*, the invasion of the Soviet Union. Next 3.(F)/Aufkl.Gr.10 moved to Neudorf, near Oppeln in Silesia, where its crews underwent final operational preparations under Generalmajor Karl Drum, the *Koluft Heeresgruppe Süd*, under whom it would work in support of the drive east by *Heeresgruppe Süd* on the southern sector of the German advance. By this stage, the *Staffel* was equipped with nine aircraft and three reserve machines, and was primed for operations in the vast expanses of the Soviet Union, being able to draw upon a fleet of around 30–50 heavy support vehicles. It had a strength of some 320 officers and men. At the beginning of June 1941, however, 3.(F)/Aufkl.Gr.10 moved farther east to Rzeszow-Jasionka in Poland and, following the commencement of *Barbarossa* on 22 June, it had transferred to Berditschew.

For the rest of 1941, and based initially at Starokonstantinow and then Zhytomir, the *Staffel* carried out longer-range reconnaissance missions in direct cooperation, through the *Koluft*, with the staffs of *Heeresgruppe Süd*.[3] 'Targets' included the photographing of enemy troop movements and concentrations behind the main battle area, roads, railways, bridges and the traffic passing over them, airfield activity, towns and factories.[4] These missions involved the Dorniers climbing to an altitude of between 3500 and 6000 m and making course directly for the target area, but as Soviet air opposition gradually stiffened, operational altitudes had to increase to 6500–8000 m. The crews of the *Staffel* were briefed to avoid combat if at all possible, but in case of attack by the enemy, the tactic was to make for home, dropping altitude rapidly in a series of violent evasive turns.[5]

In September 3.(F)/Aufkl.Gr.10 was operating from Lviv (Lemberg) in the western Ukraine, and in November it moved much farther east to Mariuopol on the Sea of Azov in the area of *Luftflotte* 4.

At the beginning of 1942, the *Staffel* handed over its Do 17s and was briefly pulled back to Ohlau in Silesia, where it converted to the new and much vaunted, high-speed Ju 88D-1. Powered by a pair of 1,350 hp Junkers Jumo 211J-1 or J-2 engines, the Ju 88D-1 was based on the A-4 fast-bomber and was able to carry the same external stores, including long-range drop tanks, but was fitted with remotely controlled Rb 50/30 high-altitude and/or Rb 20/30 low-altitude cameras in various combinations mounted in the fuselage immediately aft of the bomb-bay. Extra internal fuel tanks were fitted instead of a forward bomb-bay. The Ju 88D-1 quickly became the most common reconnaissance variant.[6]

Still under the command of Major Rainer, 3.(F)/Aufkl.Gr.10 then returned to Russia from late January 1942, assigned to FAGr 4 under Major Friedrich Alpers as its parent unit, operating from Poltawa in central Ukraine until June.[7]

In the late spring of 1942, the tactical chain of command for Luftwaffe reconnaissance operations was revised and saw the end of the *Koluft* system. The *Koluft* was replaced by the *Flivo* (*Fliegerverbindungsoffizier* – Air Liaison Officer), usually a field-grade officer with the rank of Oberst who was assigned to an army group, army or Panzer Army. The *Flivo* and his small staff held no command over local air units, but rather acted as a liaison between the regional army and air force commands, as well as preparing situation reports for the Luftwaffe and passing on requests for reconnaissance on behalf of the Wehrmacht. Under such a set-up, the deployment and decisions relating to long-range reconnaissance operations conducted by units such as 3.(F)/Aufkl.Gr.10 remained within the domain of the *Luftflotte* command.

The Ju 88s tended to fly from their bases at very low level and then climb to around 9000 m as the target was approached. Once the required photographs had been taken, they would immediately turn for home, returning once more to low altitude.

The crews of 3.(F)/Aufkl.Gr.10, each comprising pilot, observer/navigator, flight engineer/gunner and radio operator, became very experienced at these kind of missions, and several pilots, including Oberleutnante Herbert Abel and Hans Ascheid, and Leutnant Günther Korn, were awarded the *Ehrenpokal* (Honour Goblet) 'For Special Achievement in the Air War'.[8] All of these pilots would go on to fly long-range missions over the Atlantic with FAGr 5.

In August 1942, 3.(F)/Aufkl.Gr.10 moved to Kharkov and then south again to Mariupol, from where long-range missions were flown on behalf of the army to targets in the Don bend, for example, to obtain photographs of the railway lines leading to Saratow, the fighting in the area around Stalingrad, and as far east as Astrakhan and the Northern Caucasus. The dangers of such missions were highlighted when the Ju 88D of Oberleutnant Hugo Oechsle went missing in action from Tazinskaya in December.[9] But with the aforementioned Soviet counter-offensive, which commenced in November, on 21 December, the *Staffel* was forced to abandon its base at Tazinskaya, the more fortunate members of the unit's personnel escaping in the unit's motor vehicles, the less fortunate resorting to a long march on foot as far as Rostov. All but three of the eight Ju 88D-1s and D-5s of the *Staffel* were left behind.

From Rostov, Major Klinger, who had taken over command from Rainer in October, led his men on a long journey back to Gutenfeld in East Prussia where, in early 1943 under the coordination of one of the unit's pilots, Leutnant Hellmut Nagel, they were to prepare for conversion to the new, but troublesome, Heinkel He 177 long-range bomber. Nagel would soon be replaced in this task, however, by Leutnant Josef Augustin. The latter, an experienced reconnaissance pilot, had flown with 2.(F)/Aufkl.Gr.123, and more recently had served as a photographic intelligence officer on the staffs of *Luftwaffenkommando Don* and I.*Fliegerkorps*.[10]

Also based on the Eastern Front at this time was 3.(F)/Aufkl.Gr.100 under Hauptmann Karl-Friedrich Bergen, who had previously flown with *Aufklärungsgruppe* 121. Bergen was an experienced reconnaissance pilot, who had flown several types of aircraft, including the relatively rare Dornier Do 215, in an example of which he had suffered light injuries on one occasion as a result of an emergency landing in Belgrade in April 1941.[11] The 3.(F)/Aufkl.Gr.100 had only recently been formed, or more specifically been renamed, from 3.(F)/Aufkl.Gr.Ob.d.L. (the Long-Range Reconnaissance Group of the Commander-in-Chief of the Air Force), a unit that had carried out covert, long-range, high-altitude, deep penetration reconnaissance missions over Soviet territory before *Barbarossa*. Since October 1942 it had been based at Seshchinskaya, south-east of Roslavl. Like 3.(F)/Aufkl.Gr.10, it operated Ju 88D-1s and D-5s, but also numbered two of the new pre-production, twin-engined, two-seat Arado Ar 240A-0s, which had been converted from a fighter configuration with advanced, remotely controlled gun barbettes, as reconnaissance aircraft, with which it conducted long-range missions over western Central Russia. Earlier, this aircraft type had been used to fly similar missions over the British Isles.[12] Also, like 3.(F)/Aufkl.Gr.10, 3.(F)/Aufkl.Gr.100 had accumulated some very experienced pilots within its ranks. Oberleutnant Hans-Otto Heindorff, for example, who had served with 3.(F)/Aufkl.Gr.Ob.d.L., had been awarded the *Ehrenpokal* and the *Deutsche Kreuz*, and would receive the *Ritterkreuz* on 21 October 1942.[13]

But in February 1943, on instructions from the *Oberkommando der Luftwaffe*, the *General der Aufklärungsflieger*, Oberst von Barsewisch, ordered elements of 3.(F)/Aufkl.Gr.100 to be withdrawn from the front and returned to the Reich, while some personnel were reassigned to the Ju 88-equipped 4.(F)/Aufkl.Gr.121, which had recently moved to Seshchinskaya from Orscha-Süd under Hauptmann Günter Kratzmann. This amounted, in effect, to a partial disbandment of 3.(F)/Aufkl.Gr.100. Furthermore, the *Staffelkapitän*, Hauptmann Bergen, was also ordered to return home, whereupon he was then reassigned temporarily to the 4. *Verbandsführerlehrgang* (Unit Leader Intake) at the *Verbandsführerschule/*KG 101 at Tours in France for a brief period of introductory classroom training on very long-range reconnaissance using larger, four-engined aircraft.[14]

Meanwhile, at Gutenfeld, after only a short period of He 177 conversion training under the coordination of Leutnant Augustin, the former crews of 3.(F)/Aufkl.Gr.10 were informed that they were to be transferred west, still under the leadership of Augustin, to Achmer airfield, near Osnabrück, where they would be reassigned to a newly formed unit for very long-range reconnaissance missions on a special, four-engined aircraft.

Over the coming weeks they would be joined there by selected personnel from 3.(F)/Aufkl.Gr.100. In June Hauptmann Bergen completed his course at the *Verbandsführerschule* at Tours and he too headed for Achmer. The nucleus of men who would form the new long-range, maritime reconnaissance unit of the Luftwaffe had been gathered. It was now time to acquaint them with their aircraft, the Junkers Ju 290, and to train them to offer the badly needed reconnaissance support for Dönitz's U-boat campaign – a very different form of operations to that with which they were accustomed.

CHAPTER FOUR

FORMATION

Achmer, March–November 1943

Mit Gewitter und Sturm aus fernem Meer...
(With tempest and storm on distant seas...)

Richard Wagner: from the Steersman's aria, Act I, *Der Fliegende Holländer*

The regional airport of Achmer lies just to the south of the eponymous village and 15 km north-west of the city of Osnabrück in Lower Saxony. A comparatively large airfield for the time, in 1943 it functioned as a base for Luftwaffe bomber units and was known officially as Achmer-Bramsche after the slightly larger settlement of Bramsche, just over 5 km to the north-east.

Construction work at Achmer airfield began in 1936 and was completed in 1939, but there was a continuing programme of development and improvement running through to 1943. The site stretched for 2380 x 1370 m and comprised three concrete runways in the form of a triangle measuring 1800 m (with a 550-m prepared strip at one end) x 1700 m x 1550 m. Fourteen paved servicing hardstands, each fitted with refuelling points, led off the southern boundary. In 1943, the airfield was adequately and necessarily well camouflaged, and equipped with runway, perimeter and obstruction lighting, as well as a Lorenz guidance system for night landings. Achmer's 50 or so open aircraft shelters and six perimeter parking sites were supported by a strong airfield infrastructure, which included two workshop hangars along the north-east boundary, an airfield headquarters building, along with administration buildings, barracks, flying control at the centre of the southern boundary, a motor pool and associated garages, and further barrack accommodation on the outskirts of Achmer village. Additionally, the airfield benefited from a rail spur which ran into the buildings area, and also served the fuel and munitions dumps, the latter being located to the southern and northern edges of the field. In 1941, a camp had been built to house Soviet PoW workers to the north-west of the airfield and further accommodation was built throughout the war on wooded sites in the airfield vicinity.

On 18 August 1942, the 'hot' war came to Achmer for the first time, when the airfield suffered an attack from RAF Bomber Command. From August 1940, Achmer had been a base for the Dornier Do 17 and Do 217 bombers of *Stab*, II., III., and IV./KG 2 and during the 1942 attack, a Bü 131 of the IV.*Gruppe* of the *Geschwader* was destroyed. The airfield defences were stiffened and by the autumn of 1943, four 12.8-cm Flak guns had been set up on the Bramscher Berg just to the west of Bramsche, which were augmented by at least 12 light Flak positions located around the airfield, including some in specially built Flak towers. At that time there were nearly 1,200 NCOs and enlisted men based at Achmer in various capacities.[1]

This was the airfield to which Oberleutnant Oskar H. Schmidt was despatched in early 1943 on orders of the staff of the *General der Aufklärungsflieger*. Schmidt had previously served as *Offizier zur besonderen Verwendung* (Offz.z.b.V. – Officer assigned for special duties) with 3.(F)/Aufkl.Gr.Ob.d.L., but as a result of his duties in Russia, he had been hospitalized for a period in Braunschweig. Upon recovery, he was instructed to report to Achmer where he was to establish a *Stabskompanie* in readiness for the building up of a new long-range reconnaissance *Gruppe* to be known as *Fernaufklärungsgruppe* 5 (FAGr 5) which was to commence operations over the Bay of Biscay, the eastern Atlantic, and western Mediterranean with an official strength of 40 Ju 290s. The purpose of the unit was to conduct reconnaissance and shadowing missions as required by the *Befehlshaber der Unterseeboote* and to report to the *Fliegerführer Atlantik* who, based on information obtained from FAGr 5, would direct the crews of the Fw 200s and He 177s of the Luftwaffe anti-shipping *Geschwader*, KG 40, based at Bordeaux-Mérignac in Western France.

Fernaufklärungsgruppe 5 was to track the enemy's northern convoy routes between Britain and North America, westwards from the north coast of

Ireland, and the southern supply lines from Gibraltar, to and from the African coast, and westwards from south of Lisbon. It was to record and report on shipping movements through the means of visual observation, photography and use of FuG 200 *Hohentwiel* search radar. As a further function, the unit was also to provide regular weather reports. Schmidt was advised that personnel for the unit would be drawn from reconnaissance units presently operating 'in the Crimea'.[2]

The *Stabskompanie* was to include the unit's *Bildstelle* (photographic), signals and motor transport sections and was to be formed mainly from personnel reassigned from 3.(F)/Aufkl.Gr.Ob.d.L. and 3.(F)/Aufkl.Gr.10. Schmidt was soon joined at Achmer by Hauptmann d.R.z.V. Karl Nather as *Bildoffizier* (Photographic Officer) and Leutnant Hans Wessel as *Nachrichtenoffizier* (Signals Officer). For the next four months, until the end of June 1943, Schmidt and his colleagues worked hard to prepare support facilities, accommodation, supplies and equipment for the new unit. Although Nather was in nominal command of the *Stabskompanie*, it is to Schmidt's credit that he worked very much on his own initiative to set things up and without the backing of a *Gruppenkommandeur*, since one would not be appointed until June.

However, Schmidt was assisted, eventually and to a great extent, by the arrival at Achmer in June of Hauptmann Karl-Friedrich Bergen, the erstwhile *Staffelkapitän* of 3.(F)/Aufkl.Gr.100. Fresh from his large-aircraft training course at the *Verbandsführerschule*/KG 101 at Tours, Bergen had been appointed as the commander of 2./FAGr 5, the first *Staffel* of the new *Gruppe* to be formed. On 15 June, the first of his officers also arrived in the shape of Oberleutnant Herbert Daubenspeck, who would fill the role of Navigation Officer and Instructor in 2.*Staffel*.

Following in the footsteps of Bergen and Daubenspeck, throughout June and July came the crews of 3.(F)/Aufkl.Gr.100 from the East, who would form the first cadre of personnel for 2./FAGr 5, although Achmer had still not yet seen the appearance of its first Ju 290.

Meanwhile, in Berlin, Oberst von Barsewisch had appointed a member of his staff, Hauptmann Hermann Fischer, a very experienced reconnaissance pilot, to command FAGr 5. Born in March 1913, Fischer joined 1.(F)/Aufkl. Gr.120 at Neuhausen as *Adjutant* in late 1938. His first wartime assignment was with 2.(H)/Aufkl.Gr.13, a short-range army-support reconnaissance *Staffel* equipped with the Henschel Hs 126. The unit took part in the Western campaign and was later sent to Russia. In early 1942, Fischer was promoted to Oberleutnant and appointed *Staffelkapitän* of 3.(F)/Aufkl.Gr.22 based at Dno, where he transitioned to flying twin-engined Ju 88s. On 30 January 1942, he was wounded during an attack on Dno airfield by Soviet fighters.

Promoted to Hauptmann, on 2 March 1942 he was awarded the *Ehrenpokal*, followed by the *Deutsche Kreuz* on 27 July that year. At some point thereafter he was recalled to Berlin to join the Staff of the *General der Aufklärungsflieger*.

On 24 June 1943, Fischer flew to Achmer to inspect the facilities there and to hold discussions with Schmidt, Nather, Wessel, Bergen, and Daubenspeck, and the newly appointed *Stabskompanie* 'Spiess' (senior NCO), Hauptfeldwebel Heinrich Meyer. It was to be a brief visit, for it seems Fischer quickly became aware that he had not been fully informed of what was required of him. The next day he returned to Berlin to seek clarification and to discuss the role of FAGr 5 further with von Barsewisch. At that point things became sufficiently quiet at Achmer that the men of the *Stabskompanie* were allowed to take leave.

Possibly as a result of Fischer's return to Berlin, on 6 July, von Barsewisch, accompanied by Fischer, travelled to Achmer to inspect the new *Gruppe* and to address the small number of personnel in place there. Then, six days later, Fischer held his first major meeting with three of his senior officers with the purpose of devising operational tactics and the unit's modus operandi. Meanwhile, as the worrying news came in that the Allies had landed on the southern coast of Sicily, the slow pace of the unit's development meant that on 19 July, a number of men were released temporarily from service in order to join local crop-harvesting teams, whose labours were vital to the war effort. The Luftwaffe men were more than happy to oblige in this task; it was an antidote to boredom, it offered a pleasant break from service, it meant that there was opportunity to obtain some extra foodstuff, and there was even some romance between the men of FAGr 5 and some of the local girls.[3]

Meanwhile, the arrival of crews to train on, and actually fly, the Ju 290s was proceeding at a snail's pace, to a great extent because several key flying personnel from 3.(F)/Aufkl.Gr.100 had been assigned, temporarily, to other reconnaissance units. One pilot, Oberleutnant Helmut Eberhardt, who had flown with the 3.(F)/Aufkl.Gr.100 and the *Führerkurierstaffel*, was assigned to 2./FAGr 5, but spent only a brief time at Achmer before being transferred to another long-range reconnaissance unit. On 18 July, Oberleutnant Karl Schöneberger, a recent recipient of the *Ehrenpokal*, and his crew arrived directly from Russia to be joined three days later by pilot Oberleutnant Karl-Heinz Schmidt, with his observer, Leutnant Hermann Barth, and their crew. Another observer, Oberleutnant Horst Degenring, reported for duty a few days later. On the 21st, Oberleutnant Hanns Kohmann, Leutnant Hans-Roger Friedrich, Leutnant Hermann Kersting, Oberfeldwebel Gustav Albers and Oberfeldwebel Willi Wittemann, all greatly experienced long-range pilots formerly of LTS 290, arrived at Achmer.[4] These men were assigned to 2./FAGr 5 with the express task of training pilots on the Ju 290 – when such aircraft eventually arrived. The *Staffel* did, at least, take delivery of some vehicles and lorries, including some heavy-duty Czech-made Tatra trucks intended for towing the big Junkers.

A formal muster and inspection of the *Gruppe* was held on 23 July to mark the official commencement of Hauptmann Fischer's assumption of command.

Thirteen officers of 2./FAGr 5 used the pretext of making the first 'long-range training flight' to fly one of the unit's new Ju 290s to Dresden-Klotzsche on 25 August. Having arrived in Dresden, they promptly caught a tram into the city centre, where they joined in the celebrations of their fellow *Staffel* officer, Oberleutnant Günther Pfeiffer, another former member of 3.(F)/Aufkl.Gr.100, who had married the daughter of Generalmajor Helmuth Mentzel, previously an instructor and commander of the *Aufklärungsfliegerschule* at Hildesheim and Braunschweig-Grossenhain.[5]

It would not be until 16 August 1943, however, that FAGr 5 took delivery of its first Ju 290 when the A-2 model Wk-Nr 0158 SB+QH joined the *Gruppe* at Achmer and was assigned to Bergen's recently formed 2.*Staffel*. This aircraft had first flown on 7 June 1943 and was fitted with FuG 200 *Hohentwiel* radar. It would be recoded with FAGr 5's unit indentifier as 9V+BC. Two days later, the next aircraft flew in, in the form of Ju 290 A-2 Wk-Nr 0159 SB+QI, which was recoded for operational purposes as 9V+CC and also assigned to 2./FAGr 5.[6] The *Gruppe* had to wait another month until a third Junkers, the A-3 Wk-Nr 0160 SB+QJ, finally arrived. This machine was recoded 9V+BH and assigned as the first aircraft to 1./FAGr 5, which was still in the elementary stages of training at Achmer under the leadership of the recently promoted Hauptmann Josef Augustin. The *Gruppe Stab* was assigned a single Ju 88.[7]

A 3.*Staffel* was planned to expand the *Gruppe* and to be equipped with the Ju 88H-1 fitted with FuG 200 for long-range reconnaissance/anti-shipping operations as and when the type became available, but the *Staffel* was never formed. A 4./FAGr 5 would be formed in the spring of 1944 (see Chapter Twelve).

The Germans were very aware that the air war at sea required high standards of training for long-range reconnaissance aircrew, particularly in navigation. Captured logs and documents from Allied aircraft and aircrew revealed, comparatively, just how advanced and meticulous the skills were amongst Allied airmen operating over the Atlantic and the Bay of Biscay. In the case of Luftwaffe crews, the most successful were those whose proficiency had been maintained by constant practice in the use of navigational aids and techniques in long-range operations.

'In contrast to this,' lamented a Luftwaffe report in early 1944, 'the formations that have been employed for years in support of the army not only lack professional dexterity, but often also the right temperamental approach for carrying out the precise manouevres of navigation that are needed in locating targets on the sea. The crews are not to blame for this as they are usually concerned with terrestial navigation.'

By late 1943, the Luftwaffe endeavoured to place emphasis on navigational training, including astro-navigational training, as well as instilling a rudimentary understanding of naval tactics and the composition of naval forces in order to recognize and understand tactical situations and the best opportunities for attack.[8]

During training at Achmer, considerable importance was placed on such skills, since in undertaking missions which would range 3000 km from a home base, and in order to maintain mission secrecy and security, dependence could not be placed on radio navigation, which gave out emissions and which could be picked up by the enemy. Thus, as at sea, the navigator aboard the aircraft would have to make use of a sextant, and as with the practice employed aboard a ship, readings and course depended on the sun, or at night, the stars. A good navigator would be able to determine a fairly accurate position of his aircraft after five minutes of readings.

In this regard, several very long-range triangulation flights were made in the early autumn of 1943, starting from Achmer and flying out to Mykolajiw in the Ukraine, then to Helsinki, before returning to Achmer. Much to the delight of the personnel of the *Gruppe*, crews returning from these flights often brought back with them fresh food and produce from the Ukraine.[9]

The personnel of 2./FAGr 5 gradually strengthened. On 6 September, an intake of Unteroffiziere was drafted in and trained up under the supervision of Oberleutnant Schmidt of the *Stabskompanie*. That day also, Oberleutnant Kurt Baumgartner arrived at Achmer. Baumgartner was another former 3.(F)/Aufkl. Gr.Ob.d.L. pilot, but he had been injured on 6 August 1942 in an accident when the Bf 109F-4 he was flying had crashed on take-off from Gostkino-Kharkov as a result of a servicing fault and he had only just returned to duty following a lengthy spell in hospital. Just over a week later, on 15 September, the first of two observers and recipients of the *Ehrenpokal* joined the unit in the form of Oberleutnant Oskar Nau, who was followed on the 26th by 28-year-old Hauptmann Richard Schmoll. Also joining 2./FAGr 5 in September was pilot Oberleutnant Karl Otto Kremser, who had flown previously with KG 40.[10] With his experience at the Fw 200-equipped bomber wing, with whom it was intended that FAGr 5 would cooperate, Kremser, along with some other specialist KG 40 personnel, was assigned to FAGr 5 to advise on long-range, over-water operations.[11]

The early nucleus of command for *Fernaufklärungsgruppe* 5 in September 1943 was as follows:

Kommandeur:	Hauptmann Hermann Fischer
Gruppenstab	
Adjutant:	Oberleutnant Herbert Abel (prev. *Staffelführer* and Offz.z.b.V. 3.(F)/Aufkl.Gr.10)
Gruppe Technical Officer:	Oberleutnant Hans Müller, DKG (prev. 3.(F)/Aufkl.Gr.22)
Meteorologist:	Unknown at this stage
Navigation Instructor:	Oberleutnant Herbert Daubenspeck
Signals Officer:	Oberleutnant Siegfried Frank (prev. 3.(F)/Aufkl.Gr.Ob.d.L.)
Senior Staff Administration Officer:	Stabs.Int. Heinrich
Senior Medical Officer:	Oberarzt Dr. Rückstahl (prev. 3.(F)/Aufkl.Gr.10, but replaced by Stabsarzt Dr. Willi Spiesmann after only a short time)
Gruppe Operations Officer:	Various appointments, unclear for this time
Stab pilots:	Hauptmann Jochen Wahnfried
	Oberleutnant Ludwig Herlein (prev. 3.(F)/Aufkl.Gr.22 and RLM (L.In.1))
Stabskompanie	
CO and Photographic Officer:	Hauptmann Karl Nather (prev. *2.Schüler-Kp./Fliegerbildschule* Hildesheim)
Signals Officer:	Leutnant Hans Wessel
	Oberleutnant Oskar H.Schmidt
1.Staffel	
Kapitän:	Hauptmann Josef Augustin (prev. *Staffelkapitän* 3.(F)/Aufkl.Gr.10)
Offz.z.b.V.:	Oberleutnant Beuthel
Technical Officer:	Oberleutnant Günther Korn (prev. 3.(F)/Aufkl.Gr.10)
2.Staffel	
Kapitän:	Hauptmann Karl-Friedrich Bergen (prev. *St.Ka.* 3.(F)/Aufkl.Gr.100)
Offz.z.b.V.:	Oberleutnant Ernst Treskatis
Technical Officer:	Oberleutnant Konrad (Kornelius?) Mildenberger, DKG (prev. 3.(F)/Aufkl.Gr.Ob.d.L.)

Any notion of relaxation that may have existed as a result of the relatively casual progress of training and preparation for operations, ended abruptly on 14 September when the pace shifted up a gear. That day, the *Kommandeur*, Hauptmann Fischer, ordered the *Gruppe* to assemble on parade. He informed his men of orders issued by OKL to the effect that discipline on the part of aircrews was of paramount importance and that carelessness displayed on flying operations would not be tolerated under any circumstances. The fact, Fischer told them, was that in this fifth year of war, aircraft and trained airmen were too precious to lose because of inattention or negligence.

Duly dismissed, the flying crews were despatched in small groups to the *Ergänzungs-Fernaufklärungsgruppe* (or Long-Range Reconnaissance Operational Training Group) under Oberstleutnant Hans-Günther von Obernitz at Posen in western Poland, from where, using Ju 88s, it was intended that they would carry out the first excercises in cooperation with the U-boat arm's tactical training flotilla, the 27.*Unterseebootsflottille* under the command of the U-boat ace, *Korvettenkapitän* Erich Topp, using the Baltic Sea as their training area.[12] A small number of officers from FAGr 5, including Oberleutnant Siegfried Frank, of the *Gruppenstab* and a former signals officer with 3.(F)/Aufkl.Gr.Ob.d.L., observer Leutnant Heinrich Morf, and pilot Leutnant Hellmut Nagel, both of 1./FAGr 5, also spent some time on board U-boats in the Baltic in order to familiarize themselves on how the submariners depended on, and communicated with, aircraft.

Simultaneously, Fischer also asked all members of FAGr 5 for their suggestions for an appropriate emblem for use by the *Gruppe*. An emblem 'committee' reviewed all the proposals and decided in favour of '*Der fliegende Holländer*' (Flying Dutchman), which took the form of a black cog on the high seas under full sail, after the ghost ship of legend that was doomed to sail the oceans for ever. The emblem, with slight variations in colour, would be used on some of FAGr 5's aircraft.

Fischer also began to consider suitable bases in the West from which FAGr 5 could undertake its military operations. In this regard, he sent a small *Vorkommando* (advance unit), headed by Oberleutnant Ernst Treskatis, an observer from 2.*Staffel*, and Hauptfeldwebel Heinrich Meyer, the *Spies* of the *Stabskompanie*, to conduct a preliminary assessment of the pre-war civil airport at the town of Mont de Marsan, located some 100 km south of Bordeaux, and around 80 km from the Atlantic coast in western France. Following a positive initial opinion from the *Vorkommando*, Oberleutnant Schmidt, together with other officers from the *Stabskompanie*, flew to Mont de Marsan on 24 September to inspect potential accommodation should the *Gruppe* transfer there. It was decided that a local junior girls' school could provide acceptable quarters for the *Stab*, while a building on the Rue de Manon could accommodate 1.*Staffel* and the girls' High School could take 2.*Staffel*. Following further discussions between Fischer and von Barsewisch, it was decided that Mont de Marsan would become FAGr 5's operational base. Subsequently, Fischer instructed Schmidt to begin preparations for a transfer of the whole *Gruppe* to France.

Meanwhile, Oberst von Barsewisch arranged for a delegation of technical and engineering personnel from Junkers, headed by Professor Diplom-Ingenieur Heinrich Hertel, the firm's very capable Technical Director and head of development, based at the Dessau plant, to visit FAGr 5 at Achmer on 23 September. It was hoped that both sides would gain benefit from such a visit, and, after inspecting the unit's aircraft, workshops and other facilities, as well as watching some flight demonstrations, on the request of the Luftwaffe personnel, Hertel and his team rejoined to the mess hall where they took part in discussions with the crews on how the Ju 290 could be further developed for the purposes of long-range, over-water reconnaissance missions.[13]

By the end of September, *Stab*/FAGr 5 was still operating its Ju 88 but had also taken delivery of a Do 17P, while 2.*Staffel* reported one Ju 290A-2 and three A-3s. On paper at least, 1.*Staffel* had been assigned one Ju 290A-2 and one A-3.[14] As September gave way to October, 2./FAGr 5 sent its Ju 290s and crews to Rerik, a coastal airfield and seaplane station, 37 km west of Rostock on the Baltic coast, where they undertook air-gunnery practice flights over the sea.

On 13 October 1943, the *Gruppe* suffered its first aircraft damage when Oberleutnant Kohmann took off on a long-distance flight in the newly assigned, but heavily laden, Ju 290A-3 Wk-Nr 0163 (PI+PQ) 9V+AK. As the aircraft attempted to leave the ground, one of its engines failed, but Kohmann was able to belly-land it, avoiding a collision with workshops close to the runway. The aircraft sustained 30 per cent damage in the process, but was repaired and assigned at the end of October to 1.*Staffel* as 9V+CH.[15] According to Oskar Schmidt: 'The training of flying personnel on the Ju 290 was delayed because of the failure of Kohmann's machine.'[16]

On 20 October, Ju 290A-4 Wk-Nr 0166 (PI+PT) 9V+BK flew from Achmer to Mont de Marsan carrying some of the unit's advance personnel and equipment along with Oberleutnant Schmidt, who went there once again in order to carry out final arrangements with regard to accommodation for Hauptmann Fischer and the *Gruppenstab*. However, the return flight was delayed as a result of the Junkers sustaining a flat tyre. No spares were available at the French airfield, so the FAGr 5 team had to wait until a new tyre was flown out in a Ju 88 from Achmer.[17]

By the end of the month, FAGr 5 was reporting an official strength of ten aircraft – one Ju 88 with the *Stab*, three Ju 290s with 1.*Staffel* and six with 2.*Staffel*.[18]

Once safely back at Achmer, Schmidt made final arrangements for advance elements of the *Gruppe* to transfer by train to France. So it was that, beginning on 3 November 1943, the men of the *Stabskompanie*, together with a section from the *Gruppenstab* and ground personnel of 2.*Staffel*, began to pack up their belongings and equipment, and to prepare their light vehicles for transport.

Early the next day, the newly promoted Generalmajor von Barsewisch once more visited Achmer to wish the unit all success in its coming operations over the Atlantic. He further announced that from now on, FAGr 5 would, appropriately, carry the unit title of '*Atlantik*'.

After von Barsewisch's address, 11 goods wagons and a single coach were shunted by the *Reichsbahn* onto the airfield rail spur. Throughout the course of the day, signals and other technical equipment, along with bedding, clothing, kitchen equipment, desks and typewriters, were loaded onto the wagons. The process took until 2100 hrs that evening, primarily because the technical section of 2./FAGr 5 had miscalculated its load-plan timing. Thus it was not until 0700 hrs on the 5th, that the motorized column containing the personnel departed for the rail station at nearby Bramsche. An hour later, the unit, comprising three officers, 81 NCOs, 158 men and 21 Russian *Hiwis*, together with their light equipment and personal belongings, began boarding. Once again, however, there were delays in bringing together the individual wagons and coaches of the train from the marshalling yard into the station. The process took until early afternoon to complete, but at 1450 hrs, the hauling locomotive finally steamed out of Bramsche in the direction of Osnabrück on the first stage of the train's journey to western France.

CHAPTER FIVE

'NOW IT'S SERIOUS'

Atlantic Operations,
November–December 1943

There can be no talk of a let-up in submarine warfare.
The Atlantic is my first line of defence in the West...

Adolf Hitler at a conference with Grossadmiral Karl Dönitz
at the Berghof, 31 May 1943

The arrival of the Luftwaffe's new long-range reconnaissance *Gruppe* in western France could not have been more timely.

In the late summer/early autumn of 1943, with his slender resources, the *Fliegerführer Atlantik* had little option but to assign increasing responsibility for convoy reconnaissance, and the attempts to shadow convoys, to KG 40, whose Fw 200s were expected, additionally, to undertake offensive, anti-shipping operations. The *Fliegerführer* could also count on the flying boats of 1./SAGr.129, but usually there were between just two and four of such aircraft serviceable at any one time. Furthermore, it was recognized at the end of October that the monthly production of six Fw 200s meant that 'the supply of this type of aircraft to the *Fliegerführer Atlantik* is inadequate.'[1]

Another example of the failure of cooperation between the Luftwaffe and the U-boats took place on 8 October 1943 when a Bv 222 of 1./SAGr.129 out of Biscarosse appeared over convoy SC.143, comprising 39 merchantmen outbound from Halifax on course to Liverpool with an escort of nine mixed warships from the Canadian Escort Group C-2, four destroyers of the British Support Group 10 and the Merchant Aircraft Carrier (MAC) ship *Rapana*.

The Blohm & Voss had taken off at 0415 hrs and was scheduled to arrive in the convoy area at 1500 hrs with the objective of homing the U-boats onto their prey.[2] On making contact with the convoy, the Bv 222 was expected to make beacon signals on one of the six aircraft/U-boat cooperation D/F frequencies to the large but fuel-depleted *Rossbach* wolfpack of 14 U-boats. Individual U-boats would then report the bearings of the shadower with their own grid positions, making possible a more reliable convoy position from the resulting D/F fix than could be counted on from the aircraft's sighting report.

At around 1340 hrs at 35° West 6785, the Bv 222 spotted the convoy moving east at eight knots. Between 1425 and 1530 hrs, U-boat Control transmitted a series of five warnings to U-boats in the area that an aircraft was in contact with a homeward-bound convoy (SC.143), instructing the boats to stand by for D/F bearings. However, it seems the D/F fix procedure failed.[3] Nevertheless, during the night of 8/9 October, the U-boats did succeed in sinking a Polish destroyer and an American freighter, but they would pay a heavy cost,when three of their number were sunk by Allied aircraft.[4]

Another such effort occurred on 27 October, when at 0945 hrs an Fw 200 shadower from III./KG 40 sighted and reported the 60 vessels of the SL.13/MKS.26 combined homebound convoy from West Africa and Gibraltar.[5] This time, over the course of the next four days, the U-boats of the *Schill* 1 wolfpack were directed to the convoy. On the 31st, *U-306* found itself close enough to gain visual observation of the enemy grouping; the U-boat radioed the rest of the pack, but its signals were picked up and the vessel was destroyed by action from a corvette and a destroyer. The Fw 200s continued their dogged, but inconsistent and insufficient efforts into November whenever serviceability and the demands of offensive operations allowed them. The SKL war diary clung to the hope that, 'From 10 November the reconnaissance situation of the *Fliegerführer Atlantik* will be considerably alleviated by the projected allocation of ten Ju 290s which have the same range as the Bv 222s and are faster.'[6]

Indeed, in October 1943, BdU had formed a new wolfpack of ten U-boats off the coast of Portugal which, as previously noted, was known as *Schill*. The *Schill* pack was to intercept convoys sailing to and from Gibraltar, the Mediterranean and the South Atlantic. Commencing operations on 29 October, by 9 November the sum total of its success was one freighter sunk, at a cost of two U-boats, one as a victim to convoy escort and the other to a B-17 air escort. That day the SKL Operations Section noted: 'The operational failure of Group "*Schill*" is to be attributed exclusively to insufficient air reconnaissance. An improvement may be expected from employment of the Ju 290.'[7] Indeed, this belief was echoed by Dönitz on 13 November when he wrote that 'Long-range reconnaissance by Ju 290s' would make a resumption of attacks against Mediterranean convoys worthwhile, 'facilitating the speedy concentration of U-boats on a convoy and hence the possibility of carrying out an attack in a single night.'[8]

Only the day before however, Dönitz's staff lamented in a report: 'the enemy holds all the trump cards. Far-reaching air cover using location methods against which we have no warning … the [Allied] air menace has curtailed the mobility of the U-boats.'[9] The failure of the Luftwaffe to provide the U-boats with the vital information they so badly needed was a significant factor in compelling Dönitz and his staff to review and revise the standard wolfpack tactics. From that point, the U-boats – in the North Atlantic at least – would adopt more varied and experimental formations, which would see them remaining submerged during hours of daylight in order to hide from enemy aircraft. Enemy shipping was to be attacked only at night. This would result in a scattering of U-boats in the North Atlantic from November 1943 onwards, a development that served to stem the tide of losses.[10] Nevertheless, as the British historian and broadcaster John Terraine has written, 'By November the writing was on the wall.'[11]

But if FAGr 5's arrival in France was timely and badly needed by Dönitz and his U-boats, the first phase of the land logistics enterprise of getting the unit there had not proved so positive. After a journey lasting four days, staging through Osnabrück, Münster, and Aachen, across the Belgian border to Montzen, then Liège, Namur, Charleroi, and into France towards Compiègne, Paris-Le Bourget, and Juvisy – where an electric locomotive replaced the third successive steam engine – then Tours and Morcenx, the train carrying the first element of the personnel and equipment of the *Gruppe* finally drew into Mont de Marsan station early on the morning of 8 November 1943. There had been problems all along the line; delays as a result of two air raid alarms during loading at Achmer, then another at Münster, along with changes in locomotives at Aachen, Charleroi and Juvisy, and when the wagons finally rolled to a stop, there were difficulties encountered in the unloading process at Mont de Marsan station.

It was not until evening that the men and equipment finally arrived at Mont de Marsan airport, located 2.5 km north-east of the town centre, within the angle formed by the Mont de Marsan–Brocas railway line and the road from the town to Bergerac.

Set in a sandy and grass-covered area amidst thickly wooded countryside, the pre-war civil airport was bounded to the west by the road to Coudère, while the town racecourse and a small lake lay beyond its north-west boundary. The airfield had undergone some expansion in 1942 and by late 1943 measured 170 m from north to south, while in May 1943 it was extended to the west to around 1830 m, this stretch accommodating a single concrete runway which ran east to west across the old boundary road in that direction. The original, narrow runway of 500 m, running north-north-west/south-south-east served as a taxi track connecting the concrete runway with the southern dispersal area. A concrete perimeter road encircled the entire original landing area and the extension to the west. Administrative and stores buildings were situated on the western boundary, while accommodation for the aircrews was located in requisitioned houses along the road running south from the airport to the town centre.[12] By the time FAGr 5 moved into Mont de Marsan, there were three large, covered dispersal areas (one to the north and two to the south) and 24 large open ones spread around the airfield. In addition, there were another nine smaller dispersal points. In September 1943, British Air Intelligence had noted shrewdly 'In view of the extensive development which has taken place, it may be intended as a base for long-range aircraft operating over the Bay of Biscay.'[13]

Indeed the first of FAGr 5's Ju 290s arrived at Mont de Marsan from Achmer on or around 10 November. That day, Hauptmann Fischer held a major briefing with his unit commanders. The *Gruppe* was to be placed under the tactical command of the *Fliegerführer Atlantik*, Generalleutnant Kessler who, despite his lingering misgivings over the effectiveness of the organization, remained in post.

It was also arranged for a small number of aircrew with experience of long-range and long-duration over-water missions to be assigned to FAGr 5 in order to give practical instruction. Over time, in addition to the cadre from the *Lufttransportstaffel* 290, this would include, from the Fw 200-equipped KG 40 at Bordeaux-Mérignac, Oberleutnant Hubert Schreiner, Oberleutnant Otto-Karl Kremser, Oberfeldwebel Gerhard Hartig and Hauptmann Heinz Braun, only recently appointed as *Staffelkapitän* of LTS 290, and Leutnant Herbert Wagner, from *Transportfliegerstaffel 5*, Braun's old unit, where he had flown both the Ju 90 and Ju 290.[14]

In September 1943, *Reichsmarschall* Göring had directed that *Fliegerführer Atlantik* was to direct and control long-range maritime reconnaissance, undertake defensive sorties in the Bay of Biscay, mount attacks against enemy convoys and single ships in the Atlantic based on the interpretation of aerial photography and reconnaissance reports, and to undertake reconnaissance of enemy submarines. Göring was of the opinion that German 'submarines and aircraft were pursuing the same aim and *Fliegerführer Atlantik* should therefore cooperate closely with BdU. Although limited forces are available at present, considerable success could still be achieved.'[15]

To comply with Göring's orders, in mid-November 1943, in addition to the arrival of FAGr 5, Kessler drew on the following principal units:

II./KG 40	With *c.*30 serviceable He 177 bombers at Bordeaux-Mérignac, in location for only around a month, under Major Rudolf Mons and intended for anti-shipping operations.[16]
III./KG 40	With *c.*45 Fw 200 Condors at Bordeaux-Mérignac under Hauptmann Robert Kowalewski and intended for anti-shipping operations and maritime reconnaissance.[17]
1.(F)/SAGr 129	With two Bv 222 (V2 and V4) and two Bv 138C-1 at Biscarosse since June 1943, intended for long-range reconnaissance.[18]
I./ZG and 7./ZG 1	1. and 2./ZG 1 at Lorient and 3./ZG 1 at Bordeaux-Mérignac with *c.*40 Ju 88C and Ju 88R-2 under Hauptmann Horst Grahl. 7./ZG 1 was also at Lorient with Ju 88C under Hauptmann Hans Morr.[19]
3.(F)/Aufkl.Gr.123	Based at Rennes with *c.*6 Ju 88 (mixed variants) for reconnaissance.[20]
1.(F)/SAGr 128	Based at Brest-Hourtin with elements at Brest-Poulmic and Bayonne with 12 Ar 196A-3 and 5 Fw 190A-3/A-5/G-2/G-3 for reconnaissance and fighter operations.[21]

As a reflection of the actual strength of this force, on 11 November, *Fliegerführer Atlantik* reported as follows:[22]

1 Bv 222
19 Fw 200 (of which 4 were operationally ready)
61 Ju 88C-6 (of which 37 were operationally ready)
6 Ju 290 (just arrived)
24 He 177

In an official German document of late 1943, the modus operandi for the *Fliegerführer Atlantik* was outlined. The command's 'general principles' were described as follows:

1)   Concentration of all appropriate forces in the right place at the right time in accordance with the operational demands of the BdU and the requirements of *Fliegerführer Atlantik*'s own operations.

2)   Most economical operational use of reconnaissance forces until the commencement of operations by BdU or *Fliegerführer Atlantik*. For this purpose full advantage to be taken of technical and weather conditions.

3)   Flights into areas where controlled enemy day or nightfighters are operating are to be avoided. Wherever possible, operations of *Fliegerführer Atlantik* are to be confined to areas where there is no enemy twin-engined fighter defence.

When it came to reconnaissance, the rationale was as follows:

1)   Reconnaissance to be carried out mainly with ship-locating radar. Reconnaissance by sectors at 1000 m altitude. Operations not to be dependent on visibility.
2)   The situation in the Atlantic will dictate the areas in which aircraft with strong defensive armament are to be used. Area of operations to be widened by exploitation of weather conditions.
3)   Navigational accuracy of aircraft position up to distances of 2000 km with a margin of error of +/- 10 to 20 km.
4)   Convoy reconnaissance. In areas requested by BdU or laid down by *Fliegerführer Atlantik*. Generally reconnaissance of area to be covered should start in the morning. On the days when operations are planned by BdU or *Fliegerführer Atlantik*, reconnaissance should be repeated in late afternoon with a view to shadowing – in the case of U-boats, reconnaissance to continue into the night.

The basic navigation method employed by FAGr 5 was to use a track plot, with air plotting used only when a dead reckoning position was doubtful or when an aircraft was being chased by enemy fighters. Distance was reckoned in kilometres. No standard navigation drill was formulated in the *Gruppe*, however, and observers were free to take drifts, find winds or obtain fixes in their own time. On returning from sorties, the observers' logbooks would be analyzed, although not marked in any way.[23]

Shadowing missions with ship-locating radar on behalf of BdU were to commence at dusk, using D/F signals as well as flares for marking the location of a convoy. The shadower was to keep as close to the convoy as possible, and shadowing was to continue as far into the night as possible.[24]

However, by 13 November, despite some sightings by German air reconnaissance, as a result of evasive routing and land-based air support, three convoys had avoided or sailed through the U-boat patrol lines. Just one merchantman had been lost for the cost of two U-boats sunk.[25] But that day, U-boats operating in the Atlantic were signalled the encouraging news that 'the Ju 290, a four-engined, long-range, reconnaissance aircraft with penetration depth of 2250 km, is now available for operations. It is hoped that its use will remedy recent failures by U-boats, which are largely ascribed to unsuccessful air reconnaissance.'[26] BdU further signalled its U-boat commanders:

> U-boat operations of recent weeks have miscarried through failure to find the convoys. We have good reason to suppose that enemy air reconnaissance picks up our disposition-lines by methods of location which in part we are still not able to get on to, and that the enemy has gone round us.
>
> The difficulty of finding convoys must be removed through far-reaching air reconnaissance on our part with location gear. From today, the first Ju 290 four-engined long-distance reconnaissance aircraft, with penetration-depth of 1,400 miles, are ready for operational use. Their number and penetration-depth will be raised. In addition to these, we have Bv 222s and Fw 200s, and also, from today, the He 177 as a bomber.[27]

Each Ju 290 would carry a crew of between nine and 11 men; two pilots, one navigator, two radio-operators, one flight engineer and up to five gunners, the latter frequently carrying out dual functions as radio-operator or flight engineer.[28]

As Oskar Schmidt recorded: 'Now it was serious! All functions of the *Gruppe* had to be coordinated (technical sections, transport sections, the signals group, the photographic section). If everything was coordinated from the start, things should run like clockwork.'[29]

The baptism of fire for FAGr 5 came on 15 November when the *Kommandeur*, Hauptmann Fischer, led the unit's first shadowing operation into the Atlantic in Ju 290 WK-Nr 0164 9V+GK, piloted by Hauptmann Heinz Braun. The mission was called as a result of intelligence emanating on 13 November from 'agents' in the Strait of Gibraltar area on the passage of convoy MKS.30 en route from ports in North Africa via Gibraltar, which it had departed on the 13th.[30] Dönitz moved quickly, ordering 26 U-boats of the *Schill* wolfpack to attack the convoy. This group of U-boats, which had been formed partly to attempt a one-night attack on a Mediterranean convoy using boats in the Atlantic and some sailing from the Biscay bases, had failed in its initial operation against MKS.28 and MKS.29, primarily because of the boats' dependence on air reconnaissance. Unfortunately, the Fw 200s involved had suffered from engine problems and radar defects. Only one ship was sunk. Hessler notes: 'These experiences confirmed our conclusions of 1941, namely, that air cooperation could only be successful if sufficient long-range aircraft were available for prolonged and concentrated reconnaissance, together with adequate reserves of aircraft and equipment.'[31]

Meanwhile, Fischer's and Braun's course took them across the French coast at 14° West 2421, out into the Bay of Biscay, then south, to the west of Portugal and then to the west of Casablanca. During the afternoon, 400 km south-west of Cape St Vincent (Cabo de São Vicente), they spotted a large enemy convoy with escort vessels. This was convoy SL.139, heading north-west and returning to the UK from the collection point at Freetown in Sierra Leone, from where it sailed on 2 November. It had subsequently rendezvoused with MKS.30 from Gibraltar, 100 miles south of Cape St Vincent the day before. This major combined convoy was sailing in 14 columns, its escort formed of the 40th Escort Group.[32]

At 1733 hrs, Fischer reported to the *Fliegerführer Atlantik* observing, at 23°W 3661, a total of 67 merchant vessels, four escort vessels and three destroyers on course 290° and moving at eight knots, but further reporting was frustrated by low fuel levels, forcing a return, and a landing at Bordeaux-Mérignac in the early hours of the 16th after flying for 16 hr 15 min.[33] A Bv 222 of 1./SAGr 129 had also located the convoy and relayed its position.[34]

At some point, however, German wireless traffic advising of the convoy's location, possibly emanating from Fischer's Ju 290, had been detected by British listening stations. Placed on alert, the Admiralty took immediate steps to increase surface escort for SL.139/MKS.30, while air support was strengthened by drawing on squadrons in England, Gibraltar and the Azores, and it soon arrived in the form of Hudsons, Fortresses and Catalinas.[35] As for the appearance of a Ju 290, the British quite correctly noted: 'This was the first occasion on which a Ju 290 is known to have operated on sea reconnaissance in any area ... Callsigns and frequency suggest a new unit, and it must be supposed that the Ju 290 is working separately from those units already known to be operating in the Bay.'[36]

Early on the 16th, in order to maintain its observation of SL.139/MKS.30, FAGr 5 despatched a second aircraft, Ju 290 Wk-Nr 0167 9V+HK of 2.*Staffel*, which was scheduled to take off from Mont de Marsan at 0315 hrs, crossing the coast at 14° West 2415. This aircraft was piloted by Hauptmann Bergen, marking the operational debut of 2./FAGr 5. At 1000 hrs, the Ju 290 spotted the convoy at 23° West 5625, moving at seven knots, but at exactly the same time the convoy reported a shadower. Bergen's crew observed that the convoy was protected by a 'battleship'; in fact SL.139/MKS.30 had been further reinforced by the seven ships of the 5th Escort Group as well as two destroyers, making a total of 19 escort vessels providing a double screen and over which there was continuous air cover. An hour later, at 23° West 6749 the crew aboard 9V+HK located another convoy, this time OS.58/KMS.32, en route for Freetown and Gibraltar respectively. They reported 44 merchant vessels altogether, with eight escorts, course 135°, at a speed of seven knots. In fact they had undercounted the merchantmen by two. At 1231 hrs, the Junkers located and reported what was probably the French battleship *Richelieu*, accompanied by a pair of destroyers, course 320°, moving at 15 knots at 23° West 4942.

Unfortunately, during the course of their mission, west of the Portuguese coast, Bergen's plane was attacked by aircraft from a British carrier, probably HMS *Biter*. One of the crew, gunner Feldwebel Walter Bauer, was wounded in the attack when a bullet struck his leg. Bergen was forced to abandon his reconnaissance and make for home.[37] The Ju 290 landed at 1900 hrs after a flight of 15 hr 45 min.[38]

Using the information gleaned from FAGr 5's flights, Generalleutnant Kessler and the BdU deployed all available forces against the convoy. To shadow the convoy, the Luftwaffe additionally deployed the Bv 222s of 1./SAGr 129 and the Fw 200s of III./KG 40.

In accordance with Fischer's new tactical directives, FAGr 5 embarked on a continuous shadowing of the SL.139/MKS.30 convoy, and at 0400 hrs in the early morning darkness of the 17th, Ju 290A-2 Wk-Nr 0159 (originally SB+QI), coded 9V+CK of 2.*Staffel*, took off, crossing the French coast directly west of Mont de Marsan and out into the Bay of Biscay. This aircraft may have been flown by Hauptmann Heinz Braun of 2.*Staffel* who had joined FAGr 5 from LTS 290. The crew reported spotting the convoy in a signal sent to *Fliegerführer Atlantik* at 1313 hrs, advising that it consisted of 63 motor vessels steaming at eight knots, course 320°, position 23° West 8881. In fact, observers in the convoy had spotted the lone Ju 290 one minute earlier at 37° 15′ North, 18° 01′ West. Braun's aircraft was also attacked by Allied aircraft and suffered a wounded crew member, before it too was forced to head back to France. In France, Generalleutnant Kessler seems to have been concerned over the certainty of the convoy's position, probably because of growing demand for information from the BdU, and at 1640 hrs, he signalled the Junkers for an update. The aircraft merely repeated its original information.[39]

So it was that, from early evening on the 17th and based on FAGr 5's reports, Dönitz ordered eight boats of the *Schill* 1 wolfpack eastwards in submerged patrol disposition to intercept the convoy between 39° 03′ North, 21° 02′ West and 39° 36′ North, 19° 02′ West by 1800 hrs on the 18th.[40] Kessler ordered another Ju 290 patrol in the early morning of the 18th to 'make early contact with the convoy with a view to improving the disposition of the U-boats submerged on patrol.' One Ju 290, possibly 9V+HK, took off at 0345 hrs on the 18th with a second, identified as aircraft '9V+IK', following around 15 minutes later.[*] This aircraft reported contact with the convoy at 0945 hrs in 24° West 9075. The convoy reported the shadow 16 minutes later at 1001 hrs in 39° 27′ North, 19° 42′ West.

At 1100 hrs on 18 November, *Kapitänleutnant* Peter-Erich Cremer's *U-333*, in position close to the convoy, was attacked by the frigate HMS *Exe*, from which Commander G.V. Legassick commanded the 40th Escort Group. Having spotted the periscope of *U-333*, *Exe* dropped depth charges: 'A pattern of ten depth charges exploded with a deafening roar round the boat,' Cremer recalled. 'The effect was terrible ... damage very great.'[41] *Exe* then rammed the U-boat with its keel. The U-boat was subjected to another eight hours of depth-charging, but it managed to return to base despite having part of the frigate's propeller embedded in its hull.[42]

At 1125 hrs, the Ju 290 identified as aircraft 'I' expanded its report, having counted the convoy as comprising '64 motor vessels in close formation, three ships and four ships, seven knots.' Based on FAGr 5's report, at about midday on 18 November, Dönitz moved the other boats of the *Schill* 1 wolfpack eastwards to intercept the convoy.[43]

Three weather reports for the convoy's area followed from the Ju 290 'I', along with two further position reports at 1400 hrs (24° West 9032, 7 knots) and 1500 hrs (24° West 9018, 7 knots). Meanwhile, the Allied ships signalled that the shadower was still lurking in the skies over the convoy at 1331 hrs. This was potentially a fatal signal for the convoy, for it was intercepted and decyphered by the *B-Dienst* (*Beobachtungsdienst* – Observation Service). Based on this information, the eight U-boats of *Schill* 1 were ordered to steer a submerged course 030° at three knots from 1200 hrs.[44] The ten boats of the *Schill* 2 pack, lying farther to the north, six of which were returning from the North Atlantic, were also moved closer in readiness for an attack.[45] During the afternoon, *U-515*, commanded by *Kapitänleutnant* Werner Henke, fired an acoustic torpedo at the 1,350-ton escort sloop, HMS *Chanticleer*, which blew its stern off. The vessel was towed to the Azores.[46] However, at around 2300 hrs, *U-515* reported being overrun by the convoy at 1300 hrs.

Immediately after its last signal on the position of the convoy at 1500 hrs, the Ju 290 'I' broke off and returned to France, and at 2015 hrs signalled that its ETA at Mont de Marsan was 2110 hrs.[47]

---

[*] The identity of this second aircraft is something of an enigma. The British listening stations picked up the transmission 'I', but the German historians Karl Kössler and Günther Ott believe that this aircraft did not enter service with FAGr 5 until December 1943, although they accept the code was used at some point with 'great probability' – see Kössler and Ott 1993, p. 191, 231.

As darkness fell over the eastern Atlantic, SL.139/MKS.30 welcomed additional protection in the form of the 7th Escort Group, while Leigh Light Wellingtons flew in to replace the daylight air escorts. One Ju 290 pilot who encountered such aircraft was Oberleutnant Heinz Bretnütz of 2./FAGr 5 who may have been piloting 'T'. On a return flight from the Atlantic during operations over the convoy, Bretnütz was pursued by an enemy 'nightfighter' which apparently resorted to using a 'searchlight' in an attempt to locate the German shadower in the growing darkness as it headed back towards the French coast. In reality, this would probably have been a Wellington bomber of Coastal Command fitted with the powerful 24-in Leigh Light searchlight housed in a retractable ventral 'dustbin' under the fuselage of the aircraft and capable of producing a beam of between 20 and 50 million candles. Intended for deployment in night attacks against U-boats on the surface, so equipped, the Wellington was considered a very manoueuvrable aircraft, offering a good view for the pilot.[48] Indeed, Leigh Light Wellingtons of the Azores-based No. 179 Squadron had already proved themselves successful against the U-boats in the Atlantic.[49] Fortunately, for Bretnütz and his crew, they managed to return to France safely.

Both during day and night, the Allied air cover blanketed the convoy, and together with the surface escort were more than a match for *Schill* 1.

Shortly after midnight on the 18th/19th, the boats of *Schill* 2 were ordered to move 100 km north in order to be in position to attack by 1800 hrs on the evening of the 19th. At the same time, all U-boats were advised that the Luftwaffe would provide air reconnaissance during the morning and afternoon, the latter being provided by a Ju 290 of FAGr 5, which would send beacon signals from 1830 hrs until well after dark. The U-boats were to watch for these signals and report bearings.

The morning patrol was to be undertaken by four Fw 200s of III./KG 40, but one of the Condors developed fuel tank problems, began to lose fuel and was forced to return to Bordeaux. The first Focke-Wulf to reach the convoy did so at 1015 hrs, placing it at 24° West 9032. Fifteen minutes later, HMS *Exe* reported an Fw 200 shadowing the convoy. The Condors returned during the late afternoon, unharmed, one aircraft at least having apparently fed the *Fliegerführer Atlantik* with what was inaccurate reporting. According to British radio intercepts, 'Aircraft proceeded to give details of the convoy's composition, describing it as "40" and "60" motor vessels, with two escort vessels and three aircraft. This intelligence evidently puzzled the *Fliegerführer*, who enquired persistently for the correct number of merchant vessels sighted. It was not till 1515 that he was told that it was 70.'

Taking over from the Fw 200s was the Ju 290 9V+GK from 2./FAGr 5. This time the aircraft successfully sent its homing signals which were picked up by six U-boats, cross D/F bearings giving them an accurate fix 32 km south of the centre of the patrol line.[50]

Far away to the east at the *Führer's Wolfsschanze* headquarters in East Prussia, Kapitän Heinz Assmann, the naval operations officer on the OKW operations staff, was present at the midday situation conference on the 19th and advised that the 'new *Aufklärungsgruppe* 290 [sic] – they didn't expect German aircraft to appear – managed to get as close as 300 m to the convoy.'[51] There was also radio traffic evidence to suggest that this aircraft also dropped flare buoys. 9V+GK returned to Mont de Marsan shortly after 0215 hrs on the morning of the 20th.[52]

The convoy battle raged during the night of the 19th/20th as Dönitz ordered more attacks. During the early hours of the 20th, one U-boat, *U-536*, was blown to the surface by depth charges from the frigate *Nene* and the corvettes of Canadian Support Group 5, *Calgary* and *Snowberry*. As the submarine surfaced, the Allied ships used all their guns to finish it off. The vessel's commander, Kapitänleutnant Rolf Schauenburg, and 16 of his crew, were later rescued by a British frigate.[53] Simultaneously, Allied air cover was strengthened as morning broke; 12 B-17s and B-24s operated throughout the day.[54]

Taking over from Bretnütz to monitor the convoy's progress was another aircraft from FAGr 5. But 20 November was to prove a black day for the *Gruppe*. The plan was for the third group of *Schill* boats to make an attack during the evening in a line 46 ° 15 ′ North – 18° 00′–21° 30′ West and to be in position by 1800 hrs. *Fliegerführer Atlantik* would provide reconnaissance during the morning with Fw 200s from III./KG 40 and by deploying a single Ju 290 from FAGr 5 during the afternoon. However it was to be a luckless deployment, for Allied intercepts indicate that no German aircraft made contact with SL.139/MKS.30 during the day.[55]

At 1145 hrs that morning, Ju 290A-2 Wk-Nr 0159 (originally SB+QI), coded 9V+CK, commanded and piloted by the recently arrived Leutnant Hans-Roger Friedrich of 2./FAGr 5, formerly of LTS 290, took off from Mont de Marsan to track the convoy in the area 24° West 8656–34° West 2656 to 24° West 9453. At some point the Ju 290 was joined by its escort of eight Ju 88C-6s from 3./ZG 1, which had also been detailed to watch over a lone Fw 200 of 7./KG 40.[56] During the afternoon, at a point off Cape (Cabo) Ortegal at the north-western tip of Spain, the German formation was spotted by a patrol of four RAF Mosquito IIs of No. 157 Squadron, led by Wing Commander James A. Mackie, which had recently moved to Predannack in Cornwall. The four fighters were crewed by Mackie and Flying Officer Leslie Scholefield; Flight Lieutenant George Dyke and Warrant Officer Charles

Aindow; Flying Officer John Clifton and Pilot Officer G. Davidson; and Flying Officer Verdun Hannawin with Pilot Officer Bill Tofts.[57] The Mosquitos were not alone: four Beaufighter Xs from No. 248 Squadron from the same base were also operating over the Biscay. The British aircraft were flying an 'Instep' patrol, intended to shield Coastal Command units from enemy fighter attack while on operations in the Bay of Biscay, and they were searching for enemy aircraft eight miles north-west of Estaca de Bares. According to No. 157 Squadron's subsequent intelligence report, 'Course was set at "0" feet for 48° North 07°30′ West. Cape Ortegal was sighted at 1351 hrs.' The weather was murky: ten-tenths cloud at 1,500–2,000 ft, with visibility for two miles.

All these units then clashed in a large aerial engagement 13 km off the Spanish coast. At 1410 hrs, having attacked and fought the Ju 88s, Wing Commander Mackie ordered the Mosquitos to re-form. No. 157 Squadron's Intelligence Officer later recorded the following in the mission debrief:

At this moment a large aircraft was seen 15 miles north of Cape Ortegal, flying north-west at 400 feet and about two miles away. When F/Lt. [George] Dyke was about 1,500 yards from the aircraft, he recognised it as a Ju 290. The enemy aircraft opened fire from a turret behind the cockpit with explosive or self-destroying shells. [Dyke] kept to the port side, out of range and waited for the other aircraft to come in on the starboard side. He estimated that the enemy aircraft was flying at 260 mph [420 km/h] and it had dropped height to about 150 feet [46 m].

W/Cdr Mackie attacked from the starboard from 600 yards [550 m], closing to 200 yards [180 m] dead astern, firing two long bursts. Strikes were seen on the outer starboard engine, along the fuselage and on both port engines. The three engines that were hit were alight and omitting black smoke, the port outer burning furiously.

As the Mosquito broke away, the Ju 290 was seen in a shallow dive. It hit the sea with a huge explosion on impact, flames going up to 100 feet [30 m]. Wreckage on the sea continued to burn for some time. The combat ended 40 miles [65 km] north-west of Cape Ortegal at 1415 hours.

F/Lt. Dyke came into attack from slightly above and from the port quarter just after W/Cdr. Mackie started his attack. He gave a 2–3 second burst from 600 yards [550 m] closing to 300 yards [275 m]. He saw that a port engine was on fire and received return fire, but could not see strikes as his windscreen had been splintered on the starboard side during the previous combat [with the Ju 88s of ZG 1]. His navigator (W/O Charles Aindow) however saw strikes on the port engine. As he broke away to starboard, the enemy aircraft fired a three-star red cartridge just before it went into the sea. F/O [John] Clifton took photographs of the enemy aircraft burning on the water.[58]

Wing Commander Mackie, and his navigator, Flying Officer Scholefield, claimed the destruction of a Ju 290. They also claimed a damaged Ju 88. Two of the other Mosquito crews claimed, collectively, a Ju 88 probably destroyed and two more damaged.[59] The Beaufighters claimed one Ju 88 destroyed and two damaged. In fact, I./ZG 1 lost only the Ju 88C-6 of the *Staffelkapitän* of 3.*Staffel*, Oberleutnant Hans Schuster.[60] But for 2./FAGr 5 the first loss of a Ju 290 represented even greater human sacrifice; Friedrich, and his crew of Leutnant Gottfried Sachse (co-pilot), Leutnant Heinz Arnold (observer), Unteroffizier Wilhelm Schief (radio-operator), Feldwebel Friedrich Gerschwitz (flight engineer), Feldwebel Adolf Martens (gunner), Obergefreiter Horst Bentke (gunner) and Gefreiter Heinz Engelleitner (gunner) failed to return. Schief's body was eventually recovered by a fishing vessel, the *Mardomingo A*, near La Coruña on 15 December. In order to identify the body, the Spanish naval command in La Coruña advised the local German consulate of the number on Schief's identity tag. Felipe Rodriguez, at the German consulate, contacted the German air attaché in Madrid who then checked with the RLM in Berlin. It was not until June 1944 that Rodriguez was able to confirm to the Spanish naval authorities that the body was that of the Köln-born NCO, Schief.[61] He was later buried at the *Deutscher Soldat Militärfriedhof* at Cuacos de Yuste, west of Madrid.[62]

As soon as news reached Mont de Marsan of the loss of Friedrich and his crew, at 1331 hrs, the *Gruppe* sent out Oberleutnant Karl-Heinz Schmidt, whose Ju 290 was loaded with extra dinghies, to conduct a search of the sea area in question, but it was a fruitless effort. Another mission conducted later that day by Hauptmann Bergen failed to locate the convoy which had altered course, but in any case, Bergen was forced to abort early because of an engine failure.[63]

Dönitz too threw in the towel on the 20th and called off his U-boats. Thirty-one U-boats had been deployed, but the sum total of the attack was the damage inflicted to *Chanticleer* and the shooting down of two aircraft.[64] Six of the *Schill* U-boats had been sunk in the action against the convoy, while another three limped away to France with severe damage and/or heavy casualties.[65] The BdU war diary noted: 'Our own air reconnaissance obtained no results on the decisive last day because of the few aircraft available.'[66]

An official historian of the U-boat war in the Atlantic, Günter Hessler, wrote:

This last operation again demonstrated the impossibility of conducting proper reconnaissance and U-boat direction with only a handful of aircraft.

The convoy's position had to be established not once or twice in 24 hours, but every four hours at least, otherwise it was impossible to manoeuvre the submerged U-boats ahead of the convoy in time, or to counter a diversionary change of course. While it was gratifying to confirm that our aircraft were able, with their radar, to maintain contact with a convoy at night, it was unfortunate that beacon signals alone did not indicate the convoy position with sufficient accuracy for the U-boats, which at night had to rely exclusively on visual sighting.[67]

The next day, 21 November, with U-boats of the *Schill* wolfpack failing to make any impact against the convoy, the Luftwaffe launched a strike, this time using He 177s of II./KG 40 fitted with new Hs 293 glide bombs. SL.139/MKS.30 was once again located, this time, firstly, by five Fw 200s of III./KG 40 which commenced their sorties from 0330 hrs and were airborne for 12–13 hours. The Condors were followed by two Ju 290s from 2./FAGr 5, the A-3 Wk-Nr 0163 9V+IK and the A-4 Wk-Nr 0158 9V+BK, which were airborne at 0400 hrs and 0915 hrs respectively. 9V+IK first reported sighting the ships at 1020 hrs in 24° West 9700. At 1100 hrs, 'I's information was passed to one of the Fw 200s which was in the vicinity and the approaching 9V+BK. Fifty-seven minutes later, the second Ju 290 was warned to watch for beacon signals. At 1215 hrs, the aircraft advised its expected arrival over the convoy as 1515 hrs. Five minutes after that, 9V+IK, still the only German aircraft with visual contact, signalled a detailed report on the composition of the convoy at 24° West 9748, advising '50 motor vessels and six escorts, speed seven [knots], one reconnaissance aircraft'. Then, 30 minutes later, the Ju 290 was forced to discontinue shadowing SL.139/MKS.30 as a result of engine problems. 9V+BK was advised of this development, but it seems that the aircraft did not make contact with the enemy ships. At 1815 hrs, this aircraft advised it was abandoning its mission, with no shadowing reports having been signalled. It returned to Mont de Marsan at around 0025 hrs on the 22nd.[68]

When the He 177s of II./KG 40 attacked using their Hs 293s, they most probably did so using the location information provided by 9V+IK at 1220 hrs. The 25 Heinkels, led by Major Rudolf Mons, took off from Bordeaux-Mérignac at 1215 hrs and arrived over the convoy some 675 km north-east of Cape Finisterre about 4¼ hours later. By this stage, the weather had deteriorated with the cloud base down to 300–400 m, and the bombers concentrated on attacking two ships that were straggling, the 6,065-ton *Marsa* and the 4,405-ton *Delius*.[69] They sank the former, leaving it burning, and damaged the latter. Two frigates, HMS *Calder* and HMS *Drury*, were also attacked with Hs 293s, but they evaded the bombs by rapid manoeuvring, defensive fire and by letting off flares. A single He 177 attempted to attack the destroyers *Watchman* and *Winchelsea*, but failed to damage them.

During their attack, the He 177s had launched 40 bombs, 25 of which failed. The unit returned to Bordeaux still in bad weather between 2100 and 2400 hrs, to discover that they had lost three of their number, with a fourth crashing on landing, suffering bad damage, and three others sustaining lighter damage.[70]

In overall terms, it had not been a particularly auspicious start to operations for FAGr 5 either, but despite fuel and range limitations and attacks by enemy aircraft, the unit's contribution, such as it was, had been key to the efforts of the U-boats. In flights averaging 17–18 hours' duration, the Ju 290s were able to radio back their observations on the convoy's composition, as well as that of its escort, plus details of its course, defence and speed. Oskar Schmidt notes how the lurking presence of the big four-engined shadowers close to the convoy had a 'surprising effect on the enemy' forcing him to introduce new defensive tactics, course and composition.[71]

Nevertheless, as Captain S.W. Roskill eloquently describes in the official history of Britain's war at sea, 'the long-awaited cooperation of the Luftwaffe with the U-boats had not achieved the results hoped for by Dönitz. The truth now seems to be that it came too late to restore the balance, let alone tip the scales in the German favour.'[72]

Tactically, Hauptmann Fischer had directed that, whenever possible, FAGr 5's aircraft were to fly as low as possible, in order to operate below enemy radar detection. Occasionally, the Junkers would climb to around 1000 m altitude to fly a search circle. A key element of FAGr 5's operations was the nose-mounted FuG 200 *Hohentwiel* air-to-surface vessel (ASV) radar apparatus. When installed, this ASV and navigational search radar was able to cover a radius of about 100 km, weather permitting.[73] Oskar Schmidt recalled:

> The '*Hohentwiel*' rendered good services in addition to visual observation, giving a good bearing on the screen at up to 60 km. In this way, an area of sea could be searched accurately. By adopting search circles at 1000 m altitude, we could detect a target at up to around 100 km away. Upon detection of enemy shipping, the strength and composition was determined and pictures taken after detection. Then a safe distance would be kept, the shipping shadowed and then reported to the *Gruppe*. Further orders were then issued and our command decided on the future course of the flight.[74]

Intended to replace the *Rostock Gerät* search equipment from the summer of 1943, and developed and manufactured by C. Lorenz of Berlin, the FuG 200 *Hohentwiel* was a low-UHF band system which had a greater range than its predecessor of some 60–80 km when used to locate individual ships. It also had less impact on aircraft speed because of its small antennae array. But production was slow and although the apparatus was intended for use in the Ju 88, Ju 188, He 111, Do 217 and Ju 290, in the case of III./KG 40, by December 1943, only 16 of 26 Fw 200s had been fitted with the radar.[75]

Externally, the transmitter antenna for the FuG 200 comprised eight end-fed, half-wave horizontal dipoles arranged in colinear pairs mounted on brackets in the nose of a Ju 290, facing forward in the line of flight. The receiver had no r-f amplification, but was connected, by means of a motor-driven switch, alternately to two antennas fitted on the right and left sides of the fuselage at angles of 30° to the line of flight. Internally, the apparatus was powered by a motor generator and consisted of a transmitter and modulator, an indicator unit (the *Sichtgerät* [SG] 200) and a control- or switch box (*Schaltkasten* [SK] 200). There was a two-tube, high-power transmitter, a superheterodyne receiver, and a cathode ray tube (CRT) indicator. The switch box fitted with four knobs was located in the observer's position in the aircraft. The top left knob controlled the zero point; the top right, the focus of the trace; the bottom left changed the range from 0 to 150 km for search and navigational aid to the 0–150-km range for approach and attack; the bottom right governed the brightness of the trace. A two-way switch at the top of the box turned the equipment on and off, while the lowermost knob remotely controlled the gain in the receiver. A lever to the right of the unit was self-centring and made a slight adjustment in the frequency. A left-hand switch was used when the *Hohentwiel* was being used at 2000 m or higher.

The range scale etched on the glass of the CRT screen coincided with the vertical timebase and was calibrated from zero to 150 km at 10-km intervals, the distance between the 10-km marks being progressively smaller as extreme range was reached. The vertical timebase took the form of a screen of perspex sheet metal with 15 parallel horizontal lines reading 0 to 150 km (from bottom to top). Because of ground returns, satisfactory readings could not be obtained at less than 3 km. To offset that, some FuG 200 sets were fitted with a switch which magnified scale so that close ranges could read off to the nearest 50 m. The device operated on a frequency range of 570 megacycles per second and had a pulse recurrence frequency of 600 cycles per second.[76]

Schmidt also remembered:

We were always on alert for Allied long-range Lightning and other types of fighters which operated from bases in Ireland or Gibraltar, to intercept our machines when they flew out and to pick them up over Cape Ortegal using British radio stations. Our machines were often intercepted on their return flights. At that stage the crew was tired after a long flight time (18 hours) and was, of course, vulnerable at the moment of landing. Therefore attention was demanded from the crews until the very last moment of landing at the operational airfield.[77]

Away from the arena of operations over the Atlantic, FAGr 5 continued to strengthen its back-up services; in late November, Oberleutnant Schmidt of the *Stabskompanie* made several flights to Achmer from where he travelled to the army vehicle repair workshops in the Osnabrück area to obtain surplus light vehicles that FAGr 5 could take on. These were then loaded into Ju 290 transports which had completed their repair and maintenance at the Achmer facility and flown to Mont de Marsan. In such a way, the *Gruppe* gradually built up its motor transport pool.[78]

More tragedy wracked FAGr 5 on 24 November when Ju 290A-4 Wk-Nr 0168 (PI+PV) 9V+FK of 2.*Staffel*, piloted by Oberfeldwebel Josef Mohr, crashed shortly after taking off on an operational mission. The aircraft climbed vertically, rolled over and burst into flames. The entire crew was lost. It was thought that the accident may have been attributable to a malfunctioning three-way control switch at a time when the aircraft was not taking off in the usual way against the wind towards the west, but rather the reverse. In this direction, the aircraft had to fly over a small knoll, which interrupted the normal initial climb.[79] On the runway behind Mohr was the aircraft of Hauptmann Fischer, 9V+BK, and he and his crew watched in horror as the landing lights of 9V+FK faded upwards into the cloud only to reappear and fall away to earth. The commander and observer of the Junkers was Leutnant Wolfgang Adler of the *Gruppenstab*, and Mohr was accompanied at the controls by Feldwebel Herbert Greihe. They, and the rest of the crew, comprising Oberfeldwebel Hans Werner (radio-operator), Unteroffizier Karl Scheurer (radio-operator), Feldwebel Paul Borchert (flight engineer), Unteroffizier Paul Fridetzki (flight enginer and gunner), Obergefreiter Theodor Wienken (gunner) and Gefreiter Josef Zelenka (gunner), were buried in the military cemetery at Mont de Marsan airport with full honours.[80]

Two days later, the aircraft of the *Kommandeur*, Hauptmann Fischer, who was on board as commander, Ju 290A-1 Wk-Nr 0166 (PI+PT) 9V+BK, made a belly-landing when the landing gear collapsed at Mont de Marsan while being piloted by Leutnant Herbert Wagner. The aircraft suffered only 20 per cent damage, but it would be out of commission for some time, thus reducing an already low unit-serviceability level; when it came back on roster, it would be assigned to 1./FAGr 5.[81]

The loss of Adler and Mohr and their crew was a grim harbinger of winter at Mont de Marsan. As autumn faded away, the days retained a clarity and a gentle warmth, but at night the temperatures dropped significantly and the men of FAGr 5 shivered in their billets. The *Stabskompanie* arranged with the local army administration for the supply of some stoves to warm up the accommodation, which provided some relief but, as Oskar Schmidt recalled: 'The temperature fluctuations in south-west France, between sun and shade and day and night bedevilled the men. There were many colds.'[82]

On the 29th, the officer cadre was bolstered when Hauptmann Georg Eckl, an experienced maritime pilot, having served with an sea-rescue unit, joined 2./FAGr 5.

Meanwhile, the *Gruppe* continued to fly operations over the Atlantic with the few aircraft it had available. From 22 November, the Germans began to track the 46-ship southbound convoy OS.59/KMS.33, which had departed Liverpool on 16 November bound for Gibraltar (OS.59) and Freetown (KMS.33). The convoy was carrying coal, coke, ammunition, aircraft, vehicles and general stores, and many of the merchantmen were armed.[83] The intention of the BdU was to deploy a newly formed group of 16 U-boats, several of which had been previously assigned to the *Schill* pack against SL.139/MKS.30, under the name *Weddigen* and which were to be in position against OS.59/KMS.33 during the night of 23/24 November.[84] Unfortunately *U-538* was sunk by depth charges on the 21st and *U-648* went missing, without explanation, the next day, while *U-586* was forced to withdraw on the 24th because it was low on fuel.[85] The pack was down to 13 boats. Worse was to come for *Weddigen* because, aware of enemy intentions, the British sent the 4th Escort Group to cover the southbound convoy.[86]

The first reconnaissance initiated by *Fliegerführer Atlantik* was undertaken by a Bv 222 of 1./SAGr 129 from Biscarosse on the 22nd. The flying boat had an 'inconclusive engagement' with a B-24, but was able to signal back details of the convoy and it returned to Biscarosse at 2244 hrs. It was not until the early morning of the 23rd that FAGr 5 despatched two Ju 290s – between 0630 hrs and 0645 hrs on the 23rd, with the third out from Mont de Marsan mid-morning.[87] All aircraft returned safely but there are no details about their observations.* In any case, by the evening of the 24th, the Germans were under the incorrect assumption that OS.59/KMS.33 was farther west than it actually was and duly moved boats farther in that direction, away from the convoy. In fact the convoy was 2° south of the line to which the U-boats had been ordered to move.

---

* Hessler (1989) notes that two reconnaissance aircraft which took off on the 23rd had to return because one had engine trouble and the other a radar defect. These may well have been the two Ju 290s.

Meanwhile, another convoy, SL.140/MKS.31, was steaming north across the eastern Atlantic towards Liverpool. FAGr 5 was placed on readiness to shadow and, subsequently, two Junkers, 9V+BH and 9V+DH, took off around 0500 hrs on the morning of 26 November. At 1550 hrs, aircraft 'B' reported that its reconnaissance was completed and that the convoy had not been found. At 1734 hrs, Mont de Marsan signalled aircraft 'D' to ask if its reconnaissance had been completed and ten minutes later it transmitted its first report on its observations. Some time later, the aircraft sent a second report in which it stated that it had observed 45 motor vessels and five escorts, steaming at eight knots on course of 270°.[88] This was not accurate as the convoy actually numbered between 50 and 70 ships. Based on FAGr 5's reports, however, the *Weddigen* boats were moved west to intercept and to a new patrol line between 37° 30′ North, 19° 25′ West and 39° 05′ North, 17° 10′ West. 9V+DH was confirmed as landed at 2206 hrs. The problem was that once this aircraft had left the convoy area to return to base, the convoy changed course to the north.[89]

This meant that on the 27th, when air reconnaissance was continued by two Fw 200s of III./KG 40 and a Bv 222 of 1./SAGr 129, still the U-boats could not make a kill because the targets were reported well to the east of them. SL.140/MKS.31 then progressed unharmed through the *Weddigen* pack on 27–28 November, thanks largely to its escort which had been strengthened by three escort-carrier task forces; the latter sank two U-boats and badly damaged two others.[90] These were losses hard to bear: on the 25th, Korvettenkapitän Bernhard Zurmühlen's *U-600* was lost north of Ponta Delgada in the Azores, as a result of depth charges, while on the 27th, *U-542*, a new Type IXC40 boat, commanded by Oberleutnant zur See Christian-Brandt Coester, was sunk by depth charges dropped from a Wellington.[91] By the 28th, with no promise of success for BdU, *Fliegerführer Atlantik* signalled the end of combined Luftwaffe/U-boat operations against the convoy and the U-boats were withdrawn from the area on the evening of the 28th.[92] The *Weddigen* group's efforts had accomplished nothing and so far Allied action had sunk a total of eight boats from both *Schill* and *Weddigen*. The latter group was dissolved on 6 December.[93]

Before its dissolution however, *Fliegerführer Atlantik* ordered FAGr 5 to undertake reconnaissance over the Gibraltar convoy route, to the south-west of Ireland, with the aim of locating another southbound convoy for the benefit of the remaining U-boats in the area. Initially, two Ju 290s, one of which was 9V+HK, were slated to take off from Mont de Marsan in the early morning of 29 November. After a postponement, possibly on account of weather conditions, the aircraft departed and one machine later reported spotting one motor vessel of 20,000 tons and one of *c.*10,000 tons in the area of 25° West 62, course 90°, at a speed of six knots, but details of the ships could not be distinguished. These may have been vessels from OS.60/KMS.34, of 48 ships plus an oiler, bound for Freetown and Gibraltar, which had sailed from Liverpool on 25 November. Both Junkers safely returned. Another aircraft went out the following day, but details of the mission are not available.

Meanwhile, the strength of the Atlantic U-boat force had grown with the arrival of 11 new boats from Germany and three brought down from the Arctic. Together with three from France, plus another two, these boats were formed into a new wolfpack known as *Coronel*, which, in turn, was divided into three sub-groups. Things got off to an ominous start on 1 December when one of the Arctic boats, *U-269*, was badly damaged by enemy action and forced to beat a retreat to St Nazaire. The remaining boats took up their positions in the Atlantic, amidst winter storms to the west of Ireland.[94]

On the 2nd, from its base at the Hotel am Steinplatz in Berlin, BdU issued a directive that *Coronel* should be deployed against a westbound convoy, ONS.24 from Liverpool to Halifax, and that the pack should be in position from 1200 hrs on the 5th. It had also been agreed between the *Fliegerführer Atlantik* and BdU that long-range air reconnaissance to locate the convoy west of Ireland on behalf of *Coronel* would commence on 4 December.[95] The usual problem manifested itself once more: only two Ju 290s were available to carry out reconnaissance between 58° and 52° North and east of 21° West. SKL was sceptical over the contribution of the Luftwaffe: 'It remains to be seen whether our weak air reconnaissance forces will be able to detect the convoy.' Indeed, a southbound convoy had already slipped through the *Weddigen* pack undetected: 'This is the third convoy that has not been detected.'[96]

The Ju 290s A-4 Wk-Nr 0169 (PI+PW) 9V+KK, which had joined 2./FAGr 5 on 25 November, having taken part in air-refuelling trials at Dessau earlier in the month, and the A-3 Wk-Nr 0162 (PI+PP) 9V+EK, also of 2.*Staffel*, were airborne to the east of a line 53° North. 25° 30′ West–56° 42′ North 25° 36′ West during the afternoon over what was believed to be the area in which ONS.24 should be, but neither aircraft could locate it.[97] This was because the convoy, which had departed Liverpool on 30 November, had been routed to the north of the U-boats' operational area as a result of Enigma decrypts which revealed the position of *Coronel*.[98] Both aircraft returned safely, but without having assisted the U-boats – a result of Allied codebreaking rather than any shortcomings on the part of the aircrews. It was to be the same story on the 5th, when 9V+HK and 9V+DH patrolled to the south-west of the area covered the previous day. Adverse weather conditions prevented a return to Mont de Marsan and both aircraft had to land at alternative fields.[99] It looked as if ONS.24 – 30 merchants and 15 escorts, including the *Ancylus*, a former Royal Dutch/Shell oil tanker which had recently been converted to a MAC ship – had slipped through the net.[100]

Despite the dissatisfaction expressed at higher levels over FAGr 5's lack of accomplishment, in early December, the safety of the still small number of Ju 290s of the *Gruppe* had become of paramount importance to the Kriegsmarine, which was indicative of the fact that it was prepared to lend its smoke-laying units to only one airfield – and that was Mont de Marsan, presumably as defence against Allied air attacks. Protection of the Ju 290s was deemed 'more important than the protection of La Pallice or the He 177s.'[101]

By 10 December, the winter weather over the Biscay and the Atlantic was beginning to curtail the operations of the *Gruppe*. That day, the attention of the BdU shifted to SL.141 and MKS.32, convoys which had rendezvoused on 4 December to become a combined grouping of 55 merchant vessels and ten escorts bound for Liverpool.[102] SL.141/MKS.32's position at 0800 hrs on the 10th was at approximately 44° 33′ North 18° 55′ West. *Fliegerführer Atlantik* sent out three Condors from III./KG 40 at around 0100 hrs to be followed later by a pair of Ju 290s from FAGr 5, which would home in a strike force of He 177s from II./KG 40. The Focke-Wulfs found the convoy at 0910 hrs which was reported to consist of 'many motor vessels and an aircraft carrier, course 360°.' But with the weather worsening, the Ju 290s would remain on the ground in France, firstly delayed, and then eventually their mission cancelled, thus ending the hopes of an ensuing action by the Heinkels.[103]

On 11 December, three of FAGr 5's six Ju 290s were serviceable, along with ten of III./KG 40's fifteen Fw 200s and one of the two Bv 222s available to *Fliegerführer Atlantik*.[104] That day aircraft from all three of these units would prepare to take part in an operation against ON.215, a 58-vessel convoy which had sailed from Liverpool on 9 December bound for New York carrying cocoa waste, soda ash, coal and general supplies, accompanied by 17 escorts.[105] Two Ju 290s of FAGr 5, an aircraft coded 'A' and 9V+EK of 2.*Staffel*, flew from Mont de Marsan, north along the French coast, to Kerlin-Bastard, near Lorient, from where they would operate. According to the subsequent British signals intelligence report for the 12th, 'Reconnaissance was evidently planned with some knowledge of the sailing of the convoy. The convoy's position was assumed to be in about 57° North 18° West at 1400 hrs on the 12th and was in fact estimated too far to the Northward, it having been routed on a more Southerly track. At 0800 hrs on the 12th, its estimated position was 53° 47′ North 14° 20′ West.' This would explain why the Ju 290s' mission, which saw both aircraft fly out over Penmarch between 0445 and 0515 hrs, proved to be in vain. At 2313 hrs, aircraft 'A' reported a problem with one of its engines. It was forced to land at Brest-Lanvéoc on three engines at 0021 hrs.[106]

Problems did not seem to be restricted to just engines; the war diary of the operations section of the SKL again blamed the absence of air reconnaissance, or rather failure of even its limited amount of equipment, for the lack of success of *Coronel* in the Atlantic. The *Hohentwiel* search apparatus on board a Ju 290 had broken down temporarily just at the point the aircraft's crew had spotted three ships. Based on dead reckoning, the *Coronel* I and II packs were moved to the area, around 800 km west of Ireland, on the evening of the 13th.

'If a close reconnaissance with double the number of aircraft had been available,' fumed the war diarist, 'there would probably have been a chance of picking up the convoy and reporting it in time. The *Fliegerführer Atlantik* had all available forces operating. This case clearly demonstrates that the number of aircraft is inadequate. The failure of a single search-gear set resulted in a frustrated operation which had been prepared long beforehand and involved a great number of U-boats. Renewed aerial reconnaissance in the area of *Coronel* is planned for 13 December, engaging all available forces, i.e., two Ju 290s and one Fw 200.'[107]

So it was that on the 13th, Generalleutnant Kessler tried once again to deploy his forces in support of *Coronel* against ON.215. This time, any attempt to fly the Ju 290s out of Lorient and/or Brest was abandoned, and two more aircraft were made ready at Mont de Marsan for a first reconnaissance, along with a single Fw 200 of III./KG 40 at Lorient. The Condor managed to sight the convoy at 0823 hrs in 25° West 7224, 420 km west of the Irish coast, but subsequently developed engine trouble and crashed near Limerick in Ireland later that evening.

Ju 290s Wk-Nr 0158 9V+BK and Wk-Nr 0169 9V+KK of 2./FAGr 5 took off from Mont de Marsan around 0430 hrs to head out into the Atlantic. At 1058 hrs, using FuG 200 radar, aircraft 'B' picked up a 'formation' of ships in 23° West 0325, some 530 km west-south-west of Clifden, in County Galway on the west coast of Ireland. Through gaps in the cloud, the crew observed seven merchant vessels all on a westerly course. This was similar to the sighting made by the Fw 200 earlier that morning.[108] *Fliegerführer Atlantik* asked for more details and at 1420 hrs the aircraft responded that the composition of the formation was unknown although its 'blip' on the FuG 200 screen 'had been large'. It is possible that the blip may have been one of the eastbound convoys, SC.148 from Halifax to Liverpool or HX.269 from New York, which the U-boats had also been warned to expect.

Four hours later, at 1810 hrs in 25° West 8248, 9V+KK sighted ON.215. The crew signalled that the convoy comprised 40 ships with ten escort vessels, on course 270° at eight knots. The Ju 290 continued to shadow the convoy, but at 1945 hrs it was warned by Mont de Marsan of a strong southerly wind and instructed to return punctually. At 2020 hrs, the Junkers were ordered to break off their mission and return.

The results of FAGr 5's reconnaissance showed that ON.215 was so far to the south of the U-boat patrol lines as to render useless further reconnaissance for the purpose of homing. The planned take-off by a third Ju 290 (to go out at 1155 hrs) specifically to home the U-boats on to the convoy, was delayed and eventually cancelled. At 2240 hrs, the *Coronel* boats, which had been ordered to surface at 1830 hrs and maintain a watch for beacon signals, were informed that such signals were no longer to be expected.[109]

On the 14th, the weather conditions in the Bay of Biscay brought almost all Luftwaffe activity in the area to a standstill, but the next day *Fliegerführer Atlantik* once again sent out FAGr 5 to hunt for ON.215.[110] The assumptions of both the *Fliegerführer* and BdU was that, since the last sighting on the evening of the 13th, the convoy was making a westerly or west-south-west course, and both reconnaissance and U-boats were deployed accordingly. A Bv 222 of 1./SAGr 129 was sent out first from Biscarosse at 0350 hours, but returned after some five hours, probably as a result of deteriorating weather.

Then, with a flight plan that would take them across the French coast at 0420 hrs, Ju 290s 9V+AK and 9V+GK of 2./FAGr 5 crossed the Biscay to the Atlantic. They were followed later that morning by 9V+KK, which was probably sent out as a replacement for the Bv 222. As the day progressed, however, the weather out at sea grew steadily worse and at 1255 hrs, *Fliegerführer Atlantik* signalled all aircraft to be aware of the ground wind on their return flights. At 1725 hrs, they were asked to signal details of wind direction and strength hourly. No sightings seem to have been made, but this would have been as a result of the erroneous aforementioned assumption of the convoy's track, which was in fact considerably farther south than thought. The Ju 290s all returned.[111]

Fernaufklärungsgruppe 5 had been at war over the Atlantic for 30 days.

CHAPTER SIX

THE *KOMMANDEUR'S* REPORT

Operational enthusiasm and inspiration is high among all the crews. The loss of two crews has not had any effect. [There is] complete trust in the aircraft type.

Hauptmann Hermann Fischer, *Gruppenkommandeur*, FAGr 5

FAGr 5's first full month of operations was marked on 15 December and it was the point at which, in a widely circulated report, Hauptmann Fischer reviewed the accomplishments, shortcomings, immediate needs and longer-term, future requirements of the *Gruppe*. By this stage FAGr 5 had flown 29 sorties against Gibraltar–UK (MKS)/UK–Gibraltar (KMS), Sierra Leone (Freetown)–UK (SL)/UK–Sierra Leone (OS) and North Atlantic convoys (HX etc.), totalling 415 hr 16 min flying time over a distance of 120,350 km.

Over a total of 11 days, six convoys had been shadowed, representing a total of 238 merchant ships, one battleship, ten destroyers, nine corvettes and 20 miscellaenous escort vessels. Fischer estimated the 'catch' of tonnage by the *Gruppe* sat between 1.7 and 2 million GRT, of which 18,000 GRT had 'probably' been sunk by the He 177s of II./KG 40, while there had been no sinkings as a direct result of cooperation between the unit's Ju 290s and the

U-boats. In his view, with the limited numbers of aircraft available, the results were 'good' and he attributed the successes particularly to the 'good work' of the FuG 200 *Hohentwiel* ASV search sets and what he termed as reports from 'reliable agents', presumably emanating from Spain and North Africa.

According to Fischer, there was a considerable difference between flying longer-range missions into the mid-Atlantic, west of Ireland, and flying missions to cover the Mediteranean and Sierra Leone convoys:

> Up to now, successful sorties against the England–America convoys have been sparse. The search area for these convoys, the location of which is especially important for B.d.U., often lie at the outermost range of the Ju 290, so that with the limited forces available, only a relatively small area can be covered. As a result of the great ranges, in general, several search sectors cannot be covered by a single aircraft. Shadowing [a convoy] at greater range is only possible for the shortest period of time.
>
> Reconnaissance sorties against Gibraltar–England convoys met with good success, as did working with U-boats and also with bomber units. Cooperation, in principle, works. Deficiencies, which are caused in training, will be remedied.[1]

Fischer also made clear in his report the need for FAGr 5 to be given an offensive capability in addition to its 'passive' reconnaissance and shadowing roles. In this regard he highlighted the *Kehl/Strassburg* radio-controlled guidance system for guided/glide-bombs. By the summer of 1943, two such weapons had reached the anti-shipping units of the Luftwaffe. The first of these was the SD 1400 X, codenamed *Fritz X*. Manufactured by Ruhrstahl, the SD 1400 X was based on an armour-piercing bomb with a 1,150-kg warhead, and was to be released from an aircraft at between 4000 and 7000 m. It then fell at near terminal velocity and was guided to the target by a bomb-aimer using the flare in the tail of the bomb as a marker. From 7000 m, the bomb took 42 seconds to reach its target, the bomb-aimer having control for the last 27 seconds.

Initial trials of the SD 1400 had proved tricky when difficulties were experienced with the control of the free-falling bombs owing to their high velocities. These initial problems were overcome by early 1942, following which the bomb was trialled in the Mediterranean. The plan was to use the bomb with the He 177, but because of production delays with that aircraft, it was assigned for initial deployment on the Do 217K-2 of II. and III./KG 100. Once examples reached operational units, the *Fritz X* resembled the standard SD 1400 bomb, but with four stubby wings added.

On 9 September, in the Mediterranean, nine Dorniers of III./KG 100 based at Istres attacked Italian warships which it was feared would be used by the Allies following Italy's surrender. Each aircraft carried an SD 1400 X bomb and all were dropped west of the Straits of Bonifacio, with two making direct hits on the battleship *Roma*, which quickly broke in two and sank. Another bomb seriously damaged *Roma's* sister ship, the *Italia*. Successful attacks would be carried out against British and American warships over the coming days.[2]

The other weapon was the Henschel Hs 293 which carried a 500-kg warhead in the forward part of a small, cylindrical fuselage, itself forming part of a small 'monoplane' with rectangular wings and tailplane. The aft part of the missile contained the control gyroscope, radio receiver, batteries and battery-driven motor generator. After launch, a small Walter rocket motor accelerated the speed of the Hs 293 to around 600 km/h at an initial thrust of 600 kg, decreasing to 400 kg. Cutting out after about 12 sec, the bomb then coasted towards its target in a shallow dive guided by a bomb-aimer in the parent aircraft.

As with the SD 1400 X, the first aircraft to deploy the weapon in action were the Do 217s of II./KG 100, which usually carried out attacks at night from 1000 m at about 320 km/h, at which the Hs 293 had a range of about 11 km, but the missile would also be used over the Bay of Biscay and the Atlantic by the He 177s of II./KG 40.

The means of controlling and guiding both the SD 1400 X and the Hs 293 lay in the FuG 203/320 *Kehl/Strassburg* radio control system. *Kehl* had been developed by Telefunken and named after a district in Strassburg, the French/German city on the Rhine. The *Kehl* I transmitter was intended for use with the SD 1400 X, while the *Kehl* III was for controlling the Hs 293. The device transmitted orders as frequency modulations on a radio frequency carrier, with each weapon requiring a different set of four orders. The transmitter operated on one of 18 frequencies between 48.2 and 49.9 MHz, separated by 100 kHz. In the case of the SD 1400 X, these were right, left, up and down, while for the Hs 293 they were roll clockwise, roll anti-clockwise, pitch up and pitch down. The later FuG 203c *Kehl* IV, built by Telefunken and Opta, could be adjusted for use with either weapon. Before take-off the bombs would be pre-set to one of the frequencies with a corresponding setting made in the launch aircraft.[3]

The system did suffer from problems associated with moisture and condensation, especially during long-range, high-altitude missions, but these were countered by incorporating a special heating system in carrier aircraft, which directed hot engine exhaust over the weapon controls. But this installation meant that the aircraft had to be specially fitted with both *Kehl/Strassburg* and the heating system, thus limiting the number of aircraft available.[4]

Notwithstanding this, Fischer recognized the tactical value that *Kehl* would have for the Ju 290s of FAGr 5 in 'armed reconnaissance' missions. He noted:

> When, despite successful cooperation, success was not achieved, with the U-boats it was due to strong defensive measures taken by the convoys, and with the bomber units it was due to unsuitable weather conditions.
>
> Equipping the *Gruppe* with *Kehl* should lead to success in operations against convoys. Since shadowing stretches over several days (with ideal weather conditions), even with light forces (6–10 aircraft), considerable success should be attained.

Fischer emphasized his point further by underlining, with some bitter irony, the first of the sentences that followed:

> The figure of reconnoitred tonnage to the figure of tonnage sunk speaks for itself.
>
> The [enemy's] defence capability allows a sortie of 6–10 Ju 290 flying in formation. A tight formation of 6–10 Ju 290 is sufficient to form a strong defence against a Pulk [formation] of 'Mosquitos'.
>
> The idea that Ju 290 missions equipped with *Kehl* strengthens the defence in areas of extreme range, is only partially correct. The defensive measures would increase anyway, and above all, when the Ju 290 is led successfully to a convoy together with Condor units equipped with *Kehl*. Ju 290 missions against convoys should take place where other bomber units, as a result of [lack of] range cannot be utilized and where U-boats, due to the defence situation, cannot operate.
>
> Quite apart from principles of leadership, with unit leaders one can set so much tactical understanding as a prerequisite, that these missions can be reduced to a minimum. The principal focal task – reconnaissance for U-boats – will in no way be affected by the carrying out of bomber operations [by Ju 290s]. The installation of *Kehl* equipment brings about a scarcely measurable loss in range. The Ju 290-*Kehl* aircraft has reached a developed stage and should be operationally ready by *c.*1.2.44.[5]

Fischer's mention of a 'Ju 290-*Kehl* aircraft' is most probably a reference to the new Ju 290A-7 variant, then under development at Junkers, which it was planned would be able to carry and deploy the new weapons technology.

It is clear that Fischer saw the role of the Ju 290 not just in terms of lone reconnaissance and/or shadowing, or in conducting those types of mission with pairs or small formations of aircraft, but also as a strike-bomber equipped with *Fritz X* or Hs 293 bombs operating in larger formations at maximum range. He viewed the rationale that Ju 290s so equipped would attract greater enemy defence as illogical. Rather, the Ju 290 would be able to operate where the Fw 200 could not. In this, he would have found an ally in Dönitz and his staff.

By December 1943, FAGr 5 was equipped with a single Ju 290A-2, four A-3, three A-4 and two new A-5 models.[6] Oskar Schmidt recalled:

> Characteristics of the aircraft were good, easy to handle. Upon loss of one or two engines, the aircraft could still be flown well and permitted among other things, side-slipping. To ease their activities over a long a mission, the *Kommandant* [commander of the aircraft] and co-pilot had the assistance of an automatic Siemens three-axis steering [or control] device. The three dimensions could be switched-in/activated by means of three lever positions and thereby hold [the aircraft's] attitude in flight.[7]

Powered by four 1,700 hp BMW 801D engines, the five-aircraft Ju 290A-4 reconnaissance series (*Fernerkunder*) differed from the A-3 only in terms of lacking its internal transport configuration and some manufacturing processes. The Ju 290A-4 had accommodation for a crew of seven, including four 'rest chairs', as well as protective armour for the cockpit, weapons and engine areas. It came equipped with FuBl 2H receiver, FuG 101 radio altimeter, FuG 200 *Hohentwiel* ship-search radar and FuG 216 radar. Armament comprised a 20 mm MG 151/20 cannon in forward and aft low-profile dorsal turrets and the tail position. Additionally, the right- and left-side waist positions each mounted a 13 mm MG 131 machine gun, while the forward ventral gondola housed another MG 151/20 (forward) and two 13 mm MG 131 machine guns (rear).

Oskar Schmidt remembers that the aircraft's armament transformed it into a 'flying fortress':

> Up top were two turrets (one directly behind the navigator's position and another further back towards the end of the fuselage). The weapons in both turrets were 20 mm MG 151, fully automatic and fully rotatable. The gunner sat at his battle position and could move his guns electrically with a steering lever and, with a reflector sight, track the target. It was possible, if necessary, to mount a twin MG 131 at one of the three windows on the port and starboard sides. These weapons gave considerable firepower; the radio operator

and flight mechanic would man these defensive guns. In an attack, range and lead-angle could be determined via the *Revi*, and the firing sequence would then be activated by means of a firing lever located on the control stick. Pre-set locks prevented hitting one's own empennage. Each turret would be occupied by an air-gunner. The cockpit accommodated both pilots and the flight engineer. Then there were two radio-operators' seats and a small, separate area for the navigator. All crew members could communicate over an intercom. Then came the built-in fuselage tank, which was passed to the side, followed by a cabin with four rest places, and near to the loading ramp was a cleverly built galley where the most suitable crew member could prepare refreshments and snacks as needed during the long flight times. At the end of the fuselage was a large dinghy with approproiate sea emergency equipment for 11 men, including SOS transmitter with kite antennae.[8]

The Ju 290A-5 was essentially a modification of the A-4 with an improved forward dorsal turret and an extra oil tank to carry an additional 225 l, and other internal additions to the fuselage. Total equipped weight increased from 20,860 kg on the A-4 to 24,085 kg on the A-5, while fuel load went up by 4020 kg to 14,220 kg. The total weight of the Ju 290A-5 was 41,305 kg. A *Flugzeug-Baureihen-Blatt* (aircraft specification drawing) issued by the RLM on 1 September 1944 shows that it was intended to fit the A-5 with an ETC 2000 bomb rack under each wing to enable it to carry a weapon such as the SD 1400 *Fritz X*. Eleven examples of the A-5 would be built.

But by the autumn of 1943, the Luftwaffe was aware of the shortcomings in its inventory. In January 1944, one report noted, 'The fact that the [B-24] Liberator has proved superior to the Ju 290 serves as another reminder of the enormous strides German aircraft development must make to enable the Luftwaffe to achieve tactical successes in spite of numerical inferiority.'

It was clear to the Luftwaffe what was needed in terms of long-range reconnaissance:

The interior arrangements of aircraft could undergo examination when new developments occur. Operations carried out far over the Atlantic call for constant navigation. It therefore seems expedient not to burden the members of the crew responsible for this with other duties. The observer and the wireless operator would then be concerned solely with navigation, while the rear gunners would be responsible exclusively for observing a rear defence. Such an arrangement and the provision of the necessary accommodation would guarantee perfect identification of targets and effective use of armament.[9]

Fischer was candid about the existing Ju 290 variants' shortcomings and how Junkers could best serve Luftwaffe long-range reconnaissance in the coming years:

> Although the Ju 290, as opposed to all previously used types, offers an increase in range, it shows, in particular, that for reconnaissance west of Ireland, and for tasks on behalf of the B.d.U., the official flight range is insufficient. Increasing the take-off weight from 41 tonnes to 45 tonnes is intended, i.e. the installation of a second fuselage fuel tank holding 3,400 l and enabling an increase in range of around 400 km.

By mentioning a prospective weight increase, it is most likely Fischer was referring to the planned Ju 290A-8, which had a capability to carry a 1930-kg 'payload', greater fuel and oil capacities over the A-5 as well as an allowance for more crew and special equipment.

Fischer seemed equally unimpressed by the proposed Ju 290B series, on which work commenced (on the B-1) in late 1943; the design removed the *Trapoklappe* ramp. Powered by 2,000 hp BMW 801E engines, it was proposed to protect the aircraft with strong defensive armament in the form of nose and tail MG 131 *Vierling* turrets, each containing four 13 mm machine guns, two dorsal turrets with MG 151s and a ventral barbette with a further pair of such cannon. However, poor technical performance and difficulties with the pressurization system forced further development on the aircraft, as well as a proposed B-2 variant, to be abandoned by November 1944.

Fischer's view was that: 'Equipping the Ju 290B with an MG 131 *Vierling* is no good. Our own aircraft will be shot down before the enemy aircraft comes within range of our own weapons.' He further commented: 'With regard to range, it is not thought that the Ju 290B, as opposed to the 45-t aircraft, will bring about a better performance, i.e. that it would attain a maximum tactical range of 2900–3000 km.'

What Fischer really wanted was the Ju 390, the six-engined development of the Ju 290, the first prototype of which, the V1 Wk-Nr 3900001 GH+UK, had made its inaugural flight from the Junkers plant at Merseburg on 20 October 1943 with Flugkapitän Pancherz and Diplom-Ingenieur Gast on board. This massive aircraft, with a wingspan of 50.32 m (more than 8 m longer than the Ju 290), had been under development since mid-1942, and was seen as an even longer-range successor to the Ju 290 as a reconnaissance aircraft, as a carrier for 'parasite' fighters and even bombers, and as a long-range bomber and transporter. Powered by six BMW 801E engines, offering a range of 5860 km, with a crew of 10–12 men, the total equipped weight of the Ju 390 at take-off was 75 t, which included 30,400 kg of fuel, 1690 kg of oil, 8400 kg of ammunition and an allowance of 120 kg for an emergency dinghy and supplies. The aforementioned *Flugzeug-Baureihen-Blatt* of September 1944 lists the 'Ju 390A-1' as being equipped with an impressive array of radio and radar equipment and armament of three double-gun MG 151 Z (*Zwilling* – twin) sets and two MG 131s, plus four ETC 2000 racks for carrying offensive ordnance.[10] According to Fischer:

> In order to take a decisive step for Atlantic reconnaissance, it is proposed that instead of the Ju 290B, mass production should go over immediately to the Ju 390. Likewise, as in the realm of high performance, the development of interim types of fighters should be abandoned in order to make an enormous leap, it would be purposeful in this case, in terms of range, to undertake the leap from the Ju 290A to the Ju 390. Besides the clear advantage of range, the Ju 390 possesses the following further advantages:
>
> (1) At great range, a longer time-span for shadowing.
>
> (2) Through great range, it can take increased defensive measures with alternating approach and return flights, taking into account greater flight distances. Constantly changing tactics negate enemy defensive measures. At the present time, in approach and return flights, the shortest approach path has to be selected on each occasion. Enemy defence is thus easily concentrated and will lead to further losses.
>
> (3) In the to-be-expected strengthening of [Allied] defensive measures in the Atlantic, the Ju 390 offers a decisive advantage in relation to its stability. It is possible, by means of armour, weapons and ammunition, to make the Ju 390 so stable that, in terms of range, it remains superior to the Ju 290B and in terms of stability, brings about decisive advantages.
>
> (4) Equipping it with *Kehl* over the furthest range is possible, and especially by internal suspension [i.e., storage and carriage of ordnance internally] only a small loss in range is to be expected.

Set against the conditions in which they operated over the Atlantic, the question of armament was of paramount importance to the crews of FAGr 5. On this subject Fischer wrote:

> To increase defensive armament, the following development is proposed:
>
> The slow-flying *Atlantikaufklärer* begins and falls with its defensive armament. [Fischer's emphasis]
>
> It must be possible to so increase defensive armament that the aircraft is able to defend itself successfully against a swarm of enemy *Zerstörer* aircraft

[long-range fighters – i.e., Mosquitos] by skilful flying. Air combat with an enemy *Zerstörer* aircraft has shown that at 2000 m range, fire was opened and that our own aircraft already received damaging hits at a range of 1500 m. It was only due to prevailing cloud cover that the aircraft escaped. This fact is unacceptable. The following weapons development is therefore considered to be correct:

1st Phase: Immediate measures:

Heckstand [tail gun position]: to be equipped with MK 103 [30 mm cannon] with greatest possible traverse of fire, in particular rearwards and upwards, as defence in low-level flight.

Seitenlafetten [lateral MG 131 barbettes]: fully extendable and traversible with firing direction vertically to the rear, parallel to the aircraft longitudinal axis as with the Bv 222, Liberator, etc.

2nd Phase: *Heckstand* MK 103. *Seitenlafetten* as under (1), except the MG 131 has 2-cm *Zwilling* [twin-gun set]

3rd Phase: *Heckstand* MK 103. *Seitenlaffetten* 2-cm *Illing;* B-1 and B-2 Stand (dorsal turrets) MG 151 *Zwilling;* all aircraft from Wk-Nr 180 [which became an A-5 (KR+LK) with 1./FAGr 5 as 9V+KH], A-Stand with 2-cm *Illing*, C-Stand MG 151 Z remote-controlled.

4th Phase: For Ju 390A-Stand (nose) 3-cm *Zwilling*
  B-1-Stand (dorsal forward) 2-cm *Zwilling*
  B-2-Stand (dorsal aft) 3-cm *Zwilling*
  Heckstand (tail) 3-cm *Zwilling*
  Seitenlafetten 2-cm *Illing*
  C-Stand (lower fuselage, aft) 2-cm *Zwilling* remote-controlled

For special tasks at extreme range, the armament can be reduced in favour of increased fuel load; escort protection on approach and return flights by strongly armed Ju 390s for this aircraft will need to be secured at all times.

There had also been sufficient time for the crews of FAGr 5 to assess the working efficiency and functionality of the Ju 290. Fischer found concern particularly with the navigator's area within the aircraft:

> On past missions, the cramped arrangement of the navigation and radio space behind the 1st and 2nd pilot has been a noticeable disadvantage. Particularly at night and in bad weather, the annoyance to the pilot because of the radioman working behind him, as well as the navigator, is considerable.

---

*   Since *Vierling* is a four-barrel arrangement, and *Zwilling* a two-barrel, *Illing* probably denotes a single-barrel, and is meant as an abbreviation for *Einling* or single arrangement.

In the cramped space of the cockpit are located the two pilots, one mechanic, two radio-operators and one observer. For the further development, the following solution is held to be unavoidably necessary:

Separation of the pilots' space from the navigator's space; place the navigator's space forward on the starboard side instead of the current radio-operators' space; the radio-operator's space to go behind Frame 3 on the starboard side behind the B-1-Stand (arrangement as suggested by the *E-Stelle* Rechlin).

Fischer was more upbeat on the standard of training and the quality of his crews:

Operations have confirmed that the methods of training adopted prior to operations from July 1943 to November 1943 were correct. The tactical understanding of the long-range reconnaissance crews, who had not previously flown over water, have been so instructed in their training that their conduct in their new reconnaissance role region can, generally, be regarded as tactically correct.

In particular, two points in training have been decisive factors:

1. Making known the experiences of KG 40 by means of a very good training crew.

2. Practice with the 27.U-boat Flotilla at Gotenhafen.

The state of training of the pilots is good. To date, flights in the worst of weather conditions have been made. Sorties, in particular that with an aircraft weighing 41 t at take-off, in bad weather conditions, calls for the best pilots and personnel. Old, tried-and-trusted long-range reconnaissance pilots who are suitably talented have shown themselves to be successfully re-trained. The most advantageous are pilots of the *Nachtaufklärungsstaffeln* [night reconnaissance squadrons].

The *Kommandanten* [pilots-in-command] are personally nominated by the *Kommandeur* and serve either as 1st pilot or observer. Decisive for this [purpose] is frontline flight experience and character.

Operational enthusiasm and inspiration is high among all the crews. The loss of two crews has not had any effect. [There is] complete trust in the aircraft type.

Fischer concluded his report with a detailed summary of the technical performance and related aspects of the Ju 290 based on experience:

Technical experience:
The flying and technical experiences of the *Gruppe* are gained from 1,482 flights and a total of 1,852 flying-hours on the Ju 290. All crews regard the

flying characteristics of the Ju 290 as good; this holds true above all for heavyweight take-offs (at 41 t) and blind-flying. Flights in storms and areas of strong gusts (wind speeds of more than 100 km/h) have been carried out. In sorties conducted to date, only one aircraft has failed to return (shot down by a Mosquito). One aircraft crashed after take-off (a night take-off) and was destroyed by the ensuing fire on impact. The cause of the crash has not been fully determined. In one night landing, an aircraft rolling to a stop suffered an undercarriage leg breakage which caused 15 per cent damage. The reason for this is still being investigated.

The experiences and defects in flying operations were in individual cases as follows:

BMW 801 ML and G engines:
In 30 sorties there were only minor defects/faults. Engine changes due to whatever causes did not have to be carried out. Cruising performance in the *Gruppe* is between 0.9 to 1.06 atm *Ladedruck* (boost pressure). With boost pressure below 0.95 and 1,800 rpm, in most of the aircraft, strong engine vibrations occur. These vibrations carry over to the airframe, and in particular to the cockpit.

In shadowing missions and for the attainment of the longest flying time, flying with a boost pressure below 0.95 and 1,800 rpm is definitely necessary.

Equipping with metal airscrews for this low rpm value, in the view of the *Gruppe*, will bring about a decisive advantage. It is recommended that the *Gruppe* be provided with one set of metal airscrews for testing purposes.

Airframe:
Damage to the skinning, sheet-metal rents, loosening/popping-out of rivets occurred mainly in the region of the landing-flap jet nozzle. In the 100-hour inspections, these were remedied. The Junkers detachment, with Ing. Glenck and nine specialists, are carrying out the strengthening requirements stipulated by Junkers. Following completion of these alterations, the defects should be remedied once and for all.

On Wk-Nr 160 it was found in the 200-hour inspection on the wing upper side in the region of the end-box, a particularly noticeable loosening/popping-out of the rivets and sheet-metal plates. It has to be awaited to see whether this occurrence is a solitary case. Should, in later 200-hour inspections these same defects occur, a special report will follow. Also on the wing upper side, loosening/popping-out of rivets occurred, in the region of the fuel tank covers.

It has been shown that, in terms of the airframe, in general, at 200 hours of operating time, a considerable amount of sheet metalwork is necessary. Together with the defects that occur subsequently on the empennage, the defects give rise to the need to partially overhaul the airframe at the 300-hour mark. Based on the defects/faults lists from the partial overhauls, a decision should be taken by the *Amt* as to whether the parts-overhaul can be raised to 400 hours.

Due to it not being watertight in rain, the airframe suffers from a large number of damp-related and moisture faults. Measurement of the insulation values, which take place after every sortie, gives, on average, a value of 15–20,000 Ohms in cases of storms. In dry weather, 40–50,000 Ohms are regularly attained. The locations endangered by dampness are in particular the plug between the TZ and the wing; in the cockpit, the seeping-in of water behind the instrument panel into the instruments and the connecting plugs for the radio equipment. There is also the prospect of failure of the course-control and remote compass installation through damp and moisture.

Failure [to function] of the oil tanks, despite a strengthening of the tank heads, is still a considerable problem. With the tanks, leakage appears in the welded joints. The *Gruppe* believes that this is down to manufacturing faults at the Raspe company. Within a short time, three fuel-draining tanks failed in such a way that the rubber seals loosened themselves from the canvas walls. Here too, the *Gruppe* surmises that this is due to manufacturing faults.

The defects described above on all the oil and fuel-draining tanks were caused in the same way as already mentioned nine months ago by Hauptmann Braun of the *Lufttransportstaffel* Ju 290. Since then, nothing in the manufacturing of these tanks has brought about any improvement.

Tank switching:
The *Gruppe* demands, other than emptying from the main-tanks, the possibility of drawing fuel from Tz 2 and 3. Further, a fuel-transfer/pumping possibility into these tanks as well as a hand fuel-transfer possibility for all switches.

The rest seats in the Ju 290 have shown themselves to be inefficient. The *Gruppe* intends to install folding seats with metal frames instead of the seats. Following their completion, photographs will be taken of this arrangement and will be forwarded via service channels. Folding seats conserve on material and still offer the crew the possibility of resting.

For on-board catering on long-range sorties, the *Gruppe* has also built a kitchen cupboard with crockery and a heating plate in the aircraft. A sample has been forwarded to Junkers.

Undercarriage:

Tyre wear-and-tear is normal; in 156 take-offs and landings, four tyres suffered damage. On the undercarriage hydraulics system there was often chafing of the hydraulic pipes which lead through the firewall. The chafing spot is at the bulkhead.

On Wk-Nr 164, despite the fact that the undercarriage switch was in the 'off' position, the undercarriage travelled past the end position on starting-up Engine No. 3. **The reason:** A short in the undercarriage electrics.

Electrics:

For safety reasons, it is urgently necessary to move the undercarriage double-pole electrics to another location. Likewise, for safety reasons, it is necessary to move the electrics for the double-pole trimming to another position.

The connections described above on electrical installations were partly to blame for the fact that in nine out of 30 sorties, the Patin three-axis control or else the remote-control emergency compass went u/s. On such occasions the emergency compass situated in the right-hand pilot's position proved to be very badly located. It would be preferable to install an OK 42 *Draufsichtkompass* (direct-view compass) at the 1st pilot's location.

Control system:

On Wk-Nr 160, 161 and 162, in the tailplane connecting points, loose joints were discovered. Should this be the case in other aircraft, it would give cause to consider that with the current state of equipment condition, where the damping-tube is no longer adjustable, that the tailplane positioning is made more stable.

The lifting jack for the rudder lever positioning on Frame 9f is too weak, so that on operating the rudder, Frame 9f is placed under considerable stress. The frame is, at the indicated position, too weak and must be strengthened. This fault was detected on several aircraft.

Course-control (Patin three-axis control):

As already mentioned above, in this control system instruments, distributors and plugs very much suffer from damp. Some of the instrument failures have been found to lead directly back to this cause. Furthermore, according to the firm's representative, *Herr* Laude, the current damping-gyro does not meet the laid down requirements. Rarely do the gyros hold out for a flying time of 18 hours, and thereafter show a zero error or else run unevenly.

Armament:

In their functioning, the *Seitenlafetten* 131 were faultless. The HD 151/2 with electric ignition and loading shows great susceptibility to disturbances. It too is mainly dependent on connections and these [gun] mounts in turn, suffer from a lack of being watertight in rain. As an immediate remedy for these problems, the *Gruppe* has altered the mounts to mechanical operation. The RLM specialist, Oberinspektor Roloff, GL/C E-6 [the RLM department for munitions], visited the *Gruppe* and was fully in agreement with this temporary solution. At the Amt, he will advocate the following measures:

Sealing of the canopy hood, installation of an emergency battery or a second ignition lead. These measures should largely take care of the faults. The *Gruppe* will then, with regard to the distributors of the electrical system, return to electrical ignition for the HD 151/2 mounts. With the HD 151/2, in ten sorties there were 12 failures in the electric loading function. In mechanical operation the stresses on electric loading should become less.

Furthermore, Oberinspektor Roloff will investigate whether, with electric ignition, the possibility exists to enlarge the *Schlussbereich* (end-stop position). At the moment, the B-2 mount weapon fires with a blockage-area of 1.5 m around the tail unit. It is precisely the electic ignition that must allow firing to be accomplished closer to the tail unit. It would be advantageous to combat enemy aircraft flying behind the tail unit.

Radio equipment:

Equipping the aircraft with FuG 10 K2 devices (transceivers for both R/T and W/T communication) was not able to satisfy tactical requirements. It therefore became necessary on all sorties to provide an additional FuG 10 K transmitter and receiver which, in the close-range region up to the limit of 1000 km, and in particular at night, enables a secure connection. In operations with these devices, however, only the trailing-antenna was able to be used.

Experiences with the current **antenna installation**, with respect to radio, shows good results. The moveable antenna masts, however, display faulty design, as they often break, and the in- and out- movement does not function well in operation. The poor accessibility to the **trailing-antenna** was shown to be a disadvantage on some flights. Relocating the installation position to an easily accessible place and its exchangeability during flight is deemed necessary.

Hohentwiel:

All tasks undertaken up to now were in regard to *Funkmeßaufklärung* (radar reconnaissance). In nine out of 11 instances, identification of convoys was by means of search equipment. In four instances, the task was abandoned due to failure of the search equipment. Initial difficulties in equipment maintenance was, following detailed instructions, remedied by specialists. Deliveries of spare parts, particularly tubes, at the present time, is especially problematic.

Neptun-R

The *Neptun-R* apparatus show a high failure rate as a result of the damp seeping in. Part of the cause was due to the poor laying of antennae lead cable and the accumulation of condensation in the couplings. Operation of the apparatus in the first four weeks had to be deferred, as no aircraft were synchronized. The currently installed vertical antennae enable a successful sortie, but however, only after reaching altitude of 1500 m. The installation of horizontal antennae with an effective scope at low flying attitudes is therefore urgently required. Nightfighters have also been observed at low altitudes.

FuG 25 a [IFF radar]

There are at the present time still no ground-based devices with corresponding auxiliary equipment in the operational area [and] experience has not been gathered.

Supply and spare-parts:

The supply of BMW 801 engines and spare-parts for the BMW 801 from Argenteuil [Paris depot] is good. Airframe spare parts have to come from series production at Junkers Dessau. Great difficulties are experienced in the supply of fuel and oil tanks. These also have to be supplied from Junkers Dessau series production.

From the abovementioned reasons, it is urgent that the *Gruppe* receives spare parts from Dessau by means of a transport aircraft (Ju 352) so equipped.

Supplies of weapons spare-parts for SD 131, MG 131, MG 151 and HD 151/1. For the HD 151/2 [there are] no spare parts being supplied. The parts will have to be procured direct from D.A.B. Berlin.

Spare-parts difficulties are likewise for FuG 200 and 216.

Signed:

Hauptmann and *Gruppenkommandeur*

Fischer[11]

It was Hauptmann Fischer's objective and hope that his report would reach, and be read at, the highest levels of the RLM and the OKL, as well as by the relevant departments at Junkers. He was successful in as much as that it did land on the desk of Generalfeldmarschall Milch, and he took immediate steps to hasten development of the Ju 390.[12] But it remained to be seen just how much even the dynamic and influential Milch could achieve as the war entered its sixth difficult year.

CHAPTER SEVEN

A BURNING
QUESTION

Atlantic Operations, December 1943

> German air operations in the Atlantic have great
> prospects of success in spite of present inferiority.

'The Operational Use of the Luftwaffe in the War at Sea 1939–1943',
Luftwaffe 8.*Abteilung* Historical Report, January 1944

By 16 December 1943, conditions in the eastern Atlantic had become nothing short of appalling. One of the *Coronel* group U-boats, the Type VIIC *U-284*, had suffered considerable damage from the weather, and its commander, Oberleutnant zur See Günther Scholz, was compelled to abort operations and signal for help. By the 17th, *U-284* had sustained bad sea damage to both of its electric motors. *U-629*, which had arrived from the Arctic, came to the vessel's assistance on the 21st, taking all of its crew aboard before *U-284* was scuttled.[1]

After two fruitless weeks, BdU dissolved the *Coronel* group and repositioned it into three other patrol lines, *Sylt*, *Amrum* and *Föhr*.[2]

On the morning of 17 December, a day when bad weather again curtailed any operations by FAGr 5, Kapitän Heinz Assmann, the naval operations officer on the OKW operations staff, delivered a personal teletype message from Dönitz to Adolf Hitler on the 'burning question of long-range reconnaissance for submarine warfare.' The Admiral was straight to the point:

The superiority of the enemy air force due to the employment of the radar has forced our U-boats in the Atlantic more and more below the surface. For the time being it has become necessary to renounce surface operations by day, and for U-boats to surface only by night, not only in the approach, but also in the main operational areas. Even if we succeed in reducing the possibility of locating submarines or in opposing enemy radar by our own active radar, there is on the whole little scope for change along this line of development ...

Surface tactics by U-boats are a thing of the past. In the future, operations will be carried out underwater ... The finding of the enemy constituted the main problem even during the best times of submarine warfare, where operations were carried out on the surface only. In the present enforced mode of operations, the chances of finding the enemy are, as recent experience has shown, reduced by more than a half, since surface operations by day – and therewith the large reconnaissance area of the individual boat – have been discontinued.

Even now, operations without air reconnaissance hold no promise of success. The past two months have, however, clearly confirmed that the extremely weak forces at the disposal of the *Fliegerführer Atlantik* cannot carry out the minimum reconnaissance requirements necessary for a U-boat operation, even when strained to the utmost. Nine out of fourteen joint operations already carried out were failures only because the reconnaissance forces were so weak that they could not detect the convoy sailing close by the U-boat patrol line. The long-term assembly of many U-boats will be an economic waste if the necessary number of reconnaissance forces are also not available.

The last operation by Group '*Coronel*' constitutes an example of this; for this operation in which 25 U-boats were engaged, the small number of only three aircraft was available on each of two days, and after one day's interval, only three further machines could be made available. Owing to this weak reconnaissance, the convoy was not detected on two days, and on the third day it was too late and uncertain for the boats to operate.

It must be emphasized that even now, successful submarine warfare is greatly dependent on our air reconnaissance, so that the latter becomes an absolute necessity with the employment of the new types of U-boats, which will be operating almost exclusively under water. The old demand made by BdU to have at least 12 machines [aircraft] ready for operations daily, will scarely suffice for the U-boat war with the new types. According to the present planning, and taking into account the new constructions and losses even until the end of 1944, the total number of long-range reconnaissance aircraft (Ju 290) which can be reached and attained by the *Fliegerführer Atlantik*, will amount to only 20.

I therefore beg an investigation as to whether the production of Ju 290s cannot be given priority and I furthermore ask whether the whole production of Ju 290s could not be placed at the disposal of U-boat warfare for long-range reconnaissance.

I deem it my duty to report that even with the new types of U-boat, the U-boat war can be raised again to higher level only when the air reconnaissance absolutely indispensable to it is available in sufficient numbers.

That evening, Hitler declared his agreement with Dönitz: in his view 'the cited number of Ju 290s to be completed is ridiculously low and must be increased by every means possible, as U-boat warfare is in urgent need of this air reconnaissance.'

The next morning, 18 December, Assmann advised General der Flieger Günther Korten, the Chief of the Luftwaffe General Staff, of this development. Korten, caught between a rock and a hard place, took the news to his superior, Reichsmarschall Göring, who brushed it aside, proclaiming it to be impossible to increase production of the Ju 290 as construction capacity for the Luftwaffe was already at full stretch. Korten went back to Assmann and advised him of the present state of Ju 290 production at Dessau as well as his 'willingness to examine the possibility of increasing production.'[3]

Just 68 reconnaissance flights had been made by the Luftwaffe over the Bay of Biscay and Atlantic in the period 15 November to 18 December 1943, an average of two per day and far, far fewer than the number achieved by RAF Coastal Command.[4] On 20 December, FAGr 5 reported the following strength:[5]

	Aircraft available (ready)	Crews available (ready)
Stab	1 (1)	2 (2)
1.*Staffel*	4 (1) + 1 Ju 88 (ready)	8 (3) (*Staffel* still in the process of transfer from Achmer)
2.*Staffel*	7 (4)	12 (10)
Total:	13 (7)	22 (15)

That day a Naval Operations Staff memo noted:

All operations carried out during the past weeks in cooperation with the *Fliegerführer Atlantik* and the BdU against the north–south and west–east convoys in the North Atlantic were frustrated. According to the view of the

Naval Staff, the failure is not attributable to any deficiency in the crews of the *Fliegerführer Atlantik*, but was due to lack of forces. It is impossible to carry out adequate reconnaissance of the large sea areas in question several days in succession with only one, or in maximum case, with three aircraft even when equipped with ship [search] gear. The convoys were, if at all, detected only by chance, and then so late that a change of the U-boat dispositions was no longer possible. Thus each of these operations is fresh proof that only with adequate air reconnaissance will U-boat warfare be able to achieve new successes. The Luftwaffe Operations Staff and the Reichsmarschall were informed of this necessity by the Chief of Naval Staff in numerous letters and personal discussions. A demand was made for 12 operational aircraft to be placed at the disposal of U-boat warfare daily. This demand was acknowledged as practicable and possible to carry out within a short time. Generalfeldmarschall [Erhard] Milch [the *Generalluftzeugmeister* and Secretary of State for Aviation] promised that the projected monthly production of 26 aircraft would be raised to 50 aircraft monthly if possible.

Against this, a production target sent in by the *General der Aufklärungsflieger* provides for ten Ju 290s as the monthly maximum for 1944, and ten Ju 290 reconnaissance aircraft for 1945. Thus the number of aircraft available to the squadron [FAGr 5] can be raised to 20 at most only after eight months, and only then by reckoning with a minimum of losses.

At the same time the *General der Aufklärungsflieger* reported that this [new type of] Ju 290 will also be built as a bomber, its construction will start in January 1944 so that already in December 1944 ten bombers will be completed monthly, and in December 1945, 30 bombers monthly. This means that of this type, which is of decisive importance to the U-boat war, only one-third will be placed at the disposal of long-range reconnaissance in the Atlantic.

The Naval Staff thus urgently requests:

a. That production be raised to at least 25 aircraft per month as soon as possible.

b. That the building capacity used for it be used exclusively for the reconnaissance type, while the bomber production of this type be discontinued until a daily minimum of 12 operational Ju 290 reconnaissance aircraft is guaranteed.

The Chief of Naval Staff will discuss this matter with the *Führer*.[6]

Dönitz was true to his word and met with Hitler at the *Wolfsschanze* the same day to discuss submarine warfare. Göring was also in attendance. Dönitz banged the drum for 'very extensive long-range air reconnaissance.' He also stressed that aside from a shortage of aircraft, the German war effort in the Atlantic was suffering from insufficient training in navigation and communications, something which, in his view, had 'hampered the effective functioning of our aerial reconnaissance during the past few weeks and has shown the need for a coordinated training programme.' He warned Hitler that the introduction of new and improved types of U-boats would be nullified without adequate air reconnaissance.

An indignant Göring insisted that the Luftwaffe could not be held solely responsible for any failures so far, but Dönitz went further and again 'demanded' that the entire production of Ju 290s should be turned over to long-range maritime reconnaissance and not for bombing. Hitler 'promised' to discuss the matter with Göring.[7]

While such high-level discussions were taking place, the situation at Mont de Marsan had been buoyed in late December by the arrival from Achmer of the men and aircraft of 1./FAGr 5 under Hauptmann Josef Augustin, whose officers were billeted in properties on the Rue de Manon. Since the departure of 2.*Staffel* to France in early November, 1.*Staffel* had continued with its training in Germany.[8] Like 2.*Staffel*, its crews spent time at Rerik on the Baltic coast from where they undertook over-water training and air gunnery flights. For example, one pilot of 1./FAGr 5, Leutnant Hellmut Nagel, spent several days in late November 1943 flying Ju 290A-3 WK-Nr 0163 9V+CK from Rerik for the benefit of the gunners of his *Staffel*.[9]

Just one Ju 290 equipped with ship-search gear was deployed south-west of Ireland on the 21st, the results of which are not known.[10] That evening, the officers of FAGr 5 did their best to create some early festive spirit by celebrating the opening of the officers' mess; it had been set up in the villa of a local timber magnate in Mont de Marsan, whose family continued to live on an upper floor of the building.[11] The next day it was business as usual, however, when four Ju 290s took part in a reconnaissance mission, this time probably to discover the positions of Allied naval forces on behalf of German blockade-runners inbound from the Far East.

At sea, during December, attempts by the Allies to prevent German blockade-runners bringing in their vital cargoes to the Biscay ports from the Far East escalated into a small campaign. Commodities such as tungsten (wolfram), rubber, tin, molybendum, zinc, opium and quinine were crucial to the German war effort, yet they were not available within the Nazi-occupied territories. The solution lay with Germany's Axis ally, Japan. When the previous means of bringing such supplies in via the Trans-Siberian Railway was terminated by the Soviets following the German invasion of the USSR, the only option was to use merchant ships. However, under the name

Operation *Stonewall*, Allied naval and air forces had made concerted efforts to locate, identify and sink the merchantmen, to which the Germans reacted by despatching destroyers to meet and escort them to French ports. The Allies then deployed their ships to intercept the German escorts. In turn, the Luftwaffe readied the Fw 200s and He 177s of II. and III./KG 40 to conduct attacks against the enemy naval vessels using Hs 293 glide-bombs.[12]

To both search for the runners and render reconnaissance for the Luftwaffe strike force, Ju 290A-3 Wk-Nr 0164 9V+GK, the A-4 Wk-Nr 0169 9V+KK and Wk-Nr 0161 9V+DK took off from Mont de Marsan between 0630 hrs and 0730 hrs on 22 December. 9V+DK returned prematurely, while 9V+GK made the only known sighting of the day at 1435 hrs, which on this occasion was an American Task Group, TG 21.15, in the eastern Atlantic, which was reported as comprising one aircraft carrier USS *Card* (CVE-11), one destroyer and several escort vessels, course West. Indeed, the Americans reported being shadowed by an enemy aircraft between 1326 hrs and 1458 hrs in position 46° 56′ North 17° 40′ West. The aircraft, along with 9V+KK, was then instructed to patrol a line 34° West 3749–24° West 9737 and to look out for enemy vessels. A fourth aircraft, the A-4 Wk-Nr 0158 9V+BK, is believed to have operated much later, and did not return until early on the 23rd, landing at Bordeaux-Mérignac at 0645 hrs.

Later on the 23rd, 9V+DK was airborne again as part of a larger force of eight Fw 200s and a single Bv 222. This time Kessler wanted the Ju 290 to act as a homing aircraft for six He 177s of II./KG 40 in a strike against TG 21.15 and the *Card* during the afternoon. The lone Junkers crossed the French coast at 0645 hrs and at 1425 hrs it sighted ships of the task group: the crew reported observing one aircraft carrier and one cruiser at 1425 hrs as well as advising on prevailing weather conditions. At 1515 hrs Bordeaux-Mérignac, home base to II./KG 40, relayed the Junkers' observations to a formation of He 177 bombers and ordered an attack, also advising them to watch out for beacon signals on 446 kc/s. *Fliegerführer Atlantik* instructed the Ju 290 shadower to remain in contact with the task group and to send signals on its progress, which it did for several hours until it had to break off suddenly to return to base.[13] The reason for its break-off was because of heavy attacks by enemy fighters, which meant that it was not able to send D/F signals and thus the planned attack by the Heinkels was aborted.

In December 1943, FAGr 5's *Kommandeur*, Hermann Fischer, recorded the challenges associated with the transmission of D/F signals, or *Peilzeichensenden*:

> The most difficult task of the *Aufklärer* is, without doubt, shadowing and the *Peilzeichensenden* for detection of a convoy. In D/F transmission, the entire defence [of a convoy] is concentrated on the single shadowing aircraft, which

acts like a radio beacon. New orders regarding D/F transmission eases the situation, but still represent a very high level of danger for the shadower. Shadowing with cloud cover, and at night, can be carried out by the instructed methods; with less cloud cover, or else in cloudless weather, the instructed method is only possible using the *Rotte* [two aircraft] or *Kette* [three aircraft] formations in order to increase defensive capabilities. In order to lighten the burden for the shadowing aircraft, other means have to be found which detect the position of the convoy: increased use of *Schwan-See* [air-dropped radio buoys] sorties and similar methods; additionally at night, using optical means (parachute-flares, Lux lights, etc.).[14]

Navigation skills were another vital area of FAGr 5's work, as Oskar Schmidt recalled:

With extensive flight routes and long flying times, the navigator had to be well trained in astronomical navigation. Radar navigation using beacons was not possible at such distances and to camouflage radio navigation was not possible. For this reason, the navigator took with him – just like his comrades at sea – 'his instruments'. There were 'shots' made using the sun, the moon and the stars. The sextant was a special development with a 'mechanically balanced averager'. The mean fixed-point measurement value was entered into an electronic measuring device which processed all values in about five minutes and gave the required course. With a good navigator, course deviation was, at the most, 20 km!'[15]

On Christmas Eve, the blockade-runner *Osorno*, inward-bound from Kobe, Japan, to Bordeaux, carrying 3,882 tons of rubber, 1,797 tons of tin and 177 tons of tungsten, was met by destroyers from the 8.*Zerstörer-Flottille* and torpedo-boats from 4.*Torpedo-Boot Flottille*. On 26 December, despite having to be run aground as a result of striking the wreck of another vessel in the Gironde Estuary, which damaged its hull in the process, to the Germans' delight, despite sustained Allied air attack, the *Osorno* had shot down a Sunderland and made it to France; the blockade-runner had benefited from the protection of German surface vessels, and air cover from the Ju 88 long-range fighters of the *Fliegerführer Atlantik*.[16] Dönitz cabled the ship's master on the 27th, 'I welcome the *Bernau* [codename for the *Osorno*] home and express my special acknowledgement to the captain and crew for their achievement which will be of decisive value to the war.'[17] Thus far, *Stonewall* had failed.

At Mont de Marsan, for the crews and personnel of FAGr 5 *Atlantik*, Christmas 1943 passed as a subdued occasion, as Oskar Schmidt remembered:

'Christmas celebrations took place in the individual units. It was a very quiet Christmas. Everyone was thinking of the war and their loved ones at home.'[18]

But there was little time for rest. On 26 December *Fliegerführer Atlantik* organized long-range air reconnaissance for another blockade-runner, the 2,729 GRT cargo ship MV *Alsterufer*, also inward bound from Japan with a precious cargo of 344 tons of tungsten concentrate that would have been sufficient to meet the needs of German industry for a year. The *Alsterufer* was believed to be in the outer Biscay, and, once located, as with the *Osorno*, vessels from 8.*Zerstörer-Flottille* and 4.*Torpedo-Boot Flottille*, as well as Luftwaffe aircraft, could be deployed as escort for the ship. To this end, a first Ju 290 took off at 0230 hrs, followed by three more at short intervals between 0445 hrs and 0745 hrs. The aircraft involved were 9V+AK, 9V+BK, 9V+DK and 9V+KK, all of 2./FAGr 5. At 1735 hrs, one Ju 290 equipped with FuG 200 detected a large formation of ships in BD 6260, giving no details, and, according to another report, in BD 6610. The Operations Division, Naval Staff did not learn of this report until after 2300 hrs when *Marine Gruppe West* sent a radiogram to the *Alsterufer*, ordering the vessel to switch off its Metox high-frequency warning receiver.[20]

Between 1800 hrs and 1930 hrs, Ju 290s 'A' and 'B' were heard by Allied radio intercept operating in an area 46–48° North, 16–18° West, but, despite attempts to contact 'D' regularly throughout the afternoon and early evening, there was no response.[21] In fact, Ju 290A-3 Wk-Nr 0161 9V+DK, piloted by Oberleutnant Werner Nedela, had turned for home at the end of its mission, but, because of the bad weather, its crew had decided to take a direct course back to Mont de Marsan. Flying over Spanish territory, the aircraft flew into the side of a mountain between Bilbao and San Sebastián, just below its summit, to the east of the Pyrenees. The whole crew was killed, possibly as a result of an incorrect altimeter setting.

Werner Nedela was a veteran airman, having flown Ju 52s with KGr.z.b.V.102 in Norway in 1940. The commander of the Junkers had been Hauptmann Werner Schmoll, a long-time former member of 3.(F)/Aufkl. Gr.Ob.d.L., who had served under Karl-Friedrich Bergen as a photo-officer and observer in Russia and who was regarded as 'a capable and brave officer'. They were lost along with Leutnant Hans Fliege (co-pilot), Unteroffizier Alfred Gudde (navigator) Feldwebel Aloisius Rekersdress (gunner), Unteroffizier Oskar Matt (gunner), Feldwebel Adolf Widra (flight engineer), Unteroffizier Franz Margowski (gunner), Unteroffizier Gerhard Schramm (gunner) and Unteroffizier Valentin Sobotzki (gunner). As some measure of closure, under special arrangement with the Spanish government, a detachment from the *Stabskompanie* of FAGr 5 was permitted to travel to the site of the crash, recover the bodies and return them to Mont de Marsan, where they were buried in the airport's military cemetery.[22]

The 26th also saw Oberleutnant Otto-Karl Kremser of 2./FAGr 5 undertake a long-range weather flight in 9V+KK to 31° West. The aircraft took off from Mont de Marsan at 0224 hrs and returned at 2141 hrs, after flying for 18 hr 17 min.[23]

On 27 December, along with a Bv 222 and four Fw 200s, FAGr 5 sent up two Ju 290s at 0400 hrs to reconnoitre for enemy shipping on behalf of the *Alsterufer* now approaching the French coast, but at 1055 hrs one of them, 9V+EK of 2.*Staffel*, reported that its compass was malfunctioning and was forced to break off the mission. The aircraft returned safely, though whether its findings were of any significance is unknown.[24] What the Germans did not know by this stage was that, as part of the ongoing Allied air operations against the blockade-runners, a Czech-crewed Liberator from No. 311 (Czech) Squadron, RAF Coastal Command out of Beaulieu, had found the *Alsterufer* early that morning, 'making a most determined low-level attack with rockets and bombs' and sunk it, before the German surface ships could reach the freighter. The ship was set on fire and abandoned.[25]

The next day, as a measure of just how important the *Alsterufer* was, despite its destruction the day before, a force of no fewer than 13 Fw 200s of III./KG 40 took off from Bordeaux between 0445 hrs and 0545 hrs to search for the vessel and to locate it, so that German coastal naval forces could be guided to it. The Condors were supported once again by Ju 290A-3, Wk-Nr 0162 9V+EK from 2./FAGr 5, presumably with a repaired or replacement compass, which left the French coast at 0640 hrs. Once located, these aircraft were to report the position of the blockade-runner using a system of points of reference. However, by now, British warships, including the cruisers HMS *Glasgow* and HMS *Enterprise*, were on course to intercept the German surface force of five destroyers and six torpedo-boats that had set out to reach the vessel.[26] The British ships were spotted by an Fw 200 shortly after 1300 hrs in 24° West 2735, course 30°, which apparently made an attack that seems to have been ineffective. Ten minutes later, the other Condors and 9V+EK were advised that there were two enemy cruisers in the vicinity. At around 1415 hrs, the Ju 290 was ordered to shadow the warships and an hour later, the crew reported that 'enemy fighters' had arrived in the area. However, it seems the Junkers remained in position, because when, at 1645 hrs, *Fliegerführer Atlantik* asked for updated details of the enemy naval activity, the aircraft responded, since 16 He 177s of II./KG 40 from Bordeaux, each carrying two Hs 293s, were making their approach for a dusk attack. A few minutes after that, 9V+EK was asked to send beacon signals from 1700 hrs in order to home the bombers. At 1717 hrs, the *Fliegerführer*, still anxious for information, requested a further update on the position, speed and course of the enemy vessels, but he received no immediate response. At 1750 the Ju 290 signalled that it had been driven off by the fighter screen and had lost contact with the ships. At 1825 hrs, the Ju 290 crew did signal to advise that they were at 24° West 286, and the *Fliegerführer* relayed this information to the He 177 leader who was told to look out for beacon signals. But by then the initiative had been lost and the bomber attack miscarried completely. Poor weather hampered the 'half-hearted' attack, allowing only nine of the Heinkels to reach the British ships. One bomber was shot down by fighters and another damaged.[27] As late as 2004 hrs, 9V+EK signalled that it was still over the Atlantic, but it landed back at Mont de Marsan at 0043 hrs on the 29th.

FAGr 5 returned its attention to the U-boat war on the 30th. A new wolfpack, *Borkum*, comprising 15 boats, had been formed in mid-December and positioned west of the Bay of Biscay. Here, BdU believed, aside from saving fuel, it would be in the optimal location to receive Luftwaffe assistance as well as being a sufficient distance away from Allied air squadrons in the Azores, French Morocco and Gibraltar. As with the *Schill* and *Weddigen* groups, *Borkum's* orders were to intercept convoys staging through Gibraltar and going to, or from, Sierra Leone.[28] Around 0400 hrs on 30 December, Ju 290A-3 Wk-Nr 0164 9V+GK of 2./FAGr 5 took off into the early morning darkness to search for SL.143/MKS.34, a northbound convoy of some 45 merchant vessels and 20 escorts bound for Liverpool. The two convoys had linked up on Christmas Day and the merged group was expected to be at 3940 North, 1850 West at 0800hrs on the 30th.[29] *Borkum*, which was waiting along a line some 4° to the north of this, hoped to intercept it that morning. Unfortunately, it seems that 9V+GK suffered some kind of mishap, for at 0540 hrs, the aircraft transmitted distress signals. The crew had wanted to put down at Bordeaux-Mérignac, but bad weather regulations were in force there and at Cognac, and so they were compelled to head for Mont de Marsan, where they landed successfully at 0721 hrs having aborted their mission. Once again the U-boats were informed that air reconnaissance over the convoy had failed; once again there were too few aircraft.[30]

And so ended a somewhat inglorious and unlucky first two months of operations for *Fernaufklärungsgruppe* 5 '*Atlantik*'. However, experience had been gained, lessons learned and there was much to build on.

Irrespective of the meagre scale of German air reconnaissance, by the end of 1943 it had become clear to BdU that it was no longer safe, or possible, for large groups of U-boats to operate in mid-Alantic waters between the Azores and Portugal. The Allies drew on air support from naval bases in French

Morocco and the Azores, as well as from increasing numbers of escort carriers. Farther north, because of the vast, violent seas, the boats of the *Sylt*, *Amrum* and *Föhr* groups were unable to mount their Flak guns and so they were ordered to remain submerged during daylight. This, in turn, drastically nullified their ability to find convoys, most of which had been diverted south anyway. On 22 December, these three packs were divided into six groups of three boats, to be known as *Rügen* 1 to 6.[31]

Such isolated U-boat actions against convoys that there were, were dealt with swiftly by these air and surface escort forces. This meant, in effect, that the wolfpack – the scourge of Allied shipping since the winter of 1940/41 – had been conclusively defeated. The proof of this lay in the tonnage figure which, admittedly does vary according to which source is consulted; according to Roskill, in March 1943, 108 vessels of 627,377 tons had been lost to U-boats, but in the four months from September to December 1943, the loss amounted to 67 ships of 369,800 tons – an average of 17 ships and 92,450 tons per month, or less than one-sixth of the losses suffered in March.[32] Blair states that in the last quarter of 1943, BdU had committed 37 upgraded Type VII and IX boats to the *Schill*, *Weddigen* and *Borkum* groups in the area between the Bay of Biscay, Gibraltar and the Azores. These groups accounted for a 3,000-ton Norwegian merchant vessel, a British destroyer (HMS *Hurricane*) and an American destroyer (USS *Leary* (DD-158)) and irreparable damage to a British sloop (the *Chanticleer*). Nine of the U-boats were lost in the aforementioned area, plus two more brought in from the North Atlantic, representing 550 crew.[33] Another source states that by the end of 1943, at least one U-boat was lost for every merchant ship sunk.[34]

Adding to the German scenario, was that no matter how much BdU complained about any lack of performance or assistance on the part of FAGr 5, the operational reality was that, at all times, the unit suffered from a low strength and serviceability rate – far lower than that envisaged by OKL. That was not an operational responsibility in itself, but rather a greater problem involving production levels at Dessau and other Junkers plants, and Junkers was at the mercy of supplies of materials and parts, labour availability and tranpsort.

Furthermore, out in the skies over the Atlantic, on several occasions, the *Hohentwiel* search equipment provided to FAGr 5, only available in small numbers anyway, proved unreliable, often at a critical moment, thus negating the unit's ability to locate enemy shipping.

Then, once out in the Atlantic, the Ju 290s, at least for the early period of their operations, frequently had to contend with adverse weather as well as the overwhelming Allied air 'umbrellas' which prevented close tracking of convoys. In addition – and this was a crucial factor – Allied signals and naval intelligence was frequently able to intercept and decrypt German air and U-boat radio traffic and thus take pre-emptive action to move convoys away from a detected wolfpack, so that when the Luftwaffe arrived in the supposed area of an enemy convoy, they often found only empty sea.

With the Allied strategic air offensive against the Third Reich and its occupied territories ramping up in late 1943, opening up a new battlefront in the skies over the German homeland itself, from a German perspective, any sense of optimism over the coming year required considerable fortitude or a lack of reality, or both.

CHAPTER EIGHT

TO SEE, OR NOT TO SEE

Atlantic Operations, January 1944

Even if our U-boats cannot overcome the present difficulties
and do not reach the goal set for the number of sinkings in
1942, every assistance must still be given to them… Above all,
it is necessary to give the U-boats 'eyes'. That is, adequate air
reconnaissance by the Luftwaffe.

'The Importance of Long-Range Aerial Reconnaissance in U-boat Warfare',
Luftwaffe 8.*Abteilung* Historical Report, April 1944

Perhaps it was General Henry 'Hap' Arnold, the Commanding General of the
US Army Air Forces in Europe, who best encapsulated Allied sentiments and
strength when, on the first day of 1944, he sent a simple, confident message to
his commanders to welcome in the New Year: 'Destroy the enemy air force
wherever you find them; in the air, on the ground, and in the factories.' That
message may have been directed at the American airmen tasked with destroying
German airpower over North-West Europe, but it applied to Allied air forces

everywhere and, for the Luftwaffe, it was an ominous portent of things to come. To the East, where the Axis war effort was flagging, the Red Army, by early 1944 the most powerful field army in the world, had embarked upon a four-month offensive in the Ukraine. On 31 December, the Soviets had recaptured Zhytomir. It was the beginning of the end.

In western France, Generalleutnant Kessler was having to work with ever-diminishing forces as a result of a 'sudden reduction in the number of aircraft at operational readiness.' This was largely attributable to raids in which a force of 257 B-17s and B-24s of the USAAF's VIII Bomber Command struck at Bordeaux-Mérignac, Cognac-Châteaubernard, Landes-de-Bussac and Saint-Jean-d'Angély (La Rochelle) airfields on 31 December.[1] This was perhaps both a flexing of muscle and a show of intent on the part of the Allied air forces that the irritant and menace that was the Luftwaffe in the Bay of Biscay and over the Atlantic would be dealt with. On 6 January, Kessler informed the SKL that as a result of the bombing, III./KG 40 would not be operational for five weeks, meaning no Fw 200s would be available for reconnaissance, and that the few Fw 200s equipped with *Kehl* and Hs 293s were out of action. The *Fliegerführer* also projected that by 20 January it was likely that only five Ju 290s, two Bv 222s and three Ju 88s would be available to undertake reconnaissance. 'This means,' recorded the SKL war diary, 'that on an operation lasting several days, only four aircraft can be employed each day.'[2]

New aircraft did continue to arrive with FAGr 5; in early January, for example, Leutnant Hellmut Nagel and his entire crew travelled from Achmer to Junkers at Dessau to collect the recently completed Ju 290A-5 Wk-Nr 0177 KR+LH, which had made its first factory flight on 17 December. At 0900 hrs on the morning of the 7th, Nagel took off in this machine and returned to Achmer. The next morning at 0945 hrs, he left Achmer to make the 1,800-km flight to Mont de Marsan where he arrived at 1547 hrs and where the aircraft was assigned to 1./FAGr 5 and coded 9V+DK.[3]

Some days previously, based on information from 'local agents', BdU made plans to deploy the *Borkum* group of U-boats to attack a northbound convoy heading out of Gibraltar.[4] It was envisaged that the attack would take place in the mid-Atlantic on 6 or 7 January. BdU requested reconnaissance from *Fliegerführer Atlantik* and on the afternoon of the 5th, the *Borkum* boats were advised to expect Ju 290s to operate the following day to the south of their patrol line at approximately 45° North, 16° 30′–21° 40′ West to look for the convoy.

The reality was that the anticipated northbound 'Gibraltar' convoy was actually a convoy heading west for North America that had sailed from Gibraltar on the 3rd, and so the Germans had both misidentified the target and its departure dates. The next northbound convoy (SL.144/MKS.35) did not leave Gibraltar until the 6th. Notwithstanding this, FAGr 5 sent two Ju 290s out at five-minute intervals, crossing the French coast at around 0400 hrs on the morning of the 6th. Thankfully, Mont de Marsan had escaped the American raids of 31 December and thus, in what may have been one of the first missions for 1./FAGr 5, 9V+DH (previously the damaged Wk-Nr 166 9V+BK reassigned to 1.*Staffel*) was heard transmitting a weather report for 24° West 2089 at 1219 hrs. British radio intercepts indicate that the other aircraft was 9V+BH, also of 1./FAGr 5.

Eventually, SKL realized its error: 'In the meantime it was learnt that the convoy seemed to have left Gibraltar two days earlier than expected. The air reconnaissance was therefore too late.'[5] The U-boats were signalled that no further reconnaissance could be expected before 10 January, the date that the next convoy was expected to reach their patrol line. Meanwhile, the two Ju 290s returned to Mont de Marsan having carried out a wasteful and fruitless search, due to no fault of their own.[6] Later, during the night of the 6th, the SKL war diary noted:

Our air reconnaissance for the *Borkum* group brought no result. According to an intelligence report, the expected MKS convoy probably left Gibraltar on 6 January. This, and other information reveals that the Gibraltar convoys are changing from a ten-day to a fourteen-day cycle. Therefore, the next air reconnaissance off Gibraltar has been planned for 8 January. The operation against the convoy will take place on 10 January, in approximately the centre of grid square CF. The *Borkum* group will move about 150 km south.[7]

But the knives at SKL were well and truly out. On 7 January, a senior naval staff officer wrote: 'Due to the lack of sufficient air reconnaissance, the boats of the *Rügen* [North Atlantic] group are being disposed individually. We shall have to accept the resultant disadvantage that the attacks will always be carried out by one U-boat alone.'[8]

The *Gruppe* despatched Ju 290A-3 Wk-Nr 0164 9V+GK on the morning of the 8th to look for the next convoy. At 1850 hrs, the aircraft signalled its position at 23° West 2868, adding the frustrating message, 'Convoy not found'. The Junkers returned to Mont de Marsan at 0012 hrs.[9] In fact, the elusive SL.144/MKS.35, comprising 45 vessels carrying iron ore, copper, tea, wheat, oranges, cotton, groundnuts and sardines, had sailed on the 6th but was still en route from the Strait, well to the south of the search area.[10]

The next day, the naval staff recorded: 'At noon our air reconnaissance reported a northbound convoy in CF 9311. The *Borkum* [Mid-Atlantic between Gibraltar and the Azores] group is waiting for it in the patrol line extending from CF 2945 to 3556.' Indeed, Ju 290s 9V+BH and 9V+EK crossed the coast at 0545 hrs with instructions to carry out reconnaissance south of a U-boat patrol line between the approximate positions of 39° 55′ North 20° 20′ West and 41° 15′ North 16° 00′ West from 1400 hrs. At 1336 hrs, 9V+EK reported the weather for 23° West 6831 and three minutes later spotted SL.144/MKS.35, but was unable to ascertain the convoy's course, speed or details of its composition. At 1544 hrs, ground control asked the aircraft to advise whether the ships were heading north or south, and even on this question, the crew on board the Junkers seemed uncertain.

The Navy assumed that this was a sighting of SL.144/MKS.35 and, based on that, *Borkum* was ordered to take up a shortened patrol line between 40° 40′ North 19° 40′ West and 41° 35′ North 16° 40′ West to be reached at 0400 hrs on the 10th. This was the 'vital day' for the *Borkum* group in its attempt to strike at the convoy.[11] To attempt further support for the redeployed boats, FAGr 5 sent up another aircraft, possibly the A-5 Wk-Nr 0177 9V+EH of 1.*Staffel*, at 2230 hrs, and it crossed the coast outward bound 20 minutes later. It was anticipated that the Ju 290 would make contact with the convoy at about 0300 hours, giving the U-boats plenty of time to prepare their attack. The hours slipped by and at 0830 hrs, signals were sent to the effect that this mission had also failed. Thirty-five minutes later, the Ju 290 confirmed that the convoy had not been found.[12] This time the antennae on the FuG 200 *Hohentwiel* had been incorrectly adjusted and their pick-up capability had been drastically reduced.[13] According to the SKL war diary: 'The long-range Ju 290 reconnaissance aircraft which started on a flight for the *Borkum* group on the night of 9 January did not detect anything in the operational area between 0400 and 0830. On return its radar gear was found to be defective.'[14]

The BdU urged the Luftwaffe to increase the number of aircraft in its patrols, especially since the guiding of U-boats towards a target was 'dependent solely on the results of air reconnaissance and that finding convoys cannot be based on luck.'[15]

Two more Ju 290s, 9V+GK and 9V+EK of 2./FAGr 5, were sent out and the U-boats were instructed to surface at 1930 hrs to watch out for beacon signals from the shadowers. However, once more the convoy evaded the Germans and eventually *Fliegerführer Atlantik* instructed the aircraft to cease sending beacon signals in the event that the ships were located, possibly because it was thought that by evening the convoy was too far from the U-boat line for medium frequency cooperation with the U-boats to be effective. At 2046 hrs, following repeated queries from *Fliegerführer Atlantik*, the crew of

9V+GK reported that they had not located the convoy.[16] Both aircraft eventually returned to base. BdU noted: 'The three Ju 290 sighted nothing when out on reconnaissance. When the third Ju 290 flew over *Gruppe 'Borkum'*, it was fired at by *U-305*; recognition signals were then exchanged.'[17]

'Once more,' wrote the SKL diarist, 'it is obvious that the number of long-range reconnaissance aircraft is completely inadequate.'[18] Curiously, a comment in the British radio intercepts for that day reads:

Aircraft 'E' called 03.43-04.27/11 without success may have succumbed to Flak from a U-boat which reported on the evening of the 10th that it had beaten off an aircraft which it subsequently recognized as a Ju 290 and with whom it exchanged recognition signals. On the morning of the 11th, two Spanish destroyers were searching in sea area as far as 100 miles N.W. of El Ferrol to give search and rescue assistance to crew of a German aircraft – possibly the Ju 290 'E'.

This situation is not, as far as is known, borne out by any losses of FAGr 5 from that day.

Another attempt to locate the convoy was made in the early afternoon of the 11th, when two Ju 290s, 9V+DH of 1./FAGr 5 and 9V+EK of 2.*Staffel*, crossed the coast between 1245 hrs and 1330 hrs. They had instructions to be south of the *Borkum* patrol line which, by this point, lay between 41° 27′ North 22° 14′ West and 42° 21′ North 19° 26′ West by 1830 hrs. The eight U-boats were to surface an hour later and set watches for beacon signals. In fact, the most westerly boat, *U-305*, commanded by Kapitänleutnant Rudolf Bahr, had found and reported the convoy and had endeavoured to shadow it, but it had been driven off by a destroyer and Bahr lost contact. Bahr had probably found the southbound OS.64/KMS.38 on its way to Freetown and Gibraltar.

But in the air there was disappointment; British intelligence analysis reported that, 'No help in following up these was obtained from the G.A.F. [German Air Force] although boats were informed at 2050 that they could still reckon with beacon signals; at 2200 however, they were warned there would be none.'[20] Indeed, a summary of Ju 290 operations between 8 and 11 January in the war diary of the BdU did not make encouraging reading:

Summary of operation:

8.1: Radar reconnaissance made by one Ju 290: Convoy not found.

9.1: Radar reconnaissance made by two Ju 290s: Convoy found! Attempt to re-contact made by one Ju 290. Radar gear broke down, convoy not found.

10.1: Attempt to re-contact made by one Ju 290 (morning). Radar gear broke down, convoy not found. Attempt to re-contact in order to send out beacon signals made by one Ju 290 (evening). Convoy not found.

11.1: Radar reconnaissance made by two Ju 290s (evening). One aircraft had to break off search because of engine trouble.

Total: eight Ju 290s

The result of this reconnaissance shows that the number of aircraft was insufficient. At least twice as many are necessary, as apart from the fact that more aircraft can cover a larger area, if the radar gear on one aircraft breaks down, the other aircraft can be directed to the focal point and maintain successful and constant patrol.

It is not possible to concentrate reconnaissance for a short time as the submarines must be given time to change their position. With the few aircraft at present available, such hard driving for long-distance reconnaissance prevents proper servicing (on 11.1 one Ju 290 had to break off operation because of engine trouble).

Once again the BdU referred to 'luck' as a factor: 'As submarines within the scope of our own air reconnaissance are entirely dependent on its results, we cannot afford to rely on luck in finding the convoys. The number of aircraft used for each operation must be at least double.'[21]

Next day, the British codebreakers surmised: 'The Ju 290 failed to locate [the northbound convoy] although it must have been in the vicinity.'[22] Hessler comments that FAGr 5's operations for the four days from 8 January, which saw two aircraft per day operated, were achieveable only by a 'strenuous effort'.[23]

It was not a good day for the Kriegsmarine in the mid-Atlantic; U-641 suffered diesel problems and was forced to dive to make repairs. U-382 was depth-charged and forced to abort operations, while U-953 was hunted for no fewer than 13 hours with depth charges, but survived. From the 'jeep' carrier, USS Block Island (CVE-21), two Avengers attacked U-758 with depth charges and new 3.5-in rockets, damaging the U-boat and forcing it to abort as well.[24]

Indeed, by the conclusion of its operations later in January, Borkum had lost three of its eight boats to the Allies, with another lost to unknown causes, while three more were forced to abort following action by Allied aircraft. Just one U-boat completed its patrol. For these casualties, Borkum had accounted for one British frigate and a B-17 of Coastal Command shot down.[25]

Meanwhile, BdU had stretched its 20-plus boats in a wide arc from the Faroes to Brest, disposed singly about 50 km apart, a policy that was unlikely to have much effect against heavily defended convoys. Dönitz had instructed his commanders to make diving patrols and to surface only to recharge batteries, and they were further advised that Luftwaffe reconnaissance aircraft would be searching for the convoys, and when found they would signal positions to the boats. It was the first time that the U-boats had operated in the Western Approaches since they had been forced out farther into the Atlantic back in 1941.[26] But FAGr 5 would not appear, at range, over the Atlantic for a week and the six to eight available Ju 290s of the *Gruppe* had been suffering from engine problems.

On the evening of the 17th, an He 177 of 5./KG 40 returned from an offensive patrol having sighted the Liverpool–New York convoy ON.220. It was not until after the Heinkel crew had landed, however, that they reported their sighting.[27]

ON.220 had departed Liverpool on 15 January made up of just under 60 merchant ships with 25 escorts; on the morning of the 18th, the Germans estimated that it would be in the area of 25° West 3646, based on a reported course of 250°.[28] Two Ju 290s were sent out to search for it. At 1001 hrs, Hauptmann Hubert Schreiner of 1./FAGr 5, as commander and first pilot, with Leutnant Hellmut Nagel as his second pilot, took off in Ju 290A-4 Wk-Nr 0166 9V+DH to shadow the convoy.[29] However, at 1145 hrs on the 18th, while the Junkers were making their way towards the search area which was, in reality, to the south of ON.220, 9V+DH was signalled to advise of a new estimate of the convoy's position at 25° West 7559. Despite being to the south, at 1803 hrs, one of the Junkers made RDF contact with the convoy in position 55° 50′ North 17° 30′ West. The course could not be determined however, and BdU remained sceptical about this pick-up, or even whether the Junkers had located the convoy, or possibly that it was an eastbound grouping. Neither aircraft made any more reports and it seems that at 1930 hrs, at least one of them broke off their mission.[30] Part of the failure of this mission may have been attributed to the fact that at least one FuG 200 set became 'covered with ice'.

When Schreiner and Nagel returned at 0134 hrs on the 19th after 15½ hours in the air, Nagel noted in his logbook: 'Sea reconnaissance west of Ireland–Scotland. No sea targets detected.'[31]

'We have no information about its course,' the SKL war diary noted, 'Hence we cannot be sure this is the expected westbound convoy.'[32] British intelligence remarked in a summary the next day: 'No Allied convoy exists to comply with the German expectations, which were evidently based on a preconceived theory of the North Atlantic convoy cycle.'[33]

On the 20th, 1./FAGr 5 despatched two Ju 290A-5s, Wk-Nr 0172 (KR+LC) 9V+BH and Wk-Nr 0174 (KR+LE) 9V+EH, from Mont de Marsan at around 0600 hrs and they crossed the French coast 20 minutes later. The Junkers were to search the area 54° 57′ North 13° 30′ West in order to assist the *Rügen* pack, which had been directed to make maximum speed, even in daylight, in order to catch OS.65/KMS.39, which had left Liverpool on 14 January with 55 merchantmen and 18 escorts. The U-boats were intending to attack the convoy that evening. Earlier Luftwaffe reconnaissance failed to locate the convoy, although one U-boat, *U-641*, did get close to it, but it was destroyed in the process by a British corvette escort on the 19th.[34]

Once again, no convoy was actually in the assigned search area, so the air search was pointless and fruitless; but hardly the fault of the Luftwaffe. The most that seems to have been accomplished was a weather report signalled from 9V+EH at 1800 hrs; indeed, SKL reported, 'air reconnaissance for the operation by the "*Rügen*" *Gruppe* was without result. Two Ju 290s will repeat the reconnaissance on 21 January.'[35] The Ju 290s returned with 9V+BH landing at Mont de Marsan at 2336 hrs, having been in the air for 17 hours.[36]

The U-boats moved closer to the Irish coast, between 15° and 17½° West, but only under the watchful eyes of Coastal Command Liberators and Leigh Light Wellingtons.[37]

Next day, the 21st, according to the SKL war diary, of four aircraft from FAGr 5 assigned to search the Atlantic on behalf of *Rügen*, two were unable to take off because of technical difficulties and the result was not 'exhaustive'.[38] However, 2.*Staffel* sent out Ju 290A-4 9V+HK and A-3 9V+EK to hunt for convoys west of the North Channel (the strait between north-eastern Ireland and south-western Scotland). One of the aircraft located the Canadian C2 escort group, describing it as 'five destroyers in line abreast, speed 15 knots, course 60° in position 25° West 5475', but no merchant shipping was sighted. 9V+HK returned to France to land at Kerlin-Bastard at around 2050 hrs, while 9V+EK touched down at Mont de Marsan at 2145 hrs.[39]

On the 22nd, two Ju 290s were sent out, as part of a larger force comprising an He 177 of II./KG 40 and a Ju 88 of 3.(F)/Aufkl.Gr.123 detailed to search for convoys for *Rügen* to the west of Ireland. The Junkers flew out over the coast at about 0630 hrs, but at 0854 hrs one of them, aircraft 'F', reported from its position at 14° West 8766 that its gyro compass was out of order and that the crew was forced to abandon its mission. Several hours later, at 1740 hrs, aircraft 'E' – it is not clear whether this was the 1. or 2.*Staffel* aircraft – sighted a '10,000-ton motor vessel accompanied by a destroyer and an escort vessel' in 25° West 6432. The motor vessel was the 7,040-ton SS *Empire Treasure* operated by the British Ministry of War Transport. On 15 January, whilst on a convoy voyage from Liverpool to Halifax and New York, its stern frame fractured and the vessel lost a propellor blade and the use of its rudder. By the time the Ju 290 spotted the ship, it was under tow to the

Bristol Channel by the rescue tug, *Bustler*, and escorted by the corvette HMCS *Giffard*.[40] The aircrew duly reported its observations to the *Fliegerführer Atlantik* and made for home where, after an initial instruction to land at Bordeaux-Mérignac, the aircraft put down at Mont de Marsan at around 0045 hrs on the 23rd.[41]

At 1000 hrs on the morning of the 23rd, Ju 290A-4 9V+DH of 1./FAGr 5, took off for an intended 15-hour flight on behalf of the U-boats gathered to the west of Ireland. Between take-off and 1335 hrs, the Junkers signalled three weather reports, before it seems it was recalled by *Fliegerführer Atlantik* for reasons unknown.[42] There was another lacklustre mission two days later on the 25th, when the *Gruppe* again sent up two aircraft to patrol the convoy routes over the Western Approaches, but aside from further weather reports, SKL reported that 'air reconnaissance for the *Rügen Gruppe* was without result'.[43] This, despite the fact that FAGr 5 was now working in close cooperation with the Ju 88s of 3.(F)/Aufkl.Gr.123 based at Rennes to provide 'intensive' reconnaissance – presumably as a result of the pressure from BdU earlier in the month.

9V+DK of 2./FAGr 5 was airborne on the 26th to reconnoitre the Western Approaches, once more working with a Ju 88 of 3.(F)/Aufkl.Gr.123. The Ju 88 was assigned to look out for convoys, which it did, successfully sighting ON.221 en route from Liverpool to New York, while the Ju 290's main task was to undertake weather readings, which it completed at 1610 hrs.[44] The *Gruppe* sent out aircraft 'D' on the night of the 26th/27th to maintain observation to the west of Ireland, and this was probably 'DH' from 1./FAGr 5, but its efforts were plagued by malfunctioning radio equipment.[45] As BdU recorded: 'Ju 290 sighted convoy in AM 5168 at 1220, southerly course. No speed given. The Ju 290 detailed to shadow convoy at night reported results for the first time after landing, owing to wireless telegraphy breakdown.'[46]

Over the next 24 hours, the situation would become confusing and challenging for the German reconnaissance and U-boats as two outward-bound convoys, ON.221 and OS.66/KMS.40, crossed *Rügen's* area combined with the fact that they assumed the inward-bound HX.275 was also in the area too. Furthermore, ON.221 had become scattered, giving BdU and *Fliegerführer Atlantik* cause to think that it was in fact two convoys, one of which they believed was bound for Gibraltar. Finally, a fast, homeward-bound military convoy from the US, UT.7, was sighted at least twice, but seems to have raised little interest.

At 0900 hrs, 9V+DK spotted the 100 or so vessels of ON.221 stretched across the ocean on what the crew described as a 'southerly course', indicative again of malfunctioning search and radar equipment. Later on the 27th,

9V+DK was replaced by aircraft 'F' (either 9V+FH of 1.*Staffel* or 9V+FK of 2.*Staffel*) and, at 1150 hrs, this machine was ordered by the *Fliegerführer* to shadow the convoy spotted by 9V+DK earlier. It is possible had 'F' had already found it, however, for at 1115 hrs it had sighted a grouping of 20 motor vessels, one destroyer and three escort vessels, possibly a part of ON.221. The Ju 290 continued to shadow various ships, signalling three locations at 1529 hrs at 25° West 4422, then at 1715 hrs at 25° West 5442, at which point the crew reported counting 55 motor vessels and nine destroyers, which it wrongly assumed were heading for Gibraltar. *Fliegerführer Atlantik* instructed the Junkers to continue shadowing this grouping and to send beacon signals, but fuel shortage compelled the aircraft to break off and head back to Mont de Marsan. As it did so, it transmitted a final sighting at 1750 hrs at 25° West 3473, comprised of 39 motor vessels and five destroyers on course 50°, which was probably UT.7.

A third Ju 290, identified as 'D' and thus possibly 9V+DH of 1./FAGr 5, took over duties for the evening and was expected to be over the convoy area at 2330 hrs. At 2210 hrs, this aircraft was picked up receiving a list of positions, probably as a route of approach. In the early hours of the morning of the 28th, the aircraft picked up two groups of shipping at 25° West 2449 and at 25° West 3557.

The BdU war diary demonstrates the pattern of reporting from the Ju 290s on the 27th:[47]

Aerial reconnaissance confirms westbound and northbound convoys in:

1)	Ju 290	04.55	convoy in	AM 4938	course	230	degrees
		09.55	" "	AM 4955	"	230	"
		11.15	" "	AM 7928	"	230	"
2)	Ju 290	15.29	" "	AM 4872	"	230	"
		17.12	" "	AM 7212	"	270	"
		17.50	" "	AM 7346	"	50	"
3)	Ju 290	00.23	" "	AM 7128	"	270	"
		00.46	" "	AM 4917	"	North	"

At 0230 hrs, *Fliegerführer Atlantik* instructed the Junkers 'D' to shadow the first group and to make beacon signals. Two minutes later, the *Rügen* boats were signalled that the Ju 290 had found a convoy and was beaconing.

Though nothing is known of the results of this shadowing operation, the presence of the Ju 290s in the area prompted the RAF's No. 19 Group, covering the south-western British Isles, to intensify its over-water fighter sweeps, and it moved No. 235 Squadron equipped with Beaufighters from Portreath to St Angelo in Northern Ireland specifically to counter the Junkers and Bv 222s. [48] Additionally, the C-in-C Western Approaches was able to draw upon a healthy number of well organized escorts and escort groups as well as eight escort carriers – the American-built convoy veteran *Biter*, together with *Fencer, Tracker, Striker* and *Pursuer,* and three British-built vessels, the *Activity, Vindex* and *Nairana.* The Fleet Air Arm fighters aboard these carriers were now placed on high alert.[49]

A review of the air reconnaissance against the convoys over 26/27 January in the BdU war diary reveals a damning indictment of the FuG 200:

Convoy was picked up at long range. Indications on the radar gear were insufficient, no exact details of the convoy. When aircraft made their run-in and obtained more precise orientation on the targets, it was established that the radar gear did not indicate at short range. When the aircraft moved away to N.E. in order to approach the targets from longer range, a second convoy was observed. When it was realized that the second convoy in AM 4917 was a northbound one that had been picked up by a Ju 290 at 1115 in AM 7928, a fresh run-in was made on the first convoy. It was then noted that the radar equipment was not working properly and gave no further indications. Visual observation was not possible because of weather conditions. The pilot decided, although the targets were not definitely established, to send a radio report of the position located as 'convoy report reconnaissance blue' and then broke off his task.[50]

Thick fog blanketed the waters of the Bay of Biscay and the mid-Atlantic during the last days and nights of January 1944, suspending all Luftwaffe long-range reconnaissance. At Mont de Marsan the only flying was limited to night-flying training flights. In a typical such exercise, Leutnant Hellmut Nagel of 1./FAGr 5 was airborne in Ju 290A-5 Wk-Nr 0172 9V+BH with a full crew on nine flights of between seven and 13 minutes duration over the space of just over three hours during the evening of the 28th, probably to practise night take-offs and landings, and equipment procedures.[51]

But in the coming weeks, the stakes were about to rise very dangerously for the crews of *Fernaufklärungsgruppe 5.*

Supreme Command of the Navy.

Naval War Staff (2.*Abteilung*)/B.d.U. Op.   Staff Headquarters 'Koralle'

[Bernau, nr. Berlin]

25 March 1944

Operation against MKS.35 from 8–11.1.44 ('Borkum')

A. Aim of air reconnaissance: To pick up the convoy two days after it had sailed; to pick it up again at 12-hourly intervals until U-boats had been brought up by means of beacon signals.

B. Forces available: There were six Ju 290 available belonging to *Fernaufklärungsgruppe* 5. By great efforts on the part of this unit, the number was raised to eight by 10.1.44.

8 January:

Situation at sea:

U-boats in patrol lines:

I from CF 5229 to 5318

II from 2958 to 3758

III from 3574 to 3676

Air situation:

Reconnaissance by one Ju 290.

Take-off: 0827, landed: 0016/9/2.

Area covered: DJ 1237 – CG 7855 – CG 4889 – CG 8192. Convoy not found.

9 January:

Air situation:

Reconnaissance by Ju 290.

Take-off: 0530. Landed: 2150 and 2236.

Area covered: CG 5757 – CG 7877 – CG 7771 – CG 4467 and CG 4139 – CF 9597 – CF 9575 – CF 6355 not being covered.

1339 convoy in CF 9311. Strong air escort, clear weather. Course (estimated by wake): N.W. Composition: about 39 merchant ships.

Situation at sea:

U-boats, as Group '*Borkum*', in patrol line from CF 2945 to CF 3556.

10 January:

Air situation:

Reconnaissance by three Ju 290s. First Ju 290 entered reconnaissance area 0425, left 0931. Second Ju 290 entered reconnaissance area 1241, left

1950. Third Ju 290 entered reconnaissance area 2040, left 2249 after being fired upon by one of our own boats.

Area covered: CF 9365 – CF 8345 – CF 5821 - CF 5293 – CF 5133 – CF 3188 – CF 3465 – CF 2975 – CF 5337 – CF 3663 – CF 3936 – CF 3946 – CG 4145. Convoy not found. Convoy was not picked up by patrol line by 0100/11.1.

Situation at sea:

As air reconnaissance was unsuccessful and no further information was available, it was assumed that the convoy had made a detour to the west. At 0100 Group 'Borkum' was ordered to form a new patrol line from CF 2447 to 2357 at high speed. This might catch the convoy on the evening of 11.1 if it had been diverted to the W.

11 January:

Air situation:

Reconnaissance by two Ju 290s, take-off 1302 and 1310, landed 1809 and 0149. First Ju 290 broke off because of engine trouble, second Ju 290 broke off in CF 2253 because radar had failed.

Area covered: CF 3471 – CF 2558 – CF 2252 – CF 2399. Convoy not found.

Situation at sea:

While Group 'Borkum' was proceeding W., the most westerly boat of the line sighted the convoy at 1819 in CF 2452. The remaining boats were directed against the convoy. Except for the sighting of one destroyer, no further reports were received. It must be assumed that the boats, which were approaching from the east individually at considerable distance from one another, passed the convoy.

Conclusion:

The fact that the boats picked up the convoy shows that it must have passed through both reconnaissance areas on 10.1 unnoticed. It was afterwards discovered that the *Hohentwiel* aerials in the aircraft fitted with radar had been wrongly adjusted by the manufacturing firm and the range of the set had thereby been greatly reduced. This was the reason why these aircraft did not detect the convoy.

According to dead reckoning the convoy made 6.8 knots from 9.1. and steered a practically straight course between the sighting on 9.1 and 11.1. It could not have skirted the area reconnoitered, as it would otherwise have had to make nine knots, a speed impossible with this collection of ships.

The operation failed:

a) because owing to an undetected failure in the Radar set air reconnaissance did not find the convoy in spite of the full use made of the few available aircraft.

b) because, for this reason, the boats were in unfavorable positions and too far one from the other, so that even when one boat made contact the others could not get there.

Additional review of Operation:

8.1	Radar reconnaissance with one Ju 290. Convoy not found.
9.1	Radar reconnaissance with two Ju 290s. Convoy found.
10.1	One Ju 290 Set failed. Nothing found.
	One Ju 290 (morning) Set failed. Nothing found.
	One Ju 290 (evening) Set failed. Nothing found.
11.1	Radar reconnaissance with two Ju 290s (of which one had engine trouble). Nothing found.

Total: eight Ju 290s

The results of this reconnaissance show that, apart from the unnoticed failure of the radar set, forces for individual operations were too weak. At least twice the number of aircraft are necessary. Besides extending the reconnaissance area, this would have the advantage that if one aircraft's radar set failed, the other would be able to carry on and the continuity of the reconnaissance would not be interrupted. It is not possible to shorten the period of reconnaissance in order to concentrate the aircraft, as there must be time enough left to improve the positions of the U-boats. As the operation of U-boats within range of our air reconnaissance depends entirely on the results of this reconnaissance, we cannot leave anything to luck as far as finding the convoys goes. It is necessary to get more operational reconnaissance aircraft.

(Signed): GODT*
Chief of Operations Department
For B.d.U.

---

* Konteadmiral Eberhardt Godt, Chef der 2. *Abteilung* OKM/SKL (BdU-op).

CHAPTER NINE

BLACK FEBRUARY

Atlantic Operations, February 1944

Our tail-gunner, Hans Roth, had made out three dots behind us
which, as they came closer, turned out to be fighters. We called
them bumblebees, because they were so small and quick…

Feldwebel Herbert Littek, radio operator, 2./FAGr 5

Feeling dispirited and under-resourced, in early February 1944, General der
Flieger Kessler attempted to seek an audience with Hitler to relay his concerns
over the hopeless military situation facing the *Fliegerführer Atlantik*. In this
he failed, but his feelings of discontent had become increasingly well known
within the Luftwaffe leadership. Göring was attuned to this, particularly
since Dönitz had been lambasting the shortcomings of the maritime
operations of the Luftwaffe and its lack of support for the U-boat campaign
at the *Führer*'s headquarters for some time. This was embarrassing for Göring
and he also felt that Kessler had been a moaner for too many years, constantly
(although justifiably) demanding more aircraft for his command, in the full
knowledge that the most urgent need was for fighters to defend the Reich and
the Eastern Front. Kessler thus became a victim of Germany's worsening

multi-front military predicament. On 7 February 1944, the position of *Fliegerführer Atlantik* was disbanded, although, bizarrely, Kessler was not informed of this for another three weeks.[1]

There had been changes within FAGr 5 as well, possibly as a reflection of the times. Many units, including reconnaissance units, were being urgently combed for their qualified personnel to bolster the fighter *Gruppen* of the Luftwaffe. On 21 January, the *Gruppe* lost its experienced signals officer when Leutnant Hans Wessel, a veteran of 3.(F)/Aufkl.Gr.10, was posted to JG 51 on the Eastern Front. As Oskar Schmidt recalled, 'It was a difficult farewell.' The unit's senior technical/maintenance NCO, Oberfeldwebel Jung, went to JG 1 operating in the defence of the Reich. He was replaced by Feldwebel Merz, but there were new arrivals in the form of senior NCOs Hauptfeldwebel Meyer (to the *Stabskompanie*) and Willi Proch (to 1.*Staffel*).[2] On 9 February, Hauptmann Konrad Mildenberger of 2./FAGr 5, a veteran of 3.(F)/Aufkl. Gr.Ob.d.L. where he served as Technical Officer, and who had flown as Karl-Friedrich Bergen's observer in Russia, departed to become Technical Officer in FAGr 101.

Despite the generally adverse weather conditions prevailing over the Atlantic at the beginning of the month, the *Gruppe* did engage in training flights closer to home, with at least one crew, that of Leutnant Hellmut Nagel of 1./FAGr 5, using the Ju 290A-4 WK-Nr 0166 9V+DH to fly out of Mont de Marsan over to KG 40's base at Bordeaux-Mérignac in order to carry out air gunnery practice over the Biscay on 1 February.[3]

Operational missions recommenced on 4 February, the first time since 27 January that the *Gruppe* had put aircraft into the air. However, as the British radio intercept report for that day noted, the two sorties mounted by FAGr 5 that day were, 'not, as might be expected, to the west of Ireland where U-boats are now disposed, but in the sea area west of Portugal where there are, at present, no boats.' The British report identifies the two aircraft as 'B' and 'F', and the evidence points to these being from 1./FAGr 5. At 1250 hrs, 'F', possibly Ju 290A-5 WK-Nr 0175 9V+FH, picked up a radar contact on the convoy SL.147 bound from Freetown to Liverpool in 23° West 3839, course 320°/330° to 350°, but its composition could not be determined. At 1549 hrs, the aircraft signalled the convoy's speed as being seven knots, course 340°. This aircraft landed back at Mont de Marsan at 2221 hrs.

As far as aircraft 'B' (possibly Ju 290 A-5 Wk-Nr 0172 9V+BH) was concerned, the British report commented, 'No signals of interest were made by aircraft 'B' which stated at 1357 hrs that it had carried out a reconnaissance task. ETA [Mont de Marsan] was 1915 hrs. NOTE: The object of reconnaissance in this area is obscure, since as stated above, there are no boats in the area.'[4]

However, an account by Hauptmann Josef Augustin, *Staffelkapitän* of 1./FAGr 5, indicates the purpose of such a sortie at around the same time:

Early in 1944, together with my crew, which included Leutnant Günther Dittrich (pilot) and Oberleutnant Hans Rehne (observer/navigator), I received the following task: According to a report from one of our agents, there was a British convoy (Gibraltar–England) to the west of Lisbon. We had to find out the location, size and composition of the convoy, its speed, route and course. We also had to signal a weather report from the target area.

It is most likely that, following receipt of the agent's information, Augustin and his crew had been despatched to gather information on the convoy so that both the He 177s of II./KG 40 and the U-boats waiting farther to the north of the Portuguese coast could plan attacks. In all probability, the convoy would have been the merged SL.147/MKS.38, which had rendezvoused on 2 February and comprised in excess of 60 vessels. Augustin recalled:

In tolerably good new year's weather, we flew to the west along the north coast of Spain. Maximum altitude was 200 m above the sea so as, if possible, to evade enemy radar. Also at Cape Ortegal we went down to low level because there had been reports of a British radar station operating on the Spanish mainland.

Then we turned to a southerly course, to go along the Portuguese coast. At the time Portugal was neutral. During this part of the flight, we usually went to 1000 m in order to search for enemy ships with the ship-search gear (*Hohentwiel*). But neither with radar nor with visual observation by the members of the crew could an enemy convoy be made out. Time passed, continually under tension as a result of searching for ships and being on constant alert for attacks from enemy long-range fighters, until we had covered a large area from Oporto to the west of Lisbon.

We searched the area of sea thoroughly once more, but we could not trace a convoy. We flew out further into the Atlantic, in great search circles, until we again took a general course to the north, during which we would fly back across the Spanish mainland at night. Around 0500 hrs in the morning we reached the north coast of Spain and pivoted over the Bay of Biscay in the direction of our base at Mont de Marsan to the east. The experience of our crews was that the enemy would try to trap individual machines on their return flights across the Biscay using patrols of Beaufighters of about six machines. That's why we made the remainder of the flight at the lowest possible height above water (10–20 m) in order to reach the French coast.

Even here though, once more over our own occupied territory, we had to take hellish care, because on more than one occasion enemy fighters still overwhelmed and attacked our returning machines. We reached base without any credible military success, but we were dead tired and happy to be back 'home'.

Any attempt by He 177s of II./KG 40 to attack the target was abandoned.[5] But as Augustin concluded: 'Unfortunately, the flight was unsuccessful. Either the agent's report was false or the stated convoy had left the specified area long before.'[6]

Next morning, attempts to locate SL.147/MKS.38 continued: an aircraft, coded 'D', possibly Ju 290A-5 Wk-Nr 0177 9V+DK of 2./FAGr 5, sortied south towards the Gibraltar route. The Junkers made contact with the convoy at 1030 hrs at 24° West 5081 and reported its composition to be 100 ships with 20 escort vessels, speed 15 knots, course 340°. An hour later, the aircraft was still shadowing when it was reported by ships of Escort Group B3 in 39° 52′ North 14° 40′ West. From then on it seems the Junkers made no further sighting reports, possibly as a result of problems with two of its engines, although when asked by control at 1617 hrs whether its task had been completed, the aircraft responded affirmatively and reported the convoy's position as 24° West 5021. The Ju 290 landed back at Mont de Marsan at 1835 hrs.

The *Gruppe* sent another aircraft to undertake weather reports to the west of Ireland, advising at 1344 hrs that it had completed its task. However, U-boats to the west of Ireland were advised that the Ju 290 had also sighted one destroyer and three steamships in 25° West 2686 at 1155 hrs on a course of 260°. In its initial period of operations, FAGr 5 flew its missions without trained meteorological observers on board its aircraft, but from February 1944, as 1./SAGr 129 undertook fewer such operations, weather – or *Zenit* – flights over the Atlantic were becoming a more regular feature of the deployment of the *Gruppe* in addition to shadowing and long-range reconnaissance. Subsequently, more specialist meteorological observers joined the *Gruppe* from this time for that purpose.[7]

That afternoon, at around 1615 hrs, Ju 290A-4 WK-Nr 0167 (PI+PU) 9V+HK of 2./FAGr 5 left Mont de Marsan for Kerlin-Bastard, from where it was probably intending to operate over the Atlantic the following day. Adverse weather prevented the aircraft from landing there, however, and it re-routed to Rennes, which it reached at 1817 hrs.[8]

Two more Ju 290s, probably including 9V+HK, were sent out on weather flights on the 6th and then, based upon the series of reconnaissance missions flown by FAGr 5, 3.(F)/Aufkl.Gr.123 and 1./SAGr 129 since the 4th, an attack was planned against SL.147/MKS.38 on 7 February using the Fw 200s of III./KG 40. Although the Focke-Wulfs got under way, it seems they were recalled during the afternoon, probably as a result of the Allied air screen over the convoy.[9]

Over the night of 7/8 February and during the course of the following day, FAGr 5 contined to send up pairs of aircraft with the dual missions of shadowing for anti-shipping strikes by KG 40 as well as on behalf of the U-boats. By this day there was considerable convoy activity in the eastern Atlantic; the large SL.147, accompanied by the B3 Escort Group, was directly west of the Bay of Biscay. HX.277 from New York, comprising 67 merchantmen, with 29 escorts from the B1 and B2 groups, was to the north of it, while OS.67/KMS.41 with 65 merchants had departed Liverpool for West Africa and Gibraltar on the 6th and was heading south off the west coast of Ireland accompanied by Escort Group 39 and the new carrier *Pursuer* with its contingent of Martlet fighters.[10]

Shortly after 2245 hrs during the evening of the 7th, the first of two Junkers left Mont de Marsan for the Atlantic, followed at 2329 hrs by the second, Ju 290A-5 Wk-Nr 0174 9V+EH, piloted by Leutnant Hellmut Nagel of 1./FAGr 5.[11] At least one of the aircraft, 'E', was carrying *Schwan-See* D/F radio buoys.

The FuG 302 C *Schwan-See* ('Swan Lake'), referred to usually as just '*Schwan*', was a droppable radio buoy developed by the *Flugfunk-Forschungsanstalt* (Research Institute for Aeronautical Radio) at Oberpfaffenhofen and the *Gesellschaft für Technisch-Wirtschaftliche Entwicklung* (Society for Technical-Economic Development) at Reichenau. This was a bomb-shaped buoy measuring 1,920 mm in length and 470 mm at its widest point, including its four tail fins.

The buoy would be dropped vertically into the water, and on impact, a telescopic rod antenna would extend from the end of the body, which was exposed above the surface. After release, for a period of ten minutes, the aircrew could turn the transmitter on and off as a test and make minor adjustments. The beacon could then be set to transmit for up to 72 hours as it floated in the water. The crystal-controlled transmitter beamed at 3 W on a fixed frequency, but the device was not always efficient.[12] The first trials, involving five drops, were carried out between 10 and 16 October 1943 over the Ammersee, but in early May 1944 further tests are known to have been conducted from early Ju 290A-7 variant (see Chapter Ten) Wk-Nr 0189 KR+LT/9V+KK, flown by Oberfeldwebel Otto Joas of 2./FAGr 5 in cooperation with *Flieger-Stabsingenieur* Paul Bader of the *Erprobungsstelle* Rechlin.[13] Thereafter it had become usual for a Ju 290 to carry one FuG 302 C on an operational mission. The buoy would be dropped without a parachute, and from a low altitude, through a hatch in the floor of the gondola.[14]

At 0610 hrs on the morning of the 8th, *Fliegerführer Atlantik* signalled to Ju 290 'E' the estimated position of what was believed to be SL.147/MKS.38 at 24° West 9743, where the crew was instructed to drop a *Schwan* buoy, before heading north-west to continue on weather reconnaissance. An hour later, the convoy reported spotting the shadower, and five minutes after that, the Ju 290 signalled that it had located the ships in 24° West 8739. At 0830 hrs the Junkers dropped a buoy and flew off to the north-west as per orders. A little later, the aircraft signalled weather reports for 24° West 98 and 34° West 19.

The companion of 'E' was Ju 290A-5 9V+FH of 1./FAGr 5, which was instructed by *Fliegerführer Atlantik* to take over the shadowing of the convoy from 0715 hrs for the 'benefit of an air striking force'. The Junkers continued to shadow until 1200 hrs, when it gave the convoy's position as 24° West 9866, at which point it broke off and made for home.

Both aircraft also sent regular *Zenit* reports on their outward flights and from the area of the convoy, which were indicative of an intention by the Luftwaffe to conduct an air attack against the vessels. Once again, however, it seems adverse weather conditions prevented a bomber strike.

Meanwhile, BdU had rearranged the tactical grouping of its U-boats in the eastern Atlantic. The *Rügen* group had been split in early January into two short-lived sub-groups, but on 3 February these were consolidated into new groupings known as *Igel* (Hedgehog) I and II. These groups, comprising at any one time between 25 and 30 boats, were deployed in a looser fashion than *Rügen* or its successors, but with the sheer volume of Allied warships and aircraft operating in the area, the *Igel* groups would have their work cut out.[15]

As an early move to support *Igel*, FAGr 5 sent out another two Ju 290s during the afternoon of the 8th to track the convoy. These aircraft were identified by Allied radio decrypts as 'B' and 'D' and may therefore have been from 1.*Staffel*. Aircraft 'B' was to be with the convoy from 1900 hrs, but it had to break off its mission at 2319 hrs because of problems associated with its fuel tank. Aircraft 'D' located SL.147/MKS.38 at 2120 hrs in 24° West 9948, reporting its course as 350°. At 2158 hrs, *Fliegerführer Atlantik* requested the aircraft to transmit D/F signals, which it did once every hour until 0442 hrs when it landed at Mont de Marsan. The convoy reported that it had been shadowed throughout the night, though whether the *Igel* boats acted on the Ju 290s' information is not known.[16]

Despite the presence of four large convoys to the west and south-west of Ireland, the Luftwaffe mounted no long-range reconnaissance sorties between

9 and 11 February, but on the 12th an intention to send out a Bv 222 flying boat of 1./SAGr 129 at 0240 hrs seems to have been frustrated and so FAGr 5 was called in to take over. The reconnaissance was required to pave the way for a dusk attack by a combined force of Fw 200s and He 177s of KG 40 against convoy OS.67/KMS.41.

At 0511 hrs, Ju 290A-5 9V+DK once again took off from Mont de Marsan for the Atlantic to shadow the convoy. The 2./FAGr 5 aircraft was commanded and piloted by Oberleutnant Otto-Karl Kremser with Oberfeldwebel Sbresny as co-pilot and a crew comprising Leutnant Robert Stein (observer), Oberfeldwebel Fietje Müller (flight engineer), Feldwebel Herbert Littek and Oberfeldwebel Willi Joswig (radio-operators), and Unteroffizier Hans Roth and Obergefreitern Trapp and Kozorek (gunners). Herbert Littek recalled the mission:

We flew a rigid, westerly course, very low across the Bay of Biscay. Our giant bird was thus very exposed. The turrets, equipped with 2-cm cannon, sparkled in the sun. Normally, it would be ideal flying weather, but as operational weather?

We talked over the intercom and Roth said: 'Let's hope there are no aircraft carriers, because we're a nice target for fighters.'

Sitting at the radio equipment, and at the request of the crew, I played the song, 'Heimat, deine Sterne' ('Home, your Stars') – naturally on the harmonica. It sounded pretty good, and with the help of the intercom, everyone could hear it. The mood was good, but there was a strange feeling. Firstly, we did not know where the convoy was, and secondly, how strongly it would be defended. In their minds, everyone envisaged aircraft carriers, cruisers, and, of course, lots of destroyers.

North-west of La Coruña, we saw a Sunderland above us, a huge flying-boat, but very cumbersome. We had a great desire to attack it, but that wasn't a recommended course of action. So the Sunderland was able to fly away to the south without incident. Our co-pilot, Sbresny, reckoned that perhaps it was Mr Churchill flying in the direction of Casablanca. Who knows if the English crew had even seen us.

At 1054 hrs, 9V+DK spotted the first ships in 24° West 9585. Littek described the events that followed:

And then it was business. In Grid 9427/24 West we saw a cargo steamer. We knew all freighters were now equipped with Flak and so we remained at a distance. From the bridge of the freighter, a signal flashed at us; it was the same letter continually. Willi, our other radio operator, was well aware what these signals meant, and later it would be very important.

The clouds hung low over the Atlantic, a deep, thick grey. That was to our advantage. We flew further and then after the next bank of clouds we discovered, just south of us, a cruiser. Using our flash-signaller as a safety ruse, Willi sent the letters used by the freighter to the cruiser, and this was replied to promptly with specific letters. So that was the daily watchword for the convoy.

However, the crew of the cruiser must eventually have recognized our [wing and fuselage] *Balkenkreuze* and now opened up on us with all barrels. But their range fell short, and Oberleutnant Kremser applied full throttle to get us out of the danger area.

Robert Stein handed me a piece of paper with details of the identified freighter, some destroyers, one cruiser and an aircraft carrier. I encrypted the information and sent the report to Quickborn and Mont de Marsan on the shortwave.

But we weren't able to celebrate for long, because suddenly the clouds parted and we were in blue sky. Then our hearts began to beat quickly, because our tail-gunner, Hans Roth, had made out three dots behind us which, as they came closer, turned out to be fighters. We called them bumblebees, because they were so small and quick.

Oberleutnant Kremser went pale. There was only one possibility, if we did not want to go swimming in the Atlantic: escape at full power. In the meantime, the three fighters had drawn nearer and opened fire on us. Our three gunners, and Willi in the turret, answered them with the 2-cm cannon … Still blue sky all around us. Where was the cloud cover?

But the sky was merciful. To the north-west we plunged into a real pea-souper. Rescue when we needed it. We immersed ourselves into it, and I brushed the sweat from my forehead. My God, we were nervous. Some would have said 'lucky'. Following us must have been too risky for our pursuers and they left us alone.

Indeed, shortly after having sighted the convoy, British carrier-borne aircraft reported 'having driven off the Ju 290.'[17] Littek continued:

Breathing sighs of relief, we hear the voice of our commander: 'Müller, how much fuel have we left?'

'It'll get us to Mont de Marsan,' replied our flight engineer, Fietje Müller. 'And now we could all use a cup of coffee! That is, if things are OK.' I agreed and went to make some coffee. The job of on-board cook was entrusted to me. Water and coffee were available and our electric stove with two rings was still working. As I served coffee, Sbresny drank his cup empty and said, 'Man, what a pig of a mission.'

At 1210 hrs, the *Fliegerführer Atlantik* ordered 9V+DK to act as a shadower for an air-striking force and to expect a relief at 1730 hrs. At 1536 hrs, the aircraft signalled the convoy's position as still being 24° West 9427 as well as the presence of more enemy fighters. This warning was, in turn, relayed to the Condors and He 177s which, by this time, were airborne. At 1800 hrs, it was decided to break off:

Now we flew an eastwards course home. This time Hans Roth played his harmonica: 'One Day You'll be with Me!'

It was already getting dark, as we made our way across the Bay of Biscay. Otto-Karl Kremser admonished us: 'Boys, watch out and don't fall asleep – we're not safe yet!' I was damned tired and took a Pervitin tablet.

When we landed at 2247 hrs at Mont de Marsan, all was forgotten. The technical personnel patched up a few hits in our dear old Ju 290 9V+DK. We hadn't noticed them. That mission lasted 17 hr and 36 min.[18]

Significantly, 9V+DK's relief did not locate the convoy until 2020 hrs in 24° West 8457, by which time darkness had very much fallen and the KG 40 strike force had already been in the area for some eight minutes. The strike force was now down to just the He 177s of II.*Gruppe*, four Fw 200s having also been despatched, but one of which was shot down en route to OS.67/KMS.41, while the other three were unable to locate it and aborted.

At 1857 hrs, *Pursuer* scrambled four Martlets from 881 Naval Air Squadron (NAS) to intercept the seven Hs 293-carrying He 177s, and they engaged the bombers close to the convoy, 650 km west of Cape Finisterre. By the end of the attack, II./KG 40 had lost the aircraft of its *Kommandeur*, Hauptmann Walter Rieder, which plunged into the sea some three kilometres from the ships. Another Heinkel had been attacked by nightfighters on the flight out and crashed into a forest, having glided for some four kilometres. It was destroyed. The remaining aircraft were not able to execute the attack and aborted. British Intelligence concluded that: 'Owing probably to the failure of the shadower's relief to reach the convoy at the specified time, the striking force did not arrive in the convoy area until 2012 by which time the light must have been unfavourable and no attack developed.'[20]

On 14 February two Ju 290s were sent out to shadow the ONS.29 Liverpool–Halifax convoy to the west of Scotland and Ireland for the *Igel* group of U-boats. Commencing at 1130 hrs, Ju 290A-5 Wk-Nr 0179 9V+FK of 2./FAGr 5 was instructed to cover an area immediately to the west of the North Channel from 25° West 4666 to 25° West 1834 to 15° West 0857 to 25° West 2677, although there were problems in contacting the aircraft by radio and the instructions were delayed. Then, at 1340 hrs, in 46.40 North 09.45 West, the Ju 290 encountered a Sunderland flying boat, but after a brief engagement, both aircraft took cover in clouds without damage. The Junkers also made various weather reports from the area of 15° West. However, no sightings were made by either aircraft and both returned safely.[21]

On the 15th, mechanical problems continued to plague the *Gruppe*: at 0821 hrs, Ju 290A-5 Wk-Nr 0176 9V+GH, flown by Leutnant Hellmut Nagel of 1./FAGr 5, took off from Mont de Marsan for the Atlantic, but was forced to return after just 31 minutes because of 'damage to the propellers'.[22]

A single Ju 290 o FAGr 5, 'E', was detailed to track the southbound convoy OS.68/KMS.42 of some 30 vessels, which had been first sighted by a Ju 88 the day before, although one source claims the Germans had believed it to be the New York-bound ON.224 which had departed Liverpool the day before.[23] The escort for the convoy picked up a shadower by radar in 55° 07′ North 12° 15′ West at 1515 hrs at 16,000 ft. 'E' subsequently reported contact with the convoy at 1730 hrs in 25° West 4546. Twenty-five minutes later, radar operators on board the carrier HMS *Biter*, escorting OS.68/KMS.42, reported that the convoy was shadowed from 1755 hrs to 1811 hrs. At 1800 hrs, 'E' reported to the *Fliegerführer* that the convoy was making six knots and, five minutes after that, provided a weather report. At 1840 hrs, ONS.29 also reported a shadower in 54° 34′ North 13° 30′ West, but there was no report made about this convoy by the Ju 290. Possibly as a result of technical problems, the Junkers was not able to report full details until much later, and closer to home, when it advised that the convoy (OS.68/KMS.42) consisted of '40 motor vessels, two especially large units, several escorts, course 220°, six knots.'[24] The 'large units' were probably the escort carriers HMS *Biter* and HMS *Tracker*, which were operating alongside the 7th and 9th Escort Groups.[25]

Over the next three days FAGr 5 made all efforts to maintain a shadow over the convoys. But 16 February was to be the costliest day thus far for the *Gruppe*. Two aircraft were assigned to fly operations, the first being Ju 290 A-5 Wk-Nr 0175 9V+FH of 1./FAGr 5, commanded and flown by Leutnant Eberhard Elfert with Oberfeldwebel Conrad 'Toni' Oberhauser as second pilot, which was briefed to fly out over the coast at 0500 hrs in 14° West 5978. A second aircraft, Ju 290A-5 Wk-Nr 0177 9V+DK, flown by the *Staffelkapitän* of 2./FAGr 5, Hauptmann Bergen, with co-pilot Oberleutnant Kurt Baumgartner, was to fly out at 0840 hrs in 14° West 2421. A point of note here is that, as the winter weather raged in the Atlantic making conditions difficult for U-boats and aircraft, in addition to its shadowing and reconnaissance duties, around this time the *Gruppe* assumed greater responsibility for weather surveying and in this regard, from February 1944 a number of meteorological observers were assigned to FAGr 5.[26] Joining the crew of Bergen's aircraft on the 16th was Referendar (clerk) Werner Cordes from the *Wetterwarte Atlantik* (Atlantic Weather Station) of the *Fliegerführer Atlantik*, based at Angers.

Both aircraft were assigned to relocate OS.68/KMS.42, which had last been sighted at 54° 54′ North 12° 29′ West at 1800 hrs the previous evening.[27]

Hauptmann Josef Augustin, *Staffelkapitän* of 1./FAGr 5, recorded: 'Both crews were tasked with finding enemy shipping west of Ireland in the Atlantic. Enemy convoys were passing regularly through the area between America and England in both directions.'[28] Indeed, by the morning of the 16th, OS.68/ KMS.42 and *Biter* were 'zig-zagging' southwards some 170 miles to the west of Ireland.

At 1040 hrs, Elfert and his crew made contact with the convoy, and one minute later his aircraft was spotted by the Allied vessels in 55° 39′ North 14° 51′ West. According to a subsequent Allied report, the Ju 290 'crossed the convoy's stern twice at a distance of 7–8 miles and released one glider bomb which fell into the sea between the aircraft and the convoy.'[29] This is unlikely because the Ju 290 variant intended to carry the FuG 203/320 *Kehl/Strassburg* radio control system, and thus able to launch and control an Hs 293 glide-bomb, was the A-7, still under construction at that time (see Chapter Six).[30] Most probably what the Allied crews had witnessed was the Junkers discharging a FuG 302 C *Schwan-See* radio buoy for homing by U-boats in the area.

But in the first of two occasions that day, FAGr 5's nemesis was to be the Avenger-class escort carrier (based on the US Navy Long Island class Auxiliary Aircraft Carrier) HMS *Biter* – formerly the 9,100-ton C3-type passenger cargo vessel the *Rio Parana*, which had been acquired by the US Navy in May 1941 and converted in New York. Following repairs at Rosyth Naval Dockyard on the Firth of Forth, needed as a result of damage to its rudder inflicted by a rogue torpedo carried by a ditched Swordfish biplane in November 1943, *Biter* had returned to duty in January 1944. On the 12th of that month, the three stubby, radial-engined Grumman Martlet IV fighters of 811 NAS, a composite squadron under Lieutenant-Commander E.B. Morgan comprising both Martlets and its main equipment of Swordfish intended for anti-submarine work, re-embarked from RNAS *Inskip*. A month later *Biter* commenced convoy support operations west of Finisterre together with HMS *Tracker* and the 7th and 9th Escort Groups.[31]

Upon sighting Elfert's Ju 290, 811 NAS began to warm the engines of two of its Fighter Flight's Martlet IVs, to be flown by that morning's duty pilots, New Zealanders Temporary Lieutenants Eric Sven Erikson and William Dimes. Shortly afterwards, the order to launch was given and Dimes powered off in Martlet IV FN252/R closely followed by Eriksen at the controls of FN168/Q.[32]

The weather conditions were cloudy and bad as the two fighters left *Biter*, but they were ably vectored towards the Junkers by Temporary Lieutenant Francis Pagan in the carrier's Fighter Direction Room. Indeed, so determined was Pagan to bring about success that in the 'final stages' of the engagement, he abandoned his radio and radar and resorted to directing the Martlets visually from *Biter*'s bridge. According to the citation for Acting Warrant Air Officer Stanley Brown: 'In one case the normal channel of communication with our aircraft broke down, but by Mr Brown's quick appreciation of the situation, and his previous foresight in preparing for such an event, this breakdown was overcome, and the action successfully completed.'

In the Fighter Direction Room, 'Leading Seaman (Radar) Percy Clipsham operated the Type 79 Radar with great ability and concentration, and in one case enabled an interception to be made owing to his excellent height-finding.'

According to Erikson's subsequent recommendation for decoration:

On Wednesday, 16th February, Lieut. Erikson took off from HMS *Biter* in heavy weather and was directed onto a large enemy four-engine aircraft. He at once attacked through defensive cannon fire and shot out one engine before the enemy entered cloud. He skillfully anticipated the point where the enemy would leave cloud, attacked once again and shot down the enemy in flames.

Meanwhile, as 'Lieut. Erikson closed in to shoot down the enemy, Lieut. Dimes did his best to draw the enemy's fire onto himself.'[33] With one of its right engines shot away, the Ju 290 crashed into the sea at 1105 hrs before its crew members had time to signal their observations to the *Fliegerführer Atlantik*.[34]

Erikson and Dimes both experienced some difficulties in landing back on the deck of *Biter*, but they eventually managed to get down safely and successfully. Erikson was awarded the DSC 'for outstanding courage and skill', while Dimes, Pagan, Brown and Clipsham were mentioned in despatches for their efforts.[35]

Grossadmiral Karl Dönitz, *Befehlshaber der Unterseeboote* (BdU – Commander of U-boats) until January 1943 when he was promoted to Grandadmiral and appointed Supreme Commander of the Kriegsmarine, although he remained in overall direct command of the U-boats. He was a staunch believer that cooperation between U-boats and the Luftwaffe was vital to the effective prosecution of the convoy war and rallied Hitler, Göring and others continuously for long-range maritime aircraft. In this endeavour, he was to remain disappointed. (Williamson)

(Above) A convoy of merchant vessels makes its way across the Atlantic in 1942. (US Navy)

(Below) In a rolling swell, a pair of Type VII U-boats lie on the surface in daylight, their crews clad in life vests. By mid-1943, such exposure was highly dangerous as land-based Allied very long-range aircraft, and gradually increasing numbers of carrier-based fighters, gained superiority in the skies over the Bay of Biscay and the Atlantic. The U-boat to the left of the photograph is equipped with a 2-cm Flak C/30 gun. (Williamson)

Junkers Ju 290A-5 Wk-Nr 0180 KR+LK is readied for its first flight on 24 March 1944 at the Junkers works at Dessau, having been towed out of the workshops across the snow by its tailwheel. This aircraft would be operated by 1./FAGr 5, but it was destroyed in a bombing raid on Rechlin-Roggentin on 10 April 1945. (EN Archive)

Some of the officers of 3.(F)/Aufkl.Gr.10 who transferred to FAGr 5 at Achmer in the summer of 1943. (Author's collection)

The roomy cockpit of a Junkers Ju 290, possibly an A-5, showing the excellent all-round visibility offered to the pilots while in the air (though not while on the ground), and the dual controls with the throttle levers visible in the central console. Also visible to the right is the edge of one of the armoured seats. (Goss)

(*Above*) Ju 290A-3 Wk-Nr 0161 9V+DK of 2./FAGr 5 flies over the German countryside on a flight from Achmer, late 1943. The short run of five aircraft in the A-3 series were powered by 1,700 hp BMW 801D engines and featured a reduced-drag, lower-profile aft dorsal gun turret, a tail gun and improved gondola design. (EN Archive)

Ju 290A-3 Wk-Nr 0160. The aircraft was originally coded SB+QJ, but subsequently it became 9V+BH (1.*Staffel* of FAGr 5) and then 9V+AK (2.*Staffel*). It is believed to have been destroyed by bombs during an Allied raid on Rechlin on 10 April 1945. (EN Archive)

(Above) With three engines running, Ju 290A-3 Wk-Nr 0160 prepares to take off from Achmer. (Knirim)

Ju 290A-3 Wk-Nr 0161 9V+DK of 2./FAGr 5 passes overhead at Achmer in the autumn of 1943. This photograph illustrates how the ventral gondola was offset to the left of the fuselage. The aircraft and its crew were lost when it crashed in mountainous terrain in bad weather while on an operational flight over northern Spain on 26 December 1943. (Wadman)

Ju 290A-2 Wk-Nr 0158 9V+AH of FAGr 5 in flight over north-west Germany in late 1943. This aircraft was passed from 2.*Staffel* (which operated it as 9V+BK from late August 1943) to 1.*Staffel* in October. It has the early style, larger dorsal HDL 151/1 turrets and has FuG 200 search radar installed. It also carries the last two digits of its *Werknummer* on its nose as was customary for many earlier aircraft. Wk-Nr 0158 is believed to have been shot down by German Flak near Oranienburg on 22 April 1945. (Knirim)

Hauptmann (later Major) Hermann Fischer, *Kommandeur* of *Fernaufklärungsgruppe 5* 'Atlantik' from its formation in the summer of 1943 to the end of the war. A very experienced reconnaissance pilot, in 1942 he became a recipient of the *Ehrenpokal* and was also awarded the *Deutsche Kreuz* that year. (Author's collection)

Major Josef Augustin, *Staffelkapitän* of 1./FAGr 5. Previously commander of 3.(F)/Aufkl.Gr.10 on the Eastern Front, he had also served as a photographic officer on the staffs of *Luftwaffenkommando Don* and the I.*Fliegerkorps*. (Author's collection)

Hauptmann Karl-Friedrich Bergen, *Staffelkapitän* of 2./FAGr 5 (seen here as an Oberleutnant), played a key role in the formation of the *Gruppe* at Achmer. Having seen service in Russia with 3.(F)/Aufkl.Gr.100, he had also undergone senior unit leader's training in France before joining FAGr 5. He would be lost over the Atlantic while on a shadowing mission on 16 February 1944. (Goss)

Oberleutnant (later Hauptmann) Oskar H. Schmidt, a pilot and observer who served primarily as commander of the *Stabskompanie* of FAGr 5. A diligent and resourceful officer, he organized and led a column of the *Gruppe's* personnel and vehicles on a journey across France to the safety of the Reich in the late summer of 1944. (Author's collection)

The *General der Aufklärungsflieger* (General of Luftwaffe Reconnaissance Forces), Oberst Karl-Henning von Barsewisch (left) discusses equipment at either Achmer or Mont de Marsan with senior officers of FAGr 5. Frequently, von Barsewisch found himself caught between the demands of Dönitz and the Kriegsmarine for Luftwaffe support for the U-boats, and Göring's reluctance to invest in long-range maritime reconnaissance. Also seen here are Major Hermann Fischer (centre) and Hauptmann Karl-Friedrich Bergen. (EN Archive)

Major Josef Augustin, *Staffelkapitän* of 1./FAGr 5, and Oberleutnant Herbert Abel, the *Gruppenadjutant*, stand in front of a line-up of officers and NCOs of 1.*Staffel* while they await the arrival of their *Gruppenkommandeur* at Achmer in the autumn of 1943. (Author's collection)

Senior NCOs of FAGr 5 enjoy a glass of wine at their billet during the early period of formation of the *Gruppe*. (Author's collection)

The officers of 1./FAGr 5 were quartered in a comfortable villa in a leafy street in Mont de Marsan, close to the airport. (Author's collection)

A Ju 290 of FAGr 5 runs up three of its BMW 801 engines on a grey day at Mont de Marsan. (Goss)

Generalleutnant Ulrich Kessler, from February 1942 the *Fliegerführer Atlantik*. A former naval officer, he subsequently joined the Luftwaffe and, among several appointments, was *Kommodore* of KG 1 at the outbreak of war. His tenure in command of Luftwaffe units over the Atlantic was an unhappy one and he never believed his role was truly understood or supported by Göring and other senior Luftwaffe commanders. He was replaced in March 1944. Perhaps in an attempt to sideline him, he was transferred to Tokyo as air attaché for the rest of the war. (EN Archive)

Leutnant Hans Wessel joined FAGr 5 upon its formation as *Gruppe* signals officer. (Author's collection)

Oberleutnant August Vaupel joined 1./FAGr 5 at its time of formation and was one of the first observers of the *Staffel*. He had served previously with 3.(F)/Aufkl.Gr.10 in Russia. (Knirim)

Officers of the *Gruppenstab*, from left to right: Oberleutnant Ludwig Herlein (pilot in *Stab*), Oberleutnant Hans Müller (*Gruppe* Technical Officer), and Oberleutnant Herbert Abel (*Gruppenadjutant*). All three men had served in reconnaissance units before joining FAGr 5. (Author's collection)

Officers and NCOs of the *Stabskompanie*, FAGr 5, Mont de Marsan, early 1944. (Author's collection)

A tow bar can just be seen on the ground, which was used to connect the tailwheel of the Ju 290 to the heavy-duty tow vehicle parked close to the aircraft. Such vehicles would be used to tow the aircraft from the runway to wooded dispersal areas on the perimeter of Mont de Marsan airport. (Wadman)

A German atlas illustrates the method of *Suchkreise* (search circles) over the eastern Atlantic as adopted by Ju 290s of FAGr 5 flying out of Mont de Marsan. Using FuG 200 search radar, aircraft would 'sweep' a circle of sea area with a radius of 80 km, before moving on to repeat the process, using a course of parallel rows as illustrated on the map with some circles overlapping. An area 500 km x 480 km would be covered, involving 19 circles. The process would take over 15 hours. (Knirim)

Some idea of the extent of the 42-metre wingspan of the Ju 290 can be seen from this photo of the A-5 KR+LA of FAGr 5. Though covered for protection here, the circular area between the two gun turrets on top of the fuselage is the location of the clear Plexiglas panel of the astrodome, from where the crew would take accurate positional fixes using astronomical navigation. (Goss)

A navigator aboard a Ju 290 makes an entry containing time and navigation data into his flight logbook. (Knirim)

Aircrew use an octant and a navigation watch to obtain a navigation fix while over the sea. (Knirim)

The NCOs of 1./FAGr 5 await the arrival of Generalfeldmarschall Sperrle at Mont de Marsan in early 1944. (Author's collection)

Accompanied by Major Augustin, *Staffelkapitän* of 1./FAGr 5, the large frame of Generalfeldmarschall Hugo Sperrle, commander of *Luftflotte* 3, strides along a line-up of FAGr 5 aircrew during an inspection at Mont de Marsan in early 1944. (Knirim)

During its relatively short operational life, FAGr 5 always suffered from a low unit strength, but wherever possible, the unit's commander, Hermann Fischer, attempted to fly shadowing patrols with pairs of aircraft in an attempt at mutual protection. It was a measure that rarely worked. Here, two Ju 290s are seen flying at a typically low altitude over the waters of the Bay of Biscay or Atlantic Ocean. (Goss)

A pair of Ju 290s of FAGr 5 out on patrol over the Atlantic. (Goss)

Hauptmann Karl Nather, senior photographic officer of FAGr 5. (Author's collection)

Leutnant Hellmut Nagel of 1./FAGr 5 flew four long-range shadowing patrols over the Atlantic, as well as numerous instructional and night flights. (Knirim)

The *Staffelkapitän* of 2./FAGr 5, Hauptmann Karl-Friedrich Bergen (left) in conversation with Oberleutnant Hans Heindorff of 3.(F)/Aufkl.Gr.Ob.d.L., who was awarded the *Ritterkreuz* on 23 October 1942. Both men wear the reconnaissance flier's operational clasp. (Author's collection)

Nemesis of the shadowers: six Sea Hurricanes are lined up on the deck of HMS *Biter* as the escort carrier pitches forward in heavy Atlantic waves. The presence of such carriers close to the Atlantic convoys meant that no airspace was safe for Luftwaffe reconnaissance aircraft or shadowers, no matter what their range. (Thomas)

A vessel of convoy OS.68/KMS.42 is silhouetted on the horizon as smoke bellows into the sky from the spot where Ju 290 9V+DK of the *Staffelkapitän* of 2./FAGr 5, Hauptmann Karl-Friedrich Bergen, crashed after being shot down by Beaufighters of No. 235 Squadron on 16 February 1944. (Thomas)

A Martlet IV fighter of 811 NAS photographed on the deck of HMS *Biter* in early 1944. Aircraft from this squadron engaged Ju 290 shadowers of FAGr 5 off convoy OS.68/KMS.42 in February of that year. (Thomas)

Martlet pilot Lieutenant Eric Sven Eriksen of 811 NAS walks across the deck of HMS *Biter* shortly after shooting down Ju 290A-5 WK-Nr 0175 9V+FH, commanded by Leutnant Eberhard Elfert of 1./FAGr 5, over the Atlantic on 16 February 1944. (Thomas)

Lieutenant Eric Sven Eriksen's Martlet IV FN168 'Q' nosed over as it returned to the deck of HMS *Biter* after the engagement with Leutnant Eberhard Elfert's Ju 290A-5 9V+FH. (Thomas)

Formerly assigned to the Luftwaffe air-sea rescue service, Hauptmann Georg Eckl succeeded Karl-Friedrich Bergen as *Staffelkapitän* of 2./FAGr 5 in late February 1944. (Author's collection)

A Mosquito passes low over the water and the semi-submerged remains of Oberleutnant Karl-Heinz Schmidt's Ju 290 9V+FK of 2./FAGr 5 after it had been shot down by Flight Lieutenant R.J. Coombs and Flight Lieutenant R.D. Doleman of No. 157 Squadron off the north coast of Spain on 19 February 1944. (Goss)

Ju 290A-7 Wk-Nr 0181 KR+LL suffered a collapsed landing gear on its first flight from the Junkers works at Dessau on 1 April 1944 while being flown by Flugkapitän Karl Friedrich Maringer and flight engineer Fritz Pflug. Despite the damage to its undercarriage and the splintered wooden propeller blades, the aircraft was repaired and flew again on 22 April. It later served with 2./FAGr 5 as 9V+GK and in the summer of 1944 was assigned to 1./KG 200. It was eventually destroyed in an Allied bombing raid on Dessau in August 1944. (Goss)

Hauptmann Hermann Fischer, *Gruppenkommandeur* FAGr 5 (left), and Oberleutnant
Herbert Abel, *Gruppenadjutant*, compare pipes! (Author's collection)

(*Below*) This Ju 290A-4 or A-5 is adorned with the *Staffel* emblem of 1./FAGr 5, a depiction
of the *Fliegender Holländer* (Flying Dutchman) ship in full sail, carrying the emblem of the
Deutschritterorden (the knightly Teutonic Order) on its sails, set against what should be a
white shield, although curiously, here it appears to be more of a yellow background – the
colour of 2.*Staffel*. (Wadman)

A member of the groundcrew works on an underwing panel between the dipole transmitter and receiver antennae of a FuG 101a radio-altimeter on a Ju 290 at Mont de Marsan. The aircraft carries the *Fliegender Holländer* and yellow shield emblem of 2./FAGr 5 and is fitted with FuG 200 *Hohentwiel* search radar nose antennae. Also visible is the barrel of the 13 mm MG 131 machine gun at the rear of the ventral gondola. (Goss)

'All that remained of the Junkers was an oil slick and a few floating pieces of debris'. Lieutenant Allen R. Burgham, RNZNVR, a Sea Hurricane pilot of 835 NAS, shot down Ju 290A-7 9V+FK flown by Oberleutnant Hans-Georg Bretnütz of 2./FAGr 5 on 26 May 1944. (Thomas)

Lieutenant Stephen Mearns (centre) of 835 NAS accounted for the Ju 290A-4 9V+GK of 1./FAGr 5, commanded and flown by Leutnant Kurt Nonnenberg, when he shot it down during the Junkers' mission to shadow convoy SL.158/MKS.49. Some of the crew survived, others were less fortunate. (Thomas)

Sea Hurricanes IIc NF700 7-T and NF672 7-K of 835 NAS on the deck of HMS *Nairana* in 1944. (Thomas)

Officers of 1./FAGr 5 partake in an al fresco meal at their quarters in Mont de Marsan on a sunny spring or summer day in 1944. (Author's collection)

To provide recreation to the personnel of FAGr 5 at Mont de Marsan during the summer of 1944, the *Gruppe* formed its own football team, seen here, which played local army and Luftwaffe units, including the team fielded by Hauptmann Walter Nowotny's JG 101. (Author's collection)

Three in-flight views of Ju 290A-5 Wk-Nr 0170 KR+LA. This machine was the first in a series of ten A-5s, which were enhanced by improved protection for fuel tanks and cockpit, as well as an emergency fuel jettison system. Shortly after completion, the aircraft was used for tests by the *Erprobungsstelle* Rechlin, which included flights as a test-carrier for the new HeS 011 jet engine, but in late November 1943 it was eventually handed over to FAGr 5, where it was assigned to 1.*Staffel* as 9V+DH. In these photographs, the aircraft is seen finished in the standard later-style splinter pattern of greens on the wing and fuselage upper surfaces with light blue/grey elsewhere. It is believed to have been destroyed in an air raid on Rechlin on 10 April 1945. (EN Archive)

Ju 290A-7 Wk-Nr 0186 KR+LQ, photographed in March 1944 at Dessau. The A-7, of which this aircraft was the second example, was distinctive for its new glazed nose, which accommodated an MG 151 as additional armament. The antennae for the FuG 200 were fitted both above and to the side of the new nose design. This aircraft was later coded 9V+FH with 1./FAGr 5, and in October 1944 it was assigned for special duties to 1./KG 200. It finally found its way to Flensburg at the end of the war, from where the British flew it to the RAE Farnborough. (EN Archive)

Their vehicles covered with foliage for camouflage, armed Luftwaffe personnel take a wary halt at the roadside during FAGr 5's move across France. The column of the *Gruppe* encountered the French Resistance on several occasions. (Author's collection)

'Every kilometre we progressed towards the east, took us closer to the homeland and safety.'
A 20 mm MG 151 aircraft cannon has been rigged to the roof of one FAGr 5's vehicles as
'defence' for the journey across France to Germany in August 1944. (Author's collection)

The FAGr 5 column suffered several breakdown incidents as it progressed across France. Here, possibly as a result of being overloaded, the wheel axle of a trailer has broken. When such incidents occurred, the *Gruppe*'s mobile workshop section proved extremely resourceful. (Author's collection)

Three officers of FAGr 5 pause for some food during the journey across France in August–September 1944. From left to right: Oberleutnant Motzkus (pilot, 1.*Staffel*), Hauptmann Oskar Schmidt (*Stabskompanie*), and Leutnant Hertel (pilot, 1.*Staffel*). (Author's collection)

The stippled nose of Ju 290A-3 Wk-Nr 0162 9V+EK of 2./FAGr 5 photographed close to the *Autobahn* at Salzburg, where it was rendered unserviceable by US forces at the end of the war. (EN Archive)

The Messerschmitt Me 264 was envisaged as a possible replacement for the Ju 290 for long-range maritime operations for U-boats. With a range of 17,500 km, the so-called *Amerikabomber* would have been able to reach the US East Coast and conduct both offensive and reconnaissance operations. Only one complete prototype was built, the Me 264 V1 RE+EN, as seen here at Augsburg or Lechfeld in 1943. The following year, officers of FAGr 5 were assigned to *Sonderkommando* Nebel with a view to lending tactical and technical expertise to the manufacturing process, but the plan was thwarted by the destruction of the prototype and two other partially completed airframes in Allied bombing raids. (Author's collection)

An Arado Ar 234B-2b jet, similar to the type flown by the *Einsatzkommando* 1./FAGr 1 at Stavanger in Norway from February 1945. The *Kommando* had its origins in FAGr 5, its personnel being drawn from that *Gruppe*, but it took delivery of only three Ar 234s, one of which was badly damaged in a landing accident at Stavanger. Nevertheless, the Ar 234 represented cutting-edge jet technology. The example seen here probably belonged to 1.(F)/33. (EN Archive)

Ju 290A-2 Wk-Nr 290110158 9V+AH of 1./*Fernaufklärungsgruppe* 5, Achmer, autumn 1943.

Ju 290A-3 Wk-Nr 290110161 9V+DK of 2./*Fernaufklärungsgruppe* 5, Achmer, autumn 1943.

Ju 290A-5 Wk-Nr 290110180 KR+LK (9V+KH) of 1./*Fernaufklärungsgruppe* 5, Mont de Marsan, autumn 1943.

Ju 290A-7 Wk-Nr 290110186 KR+LQ (9V+FH) of 1./*Fernaufklärungsgruppe* 5, Mont de Marsan, spring 1944.

Emblem of 1./FAGr 5

The '*Fliegender Holländer*' (Flying Dutchman) depicted in full sail, carrying the emblem of the *Deutschritterorden* (the knightly Teutonic Order) on its sails, set against a golden yellow shield.

Emblem of 2./FAGr 5

The '*Fliegender Holländer*'(Flying Dutchman) depicted in full sail, carrying the *Odins Raben* (Odin's Ravens – Huginn and Muninn) emblem of 3.(F)/Ob.d.L., later 3.(F)/100, on its sails, set against a golden yellow shield.

It is worth noting that sources differ on the exact colour of the shields for the two squadron emblems. According to some, both shields were golden yellow, whereas others state that the shield for 1./FAGr 5 was actually white. In the absence of colour photographs of the aircraft emblem available for clarification, the author has chosen for both emblems to be depicted in golden yellow here.

The crew of 9V+FH comprising Elfert, Oberhauser, Leutnant Albert Pape (observer), Oberfeldwebel Albert Holzmann, Unteroffizier Rudolf Dreissig (both radio-operators), Oberfeldwebel Otto Zech (flight engineer), Oberfeldwebel Wilhelm Hausmann, Oberfeldwebel Gustav Schlatthaus, Feldwebel Erich Barlau and Obergefreiter Albert Pfeffer (all gunners) failed to return.[36]

A few hours later, at 1602 hrs, Hauptmann Bergen's 9V+DK made contact with ONS.29 but the Germans assumed the Halifax convoy was OS.68/ KMS.42, although 22 minutes later that convoy did report the Ju 290 shadowing in its vicinity at 52° 55′ North 16° 46′ West. At 1610 hrs, Bergen's crew transmitted a position report at 25° West 6336 for a course of 180°, still believing the convoy to be heading south.

At 1634 hrs, however, the Junkers was tracked by the radars of HMS *Biter* as being in the area of OS.68/KMS.42 and, from that point, the German aircraft would be in trouble.

Since October 1943, Beaufighters of No. 235 Squadron, RAF, had been detached from their main base at Portreath in Cornwall to St Angelo in County Fermanagh, Northern Ireland, from where they had been engaged in regular anti-submarine operations over the Atlantic. For most of January and February 1944, the squadron had flown anti-aircraft convoy escort missions and in mid-February it had been charged with keeping a watch over ONS.29 and OS.68/KMS.42. Like the Ju 290s of FAGr 5, the Beaufighters had on occasion struggled to find the convoys. The day before, on the 15th, one Beaufighter had searched for three hours but had been unable to locate the ships. But at 0919 hrs on the morning of the 16th, Flight Sergeants T. Shaw (pilot) and R.W. Hall (navigator) took off in aircraft 'E' to cover the Atlantic convoys. Theirs was the first of what would be a relay of single-aircraft sorties. At a height of 2,000 ft, they successfully met OS.68/KMS.42, and, shortly after, the Beaufighter was detailed by HMS *Biter* 'to investigate a bogey' which may well have been Eberhard Elfert's Ju 290, but nothing was seen. Shaw and Hall were relieved by a second aircraft, 'J', and that machine, in turn, was relieved by 'K', crewed by Flying Officers J.T. Sammon (pilot) and S.S. Harris (navigator) at 1415 hrs.

Meanwhile, the fourth and last aircraft of the relay, Beaufighter 'N', piloted by Belfast-born Squadron Leader Robert R. Wright, together with his navigator, Flying Officer P.J.F. Ross, from Edinburgh, had taken off from St Angelo at 1322 hrs on their first patrol from the Irish base to join 'K' over the convoy. Wright was an experienced pilot, already credited with the probable destructions of an He 111 and Fw 200.

Once paired, the two Beaufighters circled the convoy, but very soon they were both detailed to investigate a 'bogey', which ultimately proved to be a

Fleet Air Arm Fairey Albacore. Then at 1605 hrs, Sammon and Harris were vectored to investigate yet another 'bogey', but they returned to the convoy after losing contact. For the next 40 minutes, *Biter* sought to locate the enemy aircraft. At 1641 hrs a third vector was given by the carrier and both Beaufighters went to investigate once more. This time, nine minutes later, 'an unidentified aircraft was seen flying due North at 8,000 ft, five miles distant.'[37] As the two British aircraft closed, they identified the other machine as a Ju 290 flying at 6,000 ft. This was Karl-Friedrich Bergen's 9V+DK.

Flying Officer Sammon attacked the Junkers from the rear, closing to 400 yards, but the big German aircraft 'disengaged in cloud'. Moments later Squadron Leader Wright dived to 7,000 ft, turned to port and launched a second attack, this time on the beam and out of the sun. Despite defensive fire from the Junkers at 1,500 yards out, Wright closed to 600 yards before using his guns. Once more the Junkers sought sanctuary in the cloud, but Wright did not give up. Moments later, 9V+DK again emerged from the cloud and this time 'dense black smoke' was seen 'pouring' from both starboard engines.[38] Opening fire again, Wright saw strikes on the right side of the Ju 290's fuselage and its starboard engines. After 'losing height to 1,000 ft, the Ju 290 dived vertically into the sea. No survivors were seen.'[39] According to a subsequent British report, the Junkers had impacted '40 miles from the nearest ship'. As the Beaufighters departed, having searched in vain for survivors, 'the only evidence of the combat marking the spot was the tyre of a landing wheel floating in the sea.' Throughout the whole engagement, Ross 'gave a running commentary of the attack to the ships of the convoy over the R/T.' He recalled, 'I first knew we'd found the Ju. when the skipper shouted over the the inter-com: "It's a Jerry. Here goes," and in we went. It was all over within a couple of bursts and we did not see a single survivor.'

'It was a lucky first trip,' Wright later recounted, 'We were flying at 10,000 feet, dived to 6,000 feet and saw sparks along Jerry's fuselage and starboard wing as I gave him the first burst. He was lost in cloud for a second or two, but emerged with black smoke pouring from starboard engines, seemed to glide from 6,000 feet to 1,500 feet and then dived into the sea.'

Squadron Leader Wright had fired 120 rounds of 0.5-in ammunition and in his log book he wrote: 'Hun was clueless.'[40]

Ju 290 9V+DK crashed into the sea at 53° 13′ North 14° 03′ West having made no sighting report for *Fliegerführer Atlantik*.[41] The entire crew comprising commander and pilot Bergen, second pilot Baumgartner, together with Leutnant Martin Glöckelhofer (observer), Oberfeldwebel Heinz Felleckner, Feldwebel Heinz Schacht (radio-operators), Unteroffizier Gottfried Beninde, Oberfeldwebel Ludwig (or Gottfried?) Ebner (flight engineers), Unteroffizier Jakob Daniel, Obergefreiter Karl Zinke, Obergefreiter Josef Neubauer (gunners) and Referendar Werner Cordes of the *Wetterwarte Atlantik* was lost.[42]

This was a bitter blow for both the Luftwaffe and the BdU: FAGr 5 had lost 20 of its own trained men, and the Luftwaffe a skilled meteorologist and two precious, expensive and sophisticated aircraft. Schmidt wrote: 'It was just accepted that they had been shot down by fighters. An old, experienced crew, with the *Staffelkapitän* of 2./FAGr 5...'[43]

Indeed, the *Gruppenkommandeur*, Hauptmann Fischer, took decisive action, as Hauptmann Josef Augustin, the *Staffelkapitän* of 1./FAGr 5 recalled:

> Since neither of the crews had returned, that night, I was ordered by the *Kommandeur* of FAGr 5 to prepare a machine for readiness and to fly out the next morning to mount a search. I joined the crew of Hauptmann Pawlittke, as second pilot, for the search mission, with the objective of perhaps assisting our downed comrades with the help of distress equipment.[44]

There were yet further technical problems which had affected the performance of the *Gruppe* throughout the day; at 1038 hrs, Ju 290A-5 Wk-Nr 0176 9V+GH of 1.*Staffel* took off for the convoys, but after flying for some 500 km, its compass failed and, in a repeat of his frustrated flight the day before, Leutnant Hellmut Nagel was forced to turn back to France.[45] In a separate move, that afternoon, Ju 290A-5 Wk-Nr 0173 9V+CK departed Mont de Marsan for Kerlin-Bastard in readiness for further operations over the convoys the next day.[46]

Then, as instructed, next morning, the first of two Ju 290s – an aircraft of 1./FAGr 5 flown by Hauptmann Willi Pawlittke – took off on its attempt to find the shot-down crews. Aboard was Josef Augustin, who recalled:

> Around 0800 hrs in the morning we took off from Mont de Marsan – on a North-North-West course through cloudless skies flying at low altitude (*c*.100 m) over the water towards the south-west coast of England. As we were quickly in English coastal waters, we had to pay the highest attention to the airspace around us, as the British fighter defence had outstanding radar capability and was very dangerous. One shot from an enemy fighter was usually fatal for our machines, because the fuel tank (9000 l) located in the fuselage was a hazard of the first order. For all crew-members the flight was very strained, as all stations had to be manned continuously, simultaenously monitoring the enemy airspace while searching the surface for our missing comrades.

South-west of the English coast, one of the gunners reported a British four-engined aircraft, some 1000 m higher than our machine. On board we came to full alert and weapons-readiness. If we were recognized, we had to expect that the *Viermot* would warn the English defence. The next stage of the flight took place under the highest state of tension and alert for the crew. We were lucky not to be attacked by enemy fighters. Either the English *Viermot* had not seen us, or the English fighters had not been able to find us in the vast expanse of the Atlantic.

However, although we reported finding enemy shipping west of Ireland, moving east to west, we did not find our missing comrades at sea. Nor could another successive search aircraft under the command of Oberleutnant Karl-Heinz Schmidt of 2.*Staffel* find either aircraft. Both crews were given up as lost, and we never heard from them again.

The whole flight was free of cloud. The return flight to Mont de Marsan was without any encounter with the enemy, and after 16 hours we were fortunate enough to make it back to base and to land without incident.[47]

Augustin's sortie was not the first flight out of Mont de Marsan that morning, for FAGr 5 had already despatched two Ju 290s to the Western Approaches, and followed Augustin and Pawlittke's sortie with a fourth aircraft later in the day. The situation at sea, west of Ireland, was 'busy' with, in addition to OS.68/KMS.42, no fewer than four other large convoys in the area: ONS.29 Liverpool to Halifax, comprising 46 merchants and 23 escorts; ON.224 Liverpool to New York with 79 merchants and 34 escorts; OS.67 to Freetown with 27 merchants and five escorts; and HX.278 eastbound from Halifax, comprising 62 merchants and 34 escorts.[48] The Junkers located all these convoys within an area 50° 30′ North–52° 30′ North 16° 45′ West–19° 45′ West, but as British intelligence surmised, 'The German High Command, which on the basis of previous reports expected one westbound convoy only, must have been considerably perplexed by the signals.'[49]

The first two Ju 290s were assigned to fly out over the French coast at 0645 hrs, but one of these, aircraft 'C', turned back with engine trouble from 25° West 3182 at 0924 hrs. Just over two hours later, the crew reported that its aircraft was 'flying on three engines', but they returned to Mont de Marsan safely. Aircraft 'G', which took off to replace the returning 'C', was instructed by *Fliegerführer Atlantik* during the mid-morning to change course, and at 1300 hrs, it signalled that it had spotted what its crew believed was OS.68/KMS.42 in 25° West 7135, but was unable to provide details of composition or course. Instead, only a weather report was transmitted. At 1525 hrs, the Ju 290 reported sighting another convoy from 25° West 9215, actually

ONS.29 moving on a course of 270°. Although no details of the composition of the convoy were signalled, its position was relayed to the *Igel* pack of U-boats which were then, as a result, redisposed farther north and south in an effort to intercept. Ju 290 'G' continued to shadow the convoy for an hour or so before moving off and returning to Mont de Marsan.

Another Junkers was operational over the Atlantic later in the afternoon; the aircraft was decrypted by British signals intelligence as 'F'. That being the case, with 9V+FH of 1./FAGr 5 being lost the day before, this aircraft must have been Ju 290A-5 Wk-Nr 0179 (KR+LJ) 9V+FK of 2.*Staffel*. At 1620 hrs, this aircraft reported a convoy on a westerly course in 25° West 0215 on course 270°, which was probably a part of ONS.29. The crew of the Junkers signalled that it had observed 28 motor vessels, two destroyers, eight escorts and two carriers. Just under an hour later, the aircraft transmitted a weather report and seems to have moved off.

A fourth aircraft, the second 'G', reported a convoy at 1600 hrs in 25° West 7353, and then an hour-and-a-half later it signalled the sighting of an aircraft carrier on a westerly course in 25° West 8166, which may well have been making for ON.224. At 2000 hrs, 'G' reported 'mission completed', and was back at Mont de Marsan at 0143 hrs. Tellingly however, the British decrypters noted 'the peculiar vagueness of most of the sighting reports, which suggests that [the] aircraft remained at the maximum possible distance from their targets to avoid a repetition of the previous day's disaster. The reliability of the positions given seems to be even less than usual.'[50]

Another Ju 290, 'B', was out over the Atlantic during the night, but did not reach the convoy area and was forced to return prematurely. Nevertheless, during the night of the 17th/18th, the U-boats awaited reports from air reconnaissance before finalizing the positions of their new patrol lines. Based on what information they received from FAGr 5, on the 18th they were ordered to redeploy into two parallel patrol lines ahead of the route of ONS.29 some 1000 km to the south-west of Ireland in order to carry out an 'old style' convoy attack at night. These weak groupings of 20 boats in total, formed from *Igel* and known as *Hai* 1 and *Hai* 2, included boats that had not reported for several weeks and there was little knowledge at BdU about whether they had even survived the operations of previous weeks. In fact, the *Hai* groups were severely depleted against their assumed strengths.

The reality for BdU was that this was to be a make-or-break operation. The *Hai* groups were in their positions by 1800 hrs on the 18th, and at 2000 hrs they were ordered to head south, at first submerged, but then at high speed on the surface, their instructions to get ahead of the convoy at all costs.[51] In order to avoid attracting a mass of Allied carrier aircraft, the 'main blow' was to be delivered on the first night. BdU informed the U-boats that they had to reach the convoy regardless of the circumstances and were to remain on the surface with their 37 mm Flak guns fully manned, and bow and stern homing torpedos ready to fire. If BdU considered that the operation should extend into daylight, then only boats with malfunctioning Flak armament were to submerge; whatever the case, the priority for all boats was to strike at the carriers, then the destroyers. The signal of BdU was unequivocal: 'Do your best. This long-prepared operation must succeed.'[52]

Fliegerführer Atlantik had promised air reconnaissance from 2000 hrs on the 18th onwards. At least six Ju 290s of FAGr 5 were readied, as well as a Bv 222 of 1./SAGr 129 and a pair of Fw 200s from III./KG 40, briefed to mount a search of the area 47° 53′ North 19° 26′ West. The first two Ju 290s were to fly out from Mont de Marsan during the mid-afternoon, along with the two Condors from Bordeaux-Mérignac escorted by 14 Ju 88C fighters from I. and III./ZG 1.

Aboard Ju 290A-5 WK-Nr 0174 9V+EH that day was the crew of Oberleutnant August Vaupel of 1./FAGr 5 (commander and observer, and a former officer of 3.(F)/Aufkl.Gr.10), comprising Leutnant Hellmut Nagel and Leutnant Kurt Nonnenberg (pilots), along with Feldwebel Justel, Unteroffizier Elies, Unteroffizier Heeg, Unteroffizier Roller, Unteroffizier Wischelow, Feldwebel Berndt and Feldwebel Leimenkühler. Hellmut Nagel, who was flying as the first pilot, recalled what was a typical mission for FAGr 5 at this time:

The whole crew had been on standby since the afternoon of 17 February. At about 1000 hrs the motorcycle rider comes with the operations order: take-off at 1400 hrs. My observer and I are collected at 1200 hrs by the crew bus. In the operations room the crew is instructed on the operational plan. Two escorted convoys have to be investigated, the first in every detail, while the second would only be discovered at night. Positions and courses have to be observed and reported.

The navigation watches are set to the chronometer in the operations room, then we go with the bus to the Junkers Ju 290 already prepared for take-off. The technical service personnel give us their readiness report. Including the two weathermen, we are a crew of 11. The second pilot, Leutnant Nonnenberg declares, 'All ready for take-off!' Gyro and course steering are checked. The intercom is checked with the name of each crew member, and the four engines are checked by the second pilot.

Start: flaps to take-off position, brake chocks away, windows closed and an announcement over the intercom: 'We're off!' Throttles full forward, the co-pilot and I get the steering tight in our hands to guarantee a safe take-off. It is fascinating when a colossus like the Ju 290, with all its 42 tonnes, starts rolling. The radar station, 50 m behind the runway, speeds towards us. At first, the landing gear is pulled up at a height of 50 m, then follow the flaps and the engines are reduced to cruising power.

Our two radio operators extend the antennae in order to tune the communications equipment and the first check-call from the base station is received. Meanwhile the observer, Oberleutnant Vaupel, prepares his navigation table and fixes the first-time stamps on the sea map. All navigational events, actions, radio direction findings and course changes as well as astronomical fixes are copied on the map by the observer.

The first gunner surveys the sky from his rotatable Plexiglas turret fitted with its 2-cm machine gun, watching the airspace on the starboard beam towards the aft of the aircraft. The second gunner, also in a rotatable dome, located along the last third of the upper fuselage, monitors the airspace on the port-side beam to the tail unit. The rear gunner is located at end of the fuselage and covers the airspace at our backs. At a height of 100 m, we are welcomed by a Biscay low pressure area. An escort from the fighters of JG 101 [a fighter training *Geschwader* based at Pau, 95 km south of Mont de Marsan, under the command of the *Ritterkreuz* holder, Major Walter Nowotny] is not necessary due to the weather. The British long-range Mosquitos may not be expected in this weather. Nevertheless, the three gunners and the flight engineer test their weapons by shooting some salvoes into the sea, and after ten minutes the 'weapons clear' notice is given.

The flight engineer controls fuel and oil consumption, and oversees the pumping operations between the tanks, calculating the fuel needed from the course data and fixes by long- and short-wave radio direction findings. Everything is analysed and fixed on the map. The very short time used for radio transmissions for these findings should make detection of our flight by enemy reconnaissance difficult.

Additionally, after the second geographical fix point, every 30 minutes we switch on the FuG 200 system to search for ship targets. In two tuning ranges it is possible to locate ships, their numbers and size, from 35 km to 120 km distance. The observer is busy on his navigation table and communicates results, figures and instructions to the two radio-operators, who receive or transmit to the BdU in Paris or to the weather stations and the Norddeich radio station on the North Sea coast.

We have now been airborne for two hours and south to starboard should be Cape Finisterre in Spain. For direction and location finding we use the '*Elektra*' radio navigation guidance system with its base stations in Stavanger in Norway and Sevilla in Spain. These radio bases give the navigational base for a location and our start point into the Atlantic: our position is 11° West and 43° North. The radio operators pull in the long-range antennae. Based on our electric altimeter, we change our height to 20 m, heading north.

We are now approaching the area of the convoys which stretches from southern England to the Azores, to Gibraltar and back. The low-altitude flight gives us the best protection against unexpected encounters. Every 30 minutes we climb to 300 m and fly a circle and switch on the FuG 200. Thereafter, we descend immediately to 20 m. In this way, we avoid being discovered by the ships' radars on the convoy's escort vessels. At such a height we move at a level where radar is reflected by the rough surface of the sea, so we will not be discovered.

While flying the next search circle at 300 m, the FuG 200 detects an unknown number of ship targets ahead of us. We come out of the circle immediately and we descend to 15 or 20 m and adjust our course directly for the centre of the convoy. Over the intercom system, a state of full alert is communicated to the whole crew.

The radio operator announces that the convoy is centred on the FuG 200 display screen. He picks up some 30 to 40 ships, together with a very big 'target'. Shortly thereafter, visual observation confirms a medium-sized aircraft carrier. In very good visual conditions we spot a whole convoy from the many smoke clouds; merchant vessels and their armed warship escorts. As we approach to within 18 km distance of the convoy, still with our course to its centre, we get spotted. Some of the smaller escort ships move towards us in a broad front with waves visible across their bows and they start firing at us with all their guns.

The carrier to the west side of the convoy starts its attacks well. In such a situation we fly up to two kilometres from where their shells impact on the surface of the sea, while still observing the carrier and then we turn North on course 50°. The observer, the radio-operators and the gunners try to count the number of ships accurately. With our little Robot camera with its seven-centimetre lens, the observer photographs some of the ships. We cannot see whether aircraft from the carrier have taken off, and therefore we fly for half an hour along this course for about 80 nautical miles, because the carrier aircraft can only range 50 nautical miles from the carrier.

In the upcoming dawn, the observer and the radio operators will encode the messages to the BdU at Le Bourget near Paris. A new fine-tuning of the radio signals has to be made to transmit a new location via direction finding with the radio base stations at Stavanger and Sevilla.

We had now been underway for 17½ hours and encountered the area of the second convoy. It is a westbound one, headed to the USA. Over the intercom the voice of the first radio-operator: ship targets 50 nautical miles ahead! All battle stations are manned immediately. Our FuG 200 enables us to adjust our course exactly to the convoy. We are now detectable by the ships' radars of the escort vessels, but we are not physically visible due to cloud. From the various green marks on the screen, the two radio operators are able to detect as many as 35 ships.

The convoy makes course 215° West-South-West. We fly from the rear of the convoy to its leading point, and drop a parachute flare-bomb at both ends. They fall through the layer of stratos clouds and spread a harsh light across the sea to attract the attention of the German U-boats in the area.

After that we turn back South on a course 80° to Mont de Marsan. A clear sky, filled with stars, is the best condition to perform an astronomical navigational fix. The second pilot takes over at the controls, and my observer and I go with the bubble octant and our navigation watches to the stand in the middle section of the aircraft topped with a clear Plexiglas cover [the astrodome], to 'shoot' a star transversely and ahead.

With the octant, an extra bright star ahead and one off to the side are fixed for some seconds and the levelled angles are noted on the prepared form. A standardized calculation allows centring a cross section of two lines on our map that results in the exact location at the observation time. At the same time, our two radio-operators pick up, as an additional locating procedure, two secret radio beacons off the south coast of Ireland and one near Cap Finisterre in Spain. (See below.)

Our flight engineer and the second pilot commence some fuel-pumping procedures for our way home. The radio-operators encode the messages assisted by the observer. He also controls the navigational data of the course changes made over the recent hours. A new day, the 19 February 1944 commences. It is 0130 hrs and we have seven hours' flight-time to go to Mont de Marsan.

At about 0500 hrs we give up our altitude of 2000 m and enter the Bay of Biscay at 100 m just north of the easterly low pressure area. We choose this 'uncomfortable' height, as we move into the reach of British long-range fighters. We try to detect the German Kriegsmarine coastguard boats early enough so as to give our identification signal in good time.

Just before we fly over the coast, we advise our position together with increased radio transmissions from both radio operators: QFE, QFF and we also get some weather data from the airfield at Mont de Marsan. There's voice radio connection: an 'all-clear message' from the airfield; and no activity over Bordeaux. We two pilots navigate the Ju 290 based on the navigational data supplied by the airfield radar. We proceed at 200 m over the centre of the airfield … Putting down our landing gear in pretty bad visual conditions, we at last see the airfield lights. The chief of the direction-finder station stands waving in front of the radio direction-finding hut and gives the awaited 'Z' signal.

The landing is successful and we let the Junkers roll to a stop without braking, shut down the engines and at once we have complete silence. The crew bus comes out to us, and the ground personal help us out of the aircraft and into the bus. The technical personnel ask us about the status of the aircraft and the engines as we head towards the command post to give our operations reports. The end of a long busy flight![53]

Astro-navigation was of critical importance to the crews of FAGr 5. The bubble octant to which Nagel refers was a navigation device manufactured by C. Plath of Hamburg, and was used in U-boats and long-range aircraft to aid astronomical navigation by measuring the declination, or the angular height of a star. An artificial horizon was produced by a liquid bubble, similar to that in a spirit level, which levelled the motion of the platform. The measuring time was given by a small, integrated timer.

Precise time-setting was essential for long-range aircrews for providing accurate astronomical navigation. This was also ensured by the use of an aerial navigation watch, in the case of the crews of FAGr 5, this being an IWC cal. 52T SC. The Ju 290's commander wore such a watch, while the observer or navigator operated the bubble octant. Nagel mentions a 'clear Plexiglas cover' in the central fuselage of the Ju 290; this 'astrodome' was fitted between two pivoting, protective stands and could be fully revolved. The transparent cover was free of all optical distortions. Beneath it, on the floor of the fuselage, was a rotating platform approximately 1 m in diameter. This platform could be raised or lowered.

The observer stood on this platform with the octant in his hand. It was possible to use a hook to fix the octant to the roof to assist in taking a sight, but this was not always practical because it was not always steady and the differing heights of crew members came into play.[54]

The wearer of the watch stood nearby. The two men communicated with each other over the aircraft intercom. In operating the octant, when the observer had the square of the crosshairs and a star (which could also be the sun during daylight navigation) in view, he would announce, 'Zero', and then switch on his octant timer for the corresponding observation interval of 40, 60 or 90 seconds. The moment the wearer of the watch heard the word 'Zero', he would read the hour, minute and second indicators on his watch. Prior to every mission, navigation watches were synchronized with a ground-based chronometer kept in the operations room. The measured values to be read from the octant were: ten-degree setting, degree drum, degree disc in the integrator and minute drum, height of the star observed, half of the octant's running time added to this, and the current time. When this data was entered into a calculating form that had been prepared earlier by an astronomer, the result was a location line which intersected with the course that was being flown, if the observed star was situated ahead of the aircraft, or which ran parallel to the course, if the star was situated to the right or left of the current course.[55] (See also Appendix 5.)

Meanwhile, at 1945 hrs, Ju 290 'E' sighted a convoy in 24° West 9725 that was probably SL.148/MKS.39 inbound from Freetown and Gibraltar with around 70 vessels. Despite reporting the details of the convoy, it seems *Fliegerführer Atlantik* was not interested; the priority was ONS.29, against which the U-boats were preparing to attack. 'E' was instructed to continue with its planned patrol. Just over five hours later, at 0110 hrs, 'E's' FuG 200 radar picked up ONS.29 in 34° West 3975. But the Ju 290 was unable to determine the number of ships. However, nine minutes later, the convoy's bearing, as well as the distances the aircraft was from it, were signalled back on the tactical wireless frequency. This information was passed to the *Hai* boats, but because it was only a radar fix, it lacked details of course and speed. Nevertheless, during the early hours of the 19th, the U-boats chased both ONS.29 and ON.224, which were not far apart, although the presence of Liberators in the air forced several of them below the surface.[56] The Ju 290 broke off shadowing at 0210 hrs some 40 km from the convoy. The Junker's signal was also passed to the lone Bv 222, which was also operating, and the flying boat spent time shadowing the convoy from 0600 hrs before breaking off at 0719 hrs.

According to the British radio intercept analysis:

Two bearings taken on 'E's' beacon signals at about 0200 were reported by U-boats and gave an unreliable fix. U-boats failed to include in their reports the bearing and distance of the aircraft from the convoy as reported by the aircraft on the beacon frequency – hence the order to 'E' to report these for 0200 on his tactical frequency. At 0200, however, a number of U-boats had been ordered to operate directly on 'E's' beacon signals, presumably without reporting. After this initial deficiency in reports, control at 0300 instructed the next shadowing aircraft 'D' and 'F' also to give their bearing and distance from the convoy on tactical frequency.

At 0350 hrs, once in the patrol area, Ju 290A-5 Wk-Nr 0179 9V+FK of 2./FAGr 5 under the command of its senior pilot, Oberleutnant Karl-Heinz

Schmidt, was instructed to search from 34° West 3973 on a bearing of 50°. At 0500 hrs, new orders were received for the aircraft to fly to 34° West 1976, and an hour later to 34° West 1915. But five minutes before the second of these revised instructions, the Ju 290 spotted the convoy, although it was unable to shadow it because of 'fighter opposition', which was reported on three occasions between 0544 hrs and 0630 hrs. Meanwhile, aircraft 'D' had also located shipping in 34° West 1915 and commenced making beacon signals at 0420 hrs. On this occasion, the U-boats did report bearings and the Junkers' distance from the convoy. However, both aircraft were ordered to break off shadowing at 0648 hrs, presumably because of the presence of enemy fighters.

Schmidt turned his Ju 290 around to the east and made course for northern Spain. Some four hours later, in accordance with tactical directives, as he neared the coast of Galicia, he descended to almost wavetop height to avoid detection from the menace of radar-equipped enemy fighters. On board 9V+FK, as described in other accounts, the crew would have been weary after a long night flight over the Atlantic, but highly alert, and all guns would have been manned. But for Schmidt and his crew, the worst was about to happen.

Earlier that morning, a formation of four RAF Mosquito Mk IIs of No. 157 Squadron had taken off at 0916 hrs from their base at Predannack on the south-western coast of Cornwall to fly through cloudy skies on a routine 'Instep' patrol across the Bay of Biscay to the Spanish coast between Cape Ortegal and La Coruña. According to the subsequent RAF report:

At 1152 an aircraft was sighted three or four miles ahead, flying at '0' feet in an easterly direction; the formation closed in and the aircraft was recognized as a Ju 290. When about 1,000 yards away, it turned south flying into the sun, and opened fire with self-destroying ammunition, which appeared to come from mid-upper turret.

F/Lt R.J. Coombs [with Flying Officer G.H. Scobie as Navigator] and F/Lt R.D. Doleman [with Flight Lieutenant L. Scholefield as Navigator – leading the formation] closed in to 600 yards on the starboard and the port side of the enemy aircraft, F/Lt Coombs making a beam attack of about 60° which was over-deflected. A normal curve of pursuit was carried out and another attack made from 10° to port at 200 yards. Difficulty was experienced in keeping ring in sight, due to the bumpy conditions, and the burst went beneath port wing; another burst was given as range decreased and strikes were seen along the port wing and both motors, and the wing burst into flames. A further burst was given with less deflection and strikes were seen in the mid-fuselage which appeared to cause minor explosion in the fuselage which also caught fire. Pieces of debris flew past the Mosquito which broke off its attack position to make his second attack. F/Lt Doleman attacked from 5° to port at 550 yards range; strikes were seen on the tail unit and all along the fuselage and the port wing. A second burst, with range closing to 250 yards, produced more strikes along the fuselage and starboard wing. The enemy aircraft was seen to be burning inside the fuselage and top, behind the cockpit, and the port wing was also on fire.

The Ju 290 gradually lost height and hit the sea with its starboard wing and blew up. A large aircraft dinghy upside down on the sea and two smaller ones were seen, but no survivors were observed.

F/Lt Coombs' aircraft received strikes on both wings and port engine, and he flew back to base on one engine, making a perfect, one-engine landing with no flaps. He was escorted by F/Lt B.M. Whitlock [with navigator Flying Officer M.B. Hull] and Lt J.B. Noble [with navigator Sergeant McCormick], F/Lt Doleman returning to base alone in order to organize A.S.R. should it be required, in the event of F/Lt Coombs having to ditch.

In despatching the Ju 290, Coombs and Doleman had expended a total of 2,348 high-explosive/incendiary and semi-armour-piercing rounds of 20 mm cannon and .303-in machine gun ammunition and tracer.[57] The description of the Junkers' demise in the RAF report reinforces what Josef Augustin stated in his earlier account about the danger associated with the installation of the Ju 290's fuselage fuel tank, which stood between the forward dorsal turret and the astrodome.[58]

Meanwhile, *Fernaufklärungsgruppe* 5 had lost another valued and veteran crew, many of whom had flown with 3.(F)/Aufkl.Gr.Ob.d.L. in Russia, and another precious aircraft – the third of each in three days. Lost were Oberleutnant Karl-Heinz Schmidt (pilot), Leutnant Hermann Barth (observer), Oberfeldwebel Gustav Albers (pilot), Oberfeldwebel Emil Cudock (flight engineer), Feldwebel Gerhard Hähndel, Feldwebel Max Pötter (both radio-operators), Gefreiter Helmut Eimler, Unteroffizier Andreas Hofmann, Obergefreiter Walter von Soosten and Unteroffizier Bernhard Wermes (all gunners).[59]

Two other Junkers, aircraft 'A' and 'H', were also airborne during the day, but both failed to locate the convoys on account of technical or mechanical problems.

For the U-boats, the operation against ONS.29 had been nothing short of a catastrophe. They had failed utterly to make an impact on any of the convoys. Furthermore, at 1000 hrs on the 19th, HMS *Woodpecker* and HMS *Starling*, both sloops from Captain F.J. 'Johnnie' Walker's renowned 2nd Escort Group, forced Kapitänleutnant Hartwig Looks' *Schnorchel*-fitted

U-264 to surface and its crew to abandon ship. That afternoon, the frigate, HMS *Spey*, from the 10th Escort Group covering ONS.29, sank Oberleutnant zur See Rolf Heinrich Fritz Albrecht's *U-386* having firstly blown it to the surface with depth charges, before shooting it up with gunfire as its crew leapt off their stricken boat. *Spey* had sunk *U-406* the day before. This was enough for BdU to dissolve the two *Hai* groups and to form a new group, *Preussen*, of 15 boats, four of them newly arrived from France adding to the rest formerly from *Hai. Preussen*, which was moved to a position 650–800 km north of the Azores, would be the last anti-convoy wolfpack of the war.[60]

In his history of the U-boat war in the Atlantic, written under the auspices of the US Navy and the British Admiralty, Gunther Hessler writes of the action against this convoy:

> The take-off times of the ten aircraft then available were adjusted so as to ensure continuous shadowing from dusk till dawn, but the first two aircraft to reach the area missed the convoy, probably because of navigational errors. They made only brief contact on the return flight at about 0100 on the 19th and, although the homing signals sent by succeeding aircraft were received, cross-bearings were too acute to give an accurate fix. It was not until 0500 that a good fix could be obtained, and it then became apparent that some of the aircraft had been far out in their estimated positions. Theoretically, about eight boats could have reached the convoy by daybreak; in practice, however, they merely sighted a few destroyers and established enemy radar activity. The operation was finally broken off at daylight, when the boats had to submerge owing to the presence of an aircraft carrier in the convoy.[61]

In total, the *Fliegerführer Atlantik* had deployed two Ju 88s, 17 Ju 290s, three Fw 200s and two Bv 222s against the convoys between 14 and 19 February – a total of 24 aircraft. Of the 24, the following ten aircraft dropped out (in addition to the three Ju 290s lost):

> four Ju 290s and one Bv 222 due to engine trouble
> two Ju 290s due to radar and radio defects
> two Ju 290s due to compass failure
> one Fw 200 due to other causes

In the war diary of the BdU, it was noted with some rare conciliation:

> The large number of aircraft defects which developed, especially towards the end, were caused by lack of proper maintenance, in turn due to the high

pressure under which the aircraft were operating. Reconnaissance was only made possible by doubling the number of aircraft in a flight and sending one out as a reserve. That so many flights were made, particularly on the last night, was due to the most strenuous and devoted efforts on the part of the maintenance personnel.[62]

By mid-February, the winter temperatures fell sharply at Mont de Marsan and cold winds blew in daily from the Biscay. The war news was not good. From the Eastern Front, German forces were on the retreat in many sectors: Luga, once the base of 3.(F)/Aufkl.Gr.Ob.d.L., had been lost, and from the East came the troops of the 2.*SS-Panzer-Division 'Das Reich'* who moved into the Mont de Marsan area in order to rest and re-equip after an intense period of fighting with heavy losses.[63]

With the recent losses suffered by the *Gruppe*, it was a time of sombre reflection for the men of FAGr 5. Oskar Schmidt recalled:

In the unit, the question arose as to whether the training on aircraft and armament was thorough and long enough. Could we afford to sacrifice such experienced flying personnel? In a short period of operations, five aircraft (55 crewmen) had already been lost. Reports stated that 200,000 GRT of enemy tonnage had been found in the convoys, but – as far as the *Gruppe* was aware – 18,000 GRT had been sunk![64]

He also noted, apparently with some frustration, the following:

Our flying personnel carried out some very good reconnaissance out at sea in February. But one deficiency was that the crews were not sufficiently informed by the relevant commands about their evaluations and the use of our reconnaissance by other branches of the armed services. At the time, the U-boats could hardly cross the Biscay to the open sea, let alone be expected to find the convoys. Question: were we supposed to fly reconnaissance over the Atlantic, just to monitor ships' movements and tonnage figures?[65]

There is evidence to suggest that the technical infrastructure at Mont de Marsan was not always adequate at this time. On 14 February, for example, Leutnant Hellmut Nagel of 1./FAGr 5 flew Ju 290A-5 Wk-Nr 0176 9V+GH on a flight to the workshops at Bordeaux-Mérignac, where presumably there were better maintenance facilities or supplies of tools, parts and equipment.[66]

From the 20th to the end of February, there would be no further long-range reconnaissance missions. This was partly on account of the weather, but also because U-boat operations in the Atlantic had almost come to an end as a result of Allied escort and air counter-action. In the last three weeks of February 1944, 12 large convoys had passed through the Western Approaches, at least two of which were saved from heavy attack. For Dönitz, the balance sheet made grim reading; 11 U-boats had been sunk, in return for the torpedoing of HMS *Woodpecker*, which resulted in its eventual capsizing (this sloop, it will be recalled, had sunk *U-264*), the destruction of two aircraft of Coastal Command and the sinking of a straggling merchant vessel.[67] Furthermore, the *Preussen* pack had failed to catch the Liverpool–New York convoy ON.225, which the Allies had re-routed as a result of Enigma decrypts.

At Mont de Marsan, 20 February saw the arrival of Hauptmann Georg Eckl, a former *Seenot* (air-sea rescue) flier, as successor to Karl-Friedrich Bergen as *Staffelkapitän* of 2./FAGr 5, though Eckl's presence did little to counter the increasing trend for numbers of the unit's men, mainly its ground personnel, being withdrawn from the unit to bolster other Wehrmacht and Luftwaffe front-line units which had suffered heavy losses in the ground-fighting in the East or in the Mediterranean.[68]

Next day, Hauptmann Fischer called the whole *Gruppe* out for inspection in order to read to his men a message received from Grossadmiral Dönitz via the *Fliegerführer Atlantik* commending them on the excellent performance that they had put in during their operations over the past weeks, despite mechanical, technical and meteorological adversities. After the men were dismissed, Fischer discussed operational matters with his *Staffelkapitäne* before departing the next day for Berlin. There he met with Generalfeldmarschall Milch, the *Generalluftzeugmeister*, and Generalmajor von Barsewisch, the *General der Aufklärungsflieger*, to present his thoughts on the war against the convoys and the anticipated level of losses. It was a bleak assessment:

At the present time, there are eight Ju 290s available to the *Gruppe*. Of these, half are presently in the Reich undergoing repair, so that only three to four machines are operationally ready.

On present experience, every 16th operational sortie results in a total loss. As the weather improves, so the protection of cloud cover falls away, although against radar-equipped long-range fighters, that is little defence. Also, the nights will become shorter, the days longer, so enemy long-range fighters will be able to monitor the Bay of Biscay in daylight. Our losses will inevitably increase. Also, for the U-boats, it has been a bad time. The Biscay will be covered by radar-equipped British long-range fighters by day and night, and every U-boat will be attacked by bombs and guns. The losses among the U-boats are enormous, and only a few make it out into the open Atlantic. The U-boat command expects it will be September 1944 before boats become available again in greater numbers for operations.

Decision and Proposal of the *Kommandeur* FAGr 5
It is proposed from 'above' to reinforce operations by FAGr 5 by the end of June 1944. This [interim] timespan [to September] should be used to improve training for flying personnel on aircraft and for operations. Also aircraft can be throughly overhauled during this time and the intended reinforcements take place.

The *Kommandeur* is planning for additional aircraft: February 1944 – one aircraft; March two; April two; May four; August five. That equates to 18 aircraft by the end of August (based, of course, on full production). From these aircraft a number, together with crews, will be assigned for other tasks.

Here, Fischer is probably alluding to the planned deliveries of the anticpiated Ju 290A-7 variant, while the last sentence is most probably an early, veiled reference to the rumoured intended cooperation between FAGr 5 and the Luftwaffe's covert operations *Geschwader*, KG 200 which would require Ju 290s for other long-range operations (see Chapter Fourteen). Fischer continued:

Alternatively, during this time, the aircraft could be taken out of unit service and moved to workshops in Germany for fitting out with improved weaponry.*

Results and Recommendations:
To reduce future losses in the *Gruppe*, sea reconnaissance to be carried out in greater strength (using two to three aircraft at a time). The aircraft could then give each other mutual defensive fire in the event of being attacked by fighters.

Fischer was forthright:

But the following questions need to be asked:
Why is Atlantic reconnaissance being conducted with substantial losses if a) the U-boats cannot sail and b) the Condors of KG 40 at Bordeaux, with

---

* This most likely means the fitting of external underwing wing racks to the Ju 290A-7 and the installation of *Kehl/Strassburg* equipment for operations with the Hs 293 glide-bomb.

bombs, cannot get far enough out to sea to attack? Are our losses not too high already, just to find out about convoys in the Atlantic?

These will, if reconnaissance is to continue to be flown up to September 1944, when the U-boats are expected to be operationally ready once more, make maritime reconnaissance for the U-boat arm impossible!

Is it not more appropriate, to familiarize the crews more thoroughly with the Ju 290, its armament and the *'Hohentwiel'* equipment, so that by September the maximum level of training can be achieved?[69]

Perhaps because of Fischer's visit to Berlin, on 22 February no less a figure than Generalmajor von Barsewisch returned with the *Kommandeur* to Mont de Marsan. But if Fischer and the officers of the *Gruppe* expected a sympathetic hearing from the *General der Aufklärungsflieger*, they were to be disappointed. During an after-dinner address in the officers' mess that evening, von Barsewisch simply announced that he could not countenance the concerns or wishes of FAGr 5's personnel, and that 'further ruthless operations' were expected of the *Gruppe*, particularly since the unit's results were now being studied closely by OKL and senior staffs. From that point on, the subject was to be considered closed.[70]

Three days later, on the 25th, Oberst Rupprecht Heyn, the *Kommodore* of KG 40 and a veteran maritime reconnaissance flier, was the guest at another dinner hosted by FAGr 5. Fischer endeavoured to explain to Heyn his plans for the tactical deployment of his *Gruppe* and the challenges facing it, but Heyn seemed indifferent, claiming he was not responsible for FAGr 5's operations. As Oskar Schmidt noted, 'One got the impression that the *Kommodore* of KG 40 could not, or would not, understand our difficulties.' However, generally cooperation between the two units on a day-to-day basis remained good with regular liaison.[71]

As February 1944 drew to a close, gradually the weather in western France began to improve. In order to keep the men fit and alert, the *Stabskompanie* organized various sporting activites and country pursuits, as well as setting up training sessions in weapons and gas mask drill. *Fernaufklärungsgruppe* 5 organized its own football team and, amongst other fixtures, played Major Walter Nowotny's JG 101 at Pau.

Meanwhile, at a higher level, during one of his midday situation conferences at his headquarters at Angers at the end of February, the *Fliegerführer Atlantik*, Generalleutnant Kessler, was surprised to receive an unexpected visit from Generalmajor Alexander Holle, who entered the room and promptly announced that he was assuming command as *Fliegerführer Atlantik* with immediate effect. A startled, but courteous Kessler replied that he knew nothing of this and that he would need verification from the *Luftwaffenführungsstab*. A few hours later, Kessler received a teleprint message advising him of his replacement. He packed his bags and prepared to leave.

Alexander Holle's position at this time is not entirely clear; he had been serving as commanding general of X.*Fliegerkorps* in the Mediterranean, at least until late 1943, but seems to have been transferred to Western Europe in some capacity until his takeover of *Fliegerführer Atlantik*. Holle was not a popular officer and little would change during his time in command, either with regard to what had been Kessler's staff or to the units he commanded.[72]

With recent losses, increasing Allied air activity, lengthening daylight, lack of aircraft, and the withdrawal of men for front-line duties, the spring of 1944 began a period of great uncertainty for the Luftwaffe campaign to defend and master the airspace over the Bay of Biscay and the eastern Atlantic.

CHAPTER TEN

FADING SHADOWS

March–May 1944

I pressed home my own attack, hitting the Junkers
repeatedly at close range. It crashed into the sea and
exploded. All that remained of the Junkers was an oil
slick and a few floating pieces of debris.

Lt. Allen R. Burgham, RNZVR, 835 NAS, May 1944

Commencing 19 February through to the end of April 1944, there was an almost complete absence of Luftwaffe long-range convoy reconnaissance over the Atlantic.[1] In March, most flying on the part of FAGr 5 (and other units under *Fliegerführer Atlantik* for much of that period) was restricted to air training sorties in which crews practised navigation skills and air gunnery. But even these were few and far between.

During the afternoon of 4 March, one Ju 290 was picked up by British decrypts carrying out practice-firing along the Biscay coast, but it would not be until 0730 hrs on the 22nd that the listening stations heard the intentions for another to fly out on a six-hour training flight from Mont de Marsan to 14° West 245 to 251. Otherwise very little was heard from FAGr 5.[2]

Indeed, in a summary of 'German Air Force policy against convoys' in early April, British intelligence gloated:

> There has been no convoy recce in the Atlantic since 18th February. During the week preceding this date three Ju 290s, two Fw 200s and one He 177 are known to have been shot down by 10 Group (Air Defence of Great Britain), 15 Group (Coastal Command) and carrier-borne fighters. This included both the Ju 290s taking part in one operation, and – even more impressive – two different fighter attacks on the same attacking formation of He 177s and Fw 200s by Mosquitos on its way out across the Bay of Biscay (entirely fortuitously) and again by carrier-borne aircraft over the convoy.
>
> Furthermore, several Ju 290 shadowers were driven off by carrier-borne fighters and prevented from making adequate reconnaissance reports.
>
> In his summing up after the operation, Captain U-boats attributed the failure of the U-boats to the failure of air cooperation … This appears to be a strategical success of some significance and might almost be deemed a 'turning point' in the war against ocean convoys.[3]

The month of March started badly for FAGr 5: the US Eighth Air Force made itself felt for the first time at Mont de Marsan when B-24 Liberators of the 2nd Bomb Division attacked the airfield as part of a wider-ranging operation against airfields in western France.[4]

However, it seems the *Gruppe* had received advanced warning of the raid, and managed to get its small number of Ju 290s into the air in advance, and thus they escaped destruction or damage. Furthermore, because of cloud, Mont de Marsan escaped the effects of the bombing relatively unscathed. However, it was to be a portent of things to come and a sign that western French airfields were now a target for the Allied strategic air forces.

Despite the raid, in early March, FAGr 5 mounted a few more practice air-firing flights off the French coast, with usually one aircraft up at a time.[5]

On the 10th, Generalleutnant Kessler visited Mont de Marsan to bid the officers and men of *Fernaufklärungsgruppe* 5 farewell. Oskar Schmidt recalled: 'The outgoing General thanked FAGr 5 for its operations to date and told us that we had written a glorious page in the history of the German war effort over the Atlantic.'[6] Kessler would be shipped off to Tokyo where he would serve as German air attaché. He was awarded the *Ritterkreuz* in April 1944 in recognition of his leadership skills.[7]

The quiet period continued into the second half of March, with more air gunnery and navigational exercise flights being undertaken. On several consecutive days, such practice flights were made along the Biscay coast, sometimes with an aircraft taking off every two hours.[8] On the 17th, a Sunderland flying boat of No. 10 Squadron, RAAF, was on an 'uneventful' patrol over Biscay out of Mount Batten in Devon when, according to the squadron's record book, 'a dark camouflage, unidentified aircraft was sighted flying at a height of 2,000 ft on course 180° at a distance of ten miles on the starboard beam. The aircraft was a four-engined monoplane with twin square fins. Correct recognition could not be made as the unidentified aircraft turned on a westerly course and was lost in cloud. Nothing further was seen.'[9] From their description, the crew had probably seen a Ju 290.

Another reminder of the dominating strength of American airpower came on the 15th, when the *Staffelkapitän* of 2./FAGr 5, Hauptmann Eckl, and his crew, together with Oberleutnant Schmidt of the *Stabskompanie*, flew to the supply base of the *Gruppe* at Achmer in order to collect some replacement vehicle engines from the main military vehicle park at Osnabrück. While Eckl and Schmidt were at Achmer, the airfield suffered an Allied air attack and the accommodation buildings where FAGr 5 had established itself the previous year were heavily damaged. The base had already been subjected to a bombing raid by 103 B-17s and 11 B-24s of the US Eighth Air Force on 21 February, which dropped 317 tons of bombs. Workshops to the north-east of the field had either been destroyed or left badly damaged and the runways were still scarred with hurriedly filled-in craters.[10]

On the 21st, Hauptmann Fischer initiated a wargame at Mont de Marsan in which the *Stabskompanie* played the role of 'enemy paratroops' in an 'airborne assault' on the airfield. The personnel of 1. and 2.*Staffeln* 'fought' to defend and retain the airfield, but in the process many 'shortcomings' were revealed, especially in the transmission and carrying out of orders. But aside from wargames, the airfield air raid alarm was sounded almost daily from late March 1944.

On 23 March, Kessler's successor, Generalleutnant Holle, still commander of X.*Fliegerkorps*, visited Mont de Marsan and stayed for a 'gentlemen's evening'.

'The air raid warning sounded in good time,' remembered Oskar Schmidt, 'and the airport was largely cleared of personnel and equipment. A few French civilian workers who had ridiculed our defensive preparations lost their lives through their own carelessness in the attack. Hauptmann [Jochen] Wanfried, a pilot in the *Gruppenstab*, left the *Stab* motorcycle near the main accommodation buildings and it was hit by bombs. The surrounding pine forests were set on fire by the bombing and there were some major wildfires.'

The airfield Flak defence managed to hit and damage several of the raiders. FAGr 5 suffered the loss of its single Bf 108 courier aircraft, as well as the motorcycle. While these losses may have been light, the reality was that such raids marked the beginning of a 'softening-up' process by the Allies.

By late March 1944, there was a growing recognition and acceptance within the German military, at all levels, of the fact that the Allies would probably launch an invasion on the French coast during the spring or summer months of that year. At this time, Grossadmiral Dönitz, who, on 22 March, had withdrawn the *Preussen* boats from a large area of the central Atlantic, was instructed to assemble a force of 40 U-boats intended for inshore operations in the event of an Allied invasion – what would become known as the *Landwirt* grouping, a measure which resulted in a decline in the number of boats passing across the Bay of Biscay. The reality, however, was that U-boats would have little effect against determined, strongly protected landing forces, as demonstrated off Italy in 1943 and 1944. The few boats that did go into the Atlantic in April would serve only as weather reporters or thinly veiled decoy boats to disguise the overall German withdrawal. Dönitz further told Hitler that operations against the convoys could not be resumed until improved boats were available, as well as improved Luftwaffe reconnaissance.[11]

The Allied and Soviet vices were beginning to tighten on Nazi Germany, and Oskar Schmidt recorded: 'The retreat in the East continues and the air attacks in the West grow more intensive day by day.'

Indeed, Mont de Marsan itself had been on the receiving end of its first major bombing attack on the afternoon of the 27th when 47 B-24 Liberators of the US Eighth Air Force dropped 1,500 general purpose and fragmentation bombs, totalling 137 tons, directly on the airfield, striking hangars, various buildings, stores and a dispersal area to the north of the airport. The USAAF post-mission report noted: 'There are four concentrations of fragmentation bursts running north from the wooded area in the south end of the field, across the landing area and north-east dispersal area.' Nine Ju 290s were observed on the ground, two of them under camouflage netting, but they seemed to have escaped major damage.[12]

On 29 March, as the ground personnel of the *Gruppe*, *Hiwis* and local civilians worked to clear the damage at Mont de Marsan, Hauptmann Fischer held a meeting with his *Staffel* commanders and *Stab* officers to establish contingency measures for the *Gruppe* in the event of an enemy assault against western France from the coast and/or from the air, and if necessary a plan to effect a quick relocation to another base. It was agreed that an evacuation of Mont de Marsan by air and road was preferable to, and more practical than, by rail. Railway rolling stock was not always available, it had to be prepared and it always ran the risk of air attack. However, once in the air, although a

Ju 290 could carry a reasonable load of extra men and equipment, it too would be vulnerable. In the end it was agreed that aircrews would fly out in the aircraft that were available, together with certain equipment, but that the bulk of FAGr 5's personnel and equipment would move by road.

The tension caused by a mix of anticipation and uncertainty over the future, combined with some boredom, was relieved a little by a small festival held on 5 April and organized by former KG 40 man, Oberleutnant Otto-Karl Kremser. 'For a few hours,' recorded Oskar Schmidt, 'it took the mens' minds off the war.'

On 8 April, Hauptmann Fischer held a detailed meeting with his *Gruppenstab* to discuss the short and medium-term future of the unit, and beyond that, to what extent FAGr 5 could expect to be equipped two years ahead. However, in Schmidt's view, whilst 'anticipatory planning was certainly good, to try to forecast such a period in the present war situation was hardly worth discussing.'[13]

The meeting was interrupted by an air raid warning, which although causing much disruption, brought no sign of the enemy. The following day, however, according to Schmidt, one Ju 290 undergoing overhaul at Achmer suffered 40 per cent damage as a result of enemy air action, but it is not possible to verify which machine this was.[14]

The 10th, however, did see another precious Junkers suffer damage when Ju 290A-4 Wk-Nr 0166 9V+DH, flown by Hauptmann Emil Sachtleben of 1./FAGr 5, made an interim stop at Bourges while heading for Dessau. The big four-engined aircraft was hit on the ground as B-24 Liberators bombed the airfield; it was lucky to sustain just 20 per cent damage and the crew was fortunate to escape injury.[15]

The *Gruppe* had between ten and 14 aircraft by this stage, but not all of these were operationally ready.[16] Indeed, because of the low amount of flying conducted in April and May 1944, the *Gruppe* found it economical to concentrate operational flying on just a few aircraft whilst leaving others standing idle. This policy enabled each aircraft to build up its necessary flying hours before being sent back to Achmer or Dessau for overhaul.[17]

The remainder of April saw the unit conducting a limited series of air-firing flights and navigational excercises. One such example on the morning of the 27th involved Leutnant Nagel of 1.*Staffel* flying a 90-minute air-gunnery practice flight in Ju 290 (KR+LQ) 9V+FH.[18] This is noteworthy, for it was a freshly delivered aircraft, Wk-Nr 0186, and only the second or third of the eagerly awaited A-7s to be delivered to FAGr 5 – the first being Wk-Nr 0188 (KR+LS) 9V+FK, which arrived on 3 April. In terms of size and weight similar to, and, with four BMW 801D engines rated with 1,700 hp at take-off, powered like the A-4 and A-5, this variant was intended from the outset as a maritime reconnaissance/anti-shipping aircraft. With a crew of ten, it featured an armoured cockpit, improved braking system and provision to carry two cameras in the left and right waist gun positions. It also heralded the incorporation of a distinctive, bulbous, glazed nose into which was fitted another 20 mm MG 151 cannon (semi-rigid). In addition to FuG 200 radar, the A-7 could be rigged to carry the offensive load of three air-launched Henschel Hs 293 or three Ruhrstahl SD 1400 *Fritz X* guided stand-off bombs which Hermann Fischer so badly wanted for long-range missions over the Atlantic, one such weapon mounted on an ETC rack under the outer wing panels with a third carried under the fuselage. The reality, however, was that it had arrived too late.

Adolf Hitler's birthday on 20 April was officially marked at Mont de Marsan by an award ceremony, at which Hermann Fischer was promoted to Major. This was followed by an evening celebration attended by the senior officers and staff of the *Gruppe*.[20]

On 24 April, Major Fischer and his crew flew in a Ju 290, which was also loaded with one of the unit's Czech-made Tatra tow lorries, to the *Ergänzungs-Fernaufklärungsgruppe* at Posen under the command of Oberst Gerhard Kopper, from where he liaised with the 27.*Unterseebootsflottille* to set up new forms of U-boat cooperation training. Three other Junkers followed and for most of May, the FAGr 5 crews were based at the former commercial airport of Danzig-Langfuhr in Poland. From there, along with crews and aircraft from III./KG 40, they carried out exercises in tactics and equipment coordination from the airfields at Hexengrund, Heiligenbeil, Jesau, Grieslienen and Könisgberg. Somewhat strangely, the Ju 290s involved – A-2 Wk-Nr 0157 9V+BK, A-4 Wk-Nr 0167 9V+HK, A-5 Wk-Nr 0173 9V+CK and A-5 Wk-Nr 0172 9V+BH, to be joined later by A-2 Wk-Nr 0158 9V+AH – were all older models rather than the new A-7s.[21]

At the beginning of May, temperatures in western France increased dramatically and the ground became parched and arid. Because Mont de Marsan airport was surrounded by woods, smoking was forbidden. The month opened with a visit from *General der Flieger* Stefan Fröhlich, an experienced air commander who had once served as the *Fliegerführer Afrika*, and who was deputizing briefly for the commander of *Luftflotte* 3, Generalfeldmarschall Hugo Sperrle. Schmidt described Fröhlich as 'friendly, calm and businesslike', but he stressed to the men of the long-range reconnaissance unit the prospect and dangers of an anticipated Allied invasion, especially with the improved weather and full moon.

During May 1944, FAGr 5's technical personnel were trained in how to handle Ju 290s with the heavy towing vehicles to hand, so that the unit's aircraft could be moved quickly in the event of an emergency. According to Schmidt, 'All anti-invasion measures were taken. Everyone was on full alert.' As if to validate this policy, on the 5th, Mont de Marsan was strafed by enemy long-range fighters and a shot-up Ju 88 crash-landed in flames on the airfield. A few days later, a large fire broke out close to the runway, causing danger to munitions, fuel and equipment. Arson was suspected.

Nerves became frayed. An officer pilot from 2.*Staffel* committed suicide in the mess, followed shortly after by an Unteroffizier in the *Stabskompanie* who shot himself for reasons unknown. The men were buried in the airfield cemetery.[22]

On the 16th, another senior officer arrived at Mont de Marsan in the form of Oberstleutnant Henning Wilcke from the staff of Holle's X.*Fliegerkorps*, but simultaneously serving as Operations Officer on the staff of the *Fliegerführer Atlantik*. During a discussion with the officers of 1./FAGr 5, Wilcke ordered that in view of the fact that U-boat convoy operations were very unlikely in the immediate future, the *Gruppe* was to stand down for a period of ten days to 26 May – a strange edict given that no long-range reconnaissance missions had been flown for some time![23]

However, in the late evening of 17 May, after a break of several days, over-water flights recommenced: one Ju 290 was picked up by Allied listeners flying coastal security reconnaissance, followed by another on a similar sortie the following evening, while on the morning of the 19th, two Ju 290s were involved in radio exercises with three Kriegsmarine surface ships in the Bay of Biscay.[24] That night, Ju 290A-7 9V+FH, piloted by Hellmut Nagel of 1./FAGr 5, was airborne again when it departed Mont de Marsan at 2130 hrs on a security reconnaissance over the Biscay. Ninety minutes into the flight, however, one of its engines failed, but it continued with its mission, returning at 0730 hrs in the morning after a 2,500-km flight lasting ten hours![25]

The middle of the month also saw a return to limited convoy reconnaissance operations. The absence of any meaningful form of U-boat operations in the Atlantic at this time suggests that it must have been intended to fly these missions as reconnaissance for air attack by the He 177s of KG 40.

On the 22nd, two Ju 290s, 'D' and 'F', took off during the mid-afternoon for reconnaissance to the west and south-west of Spain. The day before, the northbound convoy SL.158, which had departed Freetown on the 11th, comprising 26 merchants and three escorts, rendezvoused with MKS.49 en route from Port Said and Gibraltar. The combined convoy totalled around 45 vessels plus four escorts, two submarines, a rescue vessel and an oiler.[26] It had also been joined by the British-built escort carrier HMS *Nairana*, which, although in need of a refit and capable of only 15 knots, carried 835 NAS, a composite squadron equipped with Swordfish and Sea Hurricane IICs.[27] It was probably this convoy that the Junkers' FuG 200 *Hohentwiel* picked up shortly after 2200 hrs in 23° West 1630. The crews later reported that the convoy was 'spread out over 10–15 km.'[28] One Swordfish pilot on board *Nairana* recalled the conditions the convoy faced that day: 'The weather was foul – mountainous seas, gale-force winds, low cloud and minimal visibility.'[29] The Junkers made it back to Mont de Marsan at 0230 hrs and 0430 hrs respectively.[30]

The next day, it seems FAGr 5 aircraft did not go out into the Atlantic, and the task of shadowing the convoy fell to a Bv 222 of 1./SAGr 129 from Biscarosse which, like the Ju 290s, picked up the convoy by radar.[31]

On the 25th, FAGr 5 intensified its efforts against SL.158/MKS.49 when it despatched two Junkers from Mont de Marsan in the early afternoon. At 2038 hrs, *Nairana* reported detecting an enemy aircraft 'in the neighbourhood of the convoy'. At 2045 hrs, the Ju 290s reported the convoy as 54 merchant vessels, three destroyers and one aircraft carrier, course 360°, at six knots.[32] By 2100 hrs, *Nairana* had increased the call of enemy aircraft to four, of which one was firmly identified as a Ju 290, but they had all departed by 2109 hrs. However, the convoy reported being shadowed by another Ju 290 from 2239 hrs; this was the new A-7 Wk-Nr 0187 9V+LK of 2./FAGr 5 and it was 'attacked by fighters without observed results' which were probably Sea Hurricanes of 835 NAS operating from the carrier. Certainly, two Sea Hurricanes flown by Lieutenant Allen R. Burgham, RNZNVR, and Sub-lieutenant Charles Richardson, RNVR, were flown off to intercept and opened fire on an enemy aircraft before it escaped into cloud, after which its presence disappeared from the carrier's radar screen.[33] As Burgham recounted:

In the afternoon *Nairana* began refuelling a frigate. While this was taking place *Nairana* picked up a radar contact and ordered 'Scramble Two Fighters'. Richardson and I manned our aircraft and prepared to take off. *Nairana* continued with the refuelling as we sat in our cockpits ready to go! Shortly thereafter a Ju 290 approached from astern and flew fairly low over the starboard side. I remember feeling extremely frustrated. I am not 100 per cent sure of the timing of these next events, but after the refuelling was interrupted or completed, the radar had another contact and Richardson and I were scrambled and vectored to intercept. After a while, but a little too soon, the Fighter Direction Officer gave us a change of course onto a reciprocal, thinking we had passed the target. I turned to starboard when Charles, who by this time had been obscured by my wing, shouted 'Tally Ho', and whipped into a turn to Port. Not seeing the target or knowing its relative position, I tightened my turn and saw a Ju 290 diving for cloud, being chased by Richardson, firing at its disappearing bulk. The 290 soon disappeared from the screen and, as the light was fast fading, we were directed back to the ship.[34]

The 26th would see one Ju 290 'D' conduct a meteorological flight between 24° West 526 to 34° West 106–335–542, turning for its return course at 1200 hrs. Such flights had become more commonplace since the weather-reporting *Staffel* of the Luftwaffe covering the Atlantic coast, *Wekusta* 2, based at Nantes, had been withdrawn to the Reich at the end of March 1944 to re-equip from its Ju 88s to longer-range He 177s. The aircraft of FAGr 5, along with those of KG 40 and *Wekusta* 51 at Toussus in northern France, had taken over such duties during *Wekusta* 2's absence.[35]

The main effort on the 26th, however, came from at least three Ju 290s which carried out shadowing sorties in the eastern Atlantic, but it would prove to be another costly day. Taking off from Mont de Marsan in the early morning hours, Ju 290A-5 WK-Nr 0178 9V+DK, flown by Oberleutnant Günther Pfeiffer with Hauptmann Helmut Miersch as commander, and one of the *Gruppe*'s new Ju 290A-7s, Wk-Nr 0188 9V+FK of 2.*Staffel*, commanded and flown by Oberleutnant Hans-Georg Bretnütz, with Unteroffizier Wolfgang Bock as second pilot, headed south towards SL.158/MKS.49. Around sunrise, Bretnütz's now lone Junkers reached the area of the convoy.

HMS *Nairana* had been with the convoy since 19 May. As (then Lieutenant-Commander) E.E. 'Barry' Barringer, commander of 835 NAS, wrote: 'The protection of this large, slow and vulnerable convoy was our most demanding and eventful operation to date. The weather was bad: strong winds, heavy seas and low cloud, which meant that flying (and particularly flying at night) was never easy.'[36]

Shortly after 0700 hrs, the Ju 290 was in 40° 55′ North 18° 25′ West as it flew off the convoy's starboard beam at low altitude in order to avoid radar detection.[37] The weather had improved somewhat and the cloud had lifted, but very soon the carrier's fighter direction team picked up the shadower. On the flight deck of *Nairana*, wary of the likely presence of enemy aircraft, Lieutenant Burgham and Sub-Lieutenant Richardson were strapped into their Sea Hurricanes. Burgham recalled:

Shortly after standing to and before breakfast, at 0730, as I well remember, Richardson [Sea Hurricane IIc JS304] and I (this time I was flying in [Sea Hurricane IIc] NF672/7K '*Nicki*'), were scrambled again to investigate a contact. Some distance out on the convoy's starboard bow, we saw a Ju 290 which must have just descended to sea level to escape convoy detection. We were at 2,000 or 3,000 ft and decided to separate so that we could attack him from opposite sides. He soon saw us and turned away, putting Richardson in a position to attack first. As he committed himself to a diving attack, the Junkers took the usual evasive action by turning towards him, making it difficult for him to get a bead on it. This meant that the 290 was turning away from me and put me in an excellent position to attack. As I approached it, I could see Charles Richardson closing in astern in a very tight turn, when his wing tip hit a wave and he exploded in a ball of oily flame. As the Junkers began a turn towards me, I came within range, opened fire and began to see pieces falling from the aircraft which climbed a little, then nosed over into the sea, where it exploded.

I checked for survivors, then went to circle the oil slick where Charles' Hurricane had gone in. I could see what appeared to be his 'Mae West', but no sign of life. I circled the site until a Swordfish arrived to 'home-in' an escort vessel. As I circled Richardson's oil patch I began to reflect on what had all happened so quickly and realized that the flashes emerging from various parts of the enemy aircraft, that I had thought nothing of at the time, had actually been muzzle flashes from its guns! It made me realize that this was a little different from all the dummy attacks we used to make on poor innocent aircraft around the skies of the U.K. Before I returned to *Nairana* I dived *'Nicki'* on the remains of the Ju 290 to alert the Swordfish to its position.[38]

In another account, Burgham recalled the moments after he witnessed Richardson's aircraft explode: 'I pressed home my own attack, hitting the Junkers repeatedly at close range. It crashed into the sea and exploded. All that remained of the Junkers was an oil slick and a few floating pieces of debris.'[39]

Ju 290A-7 9V+FK came down at 41° 03′ North 18° 37′ West and was a total loss. Its crew of pilots Oberleutnant Bretnütz and Unteroffizier Bock, along with Leutnant Hans Mahs (observer), Feldwebel Fritz Wiens, Obergefreiter Friedrich Bauer (radio-operators), Gefreiter Eduard Mrowczynski (flight engineer), Unteroffizier Wilhelm Bruckhaus, Unteroffizier Herbert Möller, Obergefreiter Karl Horn and Gefreiter Karl Unger (gunners), were killed. An additional crewman – Unteroffizier Otto Schimank – was believed to have been on board the Junkers and lost his life, making this a loss of 11 men.[40]

Miersch and Pfeiffer's aircraft managed to return safely.[41]

Meanwhile, back at Mont de Marsan, two more crews were hurriedly called from their billets and briefed to fly to SL.158/MKS.49 to report its composition and course. At around 1100 hrs, two Ju 290s of 1./FAGr 5, one with the *Staffelkapitän*, Hauptmann Josef Augustin, on board as commander, with

Hauptmann Willi Pawlittke as first pilot, the other commanded and flown by Leutnant Kurt Nonnenberg, took off in an attempt to fly in the new, two-aircraft tactical formation, spaced at 50 m apart, for mutual protection. To conserve available aircraft, Nonnenberg's crew had borrowed a Junkers of 2.*Staffel*, the A-4 Wk-Nr 0164 9V+GK, one of the original machines to be delivered to the *Gruppe* while it was forming up at Achmer.[42] The Junkers' task, like that of the ill-fated crew of Hans-Georg Bretnütz, was to shadow SL.158/MKS.49. Such was the importance attached to their mission, that for the first time, the Ju 290s were given an escort of Ju 88C-6s from ZG 1 which flew with them as far as Cape Ortegal before turning back.[43]

As Josef Augustin recalled:

A ship convoy in the area west of Portugal (approximately 12° West) was to be assessed, with the number of ships, composition, course etc., and we were to report the information via radio, and for the first time this Atlantic reconnaissance was to be carried out with two aircraft ... The aircraft flew together and also for the first time on the outward flight across the Bay of Biscay, we were escorted by a Ju 88 *Zerstörerstaffel*.[44]

Both aircraft were fitted with FuG 200, and at least one was carrying a *Schwan* automatic D/F buoy. They made their way as a pair at about 400 m, with Hauptmann Pawlittke leading.[45] The Ju 88s stayed with them as far as the coast of Spain, as Augustin remembered: 'The *Zerstörer* had picked us up at Arcachon, on the coast, west of Bordeaux, and escorted both Ju 290s as far as the cliffs of the north-western coast of Spain, near Cape Ortegal, where, with a waggle of their wings, they left us. With their protection, the flight across the Biscay had been very calm and not so strained.'

The two Ju 290s were now some 2500 km from their base and over the Atlantic. They had been in the air for over six hours:

Once the fighters left us, we went down to 200 m. Since we were far out over the sea, we had to maintain complete radio silence, and we had to carry out our long approach flight [to the convoy] using astro-navigation. Once we had got to within an estimated 70 km of the convoy, I gave the order to climb to 1000 m so as to fly search circles. Actually, there were already a large number of large and small blips on the screen of the *Hohentwiel* equipment.

The theory was that, using its FuG 200, a Ju 290 would fly a series of up to 19 'search circles'. The aircraft would fly to a designated point over the sea, switch on its radar and 'sweep' a 'circle' of 80-km diameter, then switch off.

It would then fly a straight course, to a point 80 km farther on, and repeat the procedure, meaning that the radius of the new circle overlapped with the sea surface area representing the radius of the previous circle. A third and fourth circle would be swept and overlapped, at which point the aircraft would turn 90° to port and fly 160 km before activating its next sweep in the first circle of a new row of four circles running in parallel to the row of the three just covered. This meant, however, that the new circle and the last did not overlap. At the end of that row, the aircraft would again change course, and fly another row of four circles, before turning again for a fourth and final row. This way, the aircraft would sweep a net of 19 circles in three rows of five and one of four, covering an area of sea c.500 km by 480 km.

However, even before the U-boats had left the Atlantic, the function of 'shadowing', as it had been known, had been abandoned to a great extent owing to the danger posed by increasing numbers of enemy carrier-based aircraft; thus, from the early spring of 1944, most Ju 290 pilots flying lone sorties chose simply to circle a convoy at a respectable distance, some making their approaches at low altitude from the west to make their observations.

When two Ju 290s operated, and the weather conditions were clear, they would fly at a height of between 20 and 40 m, and close together for mutual protection as per recently established tactical doctrine. In cloudy weather, the aircraft would fly at a greater distance apart. The normal search method in clear conditions was a creeping line ahead, with a distance of up to 50 km between legs; on searches of this kind, the FuG 200 was not necessarily employed. In poor visibility or cloud, the search took the form of a direct course outwards and a parallel homeward course at a distance of 100 km from the outward course. In this type of search, the *Hohentwiel* was activated at intervals of 50–60 km, when the aircraft rose to make a rate one searching turn, resuming its original course at sea level.[46]

Meanwhile, HMS *Nairana* had remained on a high state of alert, as Barry Barringer recorded:

> In the afternoon there were more shadowers ... By now there was a great deal of cloud about and a little before 1600 hrs two aircraft were detected coming in from the east at 5,000 ft. Lt Stephen 'Sam' Mearns [in NF698/7D] and S/Lt Frank Wallis, who were strapped into their Hurricanes at instant readiness, were flown off and vectored towards the approaching planes.
>
> Our Hurricanes were manouevred into the ideal position: about a thousand feet above the enemy aircraft – which were identified as a pair of Ju 290s – and up sun. Mearns and Wallis then carried out a diving attack on the leading Junkers, which saw them coming, opened fire with tracer and

tried to get down to sea level. (The idea of this was at sea level it couldn't be attacked from below.) However, it had neither the manoeuvrability nor the defensive armament to escape.[47]

Augustin continues:

The convoy was located. While we were analyzing the screen, the rear gunner gave the alarm call: 'Fighters behind us.' And already the first tracer whizzed past – like a little snowball – over our left wing. The order was given 'Fire at will' and the aircraft nearly rolled over as it headed for the safety of the surface of the water. The rear gunner and the forward turret opened fire at full blast.

Barringer:

Opening fire at a range of 250 yards with high-explosive incendiaries, our Hurricanes brought a lethal weight of fire to bear on the German plane which was quickly shot down, though the pilot, with no little skill, managed to ditch his shattered aircraft before it exploded.

Augustin:

As I turned towards our companion aircraft, a long tail of fire shot out of its left inner engine. It had already been hit. Everything happened very quickly, and suddenly the tail gun position reported back excitedly: 'Enemy fighter was hit; crashed; fighter has disappeared in the water.' As we had to reckon on further attacks from carrier aircraft, we flew even closer to the surface of the water. Our companion aircraft had quickly disappeared from view. Any help from us – almost 2500 km from base – would have been hopeless.

Aboard 9V+GK, Unteroffizier Hans Baur, the rear gunner, and the gunner in the rear dorsal position opened fire at the Hurricanes, but the latter's MG 151 cannon jammed. With the port inner engine on fire and the wing damaged, the inside of the Junkers rapidly began to fill with smoke. To make matters worse, the second pilot, Oberfeldwebel Gerhard Hartig, who had been at the controls at the time, had been seriously wounded and so Leutnant Nonnenberg took over and decided to attempt to ditch the aircraft.[48]

However, Augustin's crew had been mistaken over the apparent fate of one of the Hurricanes. Barringer continues: 'Mearns and Wallis then turned their attention to the second Junkers. It, however, very prudently first sought refuge in the clouds, and then made for home.'

In this, the FAA pilots were somewhat mistaken, as Josef Augustin relates:

It was obvious to us that because of his excellent radar devices, the enemy had picked us up early on, and therefore the surprise fighter attack. But the remaining fighters had suddenly disappeared – whether because of fuel, or whatever reason, it didn't matter – we remained without further attack. Because of this, although identified by the convoy escort, I ordered the mission to continue. Probably because the enemy reckoned they had shot us down, we were then able to fly around the convoy well to the south, then switch to a westerly course and subsequently flew with sufficient safe distance in the direction of the convoy to the north. We determined the number of vessels, composition, course and its estimated speed and transmitted our encoded report, along with a weather report for the sea area, via the radio.

As the convoy steamed away far to the north, so we made course for home. It was a long return flight, undertaken entirely using astro-navigation. Thank God, the moon and the stars were shining brightly. Our instruments and sextants gave us a position, which was out by about 30 km on the whole route. However, this was something of a problematic deviation, since the Pyrenees could become a dangerous obstacle during a night flight.

During the night, around 0100 hrs, we crossed the French coast. Here, also, we experienced a sudden surprise. Though we fired a flare pistol using the daily recognition code, we took fire from our own Flak. Although the Flak shot well and we were only at a height of 80 m, on this occasion we were incredibly fortunate – it is a wonder we were not hit. Around 0200 hrs we landed at Mont de Marsan after an 18-hour flight.[49]

From the crew of 9V+GK, Oberfeldwebel Hartig (second pilot), Unteroffizier Walter Elies (2nd radio-operator), Feldwebel Erich Butschies (gunner), Oberfeldwebel Aloys Looschelders (flight engineer) and Unteroffizier Peter Demarteau (gunner) were killed when the Ju 290 crashed into the sea. Kurt Nonnenberg and Feldwebel Herbert Köhler (gunner) survived but were injured, while Leutnant Hans Koitka (observer), Feldwebel Wilhelm Meyer (radio operator) and Unteroffizier Hans Baur (rear gunner) were more fortunate to survive uninjured. The Junkers' main survival dinghy had been holed during the attack by the Hurricanes and so the five survivors resorted to using their one-man dinghies.

Barringer recalled:

As far as the Squadron were concerned the Battle of the Atlantic was fought without rancour and a Swordfish, with Joe Supple as pilot and Johnny Lloyd as observer, was flown off to locate the survivors and keep them company. Joe and Johnny found them, a tiny speck in a vast sea, and stayed circling them, waving encouragement, until they were picked up by one of the escorting corvettes.[50]

The men from FAGr 5 were shipped to England where Nonnenberg and Köhler were taken to hospital, while the three other survivors were slated for interrogation. According to the subsequent interrogation report:

> Survivors of the crew of this aircraft are unanimous in blaming the bad leadership of Hauptmann Pawlittke in the first aircraft, who flew at the dangerous height of 400 m in bad visibility. The sea was calm and visibility at sea level was good; had they flown at a height of 20/40 m, the normal height for such operations, prisoners were of the opinion that the fighter attack could not have been successful.[51]

The body of Charles Richardson, who had taken part in the earlier of the two encounters, was recovered by the escort destroyer *Highlander*. According to Barringer, on the morning of the 27th, '*Highlander* took station close on our starboard beam. Once again the squadron lined up on the flightdeck. Once again there was a moment of absolute silence while every ship in convoy, its flag at half-mast, stopped its engines as the body of Charles Richardson slid into the grey waters of the Atlantic.'[52]

The action taken by the members of 835 NAS against the Ju 290s on 26 May was recognized in the form of various citations for its pilots and personnel. Al Burgham, Stephen Mearns, Frank Wallis and Charles Richardson (posthumously) were mentioned in despatches 'for courage and skill' in engaging, driving off, or shooting down Ju 290s on 25 and 26 May that were 'menacing convoy SL.158/MKS.49'.[53]

To deal with its losses FAGr 5 had developed a policy of creating new crews by reshuffling existing crews and bringing in replacements from the *Ergänzungs-Fernaufklärungsgruppe* at Posen and who received training on the Ju 290 at Mont de Marsan.[54] But FAGr 5 was soon to experience more tragedy.

In the evening of 30 May, the recently delivered Ju 290A-7 Wk-Nr 0187 (KR+LR) 9V+LK of 2./FAGr 5 left Mont de Marsan to conduct a security reconnaissance flight over the Bay of Biscay. The aircraft's commander and 1st pilot was Leutnant Heinz Ernst. Having completed its mission, at some point on the homebound flight, the Ju 290 was over the Spanish coast when it crashed into hills near the town of Posada de Llanes, midway between the ports of Gijon and Santander. The entire 11-man crew of Ernst, Unteroffizier

Martin Steinbock (second pilot), Fahnenjunker-Feldwebel Hans Haberer (observer), Feldwebel Walter Borntrink, Unteroffizier Wolfgang Hertz (radio operators), Unteroffizier Friedrich Strobel (flight engineer), Oberfeldwebel Willi Schmalfeldt, Feldwebel Otto Borkowski, Feldwebel Kurt Bartoschewski, Unteroffizier Alfred Janke and Obergefreiter Paul Neumann (gunners), was killed. Their remains were recovered and moved to the *Deutscher Soldat Militärfriedhof* at Cuacos de Yuste, 210 km west of Madrid.[55]

The official strength figures for FAGr 5 for May 1944 were as follows:

Stab	1 A-3
1.*Staffel*	5 A-5
	2 A-7
2.*Staffel*	2 A-3
	2 A-5
	5 A-7
Total	17

But of these figures, far fewer aircraft were either being used operationally or were fully serviceable. Furthermore, two of the new A-7s, the enhanced variant needed by the unit, had been lost, one within eight weeks of being delivered, the other within six days of being received. At least 31 airmen had been killed on missions during the month.

Back in Germany, on Tuesday, 23 May 1944, the weaknesses of the Ju 290 and its planned successor, the Ju 390, came under scrutiny, by no less than Reichsmarschall Göring. He was in a bitingly cynical, though remarkably prognostic mood when he chaired a high-level aircraft production conference attended by the Reichsminister for Armaments and War Production, Albert Speer, as well as Milch, *General der Flieger* Günther Korten, the Luftwaffe Chief of General Staff and other senior Luftwaffe technical officers. Göring asked:

The following point now arises: what can be done to make possible reconnaissance at extreme ranges? What type of aircraft do I have for this purpose? There are the Ju 290 and Ju 390, types which have a colossal fuel consumption, and now – keep a firm hold on yourselves and don't fall under the table – the Me 264 [a planned long-range, four-engined reconnaissance/bomber intended for Atlantic operations]! This aircraft, which need be produced only in small numbers and could be further improved, would give us a much faster aircraft than the 290 and would make reconnaissance at extreme ranges possible. I would set a definite limit – and we have all agreed on this point – of one *Gruppe*, which could be set up to strength. This unit would be allotted special long-range reconnaissance duties and we must consider the possibilities if the 264 were especially adapted for this work. If this were done, we could exclude all the types which devour so much fuel such as the 290, the 390 and the [Junkers] 288.[56]

Indeed, the rumours stemming from such high-level discussions quickly trickled back to Mont de Marsan; on 2 June, Leutnant Herbert Wagner, a pilot of 1./FAGr 5 who frequently flew with Major Fischer, returned from a trip to Berlin to where he had accompanied the *Gruppenkommandeur*. Wagner told his comrades that there was a rumour the new, six-engined Ju 390 had been cancelled.[57]

It had been a grim end to the month, and it was not about to get any better, as Oskar Schmidt recalled:

The radar devices on the enemy fighters were getting better. This gave us greater problems, because the enemy could identify our aircraft long before we could determine the enemy. Thus more and more attacks occurred – suddenly the enemy would emerge from the cloud, and nothing is worse than surprise! We did have *Hohentwiel*, but it was meant exclusively for ship-search.[58]

On the last day of the month, as mentioned above, the *Gruppenkommandeur*, Major Fischer, was summoned to Berlin by the *Luftwaffenführungsstab*, where he was to attend a meeting to discuss FAGr 5's recent operational performance and any resulting measures that needed to be taken. In his absence, the *Gruppe* was left with a feeling of uneasiness over what might happen on his return.[59]

CHAPTER ELEVEN

FLIGHT AND FIGHT

June–August 1944

Anything that had legs had to go up in the air.

Oskar H. Schmidt, *Stabskompanie*, FAGr 5

In the early hours of the morning of 6 June 1944, three Ju 290s returned from a luckless radar reconnaissance patrol to the west of Gibraltar. No convoys had been found, and in all too familiar circumstances, one Junkers had had to return early, suffering from technical problems.[1] However, at the same time, far more momentous events were taking place, as expected, as the Allies landed in France, pouring 155,000 men along with thousands of vehicles onto the beaches of Normandy. The Allied air cover for the opening of *Overlord* was immense, with sufficient capability to fly more than 14,500 sorties within the first 24 hours, dwarfing any meagre Luftwaffe reaction that there was. For the German military, the war had taken a dramatic, alarming and irreversible new turn.

The day after the landings, Major Fischer called the senior officers of *Fernaufklärungsgruppe* 5 together to advise them of a significant decision taken in Berlin:

In the interests of the *Reichsverteidigung* (Air Defence of the Reich), production of the Ju 290 and Ju 390 is to end. The operations of the *Fernaufklärungsgruppe* are to terminate. The unit will, on occasion, continue to fly *Sicheraufklärung* (security reconnaissance) along the coast, but the original tasks are to end. No replacement aircraft for the Ju 290 and Ju 390 are foreseen for the unit. The *Gruppe* is to remain at its present location at Mont de Marsan. However, if the U-boat arm is to be re-equipped and to go on to the offensive again, will not air reconnaissance certainly be required? A '*Führer* Directive' is awaited over the further deployment of FAGr 5.[2]

But such a '*Führer* Directive' never came.

FAGr 5 continued to carry out long-range Atlantic flights during the first week of June; at 1448 hrs on the 3rd, Leutnant Hellmut Nagel of 1./FAGr 5 took off at the controls of Ju 290A-5 Wk-Nr 0170 9V+DH for the eastern Atlantic. His crew picked up the presence of what they reported as a 'west–east convoy'.[3] Over the 4/5 and 5/6 June, more patrols were sent out to track the ships. In the case of the former dates, three Ju 290s were sent out, again as a group and again escorted by Ju 88s of ZG 1 over the Bay of Biscay, to conduct a radar search to the south-west of Portugal for the SL.159/MKS.50 convoy from Freetown and Gibraltar bound for Liverpool. The convoy comprised 33 merchant vessels and had sailed from Freetown on 17 May and from Gibraltar on the 30th. The Junkers flew to Cape Ortegal, then to Cape Finisterre, then to Cape Roca in Portugal, where the group split and each aircraft flew a different patrol route before returning to Mont de Marsan. The convoy was not found, and the only vessel picked up was a lone 'independent' at 1940 hrs. All aircraft returned safely.[4]

Another attempt was made on the 5th, with three Ju 290s flying out at around 1430 hrs, escorted by six Ju 88s of ZG 1. The Junkers patrolled an area west of Gibraltar using FuG 200, but again the convoy eluded them. One of the aircraft was forced to break off early because of technical difficulties, probably connected to its *Hohentwiel* set.[5]

Over the night of 8/9 June, the crew of Oberleutnant Günther Korn of 1./FAGr 5 flew in Ju 290 Wk-Nr 0170 9V+DH to the Spanish coast, and north-west of Santander they dropped a FuG 302 *Schwan* buoy as a trial under operational conditions.[6]

After the first week of June, FAGr 5 effectively ended operations over the Atlantic, although it remained at readiness with just a few crews. For his part, Major Fischer spent his time increasingly away in Berlin, working with the *General der Aufklärungsflieger* and was rarely to be seen at Mont de Marsan.[7]

For most of June, flying was confined to security reconnaissance over the Bay of Biscay, although shortly after 0945 hrs on the morning of the 23rd, a pair of Ju 290s was despatched to search for a northbound convoy passing the Bay. Despite not returning until after midnight, once again the convoy was not located.[8]

At the end of May 1944, one of FAGr 5's aircraft and crew, Ju 290A-7 Wk-Nr 0190 9V+MK, commanded by Hauptmann Emil Sachtleben of 2.*Staffel*, was assigned a special task and ordered to fly via Dessau and Pretsch in Germany, then via Aalborg in Denmark, to Trondheim-Vaernes, the new base for the Fw 200s of III./KG 40 in Norway. While en route, at Pretsch special solar compasses were fitted to the aircraft for its forthcoming mission.[9]

Since 1941, the Germans had maintained weather stations in the Arctic. These were extremely important because the path of low-pressure areas over the North Atlantic, from west to east, is determined by the position and movement of cold Artic air masses.[10] The synoptic analysis of weather systems moving over the Atlantic was therefore information that became crucial to both the Kriegsmarine and the Luftwaffe in their campaign against the convoys, and so an attempt was made to set up a network of weather stations in the High Arctic.

One such station, under the expedition name *Bassgeiger*, was established by the Kriegsmarine in the summer of 1943 at Cape Sussi on the uninhabited, High Arctic coast of Shannon Island in North-East Greenland. *Bassgeiger* would be one of only two such stations to become active and which would winter on the remote Arctic shores. The expedition had travelled to Greenland via the *Wetterbeobachtungsschiffe* (WBS – Weather Reporting Ship) *Coburg* from Narvik in August 1943. But after several weeks of forcing a passage through the ice belt, the *Coburg* became stuck in ice eight kilometres off the nearest land – Cape Sussi at 75° 20′ North on the island of Shannon, stranding the nine-man weather team and the ship's crew of 18. Eventually, the expedition struggled its way ashore, manhandling its equipment; they established a base of tents erected inside a system of tunnels that they dug inside a large snowdrift, some three metres high and 40 metres wide, near the cape and which would house their accommodation and radio equipment.

Sporadic supply and mail air-drops to *Bassgeiger* were flown by Fw 200s of 3./KG 30 based at Trondheim from September 1943 into the spring of 1944. In April 1944, however, *Bassgeiger* fought an encounter with the Danish North-East Greenland Sledge Patrol, which resulted in the death of the German expedition's military commander, Leutnant Gerhard Zacher; in May, the wrecked WBS *Coburg*, still out on the sea ice, was abandoned and blown up. With all 26 remaining men crowded into tents in the tunnels, without a ship, and running low on supplies, it was decided that a rescue operation had to be mounted.[11]

On 2 June, an Fw 200 C flown by Hauptmann Robert Maly, the *Staffekapitän* of 3./KG 40, left Trondheim for eastern Greenland carrying 9200 l of fuel. Also on board was Emil Sachtleben, who was to survey the emergency airstrip which had been prepared by the *Bassgeiger* team. After passing over the proposed landing site, the Condor turned back for Norway and landed safely at 2055 hrs after 13 hours of flying.

The next morning, at 0828 hrs, Ju 290 9V+MK, which had been modified for very long-range flights, took off from Trondheim flown by Hauptmann Sachtleben with Oberfeldwebel Kreutzmann as second pilot. On board was a full crew, as well as a war reporter and the adjutant to a general – in all, 16 men. After a one-hour search in cloud and mist, the Junkers, weighing 37 tons, landed successfully on the one-metre thick ice at Nordenskjolds Bugt, south of Cape Sussi at 1517 hrs. It took 40 minutes for the weather team to load its equipment, then, along with the crew of the WBS *Coburg*, they boarded the Ju 290. Sachtleben took off again at 1600 hrs with no fewer than 42 men on board the Junkers, and returned safely to Trondheim at 2206 hrs, despite some damage being inflicted to the aircraft's flaps during landing on Shannon Island.[12]

On 6 June, 9V+MK left Trondheim to return to Mont de Marsan, staging via Aalborg and Ludwigslust, where the damage suffered in Greenland was repaired. By 13 June, the aircraft resumed reconnaissance operations over the Bay of Biscay.[13]

On 12 June, in an exceptional development for a Luftwaffe air unit, FAGr 5 played a direct part in the war against the *maquisards* of the French Resistance. Since early 1944, the *Maquis* had gradually intensified its activities against the German military infrastructure in France in the lead-up to the Allied invasion. In an early example in February, Resistance fighters at a Peugeot factory at Sochaux-Montbéliard, in the east of the country, making aircraft parts, inflicted sufficient damage on equipment to interrupt production for five weeks; when new machine tools eventually arrived, they were destroyed on arrival. As the anticipated invasion drew nearer, such activity saw a widespread increase; in May at Bagnères-de-Bignorre in the Pyrenees, a factory involved in producing parts for self-propelled guns was put out of action for six months after an operation by a local Resistance cell supported by British agents. In the same month, a railway locomotive depot was destroyed in the eastern town of Ambérieu and 52 engines made unusable, while at Bar in the Corrèze, a hydro-electric station was so badly damaged it was inoperative for four months. Across occupied France, German forces were on high alert, while the security forces attempted to hunt down and deal with the Resistance groups.

Then, on the eve of *Overlord*, a coded message from London, broadcast openly on the BBC, called upon the *Maquis* across France to cut railway lines throughout the country. Of 1,050 pre-planned railway sabotage operations, 950 were executed.[14] Nowhere was safe.

On the 12th, Major Fischer, back at Mont de Marsan from Berlin, once more called his senior officers for a meeting. He told them that information emanating from reliable agents warned of an attack being planned by the *Maquis* against the airfield. Furthermore, in the town of Riscle, 45 km south-east of Mont de Marsan on the River Adour, a strong group of *maquisards* had cut off and surrounded a company of Wehrmacht construction troops. It had been decided by senior command that a 'battle group' made up of elements of FAGr 5 and commanded by Fischer, together with all the unit commanders of the *Gruppe*, would 'capture' the town, engage the Resistance fighters there, and free the beleaguered construction company.

After this had sunk in, Fischer and his officers discussed the creation of a motorized column, its size and the weaponry required. The tactical method of attack was not decided upon, and although they had grave concerns about their lack of weapons training and capability, the airmen believed that a mobile attack was the only way to go. It was also decided that their route to Riscle would be via Grenade and Aire sur Adour.

That afternoon, an advance patrol of 15 NCOs and men led by Hauptmann Walter Schoof – a pilot of 1./FAGr 5, a former member of 3.(F)/Aufkl.Gr.10, and a recipient of the *Ehrenpokal* and the *Deutsche Kreuz in Gold* – departed to investigate the situation in Riscle.

At 0345 hrs on the morning of the 13th, a fully motorized main column under the command of Major Fischer together with his *Staffelkapitäne*, Hauptmann Augustin and Hauptmann Eckl, and Oberleutnant Schmidt of the *Stabskompanie*, moved off, supported by a platoon of light Flak from the airfield Flak unit. A short while later, on the country roads between Grenade and Aire sur Adour, the head of the column came upon some men of the advance troop sent out under Hauptmann Schoof. They were badly wounded. It transpired that the advance group had never reached Riscle, for, as it crossed the bridge in Aire sur Adour, it came under heavy fire from the basement windows of nearby houses. Hauptmann Schoof and eight of his men had jumped for safety into the river and escaped only by clambering along the riverbank. However, six of his men remained badly wounded in the town. Schoof and those men with him had made their way back towards Mont de Marsan along a different route of country roads, creeping carefully through roadside ditches. Unfortunately, in the process, they ran into another Resistance group and they took more heavy fire. Schoof was hit and wounded in the stomach but managed to continue, while Feldwebel Samosch of 2./FAGr 5 was so badly wounded that he simply lay in the road where he had been hit.

A short while later, the main column under Fischer found Schoof and he was immediately sent back to hospital in Mont de Marsan where his wounds were treated by both the FAGr 5 doctor as well as French medics.

The fact was that if the main column had arrived just ten minutes earlier, the *Maquis* attack could have been prevented. However, because the situation facing the main column could not be accurately assessed and in order to avoid further losses, Fischer ordered a return to Mont de Marsan. But as the column turned around, so it was fired upon from a farm close to the road. After a short period of time, the farmhouse was surrounded, entered and searched, where the only people to be found remaining were the apparently innocent owners, and a single wounded civilian who had been hit in the fight with the men of Schoof's advance group.

As the column made its way back to Mont de Marsan, so it was fired upon again from a house in Grenade, but on this occasion two armed civilians were captured. Then, eight kilometres from the airfield, while it progressed through wooded countryside, it happened again. This time, the Germans combed the woods and saw civilians making off on bicycles who managed to escape. After that, the column reached Mont de Marsan without further incident.

Oskar Schmidt recalled: 'This badly prepared "operation" had no success and resulted only in senseless sacrifice. The attacks on the column at various places showed that this was an organized and well-coordinated operation on the part of the *Maquis* … Aside, we were worried about the fate of our remaining soldiers.'[15]

At midday, the *Gruppe* received orders to mount further assaults on Aire sur Adour and Riscle with the aim of freeing both towns of the Resistance. This time, the FAGr 5 battle group would be joined by an infantry unit based to the south. At around 1400 hrs, 100 heavily armed troops led by Major Fischer moved off towards the south, but as soon as it reached Grenade, the column came under heavy fire and became engaged in a fierce battle. Deploying the Flak guns and heavy infantry weapons it had brought with it, the FAGr 5 group gradually flushed out the Resistance 'nests', including those strongly barricaded in the local police station. However, the fighting claimed casualties on the German side, both dead and wounded, with a number of vehicles damaged as well. At 1555 hrs, with Grenade free of the *Maquis*, the battle group claimed victory and was able to return to Mont de Marsan, since news came through that the infantry had taken Aire sur Adour as well with little resistance.

Also stumbling into Mont de Marsan that day was one of FAGr 5's drivers, Obergefreiter Lewan, who had been the driver for Hauptmann Schoof's reconnaissance group the day before. When Schoof's group had come under attack, their lorry was shot up, but Lewan had jumped out and taken cover in a ditch. After the battle, he remained there for several hours in the darkness, close to the *maquisard* positions and listened to their conversations as they tended to their own wounded. Lewan was astonished to hear some of them apparently conversing in German! Eventually, he managed to escape and wandered around the countryside, without a map, until he finally returned to Mont de Marsan, completely exhausted.[16]

During the action against the Resistance, FAGr 5 suffered several personnel killed or badly wounded; from 1.*Staffel*, Hauptmann Schoof died of his wounds on the 16th and was buried with full military honours in the local military cemetery the next evening, while Unteroffizier Adam Wolk, a pilot, and Untertoffizier Herbert Losch, an air gunner, were killed during the operation. Flight engineer Feldwebel Hermann Starge, observer Gefreiter Heinz-Emil Pütz and gunner Gefreiter Manfred Gierschner were badly wounded. From 2./FAGr 5, Feldwebel Horst Hille (pilot), Feldwebel Emil Broszio (radio-operator) and Unteroffizier Hans Roth (gunner) were all wounded.[17] There were other casualties among the ground personnel of the *Gruppe*, including Obergefreiter Lewan.

Over the next few days, a high state of alert and anxiety pervaded Mont de Marsan. In consequence of the Allied landings and the subsequent marked increase in Resistance activity, all leave was cancelled for German military personnel. Security at all of FAGr 5's accommodation was strengthened resulting in considerable disruption; each evening the personnel of 1.*Staffel* left their billets on the Rue de Manon to join those of 2.*Staffel* in the former girls' school building. The *Stabskompanie* was farthest from the airfield, in quarters in the centre of the town, where the guard was particularly enforced. It was later joined by the signals section of the *Gruppe*.

During the evening of the 14th, word came through that the *Maquis* were about to launch an attack on a local fuel depot, and a detachment of men from the *Stab* of FAGr 5 was sent to deal with it. By the time they arrived, the depot had already been secured by the Resistance fighters. This had been achieved by *maquisards* wearing German uniforms, driving captured German vehicles and shooting the guards on the gate. As Oskar Schmidt mentions: 'Because our men were neither equipped nor prepared for a night battle, the operation was postponed until the morning.' Schmidt also recalled:

Work continued to reinforce the defences of the individual units' accommodation and security measures generally were increased. The

Stabskompanie accommodation was strongly secured all-round. No *maquisards* could get anywhere near. There was a lot of heightened awareness and teams of men were trained up as assault troops. There was nothing else we could do and had to just watch out as the fighting in Normandy went on. However, bearing in mind the blows that our units there were taking, privately we were quite glad that we were not being sent there immediately. Of course, these were not openly expressed views![18]

On the 15th, FAGr 5 apparently instigated something of a controversial operation. Information from French informants to the local German security forces had revealed that a large group of Resistance fighters was assembling in a town to the north-east of Mont de Marsan. Subsequently, Major Fischer ordered that a Ju 290 should be despatched to bomb the town. Oberleutnant Schmidt expressed grave concerns that innocent lives would be lost in such an operation, but according to Schmidt, that night a Ju 290 was sent to bomb the unidentified town with unknown results.

On the 17th, having distributed motor vehicles, weapons and equipment, Major Fischer once again headed to Grenade and this time secured it without trouble. It seems the Resistance had pulled out. From this point, an uneasy calm settled over the Mont de Marsan area, as well as a growing sense of isolation among the men of FAGr 5 as Oskar Schmidt explains:

> We were both glad and surprised that the road and railway line from Mont de Marsan to Morcenx were still open and that our supply routes had not been cut off. Otherwise the places around Mont de Marsan seem to be in the hands of the resistance. There were too few [German] troops in our area. The few that had been there had long since been withdrawn, and sent elsewhere. We received no orders. In any case, there was probably little interest in our few remaining four-engined aircraft. Some of our crews were commandeered for special operations.

Air operations did continue on a sporadic basis, mainly in the form of security reconnaissance patrols. In the evening of the 22nd, for example, Leutnant Nagel of 1./FAGr 5 was airborne from Mont de Marsan in Ju 290 9V+FH at 2003 hrs on a patrol over the Bay of Biscay, covering 1700 km in a flight lasting over six hours.[20]

The next day, a small formation of Mosquitos attacked Mont de Marsan airfield, but the airfield Flak defences gave a good account of themselves and drove the enemy fighter-bombers off without their having caused much damage. During the raid, the *Gruppe* had also deployed some of its 20 mm MG 151 cannon which the crews had rigged up onto the backs of vehicles in an attempt to make what was mockingly referred to as a mobile 'anti-invasion weapon'.

In the meantime, Major Fischer led another heavily armed foray to Aire sur Adour, but when the column arrived, the town was quiet and apparently vacated by the Resistance. The FAGr 5 column located one of its missing vehicles in the town and set about towing it back to Mont de Marsan. Unfortunately, however, on the way, it caught fire and had to be abandoned.

The news from Normandy was grave; on 29 June, although Caen remained in German hands, the port of Cherbourg had been lost to the Allies. That day, Feldmarschälle Rommel and von Rundstedt flew to see Hitler at Berchtesgaden to demand significant reinforcements for the battle in Normandy, particularly in aircraft and Flak guns.

The Luftwaffe fighter force was also slowly being bled dry with the demands of the Eastern Front, the protection of the Reich from Allied bombing and in dealing with overwhelming enemy air operations in France. From late June, FAGr 5 began to lose some of its flying personnel for training ahead of posting to the *Jagdverbände* operating on the Western Front or over the Reich.

Certainly, the convoy war in the eastern Atlantic was over. By the end of June 1944, the statistics for the U-boat arm did not look good. The number of ships destroyed in the first quarter of the year was 41 (235,580 GRT) for the loss of 61 U-boats, while by the end of the second quarter, the sinking total was down to 25 vessels (143,978 GRT) for 72 U-boats lost.[21] Until Dönitz could take delivery of the promised new boats, there would be no meaningful operations.

July began with a sudden emergency. According to Schmidt: 'It was a case of "anything that had legs had to go up in the air".' Enemy shipping had been picked up and there was a suspicion that it was another Allied invasion fleet heading for western France.[22] Indeed, in an unprecedented action, no fewer than six Ju 290s were 'scrambled' from Mont de Marsan at 1920 hrs on a reconnaissance mission. This high number of aircraft was probably intended both to ensure a wide and effective search as well as to offer, with the prospect of so much enemy opposition, mutual protection in the air.

Six aircraft took off again from 1720 hrs on the 2nd. In fact, what these Junkers first picked up with their FuG 200 at 0007 hrs on the morning of the 3rd in 23° West 7715 was another combined Liverpool-bound convoy, SL.162/MKS.53, of around 20 vessels plus escort on a course of 330°. Another aircraft confirmed the contact ten minutes later in 23° West 7718, but the convoy's composition could not be made out. Contact was maintained until 0420 hrs, by which time the convoy had reached 23° West 8889. The Ju 290s eventually broke off and all returned safely.[23]

Also on the 3rd, Oberleutnant Paul Birnkraut of 1./ FAGr 5 took off from Mont de Marsan in a Ju 290 on a supply flight to Achmer, which demonstrated remarkably modern air–ground logistics. The Junkers was heavily overloaded: in addition to its crew, it carried 18 other personnel as well as a *Kübelwagen* and a motorcycle. While in the air, the aircraft picked up constant radio warnings of anticipated enemy air attacks on airfields, but it reached Achmer safely and was able to put down. Oberleutnant Schmidt, together with some NCOs from the *Stabskompanie*, drove off to the main vehicle park at Osnabrück to pick up some engine parts. The Ju 290 then flew on to the Junkers plant at Dessau, where it was loaded with aircraft spares. It then returned to Achmer, collected Schmidt, the *Kübelwagen* and the engine parts and landed back at Mont de Marsan at 2200 hrs.

According to British wireless intelligence, another attempt was made on the night of 3/4 July to scour the Atlantic for the convoy so that it could be attacked: 'During the night 3–4/5 it had been intended to repeat moonlight attack on convoy (SL.162/MKS.53) with all available Fw 200s (III./KG 40). Three Ju 290s (FAGr 5) were to be subordinated for battle recce. Operation was cancelled during the morning.'[24]

Far to the east, in Berlin, on 9 July, at the evening situation conference, the Chief of the Luftwaffe Operations Staff Generalleutnant Karl Koller advised that, following a visit from a naval liaison officer, he recognized there was a need for maritime reconnaissance, and while technical problems existed, the Ju 290 and He 177 would be the only aircraft available to fulfil the role in the foreseeable future with the exception of the Me 264, which would be 'built [only] in small quantities.'[25]

This may have been the case, but it did not stop the fact that in addition to transfers to ground units and day fighter units, FAGr 5 was now being required to give up crews to the special operations *Geschwader* of the Luftwaffe, KG 200. On 10 July, the crews of Oberleutnant Günther Korn (who also served as *Staffel* Technical Officer) and Leutnant Siegfried Wache of 1./FAGr 5, along with Hauptmann Hanns Kohmann of 2./FAGr 5, were ordered to report to KG 200 at Fürstenwalde with three Ju 290s for *Sonderaufgaben* (special duties). Simultaneously, in the light of no further guidance or orders being received from any higher Luftwaffe commands, Major Fischer flew again to Berlin in order to ascertain from the office of the *Generalluftzeugmeister* and Generalmajor von Barsewisch what the longer-term intentions were for FAGr 5.

'What now?' recorded Schmidt.[26] 'No aircraft. No *Kommandeur*. No U-boats. No KG 40 [that *Geschwader* was in the process of leaving France]

– and the three units more or less at full strength [in terms of personnel]! And the *Gruppe* languishing at Mont de Marsan in south-western France!"

Fischer returned from Berlin on 16 July – 'Surprisingly quickly,' noted Schmidt. He informed his senior officers that the intention was to 'further develop' *Fernaufklärungsgruppe* 5, replacing the Ju 290 with the He 177 until such time as the prototypes of a new aircraft could be delivered, probably in December 1944 or January 1945. It had been hinted that this aircraft would have sufficient range to cross the Atlantic and reach the East Coast of the United States, which serves as a strong indication that the intention was to equip the *Gruppe* with the Messerschmitt Me 264, a new, ultra-long-range, four-engined reconnaissance/anti-shipping aircraft, the first prototype of which was then undergoing testing with Messerschmitt in Bavaria. In the meantime, as long as there was no requirement from the U-boats, the crews of FAGr 5 would be released for 'special duties' – probably another reference to KG 200. Production of the Ju 290 would be discontinued.[27]

Security reconnaissance patrols and weather flights were maintained by one or two Ju 290s at a time, operating at least every two days into late July. The latter type of mission came to a gradual end when *Wekusta* 2 returned from Germany with its new, but problematic He 177s, moving in to join FAGr 5 at Mont de Marsan.[28] Just after 0530 hrs on the morning of 24 July, for example, one Ju 290 took off and flew out across the coast at 14° West 2568. It made regular weather reports between 0615 and 0950 hrs along a course 14° West 25, 35, 46, 75, 77, 87, and 88, 24° West 19 and 29, and 25° West 20, at which point the aircraft broke off its task. It also reported '2 destroyers or light cruisers' at 1140 hrs in 14° West 0462. On the 29th, Oberleutnant Hans Müller of the *Stab* FAGr 5 commanded Ju 290A-7 Wk-Nr 0191 9V+FK on a weather flight lasting 16 hr 50 min, turning back only once a point west-south-west of Ireland had been reached.[29]

Weather reporting had also taken up an increasing level of importance within FAGr 5's missions as dependence on air attacks against convoys had grown following the slump in U-boat activity. Regierungsrat Dr. Konstantin Blanck, a meteorologist attached to the *Gruppenstab* of FAGr 5, flew 11 missions between 17 May and 5 August 1944, although several of these were frustrated by aircraft or equipment failures. Blanck also conducted tests to investigate measuring cloud height from low-flying aircraft.[30]

While on daily weather flights, the Ju 290s often observed enemy shipping, such as at 0852 hrs on the 2nd when a Junkers spotted a 'convoy of 10 merchant ships up to 1,000 tons in 25° West 2061, course 210°.'[31]

---

*   Schmidt's reference to 'three units' probably includes the 4./FAGr 5, for which see Chapter Twelve.

On the 5th, Ju 290 9V+FK of 2./FAGr 5 took off at 0530 hrs for a weather reconnaissance and returned at 0007 hrs on the 6th. 'When we landed at Mont de Marsan,' the radio-operator Feldwebel Herbert Littek recalled, 'all four engines came to a stop because the fuel had run dry. But our senior command had already written us off.'[32] The same day, Oberleutnant Otto-Karl Kremser, with Regierungsrat Dr. Blanck on board, flew another weather reconnaissance mission in Ju 290A-7 Wk-Nr 0191 9V+AB as far as 54° 00´ North 25° 00´ West. On the way back to France, the Junkers suffered an engine failure as a result of an encounter with two Liberators. The Junkers landed at Mont de Marsan at 0012 hrs on the 6th, after a flight of 18 hr 43 min.[33]

On the 7th, a Ju 290 undertaking weather reconnaissance sighted what was part of SL.165/MKS.56, which had left Freetown on 20 July and Gibraltar on the 29th and comprised 37 merchant vessels. The Junkers was to the west of Ireland when it made contact with the convoy at 1030 hrs, making about five knots on a course 170° to 190° in 25° West 6348 and reported seeing 20 motor vessels, of which four or five were estimated at 10,000 tons. There were also some escort vessels and what was believed to be an escort carrier.[34] This may well have been one of the last, if not the last convoy contact for FAGr 5. Weather flights continued daily until at least the 11th.

For the record, at around this time, Major Fischer prepared a summary of the operations of *Fernaufklärgungsgruppe* 5 from the first days of its operations on 15 November 1943 to 12 August 1944:

OPERATIONS OF FAGr 5 OVER THE ATLANTIC

Operational base:	Mont de Marsan
Period:	15.11.43–12.08.44
Results:	20 enemy convoys detected (of which 14 through visual observation and with photographic confirmation, six with radar [*Hohentwiel*])
Operations (sorties) flown:	191 (approximately 640,750 km)
Flying hours:	2,438 hrs = (av.) 12.7 hrs per operation
Identified merchant ships:	650 units of *c* 4.6 million GRT (visual reconnaissance)]
Warships:	one battleship – six aircraft carriers – seven heavy and eight light cruisers – 65 destroyers – 60 escorts – 15 corvettes
Successes through U-boats:	which led to eight destroyers and one escort
Success achieved through KG 40:	three merchant ships of 18,000 GRT and two corvettes
FAGr 5 own losses:	nine crews (with 20 officers and one official; with Unteroffizier and men = 91). Of this figure, seven crews through enemy action, two crews through technical deficiencies

four operations on instructions of BdU with 54 sorties. Involved coordination with KG 40 and U-boats.
one task for *Marinegruppe West*. Gathering of blockade-runners = 17 sorties.
38 sorties for security reconnaissance.
17 sorties for weather reconnaissance for *Wekusta* 2/OKL.

Evident here is the *Gruppe's* erroneous belief in, or overestimation of, its level of success in operations against enemy naval vessels while operating in cooperation with U-boats. In fact, no destroyers were sunk as a result of such cooperation.

As operational activity gradually declined, Major Fischer was keen that his men kept physically active and alert. The aircrews of 2./FAGr 5 kept themselves busy practising emergency and survival drill with rubber dinghies in the newly completed 'swimming pool' which had been created from the old airport reservoir, although dinghy drill ended when cracks began to appear in the cement! These were repaired and at the end of July, the *Gruppe* indulged in a series of inter-unit swimming and athletic events, as well as tennis, table tennis and rifle and pistol shooting. Hauptmann Sachtleben, the pilot who had rescued the *Bassgeiger* weather team from Greenland in June, proved particularly successful in the pool, while Oberfeldwebel Jaenicke of the *Stabskompanie* excelled at diving, and Oberleutnant Hans Münsterer, a pilot of 2.*Staffel*, won the table tennis tournament.[35]

Not surprisingly, however, against a backdrop of the Third Reich's worsening military predicament, by early August 1944, the situation at Mont de Marsan had become nothing short of surreal. The prevailing sense of uncertainty had grown even stronger since the attempt on the life of the *Führer* the previous month in which Generaloberst Günther Korten, the Chief of Luftwaffe General Staff, had been mortally wounded. FAGr 5's Ju 290s and their crews had no U-boats to support, travelling in the surrounding area had become dangerous because of the ever-present Resistance, men were being posted away from the unit to bolster other units at the various battle fronts, but there was, strangely, plenty of time for sports and games. On 10 August, FAGr 5 was suddenly removed from the tactical jurisdiction of X.*Fliegerkorps*, which had relocated from Angers, north to Reims, to be placed under the command of II.*Fliegerkorps* based at Chartres, though it received no communication or orders from this *Korps* at all. Next day, the female Luftwaffe signals auxiliaries at Mont de Marsan were evacuated. In addition, most of the local *Heer* and military security units had vacated the Mont de Marsan area, to be replaced by the Free India Legion formed by the Indian independence leader, Subhas Chandra Bose, and which based itself at Lacanau, to the west of Bordeaux.

By mid-August, with the Allied armies pushing against trapped German forces in the Falaise pocket, there was serious talk of vacating Mont de Marsan. Major Fischer decided to visit the headquarters of II.*Fliegerkorps* to obtain some guidance on future operations. But as Oskar Schmidt comments: 'We, the *Fernaufklärgungsgruppe* 5, clung on at Mont de Marsan without any military purpose. It was as if we had been forgotten.'[36] On 11 August, Major Fischer returned from his visit to the *Korps*, but none the wiser: 'They don't know what is to be done with us,' he told his staff, 'We're supposed to continue as before.' Schmidt recalled:

So we were still up in the air, and no one felt responsibility for the *Gruppe*, at least at that time … Also in the area were some smaller airfields, intended for fighters, each with a staff of only 50 men. They seemed to be forgotten too. No one seemed responsible for them either. For years there had been no [air] units at these locations.

Because our assignment to the II.*Fliegerkorps* was only a formality (as the *Kommandeur's* visit had proved), did this mean that our only responsible command was the *General der Aufklärungsflieger* in Berlin? In the coming days, the *Kommandeur* wanted to fly to the Reich to get some answers, to explain our precarious position to the General, and to demand some clear orders. It was high time, because the enemy would soon advance down the Rhône valley from the north [a reference to the expected and imminent Allied landings in southern France]. The detailed plans for a retreat by road were now put in force.

The 'heroes' in the *Gruppe*, however, were of the opinion that we still had had 'time'. But we all knew what would happen, in a unit like ours, if there was a sudden command to pull out. The flying crews, the staff and the [technical] 'experts' would leave quickly with the aircraft, and the *Stabskompanie* would have to organize all the Unteroffiziere and men, along with equipment, for a retreat overland by truck.

A withdrawal with vehicles had been ordered by the *Kommandeur*, as Allied forces were advancing ever further in a large pincer movement, and we were in danger of being cut off from being able to return to Germany. But was it still possible to make a safe movement through French territory occupied by the Resistance? [37]

Despite his attempt to fly to Germany, Fischer was prevented from doing so by the Staff of *Luftflotte* 3. Thus, by 13 August, in the absence of any firm directives from high command, Fischer ordered FAGr 5 to prepare to vacate Mont de Marsan by air and by road within days and to relocate to Mühldorf am Inn in Bavaria. Yet despite all the preparations, as far as the road withdrawal was concerned, there were still challenges and difficulties to deal with as Schmidt recalled:

> The question of fuel for the land column was completely unclear. But thank God, there was some good fortune: it happened that the airfield construction company and its staff also had orders to leave, so the manager, Bauleiter Bölt, gave us all his fuel. The procurement of barrels for the petrol and diesel also to be sorted out, but we did it. For the wood-gas-powered vehicles, sufficient quantities of wood were obtained to cover at least a great part of the journey. Once underway, more could be found.
>
> Everything was very tense and understandably so, for everyone wanted an ordered departure in such a situation. The load requirements of the individual technical specialist sections were enormous and they had to be greatly reduced, not without great annoyance. The luggage of each man was, of course, very much increased from his time in Mont de Marsan – wine, cognac (not really acceptable), but we took what was possible. By feverishly feeding fuel from the construction company, we ensured the maximum number of vehicles were available.

In the midst of this, reports came through of increased *Maquis* activity across all of France. 'It was high time we moved!' Schmidt remembered.

But on the 14th, instead of ordering FAGr 5's aircraft to take off for Germany, Fischer instructed that once again the town of Aire sur Adour, now fully occupied by the Resistance, was to be bombed from the air by the unit's Ju 290s. However, as a result of persuasion to the contrary from Hauptmann Augustin and Oberleutnant Schmidt, this was never carried out.

The following day, Oberst im Generalstabsdienst Artur Eschenauer, the *Chef der 6. Abteilung* of the OKL Generalquartiermeister, issued a report which would have ramifications for personnel of FAGr 5. It was addressed to the technical officer on Göring's personal staff, the OKL *Führungsstab* and Generalmajor von Barsewisch. According to Eschenauer:

> The removal of the Ju 290 and Ju 390 from the long-range reconnaissance programme has left a hole which needs to be closed. It is possible that the large amount of assembled parts [for the Me 264] still available would be enough to build 20–30 Me 264s and make them operational. In order to actually realize this, personnel from the *General der Auflkärungsflieger* and *General der Fliegerausbildung* should be placed with *Sonderkommando Nebel* which will have the task of coordinating the testing and deployment of the Me 264.[38]

Meanwhile, 'normal' air operations continued: on the 11th, what is believed to have been the last weather reconnaissance was flown by Leutnant Hellmut Hetz of 1./FAGr 5 in Ju 290A-7 Wk-Nr 0192 9V+HH when he left Mont de Marsan with Leutnant Luc and Fähnrich Brubach on board, returning at 2315 hrs.[39] On the 15th, the day Allied forces landed on the coast of southern France, Leutnant Nagel took off from Mont de Marsan at 1845 hrs in Ju 290 9V+BH to conduct a 40-minute security flight along the Atlantic coast.[40] The aircraft returned safely to Mont de Marsan, which, because of the threat of a direct attack by the Resistance, now resembled a 'fortress'. Also that evening, disregarding the orders of *Luftflotte* 3, Major Fischer instructed the *Gruppenadjutant*, Oberleutnant Herbert Abel, to fly to Dessau and then, via whatever means he could find at his disposal, to get to Berlin. Once there, he was to make contact with Generalmajor von Barsewisch in another attempt to make him aware of the danger facing the personnel and aircraft of the *Gruppe* and to ask for further orders. Abel departed in Ju 290 Wk-Nr 0158 9V+AH, with Oberleutnant Herlein and Oberleutnant Pfeiffer sharing the flying.

'Surely, something had to happen to us?' wrote Oskar Schmidt.

In the town of Mont de Marsan, in the interests of security and safety, the *Stab* and other elements of FAGr 5 evacuated their quarters in the former girls' school and relocated to the quarters of 2.*Staffel*, where conditions became uncomfortably crowded.

Meanwhile, Abel, Herlein and Pfeiffer had made it safely to Berlin, having commandeered a motorcycle and sidecar.[41] They returned on the 17th, bringing with them the redeeming news that the *Luftwaffenführungsstab* had ordered *Fernaufklärungsgruppe* 5 to transfer in its entirety with immediate effect to Mühldorf am Inn. Quite why it had been necessary for three officers to travel to Berlin to ascertain this was a mystery to the Staff of FAGr 5. The first 'official' instruction would not be forthcoming until 21 August when 2.*Fliegerdivision* at Giebelstadt ordered the *Gruppe* to transfer to Mühldorf.[42] Nevertheless, the *Gruppe* immediately began to make preparations for a mass withdrawal from the Atlantic Coast. Many of its crews would soon be embarking on very different tasks and missions – from the testing of new aircraft, to covert operations, to flying the most advanced jet aircraft in the last days of the war.

It is perhaps poignant to note at this point that the German military historian Sönke Neitzel has commented: 'From the very beginning, the few units which operated over the sea were overtaxed to an even greater degree than the rest of the Luftwaffe.'[43]

CHAPTER TWELVE

4./FAGr 5

by Nick Beale

Hold out baits to entice the enemy. Feign disorder,
and crush him.

Sun Tzu, *The Art of War*

The 4./FAGr 5 was formed in the spring of 1944 from *Horch- und Störstaffel* (HuSSt) 2 (Eavesdropping and Jamming Flight 2), the role of which had been to monitor and disrupt RAF Coastal Command's use of radar against U-boats in the Bay of Biscay. HuSSt 2 likewise had a predecessor: *Kommando Rastedter*, which had pioneered this specialism from July or August 1944 through to February 1944. From what little is known of these formations' activity, the emphasis seems to have been on detection since, as discussed at a Kriegsmarine conference in March 1944, the Germans' one airborne jamming set, *Kettenhund* (Watchdog), covered the frequency band of the older Allied ASV radar (Mk II) but not the nine-centimetre wavelength used by the latest ASV Mk III. Any active jamming attempted is likely to have been experimental, since there was clearly a limit to the operations that one (or occasionally two) aircraft per night could achieve.

The new *Staffel* was commanded by a Hauptmann Kunz and its existence first became known to the Allies from a deciphered administrative instruction dated 21 May. Subsequently, those of its flights that became known were largely via routine warnings to the Kriegsmarine and Flak authorities about where and when aircraft could be expected to cross the coast. Four days later, an He 111 of the new *Staffel* was due to take off from Nantes at 2030 hrs and return eight hours later. The British Admiralty saw a probable connection between this flight and a badly damaged U-boat heading for port; attacked by a Liberator and unable to dive, *U-736* had nevertheless shot down a Wellington of No. 612 Squadron. It was escorted into Lorient by five minesweepers, making port on the 26th after 57 days at sea.

On the night of the 28/29th, the *Staffel* was to operate between 1950 and 0400 hrs but nothing was heard by the British Y-Service (Wireless Intercept). On 1 June, an He 111 was to make a daylight training flight over the coast west of Bordeaux from 0616 to 0845 hrs; on the 2nd, the night's operation, by a single He 111, was to take place from 2000 to 0230 hrs. Two days after that, 4./FAGr 5 was told to coordinate its operations with the Ju 88-equipped 3.(F)/Aufkl.Gr.123, which had long flown security reconnaissances over the Bay of Biscay. The intention that particular night was for an He 111 to fly out over Pointe du Raz on the Finisterre Peninsula at 2105 hrs and back at 0230 hrs. No wireless traffic was picked up to confirm that this intention was carried out, however.

Having begun May with no aircraft, during the month the unit would take on a repaired He 111H-6 along with a Do 217E-4 and a Ju 188F-1 from other units. During June, a Ju 88A-4 was added, also from repair, giving a final complement as follows:

Do 217E-4	Wk-Nr 4330 9V+AM	Undergoing repairs to a damaged engine and radio gear on 17 July, with completion of the work expected within the week.
He 111H-16	Wk-Nr 8308 9V+DM	Under its factory code (DT+YI) this aircraft had served with HuSSt 2 at least as far back as 15 February. Destroyed before it could be physically transferred to 6.(F)/Aufkl.Gr.123.
Ju 88A-4	Wk-Nr 301573 DW+OE	Armed with 1 x MG 81, 1 x MG 81Z, 2 x MG 131 and 1 x MG FF. Ferried to 6.(F)/Aufkl.Gr.123 on 12 July but absent from that formation's surviving strength returns for later dates.
Ju 188F-1	Wk-Nr 260251 9V+EM	Refitting in Werneuchen at the time of its transfer to 6.(F)/Aufkl. Gr.123 and expected to be ready for ferrying on 19 or 20 July.

Intercepted signals indicated that 4./FAGr 5 was non-operational by 20 June. Nevertheless, strength in personnel on 10 July was 103, among them 48 aircrew, as follows:

Pilots	8 (inc. 1 officer)
Observers	8 (inc. 3 officers)
Radio Operators	14
Radio Operator/Mechanics	13
Schnarrfunker	5

This last specialism offers a clue to one part of the *Staffel*'s role: the verb *schnarren* translates as 'to buzz' or 'to clatter', suggesting the transmission of noise. Another ten radio operators were to be found among the ground echelon, suggesting rather more radio gear to service than four conventionally equipped aircraft might require. An earlier strength return had listed four on-board radio operators, three flight mechanics and an air gunner as 'not belonging to crews', so the overall numbers suggest that the *Staffel* mustered eight full crews of five, each consisting of a pilot, observer, gunner and two radio operators (as carried by a Ju 188 of *Kommando* Rastedter which had gone missing in December 1943).

On 11 July, 4./FAGr 5 was in the process of dissolution; its serviceable aircraft (with the exception of the He 111) were due to be ferried away that day and contingents of personnel were to follow over the course of three days. Any special equipment that could not be taken in the aeroplanes was to be conveyed by land. This information was sent to 6.(F)/Aufkl.Gr.123, the intended recipient. Early on the morning of the 12th, the Heinkel was burned out when Lightnings strafed the landing ground at Varades, 50 km north-east of Nantes aerodrome. That afternoon, the *Staffel* reported a strength of six (1) crews; two had already been transferred to 6.(F)/Aufkl.Gr.123, three were detached and another was sick. Equipment now consisted of just the one Do 217, with damage to its engine and radio equipment. Ju 88 Wk-Nr 301573 had been ferried to 6.(F)/Aufkl.Gr.123 while Ju 188 Wk-Nr 260251 was in Werneuchen for the installation of 'special apparatus'.

A message five days later confirmed that 4./FAGr 5 was disbanding and handing over its equipment to 6.(F)/Aufkl.Gr.123. The transfer of at least one aircraft seems to have been held up, for, on 23 July, 4./FAGr 5 asked 6.(F)/Aufkl.Gr.123 for the earliest possible confirmation that Do 217, 9V+AM had landed. The remaining elements were planning to transfer by road at about 1700 hrs the next day, but the disbandment of the *Staffel* was not reported as complete until 23 August. Its successor, 6.(F)/Aufkl.Gr.123, was wound up in early September in Deelen, Holland.

CHAPTER THIRTEEN

RETURN TO THE REICH

August–September 1944

Every kilometre we progressed towards the east,
took us closer to the homeland and safety.

Oskar H. Schmidt, *Stabskompanie*, FAGr 5

In the early evening of 16 August, the first heavily laden Ju 290 of FAGr 5, Wk-Nr 0193 9V+FK, left Mont de Marsan for Germany as part of the withdrawal of the *Gruppe* from France. When it landed at Neuburg/Donau, its right-side landing gear suffered damage. Later that night, five more of the big aircraft were loaded with equipment, a process that required several vehicles, which could therefore not be contributed to the road column. After taking off, their activity was picked up by Allied radio listeners as they routed for Mühldorf am Inn via Dijon (one aircraft) and Clermont-Ferrand (four aircraft).[1] Briefly, in the autumn of 1943, Mühldorf had served as the base for LTS 290 and, more recently, for *Transportstaffel 5* with its mix of large German and Italian transports.

Next day, another aircraft, WK-Nr 0173 9V+CK, piloted by Oberfeldwebel Martin Kistler, again heavily loaded with ground personnel, was damaged when it landed at Mühldorf.[2]

By this stage, the *Gruppenkommandeur*, Major Fischer, had banned all daylight flying, the unit's aircrews now concentrating all their effort on ferrying equipment and supplies back to Germany at night. The aircraft were loaded to take their maximum payloads, making even taxiing a challenge, let alone take-off. Leutnant Hellmut Hetz was a pilot in 1./FAGr 5 and recalled: 'Only three aircraft were left parked in the woods. By this time, things were getting rather unpleasant in France with the *Maquis* lurking in the bushes. Major Fischer told us to "get the hell out of there."'[3]

Indeed, Fischer flew one of the unit's Ju 290s to Mühldorf am Inn; his aircraft was so heavy that when it touched down in Bavaria, it overshot the runway and the undercarriage collapsed.[4]

At 0315 hrs on the morning of the 18th, Leutnant Hellmut Nagel of 1.*Staffel* took off from Mont de Marsan in Ju 290 9V+BH, bound for the Junkers plant at Bernburg, 1400 km away. As the heavy aircraft left the ground, its right side mainwheel impacted with a radio mast, and was left suspended. The Junkers went on to suffer a crash-landing on the grass at Bernburg.[5] It was to be the last time he piloted a Ju 290.

GROUND COLUMN STAGE 1: MONT DE MARSAN–POITIERS, 18–20 AUGUST

At 1730 hrs that evening (the 18th), the first of a motley column of heavily laden vehicles drove out of Mont de Marsan on the first stage of what would be a long journey across France to southern Germany. The column would carry some 600 men and comprised field cars, buses, signals and radio trucks, field kitchens, tow-tractors, wood-gas-powered vehicles and light and heavy lorries of various types and functions, some with trailers. Most of the vehicles had been adorned with bushes and tree branches for camouflage and some had been rigged up to carry 20 mm MG 151 aircraft cannon on roof mounts, taken from the Ju 290s of the *Gruppe*, for defence from ground and air attack. After the recent thunderstorms, the summer evening weather was dry, warm and pleasant, and in most cases, the open vehicles had their tarpaulins pulled back in order not to hinder the ability to use the defensive guns quickly if the need arose.

The column began its drive west towards Morcenx, after which it would take the main road north to Bordeaux. But after Morcenx, it grew dark, and, acting on little more than a hunch, Oberleutnant Schmidt decided to change the planned route and to take another road. By taking such a measure, the FAGr 5 column had the good fortune to avoid an ambush by the *Maquis*, which had attacked a German fuel column on the intended road.

After Morcenx, the column pulled over to stop for the night and also to wait for a team of civilian German administration workers as well as a group from the Mont de Marsan airfield administration *Abteilung*. These groups, like FAGr 5, had received no orders and had initally decided to remain at their posts. That turned out to be a fatal error of judgement. The FAGr 5 column waited until daylight for them, but there was no sign of the civilian workers or the airfield staff. It later transpired that they too had come up against the *Maquis* and had suffered casualties.

At around 0500 hrs on the 19th, as the new day dawned, the column started up and drove towards Bordeaux, the southern outskirts of which it reached by 0845 hrs and where it paused for a brief and very wary breakfast, as well as to refuel. By 1030 hrs it had passed through the city safely, and north-west of it, crossed over the suspension bridge leading across the Dordogne. This was potentially a dangerous moment, for, as the vehicles of the column passed over the bridge, so they were vulnerable to air attack and to an ambush by the Resistance. 'We were glad once it was behind us and we continued in the direction of Angoulême,' recalled Oskar Schmidt.[6] That afternoon they stopped in some woods, where the field kitchens were set up and the men ate and washed in a stream. At 1530 hrs, the journey resumed, and, driving as quickly as possible under sunny skies with no sign of enemy aircraft, they reached Angoulême at 2000 hrs.

Through radio contact with the remaining crews at Mont de Marsan, it was learned that Bordeaux had just been declared a 'Fortress' (which meant it had to be defended at all costs) and as such, had the FAGr 5 convoy arrived there any later than it did, it would have found itself trapped in the city, where it would have been used to bolster the defences.

At Angoulême it was learned from the local German commander that any attempt to head directly east would not be possible, because all roads were being covered by groups of *maquisards*. As leader of the column, Oberleutnant Schmidt thus decided to make for the town of Poitiers, to the north, which held a strong German garrison and where it was hoped that a road could be found close to the front line that was not held by the Resistance.

As rain started to fall and with guards scanning the surrounding area and skies, the vehicles were refuelled and fresh wood loaded into the wood-gas-powered vehicles. The local military commander at Angoulême eyed the FAGr 5 column with interest and expressed his 'opinion' that it should be incorporated into his own command. Schmidt politely, but firmly, told the soldier that he had his own orders.

At 2030 hrs, and with daylight fading, the column moved off under heavy, sheeting rain, destined for Poitiers. The rain proved relentless, and those personnel driving in the smaller *Kübelwagen* field cars found water seeping into their vehicles. Brakes failed. 'As if by a miracle,' Schmidt recalled, 'all the vehicles survived the flood.' One advantage of the adverse weather, however, was that it kept the bands of *Maquis* away.

Some 15 km north from Angoulême, the column arrived at a barrier across the road to which was attached a sign that read 'Diversion', but without any further explanation. The diversion led into a forested area with some narrow ravines, which prompted a sense of growing unease among the men in the column. At about midnight, Schmidt ordered the vehicles to stop for the night and mounted guards on all sides. Every member of the column endeavoured to get some sleep, despite their wet clothes. During the night, the guard at the end of the column, under Oberleutnant Motzkus, a pilot of 1./FAGr 5, became engaged in a short exchange of fire with a small band of assailants, but deployment of the aircraft cannon against them saw them off. There were no casualties on the German side.

At 0630 hrs, on the morning of the 20th, after a hasty breakfast, the column moved again, but by now it had increased in size as a result of being joined by vehicles from other German organizations that had been operating in France such as the *Reichsbahn* and the *Organisation Todt*. In daylight, the officers of FAGr 5 were bemused to discover that hitching rides on their vehicles were a number of elderly German civilian men wearing shirts, trousers and braces; the appearance of a well-organized military column was ebbing.

As the column approached Poitiers later that morning, so it was forced to make another detour as a result of a bridge that had been blown up. Then, a little later, the lead vehicle in the column spotted a barrier across the road made from felled tree trunks, and at the same moment the column came under light fire from a nearby village. The German gunners returned the fire as the occupants of their vehicles jumped into the cover of ditches on both sides of the road. In the process some of the Germans were wounded, including an Unteroffizier of FAGr 5 who was later taken to the base of the Free India Legion for treatment and from there to a hospital.

The heavy cannon fire from the column was sufficient to cause the *maquisards* in the village to disperse, but once under way again, a bus, which had given many years of faithful service to FAGr 5 and which had even seen service with the reconnaissance units in Russia, suffered damage to one of its wheels. Lacking spares with which to repair the damage, the mobile workshop mechanics,

Feldwebel Walk and Unteroffizier Hunn, volunteered to remain with the bus to make the new part using their lathes and other tools. It was agreed that a security detachment would also remain with them for protection, and the repair work was to proceed on the basis it did not take more than two hours.

As the rest of the column continued on its way, it stopped briefly before each settlement it came to, at which the gunners would fire a short warning salvo of cannon fire over the rooftops to dissuade any *maquisards* that might be there from launching an attack.

At 1145 hrs, they reached the southern outskirt of Poitiers amidst an air raid, but well camouflaged and armed, they used the disruption to halt for a rest and to eat.

Back at Mont de Marsan on the 20th, it was the turn of Hellmut Hetz of 1./FAGr 5 to fly to Munich-Riem, as he remembered:

> Finally, on 20 August, I loaded my Ju 290 with as much as it would carry including the *Gruppe's* butchers and six to eight pigs. I knew we would be flying at reasonably high altitude and told the butchers to kill the pigs if they should start to breathe heavily (I had learned this from my father who was a vet). Then, as I began my taxiing run, another group of men came running up and we hauled them aboard. Now heavily overloaded I continued the run, but could not reach the official take-off speed. Nearing the end of the runway, I pulled the aircraft up anyway and managed to get her up into the air. As we headed for Munich, we flew through bad thunderstorms, the butchers became air sick and the pigs suffocated. The bodies of the animals soon began to smell badly, so as soon as we touched down at Munich-Riem, the crew threw them out. After we taxied to a stop the groundcrews found bushes and twigs wrapped around the undercarriage, showing how close we had been to the trees when we took off.
>
> Shortly afterwards we were ordered to fly our Ju 290s to satellite airfields in order to conceal them from enemy fighter-bombers. After an hour's flight, I landed at a tiny airfield [Mühldorf am Inn], but as the tractor pulled the aircraft into a wood, it started to sink into the mud. I quickly taxied it out again and helped the crew to cut timbers to form a platform on which it could stand safely. As far as I am concerned, it's probably still there, as I can not see how anyone could take-off in a Ju 290 from that field![7]

GROUND COLUMN STAGE 2: POITIERS–
TITISEE, 20–25 AUGUST

The news at Poitiers was not good. The local German commanders there advised the officers from the Luftwaffe column not to take the direct roads to the east from Poitiers. Everywhere in the east was now teeming with the *Maquis*. Even some of the smaller and weaker German infantry units still operating in the area had been beaten back by the Resistance. Rather, the best option was to head north, to move closer to the front, and to try to find a route through to the east from there.

The predicament facing the FAGr 5 column was made more difficult by orders from the Poitiers military command to take with them more displaced German and 'friendly' individuals who had found their way to the town – merchant seamen, railway workers, farriers and other civilian personnel. 'We were beginning to take on the appearance of a gypsy column,' recalls Oskar Schmidt. Furthermore, after waiting in vain until 1430 hrs for the repaired bus that had been left on the road south of the town to catch up, Schmidt decided to press on.

Just as they were leaving, the local military *Kommandantur* (Commandant's Office) informed the column that a large quantity of market goods had been 'discovered' in the town and that the men were welcome to help themselves. Schmidt, however, was resolved to continue regardless of this tempting offer and although he knew it was a 'regrettable omission', progress and the prospect of survival were more important.

Heading north along straight country roads towards Tours, surrounded by open countryside with few trees, the column was then strafed in a low-level attack by Mosquito fighter-bombers. The FAGr 5 gunners responded immediately with their 20 mm MG 151 cannon, and the air around the road convoy quickly became obscured with clouds of smoke. Luckily, the Mosquitos flew off, but one NCO was wounded in the foot during the attack.

Shortly after the Mosquitos departed, the column came upon a small convoy of three staff cars, in which was a senior SS officer, together with a large amount of luggage and looted goods, as well as his female secretaries. They sought refuge with the FAGr 5 column, much to the consternation of some its members, although there was little they could do about it.

Indeed, at one point during the journey, the column entered a small town and was stopped by an SS unit. Its leader, an SS Hauptsturmführer, attempted to order Oberleutnant Schmidt to use his resources to set the buildings on either side of the street ablaze. Schmidt refused on the basis that his men had not been fired at from anyone in the town. A tense stand-off between Schmidt and the SS officer followed, during which the FAGr 5 personnel made it very clear that they would use their machine pistols against 'anyone' if they were threatened. At this, the SS backed away and the column was waved on. As Schmidt commented, 'Break the Resistance, yes – but exacting revenge on innocents was not the solution.'

Fortunately, beyond Poitiers the afternoon summer skies remained clear of further prowling enemy aircraft. 'What they could have done to us!' noted Schmidt. 'Perhaps the English fighter pilots were having their tea?'

But as the column drove on, there were uncomfortable indications that they were nearing the front, in the form of burnt-out vehicles lying abandoned by the roadside. As they neared Tours, the column turned off the main road and headed for the town of Sainte-Maure de Touraine. As it did so, the coupling between one of the lorries of the *Gruppe* and its trailer snapped. It was decided that the senior occupant of the lorry, Flieger-Ingenieur Unger of the *Gruppenstab*, would remain with it together with Schirrmeister (Technical Sergeant) Limmer, until the mobile workshop and the repaired bus caught them up and could conduct the necessary repairs.

Once more, Schmidt decided to continue, leaving his colleagues behind; 'Every kilometre we progressed towards the east, took us closer to the homeland and safety.'

As night fell, the weather changed, bringing heavy rain. In the worsening conditions, the column started to break up with some of the smaller vehicles lagging behind. A halt was ordered so that the vehicles could close up and reassemble, and the personnel rest for a meal.

Under cover of darkness, at 0100 hrs the next morning, the column set off with Leutnant Klose, a pilot of 2./FAGr 5, at its head in a lorry fitted with multiple cannon, followed by Oberleutnant Schmidt in a Tatra field car. Behind Schmidt came another heavily armed lorry. Within moments, however, the second truck struck a small landmine, which although it was triggered, fortunately caused little damage apart from puncturing the two front tyres. However, above the noise of the engines, neither Klose nor Schmidt heard the small blast and continued to drive on through wooded countryside. Furthermore, because the headlights of the following vehicles had been darkened, it was some time before Klose and Schmidt had realized what had happened. When they eventually returned to the main column, Schmidt's Tatra also drove over a mine at which it 'sprang into the air'. Once again, the mine caused damage only to the tyres. But as Schmidt recalled: 'Why the *Maquis*, who had probably laid these little mines in the rain, did not try to attack the lone column leader, is a mystery.'

Once again, the column had been fortunate, but because of the delays caused and the subsequent repairs, as well as exhaustion on the part of several of the drivers, orders were given to rest until dawn.

At dawn on the 21st, the column moved off in the direction of Bourges, which it reached later that morning. The town was in chaos as the remaining German troops there were preparing to evacuate. To the north, Paris was about to fall to the Allies and the Falaise pocket had all but been closed with the loss of more than 10,000 German soldiers killed and another 50,000 taken prisoner.

When FAGr 5 arrived at Bourges, together with their various travelling 'companions', they were one of several such retreating German columns moving through the area. But their timing was good. They had appeared just as preparations were being made to destroy the local fuel dump in order to prevent its capture by the Allies or the Resistance. As such the FAGr 5 personnel were able to replenish their vehicles' tanks as well as load up the lorries with as many more drums of fuel as they could carry.

The vehicles assembled close to the railway lines in the town, where the field kitchens set up and prepared food, and the men were able to wash. There was also the opportunity to draw upon the stockpiled treasures of the local supply office, which included such luxuries as coffee. The weather improved, which made the drive easier, but once again increased the threat of attack from enemy aircraft.

The trade-off for all this replenishment came when the local military commander requested that Schmidt make the FAGr 5 vehicles and their cannon available for an assault operation to be carried out against the local *Maquis* the following evening. However, Schmidt refused, stating that both vehicles and armament were needed for other tasks in Germany, which was where they were heading. At midnight, Schmidt led the column off, towards the town of Nevers, 70 km to the east, which it reached the same day, the weather having changed markedly, with rain once again pouring down. The vehicles drove into the town park, where they were assembled into a protective rectangle and the personnel took some time to rest.

Meanwhile, the local commander summoned Oberleutnant Schmidt and told him that he required his vehicles in order to form the basis of a convoy, which was to drive east, through *Maquis*-occupied territory, 175 km, to the town of Autun. More personnel would be attached to the convoy, some with vehicles and some without, including around 100 infantrymen and some French citizens who had collaborated with the Germans. This time, Schmidt obliged, drawing on the benefit of the protection that 100 combat-seasoned troops would offer for the rest of the drive to the German border.

Under heavy guard, the column remained in the park for the night of 21st/22nd.

Early next morning, all personnel were mustered, given orders and assigned tasks. The column had become a large force of military and civilians, and it took most of the day to get the vehicles safely loaded with people and supplies. It was late on the 22nd before they took to the road.

On this leg, conditions became more dangerous. The infantry were deployed at one spot when the column came under heavy fire, and they suffered dead and wounded. Elsewhere, there were further harassing, lighter attacks, but once again, by deploying the aircraft cannon, the opposition was driven off. Often, the way was blocked by abandoned vehicles and the column had to call upon its heavy Faun tow-tractors, which FAGr 5 used to tow its Ju 290s at Mont de Marsan, to clear the road.

They overtook other retreating German columns as they moved on towards the east, but at times the road narrowed and passing another column became very challenging, slowing progress. At one point, having just cleared the road of a pile of shot-up and burnt-out vehicles, a formation of USAAF P-51 Mustangs swept in low and raked the column with machine-gun fire, causing casualties, damage and panic.

At 2100 hrs, after having shot bursts of MG 151 fire over the rooftops, the column sped past the road junction town of Autun. Beyond the town, the roads were quiet and the night was spent peacefully in the area under a strong guard.

Heading north-west on the 23rd, at around midday they drove through Dijon, having covered another 90 km. Here the vehicles were checked over and refuelled, the opportunity taken to acquire some local supplies and provisions, and at 1345 hrs the column was back on the road, making for Vesoul.

The hilly terrain area between Dijon and Vesoul was crawling with Resistance groups, and the Germans attracted fire from woods bordering the route. Bullets hit the vehicles, with at least one taking a rifle round through the cab, but no one was injured. It was only in spots where the column was held up for a period of time that the Germans resorted to responding with their own weapons. However, at one point, the radio truck suffered a broken axle, and under the supervision of Leutnant Scherp, a pilot in 2./FAGr 5, all the important equipment was removed and transferred to other vehicles. The trailer which had been towed behind the radio truck was blown up, an action which attracted more fire from the *maquisards* hiding out in nearby woods.

The route now became very steep as the road wound through the wooded hills of Franche-Comté, and the tow-tractors had to render assistance to the wood-gas-powered vehicles, although these latter machines had performed well, against all expectations, for the whole journey up to that point.

At around 1630 hrs, the column reached Vesoul. Here, 150 km from the German border, the personnel in the column began to feel more secure, more hopeful. The column came to a stop in the town and, for the rest of the day, no onward march was ordered. The night would be spent in the town. The halt was used to give the vehicles an overhaul, to fill up fuel tanks and to find more supplies.

Vesoul was bustling and busy, its ancient roads choked with other German units trying to reach the frontier, including units of the SS and the feared SD (*Sicherheitsdienst*), the SS intelligence and security service, mostly in requisitioned French vehicles laden with family, children and 'liberated' luxury items. The sight did not impress the men of FAGr 5. And yet it was at Vesoul, much to Schmidt and his fellow officers' delight, that some of the mobile elements that had 'attached' themselves to the column earlier took off or simply 'dissolved'. As Schmidt recalled: 'One could almost "smell" the border, and so some of them attempted to continue the journey on their own.'

Under a strong guard, the Luftwaffe reconnaissance men enjoyed a refreshing evening swim in a local pool, while the *Gruppe* officers spent the night in a hotel, where they observed at a comfortable distance, some of the 'wayfarers' who had joined the column during its route from the west, playing cards in the bar with a group of SD men.

On the morning of the 24th, Oberleutnant Schmidt arranged a checking of all weapons and equipment prior to embarking upon the next leg of the journey towards Belfort. He then gave final instructions on the route, but the opening of the field kitchens and preparation of a hot meal delayed departure until 1400 hrs.

As the column headed for Belfort, it became quite widely dispersed and 15 km from that town, it was ambushed by heavy gunfire emanating from a house and surrounding woodland. After a short but violent skirmish, in which two of the column's members were lightly wounded, the 'terrorists' were beaten off by the deployment of a small section of infantry supported by FAGr 5's heavy cannon.

At around 1815 hrs, the column passed Belfort, unaware of the fact that at that very moment, Marshal Pétain, *Chef de l'État* of Vichy France, was in the town, pausing, like thousands of others, on his way to the sanctuary of the German border. Forty minutes later, the FAGr 5 column reached German soil. 'It was a very comforting feeling to be back in the Fatherland,' Schmidt conceded.

It is to Oskar Schmidt's credit that, as a relatively junior officer, he had achieved a remarkable feat in assembling and leading a large, gradually expanding convoy across central France, under threat from attack the whole way, safely back to Germany with minimal human and mechanical casualties.

At the frontier Schmidt had to deal with the German border guards on behalf of the female Luftwaffe signals auxiliaries, various civilians, French nationals, Russian *Hiwis* and others – all of whom had rendered assistance to FAGr 5 during its time at Mont de Marsan, and who had journeyed across France with the column; otherwise, without sufficient papers and credentials, some personnel would have been refused permission to enter the Reich. The chaos that prevailed in France, and the reckless behaviour of certain elements of the SS and SD there was of little interest to the border officials, and, ironically, perhaps because of that, they were 'generous' in their decision to let the 'passengers' through. 'Perhaps,' reflected Schmidt, 'they wanted to keep unpleasant decisions away from their necks.'

From Colmar, they reached the Rhine by nightfall, crossing at Breisach. A short while later, they stopped outside a village and spent the night parked up in the yards of some farms, where most of the travellers slept fully clothed in their vehicles. It was the first night that they slept peacefully without alarm, incident or danger. At 0830 hrs the next morning, the column moved off, and by 1015 hrs, it had arrived in the city of Freiburg am Breisgau.

Here, Oberleutnant Motzkus delivered the remaining French nationals to the local Kommandantur and enquired about the location of the nearest military airfield. Simultaneously, Oberleutnant Schmidt bade farewell to the various railway workers, mariners and officials from the *Organisation Todt* who took leave of the Luftwaffe men to make their way to their homes and places of employment wherever they were in Germany. A little later Motzkus reported that having talked with the local airfield commander, the airfield was so overcrowded that FAGr 5's personnel could not be accommodated there.

Schmidt therefore decided to continue on to the Titisee (a picturesque lake in the Black Forest) and from there to Überlingen on the Bodensee (Lake Constance), where it was known that trains could be boarded to take them to Bavaria and the present base of FAGr 5. Unteroffizier Faller would remain in Freiburg to round up and follow on with any stragglers who might yet arrive from France.

At 1240 hrs, the now smaller column, comprising almost exclusively FAGr 5 personnel, drew to a stop in a long row under bright-blue summer skies alongside the shore of the Titisee, surrounded by wooded hills. Although the town of Titisee was known as a peaceful place with no military installations, the vehicles were nevertheless fully camouflaged with netting and tree branches to protect them against being spotted from the air, after which they were serviced before the men were allowed some time to swim in the lake and to rest and sunbathe for a few hours.

Oberleutnant Schmidt was able at last to establish a radio link with Major Fischer. Fischer promised Schmidt that he would arrange with the *Reichsbahn* for the necessary rolling stock to be assigned for the onward movement of the personnel and vehicles of the *Gruppe* at either Titisee or from the Bodensee. He also informed Schmidt that the entire *Gruppe* – flying and ground personnel – was to assemble at the new operational base of Neubiberg, to the south of München (Munich) and not as previously planned at Mühldorf, mainly because some of the heavily laden Ju 290s from Mont de Marsan had experienced problems in landing there – as in the case of Leutnant Hetz of 1.*Staffel*. Mühldorf was to remain only as a base for a small technical detachment which would liaise with Junkers and other industrial concerns. As such, Schmidt's column was to travel by train to Neubiberg at the earliest opportunity.

But there was still no sign of the mobile workshop mechanics, Feldwebel Walk and Unteroffizier Hunn, who had volunteered to remain with the broken-down bus outside Poitiers, and Unteroffizier Faller had waited in vain for any stragglers in Freiburg. He eventually left a message with the local Kommandantur about where *Fernaufklärungsgruppe* 5 could be found.

The last Ju 290 is believed to have left Mont de Marsan early on the 26th with Unteroffizier Heinrich Geye (observer) and Unteroffizier Heinrich Notz (radio-operator) among the crew. However, the night prior to its departure there was a very severe thunderstorm, which left the runway flooded. In addition, 60 soaking infantrymen arrived, together with assault equipment and baggage, and requested to be airlifted out. At 0500 hrs in the morning, with all the soldiers and their equipment loaded on board, its four BMW 801 engines throttled to full power, the Junkers dutifully lifted off the waterlogged surface of the airport amidst a wave of spray. Resistance fighters were already in Mont de Marsan. However, shortly after take-off, the outer right engine of the Junkers ceased running, but the aircraft kept flying all the way to Munich-Riem where they landed safely.[8]

GROUND COLUMN STAGE 3: TITISEE–NEUBIBERG/HOFOLDING, 28 AUGUST TO 5 SEPTEMBER

Misfortune befell the column after it departed the Titisee on the morning of the 28th when one of the large tow-tractors driven by Obergefreiter Schmander crashed into a beer lorry on the road to Überlingen, although the damage to his vehicle was light. Schmander had driven the tractor with faulty brakes, skillfully avoiding accident or mishap, all the way from central France – 'A masterful performance,' noted Schmidt.

By midday, the vehicles of FAGr 5 were parked up on the road running along the shore of the Bodensee in Überlingen. There was no other significant military presence in the town and so there was plenty of available accommodation. A classroom in the local school was set up for most of the other ranks, while the officers found quarters in the family-owned Hotel Ochsen, where they were able to enjoy comfortable beds and bathrooms. The kitchen in one local restaurant acted as a host for the cooks of the *Gruppe*, who benefited from the contribution of market goods and foodstuffs brought in by the unit from France, while some officers chose to dine on fresh fish caught in the lake, washed down by French wine, and served in the town's other restaurants.

Soon word came through from the rail transport office at Karlsruhe that wagons and coaches had been booked and the unit was to await further details about when they would be available. However, in a portent of what could be expected in the coming weeks, there was some upheaval on the 29th when, following orders received in a telephone call from Major Fischer at Neubiberg, all personnel not essential to the functioning of the unit at its new base were to be sent via the next available train to Munich, where they would be assigned to duties with other units – probably for retraining or service as ground troops. This was a difficult task to execute, but it was done. One happy event, however, was the eventual return of Feldwebel Walk and Unteroffizier Hunn and their workshop lorry together with the faithful old bus of the *Gruppe*. Their return also meant that the unit could now produce some of its own spare parts by using the drills and lathes in the workshop.

On 1 September, Schmidt was informed that rolling stock would be arriving at Überlingen the next day from Karlsruhe, so preparations hurriedly commenced to get men, equipment and vehicles ready for loading. On the morning of the 2nd, under heavy rain, the loading commenced, but, because most of the freight wagons were in poor condition and damaged, the process took much longer than anticipated and was not completed by nightfall. Loading recommenced first thing on the 3rd, but, because the wagons arrived at Überlingen station only at intervals, it again became an extended operation and it was not until 1945 hrs that all vehicles, equipment and men had embarked. Eventually, with all wagons and coaches coupled, and vehicles lashed securely, the train steamed out of Überlingen into the darkness of the night, heading through Lindau and on towards Kempten.

Next morning, the train pulled into Munich-East, and after a brief wait, it was a halting journey to Neubiberg. At Neubiberg, Oberleutnant Schmidt quickly climbed on a motorcycle and rode to the airfield to explore the facilities for unloading the train. But getting to the airfield was a challenge in itself, for in the time he had been away in France security in the Reich had tightened, and at one point he was flagged down and almost arrested for not having the required travel permit and papers.

Finally reaching Neubiberg airfield, Schmidt reported the arrival of the column at the railway station, but then discovered that the airfield had no suitable ramp for unloading the wagons. Thus this procedure would have to be carried out at the station, despite the primitive facilities there as well.

The bulk of the personnel from the column would be quartered in farm buildings around Hofolding, but they were met with a frosty reception from the local farmers and so the first night was spent in their vehicles. The unloading operation commenced at 1030 hrs and was completed by 1730 hrs.

Most of the flying officers stayed in Neubiberg with only the *Stabskompanie* moving to Hofolding, where a command post was set up in the old bus and more permanent quarters found, with the kitchens being set up in a local guest house.

By the afternoon, all personnel had been found billets. Schmidt and his fellow officers then reported to Major Fischer at Neubiberg, who thanked them for their good work and diligence in bringing the bulk of the *Gruppe* safely back to Germany. Fischer then read out a list of the names of men who were to be sent promptly, together with motor vehicles, to the *Metallbau* Offingen, a subsidiary of the Messerschmitt company, involved in the assembly of certain types of long-range aircraft. As for Oskar Schmidt, he was told he was to be posted away from FAGr 5 for further duties in the air defence of the Reich.

Fernaufklärungsgruppe 5 'Atlantik' had been assembled once more, but it had been quickly splintered and depleted. Its remaining crews and personnel would find themselves assigned to tasks very different from those which they had been undertaking in France – tasks of a covert and experimental nature.

CHAPTER FOURTEEN

'SPECIAL TASKS'

KG 200 and *Metallbau* Offingen/ *Sonderkommando* Nebel, July 1944 to February 1945

The dice were going to roll for our unit.

Oskar H. Schmidt, *Stabskompanie*, FAGr 5

Oskar Schmidt summarized FAGr 5's situation at the beginning of September 1944 as follows:

> The *Gruppe*, with its *Kommandeur*, Major Fischer, now existed practically only on paper. However, a complete disbandment was not ordered by the *Luftwaffenführungsstab*, so the hope remained that, in early 1945, operations would resume with new aircraft. Since May 1944, the unit had flown only some 'restricted' reconnaissance over the Atlantic, because the U-boats could no longer reach the open sea through the Bay of Biscay. At that time, we were slowly beginning to supply our aircraft, along with crews, for special tasks, but the *Gruppe* did not have much experience of such operations.[1]

Schmidt is referring to the operations of *Kampfgeschwader* 200, the special operations wing of the Luftwaffe.

Much has been written about the activities of KG 200 and post-war literature, both fact and fiction, has sensationalized the 'clandestine' nature of the work undertaken by the *Geschwader* during its existence. Formed on 21 February 1944 at Wildpark-Werder in Berlin (the *Geschwaderstab* moved to Berlin-Gatow in May) and placed under the command of Oberst im Generalstabsdienst Heinz Heigl, the *raison d'être* of the unit stemmed from a need for coordinated control of aircraft assigned to agent-dropping duties. Such duties had been the task of the *Gruppe Gartenfeld*, which undertook missions on behalf of the *Abwehr* (Military Intelligence Service) and the SS-controlled *Reichssicherheitshauptamt* (RSHA – Reich Main Security Office). The *Gruppe* operated a mixed fleet of transport aircraft as well as German and foreign bombers. The unit, together with its commander, Major Karl-Edmund Gartenfeld, was amongst the first to be integrated into I./KG 200 along with elements of the 2./*Versuchsverband Ob.d.L.* Gartenfeld was appointed the first *Kommandeur* of the *Gruppe*. All three *Staffeln* which constituted I. *Gruppe* were involved in agent-dropping, most of which were controlled by Amt VI, the Foreign Intelligence department of the RSHA. Based at Finsterwalde, the composition of the new *Gruppe* was as follows:

1.*Staffel* – long-range operations
2.*Staffel* – shorter-range operations
3.*Staffel* – for maritime operations; previously operating as *Sonderkommando See* with the *Versuchsverband Ob.d.L.*[2]

The operations of the *Gruppe* spanned from Finland to Persia, from Africa to Ireland and utilized such diverse aircraft as He 111s, Do 24s, Ju 252s and captured American B-17 and B-24 bombers.

A II./KG 200 became operational at Hildesheim at the end of March 1944 under Major Hans Jungwirt. This *Gruppe* would eventually undertake a variety of 'special tasks'. Its 2.*Staffel* was commanded by a former glider pilot, Oberleutnant Karl-Heinz Lange, who believed that huge damage could be inflicted on the anticipated Allied invasion fleet by committed pilots who would launch manned glide-bombs at enemy ships and who were prepared to die in the attempt. Such radical operations were referred to as *Totaleinsatz* – 'total commitment', or 'operations with expendable weapons' (and, in cases, crew) – and *Selbstopfer* ('self-sacrifice'). Lange's idea eventually manifested itself in the form of a handful of Fw 190s laden with 1,100-kg bombs, which were to be carried right onto a target. The unit trained up at Dedelstorf and Stolp-Parow and finally became ready for operations in late June 1944, by which time the whole scheme was cancelled by an order from a senior authority who apparently lacked the stomach for it.

In the summer of 1944, the various Nazi intelligence services were very active in Eastern Europe, the Soviet Union, and areas of the Mediterranean and Middle East where they attempted to promote dissent and rebellion against the Allied powers, and particularly Britain's powerful pre-war colonial and economic grip in certain regions. In July 1944, no fewer than 260 agents were dropped, 80 of these by 1.*Staffel*, at distances up to 250 km behind enemy lines, and as such there was a high demand for long-range aircraft.[3]

Probably aware that long-range maritime reconnaissance operations over the Atlantic were in decline, KG 200 was known to have turned to FAGr 5 as a source of suitable aircraft and personnel, and as early as July requested that three Ju 290s and crews should be assigned to the *Geschwader* for transport operations, although they would remain at Mont de Marsan and continue to perform their normal duties simultaneously.[4] Early plans included using a Ju 290 piloted by Oberleutnant Ludwig Herlein of the *Gruppenstab*/FAGr 5, together with his crew, to fly to Japan via the Polar route in order to collect a cargo of important raw materials badly needed by the Reich. Ultimately, however, the flight did not take place because the Japanese Government feared repercussions from the Soviet Union.

Crews placed on stand-by for missions under the jurisdiction of KG 200 at this time included those of Oberleutnant Günther Korn (Wk-Nr 0186 9V+FH) and Leutnant Siegfried Wache of 1.*Staffel* and Hauptmann Hanns Kohmann of 2.*Staffel* (Wk-Nr 0181 9V+GK).[5]

Throughout the summer of 1944, these crews flew several long-range missions for KG 200, starting in July when Oberleutnant Korn, a veteran of 3.(F)/Aufkl.Gr.10, together with his 1./FAGr 5 crew of Oberleutnant Hans Ascheid (observer and aircraft commander), Oberfähnrich Fischer (second pilot), Oberfeldwebel Schade (radio-operator), Oberfeldwebel Engel (flight engineer) and Feldwebel Seifert (gunner), were given the opportunity to fly one of the captured B-17G Flying Fortresses of the *Geschwader*, coded A3+BB, on a mission to drop three agents over North Africa in which it was intended that the aircraft would fly adorned in its USAAF markings. This aeroplane, B-17G-25-DL, s/n 42-38017, had originally flown with the US Eighth Air Force's 349th Bomb Squadron of the 100th Bomb Group based at Thorpe Abbot, but during a raid to Berlin on 3 March 1944, its crew had failed to hear a recall order, and together with the other two aircraft in its lead element, continued to fly to the target. Having been attacked by fighters, it was damaged by wreckage from the two B-17s above it. Its pilot attempted to head for neutral

Sweden, but landed at Schleswig-Jagel airfield in northern Germany in error.[6] The aircraft was repaired to flying condition and handed over to KG 200.

While taking the American four-engined bomber for a test flight, compared with the Ju 290, Korn and Ascheid, also a veteran of 3.(F)/Aufkl.Gr.10, found it heavy to handle. They were also extremely reluctant to fly the aircraft in American markings, since if they were shot down and captured, they would be treated as spies rather than soldiers and dealt with accordingly. Instead, the airmen requested, in the strongest possible terms, that they be allowed to fly a Ju 290, and their request was granted. They were then ordered to fly their Junkers, 9V+FH, from Mont de Marsan to Athens, where they would pick up the agents, in this case saboteurs who were to be dropped in the valleys along the railway line running from Tunisia to Algeria in North Africa.[7]

Preparations for their mission, which was assigned the codename Operation *Antiatlas/Sultan Alekbar*, were made very carefully, and Ascheid and his crew were briefed by a professor of geography, with specialist knowledge of the region, on pertinent aspects of the terrain as well as supplying them with detailed maps of the drop points to study.

At 1907 hrs on 25 July 1944, with the agents on board the Ju 290, Korn took off from Athens-Kalamaki and headed across the Mediterranean in the direction of the Gulf of Sidra on the coast of Libya, a course over which the *Abwehr* had picked up a gap in the enemy's radar coverage. The Junkers flew at just five metres above the surface of the sea and then turned and climbed to approach the Tunisian coast along an air corridor used by the French *Armée de l'Air* to fly supplies from Chad to Tunis. The Junkers used its full lighting to make out the first drop point. The first agent, a North African, was then parachuted, as arranged, from a height of between 200 and 400 m into a wine-growing area which lay in a basin on the outskirts of Tunis.

The second agent, a former French officer, was dropped farther along the coast, without any difficulties, between Bône and Constantine in Algeria, while the last man, another Arab, parachuted out south of Algiers. Shortly after, as dawn broke, Korn turned the Junkers back towards the sea and dropped back down to five metres. As the sea remained calm, the Ju 290 was able to maintain such a low altitude until it reached the French coast, after which it landed at Mont de Marsan at 0830 hrs the following morning. Immediately on landing, Hans Ascheid learned that he had become a father, and some time after that, FAGr 5 was advised by the intelligence services that all three agents had landed safely and had subsequently reported in by radio. This early 'agent mission' for FAGr 5 had gone well.[8]

Meanwhile, Hauptmann Kohmann had been sent in Ju 290 9V+GK to Zilistea in Rumania in order to conduct similar missions over the southern sector of the Eastern Front. On 9 August, the aircraft was flown from Medias in Rumania back to the Junkers works at Dessau, most likely for overhaul. However, this machine was lost during a bombing raid on Dessau on 16 August.[9]

Korn, Ascheid and their crew were called upon for another mission, this time codenamed Operation *Polka*, which commenced on 12 August and which would involve the dropping of 13 Turkmen nationals in Soviet uniforms into Turkmenistan. On this occasion, the Ju 290 left Mont de Marsan for Medias in Rumania, but was moved farther east to Zilistea because of the threat of another USAAF attack on the Ploesti oil refineries, in the case of which Medias would also be threatened. The plan was to drop the Turkmen in the area of the Main Turkmen Canal, a landmark easily recognizable from the air.

At 1539 hrs on the 13th, the Ju 290 took off from Zilistea and flew out across the Black Sea, but, while over the hills near Sinop on the Turkish coast, its left-side inner engine failed. Unfortunately, all efforts to try to fix the problem from within the aircraft proved in vain and Korn* and Ascheid decided to abort the mission. Despite hoping to wait for the delivery of a replacement engine to Rumania, the crew eventually ended up having to fly the aircraft in stages to the Junkers plant in Dessau where reliable repairs could be effected. *Polka* was eventually executed using another crew.[10]

Aside from adversities caused by enemy air operations, agent-dropping flights also depended to a great extent on weather conditions and they were frequently subject to postponement. The aircrews would prefer to be over a drop zone at night with as little moon as possible. The 'agents', of whom the crew knew very little, if anything, and with whom there was no communication, were usually dropped with black parachutes, as was their equipment if applicable. In an aircraft as large as the Ju 290, conditions were comfortable enough to accommodate several agents along with weapons, radio sets, clothing, and provisions. This was an advantage and complied with the requirement in particular of the RSHA not to drop just one agent per flight, but rather to land, wherever possible, two or more agents per sortie.[11] However, when an aircraft climbed steeply from low, anti-radar level to cross a hostile coast, agents would feel airsick and would frequently have to be 'encouraged' towards the fuselage exit door, especially as the aircraft flew farther and farther away from the intended drop point.[12]

Just over a fortnight after the *Polka* mission, on 28 August, the Korn crew took off from Udetfeld in Germany to fly via Lublin to the Pinsk Marshes, territory recently recaptured by the Soviets as they advanced against the retreating *Heeresgruppe Mitte* (Army Group Centre). It would be the first of three such flights. The Ju 290 carried 12 heavily armed agents wearing Soviet uniforms, who were to be dropped into an area the size of a football pitch, east of Chernihiv in northern Ukraine, which was to be illuminated by three fires.

Their route across the marshes was trouble free, because the moonlight cast a white glow on the banks of the main rivers, which acted as a great help towards navigation. But when the low-flying Junkers reached the drop area, Oberleutnant Ascheid was astounded to note that the entire forest was aflame. Suddenly, machine-gun fire rose up towards the aircraft from the ground, and Ascheid told Korn to break off the mission and turn for home. The Ju 290 landed back at Udetfeld at 0515 hrs on the 29th. For future attempts, Ascheid proposed using coloured identification markers.

Two days later, another mission, under the codename Operation *Wolf,* was devised to drop a ten-man sabotage group with weapons east of Toropets, a town some 400 km to the east of Moscow. Taking off at 1925 hrs from Udetfeld, Korn flew the Ju 290 through thick cloud – conditions which made navigation difficult – towards the target. Eventually, the aircraft reached the large, open field where the agents were to be dropped; the fuselage door was pulled open, and one by one, they left the aircraft. However, as the Junkers pulled away after the drop, searchlights suddenly switched on, bathing the drop point in bright light and Soviet vehicles started to move in towards the agents to round them up. Evidently, the operation had been betrayed. After landing back at Udetfeld at 0448 hrs on the morning of 1 September, Ascheid immediately informed military intelligence of the fiasco.[13]

On 3 September, Korn and Ascheid tried once again to reach Chernihiv, departing Udetfeld at 2025 hrs. This time arrangements had been made to light green markers at the drop point, and when the Ju 290 arrived over the spot, it had to make three passes in order for all 12 men to parachute out. The aircraft returned in the early hours of the 4th, and during the evening of the 5th, the Junkers took off for the third and last time, carrying another team of agents, who on this occasion, carried with them three tons of explosives packed into large, felt-lined, plywood containers. Needless to say, this increased the state of wariness among the aircrew.

In the Lublin area, the Ju 290 ran into a sudden thunderstorm of such severity that Ascheid thought initially of turning back, but they pressed on. Reaching Pinsk, the aircraft then attracted heavy Flak fire, something which caused great consternation because all aboard knew that felt-lined plywood would offer little protection for the explosives against a close Flak burst. Somehow the aircraft evaded being hit, and all agents and their equipment were dropped as planned. The crew was able to see them being welcomed by their comrades already on the ground. The Junkers returned to Udetfeld at 0507 hrs on 6 September.[14] This marked the end of Günther Korn's association with KG 200, for after this mission he was assigned to Alt-Lönnewitz as a pilot with the Arado firm to test-fly the new Ar 234 jet.[15]

Shortly after arriving at Neubiberg from Mont de Marsan in mid-August 1944, a detachment of officers from FAGr 5 was ordered to relocate to a subsidiary of the Messerschmitt aircraft manufacturing conglomerate known as the *Metallbau* Offingen (Offingen Metal Construction), a small production facility in the village of Offingen near Günzburg, to the east of Neu-Ulm. This detachment was led by Hauptmann Georg Eckl, Staffelkapitän of 2./FAGr 5 and included, from the *Gruppenstab*, Oberleutnant Ludwig Herlein; from 1.*Staffel*, Leutnant Günther Dittrich; and from 2.*Staffel*, Oberleutnant Horst Degenring, Leutnant Lothar Hecker, Oberleutnant Hans Münsterer, Oberleutnant Reinhard Sigel, and Leutnant Lohberg – all experienced airmen with sound technical awareness. The plan was that these officers, based at the offices of the *Metallbau* Offingen, would used their experience and expertise as aviators to work with senior civilian personnel in the aircraft industry to improve manufacturing quality, production processes and procurement methods. As Eckl recorded: 'A detachment from the crews was ordered to go to Offingen. There I would lead a "*Kommando* Nebel", which was involved in the procurement and supply of materials for the Me 262; the assembled aircraft were test-flown nearby in Leipheim.'[16]

Indeed, Professor Willy Messerschmitt's state-of-the-art Me 262 jet interceptor had first taken to the air from Leipheim using pure jet power just over two years earlier on 18 July 1942. By August 1944, small numbers of the jet fighter had been delivered to the first dedicated test unit of the Luftwaffe and there was great hope that the Me 262 would be the aircraft that would turn the tide of the air war back in Germany's favour.

However, only a short time after the reconnaissance flyers had arrived at Offingen, their brief was changed and they were ordered to report to Hauptmann Wolfgang Nebel for new tasks. Nebel was another experienced Luftwaffe reconnaissance pilot from 2./*Versuchsverband Ob.d.L.* Before serving with the *Versuchsverband*, he had flown with Oberstleutnant Theodor Rowehl in the *Versuchsstelle für Höhenflug*, a specialist high-altitude group and officially part of the Aufkl.Gr.Ob.d.L. Here, amongst other tasks, Nebel had flown a number of secret missions dropping spies and saboteurs over Iraq, Iran and other areas of the Middle East.[17] Later he was assigned from 2./*Versuchsverband Ob.d.L.* to the *Stab* of GL/C-E (the *Amtsgruppe Entwicklung*, or Development Department) at the RLM under Oberst Georg von Pasewaldt for the purposes of assessing the development of new aircraft, particularly long-range types.

In this capacity, on 25 January 1944, the then Oberleutnant Nebel travelled to the Messerschmitt works at Augsburg to discuss the building of five prototypes of the Messerschmitt Me 264, a four-engined, ultra-long-range design project instigated by Professor Messerschmitt and intended to offer the Luftwaffe an aircraft capable of crossing the Atlantic as far as the US eastern seaboard, and of operating in the roles of reconnaissance, bomber and anti-shipping aircraft. By this stage and since December 1942, the first and thus far only prototype of the Me 264 had been undergoing flight-testing at Augsburg and Lechfeld, which involved a programme of ironing out creases in the aircraft's performance. Throughout 1943, the Me 264's development had been the cause of considerable protracted debate within the RLM, as its various departments, along with Generalfeldmarschall Milch and senior Messerschmitt personnel, argued over the pros and cons of retaining the Ju 290 and the He 177 for Atlantic reconnaissance, against investing time, resources and money in other new, competing projects such as the six-engined Ju 390 and the similarly-engined Ta 400 from Focke-Wulf.

Nebel was tasked by the RLM to investigate the realities of manufacturing a short run of Me 264s. On 26 April, the recently promoted Hauptmann Nebel visited Memmingen to test-fly the Me 264 prototype on an assessment flight for the RLM. On 3 May, he made three further flights, but there were persistent minor problems with the aircraft.[18] Generalmajor von Barsewisch, the *General der Aufklärungsflieger*, was also present at Memmingen to fly the aircraft, but he judged the machine to be too slow for combat missions.

On 18 July 1944, however, aircraft of the USAAF Fifteenth Air Force bombed Memmingen and the Me 264 was destroyed. For Willy Messerschmitt and his dreams of building a long-range aircraft, the loss of the only fully assembled Me 264 prototype must have been a blow. Yet, as with so many other military and technical projects developed in the Third Reich in 1944, despite the prevailing adverse war situation and worsening conditions on the home front, the physical destruction of the aircraft did not signal the end of the Me 264 programme.

On 26 July, the *Kommando der Erprobungsstellen* authorized the establishment of *Sonderkommando* Nebel (Special Detachment Nebel) under the command of Hauptmann Nebel. The unit was set up specifically to oversee the further development of the Me 264 V2 and V3 prototypes and to assess the best use for them. It comprised engineers and personnel drawn from the staffs of the *General der Aufklärungsflieger* (with whom the *Kommandeur* of FAGr 5, Hermann Fischer, was working more closely on the long-term, long-range reconnaissance requirements of the Luftwaffe) and the *General der Fliegerausbildung*. The headquarters of the *Kommando* was to be at Offingen, the location of the V2 and V3 airframes, and its core staff was to be augmented by Georg Eckl and the aforementioned officers from FAGr 5.

No sooner had Nebel's unit been established, however, than it was given fresh orders by OKL. It was now to concentrate on the 'technical problems associated with new aircraft' – this meant not just the Me 264, but other new long-range types such as the Do 335 and the planned ultra-long-range Do 635.

The accomplishments of the *Kommando* remain unclear, but in August 1944, it is possible that, among other things, it was involved in working with the firm of Osermaschinen GmbH to carry out the design and development of a 6,000-hp steam-turbine power unit for an aircraft, and an Me 264 airframe – possibly the V2 – was to have been placed at the disposal of the firm.

On 15 August 1944, at the time Eckl and the FAGr 5 officers were assigned to Nebel, Oberst im Generalstabsdienst Artur Eschenauer, the *Chef der 6. Abteilung* of the OKL Generalquartiermeister, issued a key report on the future of both the Me 264 and the activities of *Sonderkommando* Nebel addressed to the senior technical officer on Göring's personal staff, the OKL *Führungsstab* and von Barsewisch. According to Eschenauer:

> The removal of the Ju 290 and Ju 390 from the long-range reconnaissance programme has left a hole which needs to be closed. It is possible that the large amount of assembled parts still available would be enough to build 20–30 Me 264s and make them operational. In order to actually realize this, personnel from the *General der Aufklärungsflieger* and *General der Fliegerausbildung* should be placed with *Sonderkommando* Nebel, which will have the task of coordinating the testing and deployment of the Me 264.

In a somewhat contradictory manner, Eschenauer also went on to state that no 'large' completed parts still existed with which to start construction, and that 80 per cent of the required materials had been destroyed. He also foresaw that the Me 264 V2 would not be ready until February 1945 and that the aircraft would weigh 50 tonnes and be powered by four BMW 801 engines. The workforce available at Messerschmitt to build the Me 264 was noted at 80 'constructors', of which half were foreign, with a further 20 brought in from Heinkel. If the plan of the *Technisches Amt* to use more than one manufacturer was to be realized, Eschenauer opined that, 'in order to push the matter through, a military commander should be placed in charge. For this purpose, any personnel should come from the *General der Aufklärungsflieger* or the *General der Fliegerausbildung.*'

This was obviously a reference to the employment of the men from FAGr 5.

Even as late as August 1944, Adolf Hitler still harboured thoughts of conducting air operations against the United States. On 5 August, he announced that he wanted to see the 'fastest possible production' of further Me 264s.[20] By early September 1944, however, von Barsewisch and Admiral Dönitz were forced to accept that with the imminent loss of vital airfields in France and the increasing superiority of the Allied air forces, the prospect of conducting any form of cooperation between the Me 264 and the U-boats was very unlikely. On the 7th, a last-ditch meeting was held in Berlin to discuss in what way – if at all – anything could be done with the Me 264 project on a practical level. In attendance from the Kriegsmarine were Dönitz and members of the staff of the BdU, while from the Luftwaffe, there was von Barsewisch and Hauptmann Müller from the staff of the *General der Auflkärungsflieger*, together with Major Fischer from FAGr 5, who had been asked to attend because of his recent practical experience in flying long-range operations over the Atlantic. As Oskar Schmidt noted: 'At this time Major Fischer was more frequently in Berlin, to be readily available to the *General der Aufklärungsflieger* and the RLM *Chef der* TLR for new tasks. There he was also best able to represent the interests of his FAGr 5. Events at the battlefronts, which were the cause of so many problems for the high command, meant the *Gruppe* was left, more or less, alone.'[21] It is quite possible that Hauptmann Nebel was present as well, but this is not certain.

By the autumn of 1944, the whole Me 264 project was in some state of abeyance. In late September, Dönitz diplomatically persuaded Hitler to cancel plans for the aircraft; in truth, the task of the Admiral was made a little easier by the fact that the *Führer* was too preoccupied with other more pressing matters, so that by this stage of the war, the question of transatlantic bombing and reconnaissance was no longer relevant or a priority to him. Thus on 23 September 1944, orders were issued from the headquarters of the *Führer* that all further work on the Me 264 was to be cancelled. This was followed just under a month later, on 18 October, by a stark order from Göring stating: 'Production of the Me 264 is herewith cancelled.'

In another meeting, on 16 October, Fischer presented his requirements to representatives from Dornier, Heinkel and Junkers for a strategic reconnaissance aircraft with a range of 8000 km to replace the Ju 290. This was to be based on the *Zwilling* (twin) concept as used by Heinkel in which the fuselages of two He 111s had been mated together and used to provide power and range, in that case for long-range air-towing. There was no reason why the same concept could not be used for reconnaissance. It was decided that the majority of the aircraft should be used for fuel, although one fuselage was to be used to house 300 kg of marker flares. The hope was that production should begin in January 1945, with one aircraft being delivered in that month, three each in February, March and April and four in May.

A few days earlier on 12 October, Junkers had agreed to take over from Dornier the design of a radical new *Zwilling* concept for an Atlantic *Aufklärer*, which would be able to assist the Kriegsmarine when it planned to resume a meaningful level of U-boat warfare in the late spring of 1945. The big Dornier, formed from the idea of mating two standard Do 335 fuselages to create more fuel capacity in a new wing centre section, was expected to possess a range of nearly 7000 km, enough at least to reach as far as the north of Ireland and the St George's Channel. This would work ideally to Fischer's outline specification requirement for an ultra-long-range machine. *Sonderkommando* Nebel's work was not over.

'For three days, American P-51 Mustangs have been attacking our aircraft on the *Autobahn*. They were able to pick out their dispersals despite some pretty good camouflage.' So wrote Oskar Schmidt on 9 September 1944 of events at Neubiberg. By this point, those Ju 290s of FAGr 5 that had reached Neubiberg from Mont de Marsan had been towed out to the adjacent *Autobahn*, which had been closed to civilian traffic, and pushed back into the woods edging the road in an effort to conceal them from Allied air attack.

Schmidt later recalled: 'Since there was no Flak defence at all – at least not at the time – the fighters flew low along the *Autobahn* and fired at the aircraft parked there. Of our own fighters, nothing was seen; but at that time they faced a very difficult situation. Against such overwhelming opposition, it was no longer possible for us to mount regular operations.'

Eventually, FAGr 5 set up two 20 mm cannon in dugouts on the *Autobahn* as defence against enemy aircraft.

In September, the mood at Neubiberg was one of tension and weariness. The men were aware of heavy fighting in Aachen. Yet there was little to do. Boredom created anxiety. Those personnel who were deemed by the *Stab* to be deserving were given leave (frequently disguised as a service task). Although this was risky, it meant that such servicemen could spend a short period of time with their families before whatever the war would bring in the coming weeks and months. Some men, whose wives lived in areas closer by, even managed to get them quartered in local accommodation for short periods. A nearby Flak and fighter defence radar unit made its facilities available for the men of FAGr 5 to watch the occasional evening film.

The *Gruppe Adjutant*, Oberleutnant Herbert Abel, who made strenuous efforts to keep the elements of FAGr 5 in Bavaria cohesive and to maintain morale, travelled to Berlin by train in order to ascertain how, as Schmidt recorded, 'the dice were going to roll for our unit.' He returned on the 15th unable to say much.

As September gave way to October, the men carried out work on the land, to help local farmers, and also worked on maintaining the *Autobahn*, while the mechanics and signals sections busied themselves servicing the vehicles and radio equipment of the *Gruppe*. By the middle of the month, the atmosphere at the *Stab* headquarters at Hofolding became increasingly illusory. 'The *Volkssturm* was called up – all men between the ages of 16 and 60,' recalled Oskar Schmidt, 'and our soldiers were at Hofolding in retirement! With the deterioration in the situation at the battlefronts, the satisfaction with the prevailing situation was quite noticeable. Who could blame us?'

On the 22nd, the 'peace' at Hofolding was disturbed by another low-level strafing attack by Mustangs. Cannon set up in the woods as 'AA guns' responded in defence and hits were observed on at least one of the P-51s, which veered away and disappeared behind some trees to come down in the Hofoldinger Forest. The newly promoted Hauptmann Schmidt headed off into the forest with a detachment of men and found the wreckage of the USAAF fighter lying broken up on the forest floor as a result of crashing through the dense trees. The pilot was dead in his cockpit. Schmidt posted a guard to stay with the aircraft, while he went off to advise the appropriate recovery authorities.

In early November, two of the unit's Ju 290s were pulled out of their forest dispersals and towed to Neubiberg airfield, from where they took off to an airfield in the east to collect personnel from two reconnaissance *Staffeln* which had been cut off by the now rapidly advancing Red Army.

Meanwhile, 25 men from the *Stabskompanie* of FAGr 5 had to be given up for service with the *Fallschirmjäger* (paratroops), probably for use as ground troops.[22]

On the morning of 4 October 1944, Ju 290A-7 Wk-Nr 0186 9V+FH, an aircraft which had been delivered to FAGr 5 in April, took off from the base of 1./KG 200 at Finsterwalde en route for Wien (Vienna)-Parndorf in order to undertake an operation on behalf of the *Abwehr*. The objective of the mission was to drop an Arab sabotage team, led by a Leutnant from the *Abwehr*, together with containers of explosives, into an upland region of Algeria under the codename Operation *Parzival*.

Despite having been assigned to KG 200 since 10 July, the Junkers retained its FAGr 5 fuselage code. Wien-Parndorf was the first stage-stop on its flight to Athens-Kalamaki in Greece, a country from which the Germans were about to withdraw under Allied pressure. After leaving Parndorf, the pilot, Hauptmann Emil Sachtleben of 1./FAGr 5, the man who had flown to eastern Greenland in June, together with his crew, which included observer Oberleutnant Adalbert von Pechmann, also of 1.*Staffel*, headed for their next stop at Belgrade-Semlin in Yugoslavia. They then flew on to Thessaloniki. They found the airfield there being demolished by German units who were in the process of pulling out. With no accommodation, they tried to get some rest sleeping in the open air, but this proved virtually impossible amidst an uncomfortably warm night spent under mosquito nets with the constant sound of buildings being detonated.

Furthermore, there was no transport available for Sachtleben to get into the town to report his arrival to the local Luftwaffe commander. It was fortunate therefore, that he was able to use the motorcycle that the crew kept on board the Ju 290 for just such an emergency. Upon his return to the airfield, he found it under attack from a large formation of enemy fighter-bombers, and two other transport aircraft parked either side of 9V+FH were already burning; miraculously, the Junkers remained unscathed.

Sachtleben instructed the Arabs and their German leader to board the Junkers. Once they and their explosives were safely stowed, the Ju 290 took off for Kalamaki. In a bizarre ritual, prior to take-off from Kalamaki at 1738 hrs, the Arabs performed a dance for their German *Abwehr* officer. The take-off and first part of the flight went smoothly, but as they approached Chalcis on course for Athens at an altitude of 3000 m, the local German naval Flak batteries, not familiar with the size, shape and sound of the big four-engined Ju 290, feared it was an Allied bomber and opened fire.

The Ju 290 then flew a course at low level across the Mediterranean towards the coast of Libya. To that point the weather was exactly as forecast, and the crew kept a careful eye on wind direction and speed. On reaching the coast near Tripoli, the Junkers climbed and turned to cross Tunisia and on towards Algeria. Soon after, however, the cloud suddenly thickened and the Junkers flew into the midst of a raging sandstorm. Visibility was zero. After a very worrying period, the storm passed, but the inside of the aircraft had been left coated in sand and all aboard could feel and taste sand in their mouths. It was impossible to tell if any of the engines had been damaged.

The crew members of the Junkers were now facing real difficulties, since the Allied radio transmitters on Malta, from which they hoped to pick up navigational assistance, were silent and astro-navigation was not possible.

Fortunately, however, as they crossed into Algeria, the weather started to clear and a full moon shone. In reality, this was of little help because the Germans were not familiar with the largely featureless terrain below. Eventually, the desert morphed into hills and the crew searched for a suitable drop point. After flying for some time longer, the spot was found and all the agents, as well as their explosives, were dropped.

The Junkers then turned back across the sea and, after an uneventful return flight, landed at Thessaloniki at 0601 hrs on the morning of the 8th after a flight of 12 hr and 29 min. The aircraft eventually flew to I./KG 200's base at Finow. From 29 October, this aircraft was based at the East Prussian airfield of Wormditt, from where Sachtleben and his second pilot, Oberfeldwebel Kreutzmann, would conduct further flights, with their aircraft recoded as KG 200 machine A3+OB.[23]

By late 1944/early 1945, those crews of FAGr 5 assigned to KG 200 had still not returned to their former *Gruppe* and it was assumed that, in effect, their posting to that *Geschwader* had become permanent.[24]

Meanwhile, in another initiative in November 1944, other crews of FAGr 5 were used to undertake dangerous supply flights to Skoplje (Skopje), one of the last German-held cities in Yugoslavia. Since September 1944, German forces had been vulnerable to attacks from Yugoslav partisans in the region and were increasingly at risk from a Soviet thrust through Rumania. Despite bitter fighting, by November, the Nazis' 3½-year occupation was almost over. Yet in the first half of that month, Ju 290s continued to fly supply missions from Wien-Aspern to Skoplje, from where they picked up wounded troops for the return flight.

Leutnant Herbert Wagner of 1./FAGr 5 in Wk-Nr 0157 9V+BK made five such flights up to 13 November. The *Ritterkreuz* holder Oberleutnant Paul Birnkraut, also of 1.*Staffel*, performed a mission on 3 November, but on the return flight, his aircraft, Wk-Nr 0180 9V+KH, was hit badly by enemy ground fire. He made it back to Aspern, but his Junkers had been peppered by 80 20 mm hits.[25]

In a conference on 27 November 1944, the OKL decided that 3.(F)/ *Aufklärungsgruppe Nacht* would convert to the Ar 234 jet reconnaissance aircraft rather than the original intention to equip it with the much-awaited and innovative 'push-pull' Do 335 for nocturnal reconnaissance. At the same time, it was decided that FAGr 5 at Neubiberg should re-equip with the new Dornier.[26] Simultaneously, it was also noted that a new U-boat with a reduced radius of action would soon be introduced, and that FAGr 5 should receive either the Do 335, Ar 234 or, ideally, the Do 335Z (*Zwilling* – what was actually the new Junkers Ju 635 project). A two-seat version of the Do 335 was considered ideal, but a single-seat version would be acceptable. It was hoped that the former would have a range of 4800 km and the latter 5500 km, which was more than twice that of the standard aircraft. Four Do 335s were intended to be built during each of the first four months of 1945, three Ar 234s during each of the first three months of the year, and one Do 335Z in March and April, three in May and five in each of the following months.[27] The desired range requirement would probably be achieved by a larger wooden wing, enlarged internal fuel tanks and two 900-l drop tanks beneath the wings.[28] *Stab*/FAGr 5 was to have an intended establishment of three aircraft, while the two *Staffeln* of the *Gruppe* would have 12 each. It was proposed that the *Fernaufklärungsgruppe* would operate out into the Atlantic as far as 25° West, while longer-range missions would be the responsibility of *Sonderkommando* Nebel equipped with the Me 264.[29]

The same day as the OKL conference, Major Fischer – now assigned to the Chef TLR/F1-E, together with Oberleutnant Hans Müller, FAGr 5's Technical Officer, examined a mock-up of the new Ju 635 twin-fuselage *Zwilling* project.[30] It seemed preliminarily work on the enormous *Aufklärer* was well under way. After taking over the Do 335Z/He P 1075 project, the Junkers design team had begun by installing radio equipment in late November/mid-December 1944. In addition, Fischer was informed that the FuG 200 *Hohentwiel* was to be supplemented, or replaced, with the new FuG 224 *Berlin A* target-indicating set.[31]

In December 1944, as German forces fought their last significant counter-offensive of the war in the snow-covered forests of the Ardennes, and the Red Army approached Budapest, Messerschmitt engineers continued their work on developing designs for the Me 264 at *Metalbau* Offingen. One idea being worked upon at this time was a courier version of the Me 264, with a range of 12,000 km and a payload of 4000 kg. But since virtually all the necessary parts and components for such a project had by now been scrapped or commandeered for other tasks, it seems likely that the whole idea was little more than a ruse to prevent Messerschmitt employees from being caught by military conscription teams who were combing government and civil institutions for vitally needed personnel for the war fronts.

Meanwhile, on 5 December 1944, *Sonderkommando* Nebel at Offingen was tasked by Generalmajor Ulrich Diesing, the *Chef der Technischen Luftrüstung* (Chef TLR – Head of Air Technical Equipment), with urgently taking charge of development policy with regard to all long-range reconnaissance, long-range *Zerstörer* and long-range fighter types, particularly to assist the new U-boat campaign for 1945. The *Kommando* was to cease any special priority it gave to the Me 264.[32] This was reinforced on 16 January 1945, when the *General der Aufklärungsflieger* demarcated the objectives of *Sonderkommando* Nebel as the development and operational trials of aircraft for special long-range missions for the *Seekriegsleitung* and the *Luftwaffenführungsstab* as distinct from FAGr 5, which was to work on reconnaissance for U-boats and over 'north-east England', as well as conducting operational trials with the Ar 234 jet reconnaissance aircraft (see Chapter Fifteen) and the anticipated Do 335Z.[33]

On the 12th, during a discussion between officials of the RLM, officers of the OKL and Reichsmarschall Göring, it was stated that four Ju 635s were on order and that the *General der Aufklärer* had requested the construction of 20 0-series pre-production aircraft. It was felt that this could be achieved if a number of Do 335 fuselages were put aside in May 1945.

That day, Major Fischer ordered the rest of FAGr 5 at Neubiberg and Hofolding to relocate to Offingen, but the reason for this was, and remains, a mystery, though it is believed it was to assign the unit's effectively redundant personnel to work on the assembly lines there. Whether this was on his own initiative, or whether he was acting on orders from a higher command, also remains unknown. Certainly, it seems logical to have wanted to give 'idle hands work' and possibly save them from being assigned as ground troops in the East. Whatever the case, a lack of accommodation at Offingen prevented such a move, as did a lack of fuel.[34]

Development of the Ju 635 continued, but considerable delays were experienced. Wind-tunnel testing carried out with scale models of the aircraft fitted with freely rotating propellers revealed wing-tip airflow separation but oddly, only on one side. Test pilots flying the Do 335 at Rechlin also reported complaints with the cowl-flaps and persistent problems with the undercarriage and fuselage joints. In the middle of January, the Chef TLR reported that the order for additional machines over the four already sanctioned by the Reichsmarschall had been delayed by labour problems at Junkers.[35] The first aircraft (component testing), which had been intended to be flight-tested in March and the second aircraft (radio equipment trials) probably in June, were not envisaged until July/August. The reasons for the delay were difficulties in the delivery of fuselages and problems with the wing design. On 24 January, Göring again pressed for the production of ten Do 335s with two 300-l or two 900-l long-range tanks and 20 Ju 635s.[36]

Following an order from *Hauptdienstleiter Diplom-Ingenieur* Karl-Otto Saur of the *Rüstungsstab* issued on 15 March and in agreement with Junkers, it was decided to continue with the Ju 635, but use the simplest solution for its production.[37] However, no aircraft was completed before the end of the war.

By mid-February 1945, with the worsening war situation, work on the Me 264 was dead, and there were proposals to disband *Sonderkommando* Nebel – which was known to have a strength of 388 personnel, including nine officers, presumably most of them from FAGr 5 under Hauptmann Eckl, and 44 civilian 'helpers' or auxiliaries – and assign its members to front-line service. On 12 February, at a meeting of the heads of the various operational arms of the Luftwaffe, it was decided to retain the *Kommando* as a small military unit intended to fulfil tasks for industry using civilian personnel. Its fate at the end of the war is not known.[38]

———————

From January 1945, Hauptmann Emil Sachtleben and Oberleutnant Adalbert von Pechmann of 1./FAGr 5, together with their crew and aircraft Ju 290A-7 Wk-Nr 0186 A3+OB (9V+FH while with FAGr 5), were based at Stolp-Reitz, 100 km west of Danzig in Pomerania. From this small airfield, the Luftwaffe flew occasional supply flights to the so-called 'Fortress cities', ones that had been surrounded by the Red Army, but which Hitler insisted were to be defended to the last man. However, the Ju 290, when fully loaded, required a runway of 2.5 km in length, so it was therefore not possible to fly such missions from the 1,465-m runway at Stolp-Reitz.

Thus it was, that on 3 February 1945, Sachtleben and von Pechmann took off from Stolp-Reitz for Gotenhafen-Hexengrund, the *Torpedowaffenplatz der Luftwaffe*, farther east along the Baltic coast. From here the plan was to fly to Lake Peipus (the Peipussee), the fifth largest lake in Europe, on the border between Estonia and the Soviet Union, close to which a group of Finnish officers would be parachuted. A first attempt to fly the mission, under the codename Operation *Narwa*, was thwarted by fog, but the following day, the Junkers took off at 2207 hrs. Reaching the lake, the aircraft came under fire from light Flak and over the target zone dense fog prevailed, which made it impossible to locate the exact drop point. After flying around for some time, the mission was eventually aborted and the aircraft returned safely to Gotenhafen-Hexengrund after an eight-hour flight.[39]

———————

From mid-December 1944, along with snow showers, the sight of Allied bomber formations heading north into the Reich from Italy became a regular feature in the skies over the now-named *Ausweichsquartier Hofolding* (Dispersal Base Hofolding). During this period, Major Fischer was in Neubiberg quite frequently since there was now a strong likelihood that FAGr 5 would be transferred to Scandinavia, either to Stavanger or Aalborg, from where, apparently, new reconnaissance operations would commence. Although such news was greeted with some degree of scepticism at first, this quickly changed when preliminary orders came through to prepare to transfer north in January. Preparations began immediately, but they proved challenging because *Sonderkommando* Nebel was reluctant to release those officers of FAGr 5 at Offingen. 'There was quite a tug-of-war,' remembers Oskar Schmidt.[40]

The last Christmas of the war was celebrated by the *Ausweichsquartier Hofolding* in a restaurant at Hofolding. The *Stabskompanie* of FAGr 5, together with some *Hiwis* and soldiers – 55 men in all, as well as a small group of musicians – squeezed into a small dining room to enjoy some festive music and the carefully stored fare brought back from France, including bottles of decent Cognac, together with beer and *Glühwein*. 'It was a peaceful Christmas Eve,' Schmidt noted, 'Unlike that experienced by German troops in the Ardennes!'[41]

But the rest did not last long, and, just a day later, activity centred on overhauling vehicles and equipment in readiness for the move. The problem was that the period of inactivity, during which the unit's vehicles had been left out in rain and deep snow, had taken its toll on engines and driving systems. In addition, the regional *Luftgau* had commandeered several of the cars and lorries of the *Gruppe*. Heavy snow hindered movement, but above it all was the excited, slightly apprehensive chatter and rumour over a return to operations within a new theatre and with an impressive new aircraft in what would be the seventh year of war. There was still hope of a victory, even if the offensive in the Ardennes was faltering and Budapest was threatened by the Soviets. The promised new jet aircraft and U-boats would be sure to change things.

CHAPTER FIFTEEN

DIVIDE AND FALL

The Final Months, January–May 1945

It boggled my mind to think that here was a group of our
leaders talking about aircraft production for the next few years
while we were diving into an air raid shelter every ten minutes.

Hellmut Hetz, I./FAGr 5

The Arado Ar 234 – the world's first pure jet reconnaissance-bomber – had joined
the Luftwaffe inventory in the summer of 1944. Not particularly inspirational in
appearance, yet neat and compact, this single-seat, twin-engined, high-wing
aircraft nevertheless demonstrated unprecedented performance and was able to
achieve breathtaking performance for the time. The Ar 234 had a maximum
speed of 735 km/h, a cruising range at altitude of 1600 km, and a service ceiling
of 10,000 m, making it extremely difficult to target, let alone shoot down.

One of the first pilots to fly the machine was Horst Götz of
1./*Versuchsverband* OKL on 1 June 1944. He remembered: 'It was a completely
new flying experience. Only a slight whistling noise in the cockpit could be
heard. It was really wonderful! The aircraft promised a legendary performance
… [When landing] it felt just like a glider.'[1]

Originating from an Arado 'in-house' project of 1940 for a long-range reconnaissance aircraft and designed by the company's *Technische Abteilung*, the Ar 234 was powered by two Junkers 004 turbojets, developing 900 kp of static thrust. It eventually appeared in operational units in two basic variants: the early 'A' series (actually prototypes fitted with a jettisonable take-off dolly and a retractable landing skid) and the later, mass-produced 'B' variant which had a fully functioning retractable undercarriage, which equipped both reconnaissance and bomber units. In the former role, operations commenced initially with *Kommando* Götz in France, later known as *Kommando* Sperling. The Ar 234 bomber, the world's first dedicated jet bomber, was deployed from December 1944 by the *Einsatzstaffel* of III./KG 76. In 1945, KG 76 would operate greater numbers of the aircraft against Allied airfields, vehicle columns, strongpoints and bridges on the Western Front.

On 16 January 1945, a conference was held at the RLM in Berlin, chaired by Oberstleutnant Siegfried Knemeyer, the Chef TLR/E in the *Abteilung Entwicklung* (Development Department) at the RLM, which was intended, once again, to review potential, long-range maritime reconnaissance aircraft, including a turboprop-powered version of the Me 264, the Hütter 211, which had been developed from the Heinkel He 219, a modified Do 335 featuring an enlarged wing, and the Ju 635 project. Not surprisingly, Major Hermann Fischer from FAGr 5 was asked to attend.[2]

For his part, with deep snow and temperatures in southern Germany dropping to well below zero, on 4 January 1945, Hermann Fischer had escaped to a Luftwaffe rest home in the Austrian Alps, together with a few other officers, for four days of skiing. On his return to Neubiberg on the 8th and suitably refreshed, he relayed orders he had received to prepare a *Vorkommando* (advance detachment) of 30 men led by Major Augustin, which would be destined for Norway, from where it was envisaged elements of the *Gruppe* would operate the new Ar 234. The crew of Hauptmann Miersch of 2.*Staffel* was also put on standby to fly one of the Ju 290s to transport the detachment.[3]

Accompanying Fischer to Berlin for the meeting on the 16th was Leutnant Hellmut Hetz, a former pilot of 1./FAGr 5, who had flown a Ju 290 out of Mont de Marsan to Mühldorf in August 1944 (see Chapter Thirteen). After leaving France, Hetz had been assigned to the Ago factory at Oschersleben where he was engaged as a production test pilot on the Fw 190. Then, in November he was transferred to Neuburg an der Donau as a test pilot for the Me 262. In January 1945, he received a telephone call, as he recalls:

> I had a telephone call from Major Fischer asking me if I wanted to go back into action. He told me that Admiral Karl Dönitz was considering reforming

FAGr 5 for reconnaissance duties with the Ar 234. These were to support the new Type XXI U-boats which were due to make their operational debut imminently.

Shortly afterwards, I met Major Fischer in Berlin where I was to carry his briefcase at an important meeting at the RLM. I considered the meeting completely pie-in-the-sky, and it boggled my mind to think that here was a group of our leaders talking about aircraft production for the next few years while we were diving into an air raid shelter every ten minutes. One General, I remember, was very anxious to promote a particular Junkers type, but I could not understand why he found it so impressive. When the conference finished I asked Major Fischer about it. He pulled me to a window and pointed to a beautiful new Horch sports car parked outside. 'The General was given that by the Junkers Company,' he said. I was so disgusted by this that I got blind drunk that night and had to spend the next day cleaning up the mess I had made![4]

The outcome of this conference was the proposal that *Sonderkommando* Nebel be disbanded, with Hauptmann Eckl and the other officers of FAGr 5 returned to the *Gruppe*, which was to be 're-formed' for new maritime reconnaissance operations. Pending arrival of whatever new dedicated aircraft types were approved for such operations, FAGr 5 was to be given a small number of Ar 234s sufficient to equip both Augustin's and Eckl's respective *Staffeln*. In addition to providing support for the new U-boat offensive, missions would also be flown to reconnoitre Scapa Flow, ahead of a proposed air attack on the Royal Navy's anchorage there, planned for later in January.

Meanwhile, at some point in January 1945, a special *Einsatzkommando* (Operational Detachment) was formed from 1./FAGr 5 with the intention of taking on a small number of Ar 234 jets and flying them operationally, though precisely where, at that time, the acceptance process was to take place is not clear; some sources state Quakenbrück in northern Germany, others Brandenburg.[5] By the second half of the month, weather conditions to the south at Neubiberg were harsh, with snowdrifts and temperatures falling to -25°C at night. The vehicles of the *Gruppe*, which had been given up to other units during the autumn, had been returned but were in a poor condition after continuous use. With rumours of a move to northern Germany at some point, they had to be dug out of the deep snow and overhauled in the freezing conditions. On the 29th, Major Fischer was briefly in Neubiberg and gave final orders to prepare the Norwegian *Vorkommando*, comprising a photo-section, ground-based radio-operators and signals personnel, and a vehicle team, for transfer, although its departure would be delayed by 24 hours because of a lack of railway freight wagons. Beyond that, Fischer was able to tell his *Stab* little of the immediate intentions of the OKL for the rest of the *Gruppe*. The only certainty was that the unit could expect to have to give up more men for ground-fighting duties.[6]

Quickly following this was the appointment, in early February, of Major Fischer as commander of the *Stab* FAGr 1. On 30 January, the *General der Aufklärungsflieger* had ordered that Fischer should transfer to take over control of all reconnaissance units in Denmark, specifying an initial move in connection with this, to Quakenbrück on 4 February. To this end another *Vorkommando* from FAGr 5 at Neubiberg was prepared with orders to proceed to Grove airfield in Denmark, where it was to join Major Fischer.[7]

Fernaufklärungsgruppe 1 had been formed in May 1942 and had functioned as a tactical command staff for long-range reconnaissance units on the northern sector of the Eastern Front. Its various assigned *Staffeln*, which included, at different times, 3.(F)/Aufkl.Gr.Nacht, 3.(F) and 5.(F)/Aufkl. Gr.122, 3.(F)/Aufkl.Gr.22, and 1.(F)/Aufkl.Gr.33, had operated mainly Ju 188s and Me 410s. After German forces had steadily withdrawn from the East in 1944, the *Stab* FAGr 1 finally settled at Quakenbrück in early February 1945.[8]

Josef Augustin recalled of this time:

On 30 January 1945, the '*Kommando Norwegen*' departed Neubiberg for Stavanger-Sola, under the command of Hauptmann Augustin, previously *Staffelkapitän* of 1./FAGr 5, who had now been further ordered to take over a *Staffel* of the new FAGr 1 at Grove. Actually, Hauptmann Eckl was to have led this *Kommando*, but at the time he was unable to get away from the Messerschmitt works at Augsburg [sic], so Augustin jumped in for him. It was not planned for Hauptmann Eckl to be in the new FAGr 1. Stavanger-Sola was seen as the base for operations with the Ar 234 over England.

The departure from Neubiberg was in two freight wagons. Strength 30–40 officers, NCOs and men. Besides Hauptmann Augustin there were the following officers: Hauptmann Helmut Miersch, Oberleutnant Hans Ascheid, Oberleutnant Siegfried Frank (Signals Officer), Leutnant Hellmut Hetz (Technical Officer), Leutnant Eduard Schmitt (Offz.z.b.V.) and as senior NCO, Hauptfeldwebel Meyer. On the way, while in the Hannover area, the wagons were coupled to an empty train intended for carrying V2 rockets and were attacked by enemy fighters. No losses. At Arhus in Denmark, the wagons were unloaded onto a ship for Oslo. There we were again loaded onto a train and travelled on to Stavanger-Sola. Once we had arrived, I reported to the local *Fliegerführer*. Our task was to fly reconnaissance over the east coast of England, to determine air and ship activity from an altitude of 10,000 m. For enemy aircraft, the Ar 234 was untouchable in terms of height and performance. We were placed under the command of the *Fliegerführer Norwegen*.[9]

On 11 February, Major Fischer arrived unexpectedly at Neubiberg, having travelled there yet again from Berlin; this time he brought clear new orders with him. Hauptmann Eckl also arrived from his duties with *Sonderkommando* Nebel at Offingen to take part in the briefing.

Fischer confirmed the following salient points:

- *Fernaufklärungsgruppe* 5 '*Atlantik*', which, in effect, had been in the process of disbandment for some time, was to be disbanded offically.
- Only 1.*Staffel*, under Hauptmann Augustin, was to remain active and would be strengthened from various other units.
- Upon disbandment, the *Stabskompanie* of FAGr 5 would give to 1./FAGr 5 any personnel it required, with the remainder being transferred for duties as *Fallschirmjäger* or as infantry. Hauptmann Oskar Schmidt, *Chef* of the *Stabskompanie* would transfer as Offz.z.b.V. to Augustin's new *Staffel*.
- Major Fischer was to assume command of FAGr 1, which was to be reformed at Grove. In doing so, he would assume control of the *Gruppenstab* of FAGr 1 and arrange to dissolve the *Stab* of FAGr 5, although he would be able to retain key personnel from it in his new appointment. One loss from the *Stab* would be Oberleutnant Ludwig Herlein, previously of 3.(F)/Aufkl.Gr.22, who was promoted to Hauptmann and awarded the *Ritterkreuz*. He would then be assigned to Italy as *Staffelkapitän* with a *Fernaufklärungsgruppe* based there.
- The existing *Staffeln* of FAGr 1 would be consolidated into one new, enlarged *Staffel* under the command of Hauptmann Augustin, as 1./FAGr 1.
- Hauptmann Eckl, previously *Staffelkapitän* of 2./FAGr 5 under attachment to *Sonderkommando* Nebel, was now unassigned and to be found a new appointment by Major Fischer.

Oskar Schmidt commented: 'Finally, these were clear orders, and everyone now knew what was intended of him … However, until these new commands were arranged properly and the new establishments were effected, the existing formations would remain in place.'[10]

On 14 February, Oberleutnant Herbert Abel, the *Gruppenadjutant* of FAGr 5, and Hauptmann Oskar Schmidt journeyed by rail from Munich to the headquarters of *Generalmajor* von Barsewisch at Jüterbog-Damm to discuss matters connected with the new arrangements. However, their outward and return journeys were tedious and badly delayed as a result of frequent air raid warnings.

The following day, the OKL war diary noted: 'The provision for the transfer to Norway of a *Schwarm* of 1(F)/33 contained in the directive of 1 January is cancelled. A *Schwarm* of 1(F)/5 will be provided for operations in Norway.'[11]

By late February, more personnel from FAGr 5 at Neubiberg were despatched to Norway. The *Gruppe* ensured that this was always undertaken using small groups of men with impeccable paperwork, otherwise there was always the risk that they could be 'press-ganged' during their journey through the Reich and commandeered for other purposes. The *Gruppe* also established its own radio unit at Grosshelfendorf, just to the east of the Hofoldinger Forest, from where a permament communications link was established with the new units in Scandinavia.[12]

Some training on the Ar 234 had commenced. According to Josef Augustin, every 14 days, a pilot was ordered from Neubiberg to Burg-bei-Magdeburg for training on the jet; firstly Hauptmann Miersch, then Leutnant Hetz, then Leutnant Schmitt.[13] As Hellmut Hetz recalled:

Late in January 1945 I moved to Burg where I began training on the Arado. My first five-minute flight was made on the 30th, followed by a second which lasted 51 minutes. These were both made in an Ar 234B coded 9V+GH. I then transferred to Stavanger-Sola in Norway from where I made two more familiarization flights on 25 February and 3 March.[14]

Indeed, the British had reported 'one Ar 234 of 1./(F) 5' as having arrived in Stavanger on 26 February, information that was born out by an entry in the OKL war diary for that day, which confirmed that 'the *Einsatzkommando* 1./(F)5 has arrived in Stavanger with 1 Ar 234. This means modern jet reconnaissance is available in Norway.'[15] They also picked up a radio transmission from the Kriegsmarine reporting a flight, which in itself gave the British their first signal that the Ar 234 was operating from Norway. On the 26th, the British noted that the ground echelons of *Einsatzkommando* 1.(F)/5 were at full strength at Stavanger-Sola along with a solitary Ar 234, although two more such aircraft were at Grove, having made an interim landing there. They were expected to head to Norway as soon as the weather had cleared and the skies were deemed safe enough.[16]

On 1 March, the *Stab* FAGr 1 moved to Grove, and three days later, Generalmajor von Barsewisch ordered that operations previously undertaken by 1.(F)/Aufkl.Gr.123 were to be taken over by the *Einsatzkommando* of 1.(F)/5, which comprised Leutnant Hetz and Leutnant Eduard Schmitt, both former members of 1./FAGr 5. Furthermore, 'Reconnaissance Ar 234s would be ready for operations from Stavanger in six days' time … U-boat command is to pass requests for coverage direct to the *Kommandierende General der Deutschen Luftwaffe in Norwegen* (Commanding General of the Luftwaffe in Norway).'[17]

This was the signal that, albeit in a new guise, at least some of the personnel of FAGr 5 would again be undertaking reconnaissance for the U-boat arm. Twenty-nine Type VII U-boats had sailed from Norway in February, and they had sunk 16 Allied ships of 50,000 tons, but, in the process, 16 boats – more than half the force – had been lost. This was the second month in a row that one U-boat had been lost for every Allied vessel sunk. In March, 29 boats would sail from Norwegian bases to British waters, accounting for nine enemy ships sunk of 20,000 tons, or one-third of a ship per U-boat.[18]

Although Hetz and Schmitt had made some further training flights over Norway in late February and early March 1945, it would not be until the afternoon of the 23rd that the first operational mission was flown, when the two pilots flew a photo-reconnaissance from Stavanger-Sola to the northern British Isles in aircraft carrying the FAGr 5 unit code of '9V', with Hetz covering northern Scotland in Ar 234B-2b Wk-Nr 140341 9V+AH and Schmitt in Ar 234B-2b Wk-Nr 140493 9V+CH, covering the coastal waters from the Firth of Forth south to the Tyne at South Shields. Hetz recalled: 'I took off "heavy" (loaded with two RATO and two drop tanks) at 1450 hrs for my first operational sortie over Britain. This was completed at high altitude, and although an attempt was made by Spitfires to intercept, they could get nowhere near me.'

Hetz crossed the Scottish coast north of Aberdeen and made his way towards the Firth of Forth:[19]

> Later I realized that one engine was overheating, but this didn't bother me as I was used to this happening with the Me 262. Eventually, the engine became so hot that I was forced to shut it down. Despite this, fuel continued to be consumed at a high rate as well and I realized that there must be a leak. I turned back to Norway and began my slow descent back into Stavanger, knowing that even if the other engine cut out, I could glide her in. I had flown gliders before the war and had plenty of experience in this field.
>
> Another problem came when I tried to lower the undercarriage. It just would not work so I was forced to go around again, using the manual pump until it locked down. As I came in for a second time, the other engine quit

and I did not have the speed to get the aircraft over some trees close to the runway. My Arado hit them broadside on and the sudden deceleration flung me, and the heavy seat to which I was strapped, head first through the glazed nose. I found this extremely disappointing! The flight had lasted 2 hr 20 min.

Men came running across the airfield and took me to a first aid room where I was kept under observation for two days, before being moved to a local hospital. The only really severe injury was to my right ankle which was put into a plaster cast.[20]

The following day, another Ar 234, most likely from the *Einsatzkommando* 1.(F)/5 – in which case it would have been flown by Eduard Schmitt, and probably, according to British interpreters, 'for the benefit of U-boats' – conducted a reconnaissance over the east coast of Scotland, observing firstly at 1526 hrs six small warships and one large merchant vessel eight kilometres north-east of Berwick; two small merchant vessels to the north-west; and two small merchantmen to the south. Then, at 1537 hrs, it spotted five merchant ships, while to the north, four more proceeding towards Newcastle. Elsewhere, there were only individual ships between the Firth of Forth and Middlesbrough.[21]

By late March, purposeful air reconnaissance for the U-boats was at an end. It had become clear to BdU that losses in the waters off Britain had increased steadily since the beginning of February and so it ordered the boats to pull back seaward from the coastal areas, simultaneously authorizing commanders to return to base if enemy forces proved too strong.[22] Nevertheless, Leutnant Schmitt is believed to have made one more flight on 9 April.[23]

In the afternoon of 4 May, however, the desire to fly in the Ar 234 once again was too much for the recently injured Hellmut Hetz, as he recalled:

Despite my crash, I was determined to fly once more before the end of the war. I had an argument with my *Staffelkapitän*, Major Augustin, but he eventually allowed me to take up another Arado coded BH on 4 May. I was the engineering officer for the unit at this time and I used this fact to convince Augustin, who was a non-flyer, that I should fly. I was elated that I had managed to make just one more flight before the British finally arrived[24]

Hetz was in the air for just 15 minutes.

In early February 1945, Major Fischer hinted to his senior staff that a mysterious, highly secret *Grosseinsatz* (major operation) was being planned for FAGr 5 in association with KG 200, which would involve the Ju 290s of the *Gruppe*, and that to this end, certain 'special equipment' would be needed for pathfinding missions. The result of this was that towards the end of the month, as certain preparatory work was undertaken in accordance with directives from KG 200, the personnel and aircraft of the *Gruppe*, although scattered across the Reich, still retained their cohesion and identity in readiness for the special operation – the purpose of which had still not been revealed.

On the 21st, OKL ordered that the commander of FAGr 1 was to be 'subordinated to KG 200 for two special operations.'[25] Furthermore, the earlier order to disband 2.*Staffel* was to be suspended for the duration of these operations. Fischer would be informed of details of his role in these tasks by Oberst Werner Baumbach, the new *Kommodore* of KG 200 'only as far as is absolutely necessary and as late as possible.' In the meantime, the operations of FAGr 1 would remain unaffected, and aircraft would be assigned to 2./FAGr 5 as required by the Generalquartiermeister.[26]

By early March, anticipatory rumours were rife at Neubiberg and Hofolding about how the Ju 290s of FAGr 5 would be deployed; on the 16th, two aircraft of 2.*Staffel*, the A-5 Wk-Nr 0171 9V+CH, which had been taken on by the *Gruppe* in December and was assigned to Hauptmann Eckl, and the A-2 Wk-Nr 0157 9V+BK, assigned to Leutnant Wagner and Leutnant Münsterer, were ordered to be available for 'government duties'.

There was also talk of a 'special operation devised personally by the Reichsmarchall', but on the 6th, Oskar Schmidt noted:

The 'Reichsmarchall' operation was delayed again; the organization of so many units was very difficult at that time. There were very few clear instructions. Across several airfields, our flying crews were waiting to deploy the Ju 290 (for example, at Mühldorf, Neubiberg, Rechlin, Dessau and others). But we had the feeling that our *Kommandeur*, Major Fischer was 'dancing at several weddings' and did not want to miss out on anything. He had been given orders to take over FAGr 1. He also continued with the Ju 290 as *Kommandeur* of FAGr 5, as well as being involved in the special 'Reichsmarchall' operation, mainly from Rechlin. In addition, he wanted to continue to be involved in aircraft development matters with Oberst Knemeyer. Furthermore, he did not want to be excluded from discussions with Oberst Baumbach of KG 200 and also with the *General der Aufklärungsflieger*. Of course, all this meant he was constantly travelling (although mostly in our interests), but his various command tasks left him with very little time.[27]

The possibility of launching a major air attack against the key power stations of the Soviet Union had lingered in the corridors of the OKL since 1943, when a ministerial official in the RLM, Professor Dr. Ingenieur Heinrich Steinmann, head of the innocuously titled *Bauabteilung* 10 (Construction Section 10) of the ministry's administration department, had been commissioned to produce a feasibility study on the prospects of the Luftwaffe mounting a significant bombing raid against the power supply infrastructure of the Moscow and Upper Volga regions. The Moscow area alone accounted for 75 per cent of the output of the armament industry, and so an effective attack could have considerable impact on production. Steinmann believed that by carrying out such a strike, the Soviet Union's ability to wage war would be severely impinged. However, when he submitted his report, it was met with scepticism by Luftwaffe intelligence officers, who felt that the proposed target list was too lengthy and that attacks on key industrial targets would produce more significant results. Undaunted, Steinmann set about producing a further report, this time centred around a strike against a range of Soviet hydro-electric and steam power plants.[28]

Steinmann's ideas received some support from Reichsminister Albert Speer, the armaments minister, who took the idea to Hitler. As Speer recorded in his memoirs:

> We had wooden models of the power plants made for use in training the pilots. Early in December I had informed Hitler. On February 4 [1944], I wrote to [*General der Flieger* Günther] Korten, the new Chief of General Staff of the air force, that 'even today the prospects are good ... for an operative air campaign against the Soviet Union ... I definitely hope that significant effects on the fighting power of the Soviet Union will result from it.' I was referring specifically to the attacks on the power plants in the vicinity of Moscow and the Upper Volga. Success depended – as always in such operations – upon chance factors. I did not think that our action would decisively affect the war. But I hoped, as I wrote to Korten, that we would wreak enough damage on Soviet production so that it would take several months for American supplies to balance out their losses.

Nearly a year was to pass, by which time Korten had died as a result of wounds received during the assassination attempt on Hitler in July 1944. Then, on 6 November, under the codename Operation *Burgund*, Reichsmarschall

Göring ordered that in the next full moon period a specially created force of ten He 177 bombers formerly of II./KG 100 was to carry out an attack on three Soviet hydro-electric plants.[29] The bombers would deploy BM 1000 *Sommerballon* (Summer Balloon) floating mines and were to be placed under the operational control of KG 200, which in turn would act 'in closest cooperation' with Professor Steinmann.[30] However, Steinmann was dealt another blow when KG 200's operations officers calculated that a further 150 m³ of fuel would be needed for the operation over and above what he had forecast. Furthermore, acute difficulties were experienced in servicing the He 177's Daimler-Benz 610 engines, for which parts were now in short supply. Because of these difficulties, the plan was eventually dropped.[31] Thus, attention then turned to the possibility of using *Mistel* composite bombers, which took the form of a Ju 88 lower component 'bomber' with its cockpit replaced by a hollow-charge warhead, flown to the target by a piloted and attached Bf 109 or Fw 190 upper component, to carry out a raid.

Under the codename *Eisenhammer* (Iron Hammer), Korten's successor, *General der Flieger* Karl Koller, and Steinmann once more proposed a dawn attack against electrical power production in the Moscow/Upper Volga regions to be carried out in the forthcoming moonlit period (February–March 1945), specifically at the hydro-electric power plants at Rybinsk and Uglich and the steam-power plants at Stalingorsk, Kashira, Shatura, Komsomolsk, Yaroslav, Aleksin, Tula, Balakhna, Gorki and Dzerzhinski. German intelligence believed that 90 per cent of the Soviet Union's motor vehicle production emanated from the Moscow/Upper Volga areas, along with 50 per cent of its ballbearing output and 60 per cent of its light assault-gun manufacture.[32]

As before, Koller assigned operational control of the mission to KG 200, though the *Geschwader* was to carry out its task in close collaboration with the *General der Kampfflieger* and Professor Steinmann. To prepare for the mission, OKL further envisaged production of 100 *Mistel* by February 1945, and, should KG 200 require additional crews, the *General der Kampfflieger* was supposed to supply these. Just how realistic this expectation was by this stage of the war was a matter for conjecture. Koller and OKL also stipulated that if, as predicted, the winter ice around the targets thawed by the time the mission was carried out, BM 1000 *Sommerballon* would also be deployed.

On 10 January, OKL demanded that in addition to the 100 composites required by the end of the month, a further 50 *Mistel* be ready by 15 February. However, the *Kommodore* of KG 200, the highly decorated bomber 'ace' Oberstleutnant Werner Baumbach, warned that II./KG 200 could provide only 15 trained crews and that these would be needed just to transfer completed composites from the Junkers assembly plants.[33] A possible solution was to take on crews from KG 30, the pilots of which had been undergoing fighter conversion since the autumn of 1944, and thus were experienced on both the Ju 88 and single-engined fighters.

In Berlin, however, it seems that competing interests were at work, for according to a minute from the OKL daily conference on 2 February: 'The Reichsmarschall agreed that the 100 *Mistel* aircraft planned by Reichsminister Speer, in addition to the 130 already in production or completed, will not now be built so as to allow industrial capacity to be freed for other purposes. The Reichsmarschall intends to confer with Reichsminister Speer.'

The pressure now was to build fighters and jet fighters for the defence of the Reich. Yet ten days later, the OKL diarist recorded: 'Operation *Eisenhammer* will be carried out at all costs. Preparations will be expedited. The fuel required for the operation has been promised by OKW.' The following day, 13 February, he wrote: 'After the fuel required for Operation *Eisenhammer* had been provided by OKW, the Reichsmarschall decided that the operation will be prepared and carried out as soon as possible.' Twenty-four hours later, KG 200, now assigned by Göring to supervise all aspects of *Eisenhammer*, confirmed that, provided initial preparations were completed in time, it would be ready to undertake the operation 'as early as the end of February or beginning of March.'

The effects of these developments and high-level orders filtered down to what remained of FAGr 5 in Bavaria. In early March, Hauptmann Schmidt of the *Stabskompanie* and Oberleutnant Abel, the *Gruppenadjutant*, used one of the unit's tow-tractors, to which was fitted an empty signals trailer, to collect the required equipment needed for the Ju 290 to conduct pathfinding operations from a storage facility in the Harz Mountains – a long and dangerous journey of 560 km during which they would be prey for roaming Allied fighter-bombers. Somehow they managed it and returned to Neubiberg with the equipment safe and intact.[34]

Commencing in mid-March, in halls with their walls covered with vast maps of the Soviet Union, extensive training and briefing sessions were given to the former bomber pilots slated to fly the mission. In the first leg, the whole attack force – *Mistel* led by Ju 88, Ju 188 and Ju 290 pathfinders – would fly north to Bornholm, where the course would be changed eastwards across the Baltic, to cross the coast north of Königsberg. Then, having flown over East Prussia and the old Soviet border, the second stage would take the formation along a highway from Minsk to Smolensk where it would split. One group of *Mistel* would turn south-east to attack Stalinogorsk and Tula, while the remainder would continue east towards Gorki. North-west of Moscow, one section would make for Rybinsk.

One pilot recalled:

The targeting instructions were outstanding. Every detail was thought of and by using detailed maps, photo-reconnaissance pictures and large dioramas, the targets were introduced to us. Each group spent hours working out the most efficient course of attack against the power stations. The turbine installations, as the heart of the power station, were the main target, and were to be totally destroyed. Course, headings, impact points (which were to be marked by the pathfinders) and target illumination was mentioned repeatedly and the proper documentation was handed out.

Another remembered:

Steinmann showed us that the most important part of the power stations were the turbine houses, for the simple reason that if the turbines were damaged, to repair them would take six months. The Russians were not in a position to build their own turbines. They were only capable of making temporary repairs and therefore were unable to replace them. Steinmann had the original photographs of the power-house installations. Siemens had, in fact, delivered the turbines and had supplied the photos. These photos had been taken throughout the year and thus showed all the different climatic conditions, so that the targets would be recognizable under any circumstances.

For the crews of FAGr 5, however, things were not so clear, as Oskar Schmidt recorded:

During the planning for the 'big operation', a part of FAGr 5 was based in Rechlin where its aircraft were equipped for long-range operations and the crews were instructed accordingly. Even there though, FAGr 5 had no definite direction. Although the commander of FAGr 5, and most of the crews, was assigned to the new FAGr 1 in Grove, Major Fischer remained in Rechlin where he worked with the leadership of KG 200. It all went back and forth. Although Major Fischer became the new commander of FAGr 1, he was still unable to decide (until about 20 April 1945) whether to fly to Denmark. He was very anxious to get hold of a Ju 290 with his crew for the 'big operation'. In March 1945 his crew transferred a Ju 290 from Neubiberg to Jüterbog.

Logbooks collated by the German historians Karl Kössler and Günther Ott indicate that at least five Ju 290s of 1./FAGr 5 – 9V+AH, CH, DH, IH and KH – and four from 2.*Staffel* – 9V+AK, BK, EK and FK – were in situ at Rechlin, Lärz and Roggentin airfields, and assigned for *Eisenhammer*.[35]

However, even as the *Eisenhammer* briefings were taking place, events were rapidly overtaking German aspirations. By mid-March, the Red Army was consolidating its position along the Oderbruch. The vital nodal point of the Küstrin 'Fortress', spanning both the Oder and the Warthe rivers, was still in German hands, but the Soviets were about to advance on Golzow and were poised to take Kietz. On 18 March, just one day after the selected Luftwaffe crews arrived in Berlin, Koller advised Baumbach that even though the 'enemy offensive in the East may demand operations against the Oder bridges by units set aside for *Eisenhammer*,' the operation was still regarded as of 'decisive importance even under present circumstances. Preparations for Operation *Eisenhammer* to be pressed on with determination to enable operations to be carried out during the March moon period.' On the 25th, OKL was informed that orders to disband FAGr 5 were postponed until the 'special task' was completed.[36]

By 29 March, the garrison at Küstrin had surrendered under Soviet pressure. Marshal Georgy Zhukov's forces had now punched a bridgehead some 50 km wide and 10 km deep into the crumbling German defensive line. Berlin lay in reach. For the Luftwaffe, weather conditions were now also hampering plans. On the 30th, the OKL was forced to advise Steinmann and Baumbach that *Eisenhammer* was 'postponed for the time being.' Aircraft and crews earmarked for the operation were to be released for operations against the enemy bridges over the Vistula, though they were to be 'pledged to secrecy, particularly in case of being taken prisoner. Operation *Eisenhammer* to be kept secret at all costs.'

Perhaps the final nail in *Eisenhammer*'s coffin came on 10 April, when 103 US Eighth Air Force B-24 Liberators bombed Rechlin and its satellite fields. Six Ju 290s of FAGr 5 were destroyed at Roggentin, including: Wk-Nrs 0170 (9V+DH), 0196 (9V+IH), 0180 (9V+KH), 0160 (9V+AK), 0193 (9V+FK).[37] At least four FAGr 5 personnel were killed in the raid, including Feldwebel Wolfgang Schneiders, a radio operator, together with an armourer, Unteroffizier Georg Walter, and two electricians, Obergefreiter Karl Dömsch and Gefreiter Karl Bader.[38] The bombs also destroyed 18 *Mistel*, a significant part of the *Eisenhammer* attack force. Another five were destroyed at Oranienburg. The same day, in his operational orders, Generaloberst Robert von Greim, the commander of *Luftflotte 6*, issued orders to the tactical command, *Gefechtsverband* Helbig: 'The execution of Operation *Eisenhammer* still takes priority, weather permitting, over all other missions.'

The possibility of attacking Soviet power installations also lingered on in the minds of those at the OKL. On 8 April 1945, Major im Generalstab

Sandmann of the *Führungsstab* telephoned Major von Harnier, KG 200's operations officer, instructing him that Major Fischer and the Ju 290s of 2./FAGr 5 were to be removed from Baumbach's personal jurisdiction as the *Fliegerführer* 200, and placed under the direct control of the OKL in readiness for a revised plan to be codenamed Operation *Gertraud*. A total of 200 m³ of fuel allocated for *Eisenhammer* was to be reserved for *Gertraud*.[39]

Operation *Gertraud* foresaw an attack by up to 12 Ju 290s from 2./FAGr 5 based at Rechlin-Lärz (quoted as having a range of 2,300 km) against three target groups of hydro-electric power plants most probably at Stalinogorsk, Kashira, Shatura, Komsomolsk, Yaroslavl (two plants), Aleksin, Tula, Tolon, Gorki and Dzerzhinsk. The operation was to be prepared in closest cooperation between Major Fischer and Professor Steinmann, and was to be carried out no later than 18–20 April. OKL also stressed the secrecy surrounding the operation, with informed personnel being kept to the minimum and those crews assigned to fly the operation being briefed thoroughly at the latest possible stage.[40] The Ju 290s would be fitted with external ETC carrier racks and carry BM 1000F/H *Sommerballon* and BM 1000G *Winterballon* mine bombs. These were air-dropped, *Treibminen* (drifting mines) intended to hinder the use of rivers as supply routes, but they were seen as an ideal weapon for destroying the power stations, by dropping them close to the waterway entrances which were protected by torpedo nets.

The *Sommerballon* was detonated by a passive, short-wave transmission fuze and was filled with 750 kg of Trialen. It was divided lengthways into halves, only one half being filled with explosive. When dropped, because of the location of the centre of gravity, which was low down and on one side, and because of a ballast of 1–3 kg, the bomb stood on its nose, inclined from the perpendicular and with little pressure on the ground. Entering the water up-stream of a hydro-electric power station, the bomb would be carried by a current flowing at over 0.5 m/sec to the grate of the operating turbine. It was designed to pass easily over small obstacles on the bed. If the bomb exploded at the grate of the turbine, the resulting pressure wave would have been transmitted through the induction channel and would have destroyed the cover of the turbine.[41]

The *Winterballon* was an SC-1000L bomb with a *Prallscheibe*, or anti-ricochet disc, angled at 30° and filled with 400–500 kg of Trialen explosive. It was intended to be used in icy conditions. Once dropped, the 'bomb' would penetrate the surface ice layer and then be raised by a balloon to drift with the current beneath the ice layer towards the target. The *Prallscheibe* was used to turn the nose of the bomb in shallow water. The mines could be fitted with parachute brakes and could penetrate ice up to 50 cm thick. They could be safely dropped from high altitudes into as little as seven metres of water and were intended to explode in the same manner as the *Sommerballon*.[42]

Shortly after the orders for Operation *Gertraud* had been issued, six of the twelve Ju 290s allocated for the mission were destroyed in Allied strafing attacks on north German airfields. Accordingly, on 14 April, Koller ordered that all preparations for the planned operation be abandoned, and this finally marked the end of German hopes of destroying Soviet hydro-electric power stations. However, even if *Gertraud* had taken place as scheduled, it is extremely doubtful whether, at this late stage, it would have had any effect on the final outcome of the war. The Soviet offensive against Berlin, which effectively sealed the fate of the Third Reich, commenced on 16 April 1945 and by 24 April the city was virtually surrounded and the defending German armies in disarray. The truth was that the Red Army possessed sufficient reserves of equipment and munitions to offset the possible effects of a successful Operation *Gertraud*, and could have completed the occupation of eastern Germany before any material shortages manifested themselves.

At the beginning of April, the bulk of the *Stab*/FAGr 5 and 2.*Staffel* were still at Neubiberg, although elements of the latter were also at Rechlin-Lärz.[43] At Hofolding, Hauptmann Schmidt was given, briefly, the responsibility of the local *Volkssturm* unit which was led by the head forester of the Hofoldinger *Forst*. While this may have been a source of useful additional manpower, by this stage it was accepted that if the enemy did arrive in the vicinity, as was anticipated, deployment of this last-ditch unit would serve no purpose to the people of the village.

Then, on the 6th, OKL issued the following directive: 'As part of the disbanding of units no longer fully utilized, the *Gruppenstab* of FAGr 5 is to be disbanded. With immediate effect the *Gruppenstab* of FAGr 1 will assume the immediate cooperation with B.d.U. in all matters associated with maritime reconnaissance for U-boat operations.'[44] Just what measures were actually put in place to effect this, if any, is not known.

Meanwhile, with the eventual disbandment of *Sonderkommando* Nebel at Offingen some time in the spring of 1945, those personnel of FAGr 5 under Hauptmann Georg Eckl who had been assigned to it prepared to return to their *Gruppe*'s base at Neubiberg, but for Eckl, and his A-5 Wk-Nr 0171 9V+CH, on 21 April there was a last-minute, unexpected demand that he fly a mission on behalf of the *Fliegerstaffel des Führers* (FdF) together with Leutnant Wagner in A-2 Wk-Nr 0157 9V+BK. As Eckl recorded:

Having spent the winter of 1944/45 in Offingen, the crews went back to Neubiberg. It was April 1945. There were preparations being undertaken for a large-scale attack under the jurisdiction of KG 200. But on the day of deployment, the operation was called off. It was all last-moment. After that, the last four Ju 290s were ordered to Berlin-Tempelhof. We landed there around 0230 hrs [on the 22nd] and had with us Hauptmann Eckl (*Staffelkapitän*, 2./FAGr 5), Leutnant Günther Dittrich, Oberleutnant Günther Korn and Oberleutnant Herbert Wagner, all pilots from 1.*Staffel*, and Oberleutnant Horst Degenring (observer), Oberleutnant Hans Münsterer and Oberleutnant Reinhard Sigel, both pilots, all from 2./FAGr 5, as well as Leutnant Lohberg, another officer assigned to the *Gruppe*.

Eckl described the general chaos facing the aircrews at this time as Germany declined into collapse:

At Tempelhof, some SS officers with armoured filing cabinets boarded the aircraft, along with their secretaries, and ordered us to fly to Ainring near Salzburg. On the second flight, which was the first flight to have an intermediate landing in Prague, about 100 German women and children were taken on board (later *Frau* Degenring and her mother were also there). Then came orders to fly from Salzburg via Vienna, from where we were to collect new landing gear for a Focke-Wulf Fw 200, on to Prague. Prague airfield was already under attack when our Ju 290 landed there. Because of the artillery fire, the spare parts for the Fw 200 were quickly unloaded in the centre of the airfield and we immediately took off again. Without loss or damage, the aircraft was able to take off.

Once in the air, we were instructed to fly to Lübeck. At Lübeck and at Rechlin, there had been strong enemy air raids ... By the end of April, there was only my Ju 290 at Lübeck. Meanwhile, on a flight on 22 April 1945, the Ju 290 flown by Leutnant Dittrich, with Oberleutnant Hans Rehne as observer, had been shot down by German Flak [see below]. Who expected a German four-engined aircraft to be in the sky at that time?[45]

On 10 April, the day after the city of Königsberg had surrendered to the Soviets, a signal reached Oberleutnant Abel, the adjutant of FAGr 5, who was still at Neubiberg, instructing all military personnel in the area to leave their units with immediate effect and to serve as ground troops to fight the advancing Allies or Soviets. At this, a further instruction came quickly from an apparently worried Major Fischer in Rechlin, where some of his pilots were training up on the Ar 234, to transfer there as soon as possible. Two columns were formed up: one under Hauptmann Schmidt, to move by road, the other, under Leutnant Robert Stein, an observer from 2./FAGr 5, together with Hauptfeldwebel Proch, Oberfeldwebel Limmer and Feldwebel Schartner, to move by rail. As Schmidt recalled:

> We received movement orders from the *Luftgau*, giving permission to transfer the senior technical personnel by road (in wood-gas-powered vehicles) via Rechlin to Denmark. We were issued with correct travel papers and special passes, without which we wouldn't have got anywhere at all – so stringent were the checks. Everything that was not riveted or nailed down was then taken away by local commanders.[46]

Movement of the rail column got off to a bad start when the wagons assigned for it were destroyed in an enemy air attack between Zwiesel and Bayerisch Eisenstein, but the road column, to which a few petrol vehicles had been added as well, departed Neubiberg on the 12th, routing to the east of Munich, to halt at Straubing for the first night. Progress was slow as a result of having to negotiate bomb craters and the shot-up wrecks of many vehicles on the *Autobahn*. The column then continued north, edging the Böhmerwald, via Eger, to Plauen. The Luftwaffe men noted the considerable damage done to the town from Allied bombing, but despite this, local *Volkssturm* units had erected makeshift defensive barriers in the streets in an attempt to hold back the enemy, whether they came from the east or the west. The next major town would be Magdeburg, but the place had already fallen to the enemy, so the decision was taken to veer east towards Brandenburg, before heading north to Ludwigslust. However, between Halle and Merseburg, the FAGr 5 men had their first encounter with Allied advance units. Although given *Panzerfäuste*, for which they had received no prior instruction, the column became involved only in a brief nocturnal 'skirmish' and during the night, the enemy moved away.

Schmidt was able to use the 'authority' of the Reichsmarschall Aktion to convey the column speedily and without delay through SS roadblocks and as far as Hagenow, where he allowed a halt. From Hagenow, he telephoned Major Fischer at Rechlin. 'The *Kommandeur* gave orders that the column was to go to Rechlin,' Schmidt recalled. 'He wanted to go with Oberst Baumbach and the SS to help stop the Russians on the Oder. The planned major operation with KG 200 was no longer possible and "blown out" at least in the short-term. Irrespective of whether we agreed with the *Kommandeur*'s intention, we had no choice but to make for Rechlin.'[47]

The FAGr 5 column reached Rechlin on the 18th to find the airfield badly damaged by recent American bombing raids and attacks by USAAF fighters.

The following day, several ground personnel of the *Gruppe* were killed or wounded during further low-level attacks by enemy fighters and more *Mistel* composites, intended for *Eisenhammer*, were also destroyed.

On 16 April, not that far away to the east, the Red Army commenced its main attacks around Küstrin, assisted by large numbers of close-support aircraft which hindered German response and artillery operations. They also used the massive SU-152 assault gun bearing a formidable 152 mm gun. The German 9.*Armee* had to cover a 130-km front with just 235,000 men, 833 tanks and assault guns and some 4,000 artillery pieces and mortars. Schmidt recalled:

> Why Major Fischer did not go with his new unit to Grove was a mystery to us. With some of the 'faithful', he wanted to be a hero alongside the *Fallschirmjäger* … He still believed in victory, despite the fact that on the Western Front, there was already fighting in our homeland. Abel and I demanded orders to move to the West. But none were forthcoming. After several unsuccessful requests from the *Kommandierende General der Deutschen Luftwaffe in Dänemark* [Commanding General of the Luftwaffe in Denmark], the General called Fischer and gave him a real dressing-down. He was to take immediate action and assume command at Grove, otherwise he would be put before a court martial. At that, the Utopia of heroic operations vanished. The crews – at least those with aircraft – flew to Grove the next day, while the rest joined my motor column which departed Rechlin immediately.[48]

On 20 April, Schmidt's column found itself driving through the night, past Kiel, towards the Danish border. During the journey, an address was broadcast over the radio to mark the *Führer's* 56th birthday. The men in the column wondered briefly whether this day would see the deployment of the long-promised 'wonder weapons'.

At Grove, conditions were considerably better, with decent quarters and decent food, including fare that had not been seen in Germany for a long time. The men from Schmidt's column had the opportunity to inspect the new Ar 234, although for most of the time the aircraft remained on the ground because of a lack of fuel and the inability to supply parts. But there was one intriguing development when Major Fischer suggested to the *Kommandierende General der Deutschen Luftwaffe in Dänemark*, Generalleutnant Alexander Holle, who had been General Kessler's successor as *Fliegerführer Atlantik*, that all personnel at Grove either not immediately needed for flying operations or of no immediate use should be used to create a *Panzerjagdabteilung* (Tank Destroyer Unit), armed with *Panzerfäuste* and equipped with bicycles, to be 'thrown against' enemy tanks. Hauptmann

Schmidt was duly selected to set up this ad hoc unit, but little, if anything came of it.[49]

At 0300 hrs on the morning of Sunday, 22 April 1945, Leutnant Günther Dittrich of 1./FAGr 5 took off from Rechlin in Ju 290A-2 Wk-Nr 0158 9V+AH, bound for Neubiberg. At his side in the cockpit as second pilot was Oberfeldwebel Martin Kistler, with Oberleutnant Hans Rehne as flight commander and observer. The crew was completed by Oberfeldwebel Günther Rudolph and Feldwebel Erich Frohn (radio-operators), Feldwebel Rolf Werner (flight engineer), together with Oberfeldwebel Walter Kroll and Oberfeldwebel Drescher (both gunners).[50] Also on board 9V+AH as 'passengers' were Leutnant Gustav Thomas of 1.*Staffel* and Oberleutnant Rolf Rotenburg, a pilot of 2./FAGr 5, two or three female signals personnel, as well as three or four NCOs from FAGr 5 who acted as additional gunners. Walter Kroll remembered:

The aircraft was heavily laden with *Panzerfäuste* of all kinds that were to be taken to southern Germany. The flight was reported to the *Reichsverteidigung*. The weather was bad; at around 400 m, there was heavy cloud. Because the course of the flight passed over some mountains, the crew took the aircraft up through the clouds in order to fly above them. The clouds were at 3000 m, the aircraft settled down to fly at 3200 m. Feldwebel Frohn announced over the intercom that he had received a radio signal to the effect that there was no expected enemy activity. After about 20 minutes in the air, at 0320 hrs, the aircraft was suddenly shaken, and it rocked back and forth. I was wounded in several places by Flak shell splinters. Inside the aircraft, wood, leather and fabric began to burn, as well as the parachutes which were on the floor. The intercom system packed up, so that communication between the individual crew members was not possible.

I wore the harness of an observer's parachute with a breast pack, and at that moment I fixed the parachute to the straps on my chest. Then I went with Oberfeldwebel Drescher, who emerged out of the tail-gun position, to the fuselage, extinguishing glowing and burning pieces of equipment as we went. My parachute pack fell off, and I had to hold the chute with one hand. But the fire could not be extinguished. At this point, the aircraft was hit for a second time by a salvo of Flak bursts, violently shaken about and it began to burn ferociously. The aircraft now tilted forward slightly. I clasped my loose parachute with both hands in front of my chest and stood in the open fuselage door to jump out. The violent slipstream pulled at the parachute, then pulled me down and away. Hanging on to the parachute, I saw the burning aircraft flying away in an ever-steeper dive. I came down in a field of corn. It was not yet dark, and I saw and heard the aircraft crash about five kilometres away.

I realized that the cargo in the aircraft and the fire caused by the Flak shells had caused the load to slip and block the passage through the fuselage. I managed to get up and was then picked up by a *Volkssturm* unit. I was then able to direct a local policeman on a bicycle to the crash site. But when he returned, he said that the whole aircraft was destroyed … I was taken to the hospital in Schwerin. There my right index finger was removed and several Flak splinters were removed from my body. While in the hospital, I also continued to look for any of my companions who might have been taken there, but without success. The hospital at Schwerin was later taken over by the Americans. When the Russians began to approach that area, the Americans moved the hospital with all its patients back to their territory, and they later transferred it to the British. After I had been treated to some extent, I was sent to a detention centre at Eutin, not far from Lübeck.[51]

Also departing the north that morning for Neubiberg was Ju 290A-3 Wk-Nr 0162 9V+EK, flown by Oberfeldwebel Willi Wittemann, with Leutnant Oskar Nau of 2./FAGr 5 as commander. This aircraft would make its last flight from Neubiberg at dawn on 30 April when it flew to Salzburg, where its crew left it on the *Autobahn*. Shortly before the arrival of the US Army, it was rendered unserviceable.[52] Two or three other Ju 290s, including the aircraft of Major Fischer, were left abandoned at Neubiberg.

On 21 April, the *General der Aufklärungsflieger* announced that 1.(F)/5 was being disbanded and that 1.(F)/33 was taking over the 'entire task' of reconnaissance for U-boat operations. As a result, *Einsatzkommando* 1.(F)/5 would be renamed *Einsatzkommando* 1.(F)/33 and absorbed into that parent *Staffel*. Operational control and signals channels had been set up between Stavanger and Grove, and the *Kommandierender General der Deutschen Luftwaffe in Norwegen* would also receive reports on the unit's operations.[53] At some point in early May, on paper at least, it seems the *Einsatzkommando* 1./FAGr 5 had still survived in name, but was redesignated *Einsatzkommando* 1./FAGr 1.

Then, on the afternoon of Friday, 4 May, Admiral Hans Georg von Friedeburg, the *Oberbefehlshaber der Marine* (the Naval Commander-in-Chief), and General der Infanterie Hans Kinzel, *Chef des Generalstabes vom Operationsstab Nord* (Chief of the General Staff [Operations Staff North], OKW Operatuions Staff A), signed the instrument of surrender of the German forces facing Montgomery's 21st Army Group. Immediately after the surrender, the last functioning Ju 290s of FAGr 5 left Rechlin to fly to airfields in the west, such as Flensburg and Rügen Island. On the ground, the men of FAGr 5 retained their weapons as the Danish Resistance was still thought to be 'active'.

CHAPTER SIXTEEN

'*GENIESSE DEN KRIEG, DER FRIEDE WIRD FURCHTBAR!*'

May 1945

'Enjoy the war, the peace will be terrible!'

Popular German soldier's expression at the end of World War II

In the last days of the war, Hauptmann Georg Eckl and his crew were ordered to fly their Ju 290 to Haderslev in Denmark. As Eckl recalled:

> Because of the presence of the enemy we made a low-altitude flight at about 40 m. At Rendsburg, west of the bridge over the Kiel Canal, the aircraft received fierce anti-aircraft fire from a German U-boat supply vessel, despite the fact that we gave the appropriate identification signal.

After refuelling in Haderslev, we waited for further instructions. There was talk about flying either to Oslo or to Madrid. We had two days of sitting around without orders. Then I took my own decision to go to Flensburg, along with my crew, and into captivity. There we met up with the 'old gang' from FAGr 5. From there I took a 'bicycle ride' to Schleswig to my family to pass on some supplies. I then returned to the camp to await official release.[1]

At Grove on 8 May, German units in Denmark began a march back to the German border. It was an orderly process, with the long columns of men organized into *Marschgruppen* (marching groups). Those personnel of FAGr 5 and FAGr 1 in Denmark, numbering a few hundred, were assigned to *Marschgruppe* C, destined for an assembly camp at Elpersbüttel in Schleswig-Holstein, close to the North Sea coast, from where they would be officially discharged and released. They were allowed to carry with them only their personal belongings, and curiously, their weapons, although Major Fischer and Hauptmann Schmidt had decided to take all the serviceable vehicles of the *Gruppe* along for the journey as well, including the field kitchen. Thus while the army units adhered faithfully to the order and marched by foot, the Luftwaffe men enjoyed mobility; 'marching was truly not our strength,' Schmidt recalled wryly. By the end of the first day, they had reached Herning, where they spent the night on a local sports field and where the terms of the surrender were read out to them beneath a fluttering and defiant Reich war flag. At the end of proceedings, before being placed at ease, the men lined up to give the old military salute.[2]

At this point, with tears in their eyes, the group of loyal Soviet *Hiwis*, who had joined 3.(F)/Aufkl.Gr.10 back at Kharkov in August 1942, before transferring to FAGr 5, asked to take their leave, fearing that the British would hand them over to the Soviets. If they left now, their plan was to obtain civilian clothes and make their own way to the east. The senior German officers reluctantly agreed.

Next day *Marschgruppe* C walked on to the Skarild area where some of the FAGr 5 men purchased luxuries such as milk, cream, eggs and butter. With full bellies, morale was high. The day after they journeyed south, passing through Hejnsvig to Vorbasse, where they settled for the night with hundreds of other German personnel in a large camp in woodland.

To the north, in Norway, the two Ar 234B-2b of the *Einsatzkommando* 1./FAGr 1 remained at Stavanger-Sola, along with the nine officers and 59 other ranks of the *Kommando*. They were also joined by eight Ar 234s from 1.(F)/Aufkl.Gr.123, 1.(F)/33 and III./KG 76, meaning that ten of the jets awaited the British when German forces at Sola surrendered on 8 May.[3]

The British were assisted at Sola by Hauptmann Helmut Miersch, formerly a pilot of 2./FAGr 5, who had received training on the Ar 234. It is probable that Miersch was flying an Ar 234, possibly, WK-Nr 140491, the aircraft flown briefly by Leutnant Hetz on 4 May, when it was caught in a crosswind while landing, and its nosewheel collapsed. The aircraft skidded along the runway and ended nose-up close to the waters of Sola Bay. The Arado was subsequently abandoned and later scrapped.[4]

By the 18th, *Marschgruppe* C had reached the German border where, under the eyes of relatively friendly British troops, the NCOs and other ranks were required to dispose of all their weapons by the roadside (British officers helping themselves to German pistols as 'war prizes'), while binoculars, compasses, bicycles and all other items of military equipment that were deemed useful were 'liberated'. When they crossed the border back into Germany, they did so peacefully, safely and with little fanfare.

On the 21st, in a wood not far from Flensburg, a small group of men managed to drive surreptitiously to the home of Leutnant Heinrich Morf, an observer from 1./FAGr 5, where they held an unofficial 'last post' followed by copious quantities of a 'stiff grog'.

South of Flensburg, at another huge wooded assembly camp for German servicemen, the contingent of former FAGr 5 men were delighted to run into their old comrades Georg Eckl, Emil Sachtleben, Horst Degenring, Hans Münsterer, Heinz Schlichting and Herbert Wagner. They also met Hans Wessel, the former signals officer of FAGr 5 who had been transferred away from the *Gruppe* to carry out a similar role with JG 51 in the East. Together they moved on, and at Friedrichstadt on the 28th, they crossed the River Eider where they passed long columns of British troops, vehicles and armour. Later in the day, they came to the village of Südersheistedt where, with increasing weariness, they stopped to rest in some large barns. After a short while, British troops arrived and relieved the officers of their remaining sidearms, although many had already been ditched or destroyed some days previously.

Already, at this point, the column's numbers became depleted by the departure of those men who, as residents of Schleswig-Holstein, left to return to their homes. One officer, Hauptmann Werner Breese, a *Ritterkreuz* holder and a highly experienced reconnaissance pilot who had joined FAGr 1 at Grove in the final weeks of the war, offered to take a large quantity of the officers' personal luggage to his home for safekeeping, from where it could be collected at a later date.

Marschgruppe C had now been redesignated *Bataillon* 163, and, under the command of Major Fischer, continued to head south, cross-country, the

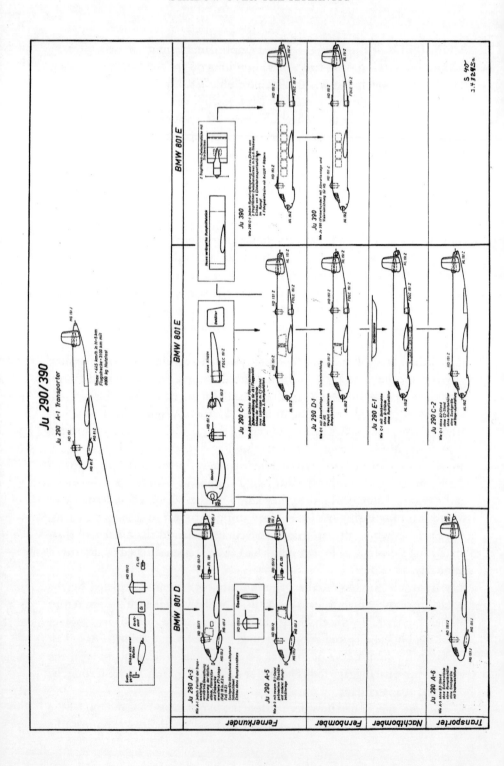

men's mood kept high by periods of singing until a British officer, evidently irritated by the apparent good mood of the defeated enemy, forbade it. On the 29th the *Bataillon* started out on the last leg of its journey to Elpersbüttel. It reached the *Endlager* two days later – groups of tents set up around the local farms. They spent the next two weeks there, staving off boredom by organizing a camp 'circus' and playing sports, including handball, in which a small tournament was played against the men of a former *Schlachtgeschwader* (ground-attack wing) at Meldorf.

In mid-June, a period of unseasonal rain drenched the tents, making conditions unpleasant. But it passed and was followed by warm, sunny weather, which prompted some of the men to take the opportunity to bathe in the sea. On one such trip to the coast, on 19 June, word came through to Oskar Schmidt that he was to make himself ready next morning for a march to Tellingstedt, 23 km away. At Tellingstedt he was discharged and by 26 June, he had finally reached his hometown of Melle in Lower Saxony. By comparison, Josef Augustin, the former *Staffelkapitän* of 1./FAGr 5, was held initially in Norway, but was later moved to France, from where he was finally released in 1948.

The Ar 234 Wk-Nr 140493 was flown out of Stavanger on 9 July 1945 to Schleswig by Squadron Leader Tony 'Marty' Martindale. Four days later, Martindale piloted the Arado from Schleswig to Gilze-Rijen in the Netherlands. On the 14th, after staging via Melsbroek and Manston, the jet arrived at the Royal Aircraft Establishment at Farnborough. From late July until late October 1945, it made a series of test flights from Farnborough, totalling 9 hr 25 min, before being ferried to No. 6 Maintenance Unit (MU) at Brize Norton on 27 November for storage.[5] It had been scrapped by 1948.[6]

Ar 234 Wk-Nr 140491 may have been damaged as it landed following a test flight at Stavanger-Sola on 1 August. By November 1945 it was known to have been scrapped at Forus.[7]

Ju 290 Wk-Nr 0186, originally 9V+FH, was among the first A-7s to be delivered to FAGr 5. It was later used by 1./KG 200 from July 1944 and recoded A3+OB. Its last flight was to Flensburg, from where it was flown on 22 June 1945 by Squadron Leader Joe McCarthy, who commanded the Royal

OPPOSITE An overview of the planned development of the Ju 290A, C, D and E variants and the Ju 390 as a reconnaissance aircraft, long-range bomber, night-bomber and transport, using BMW 801D and E engines, showing armament, radio and fuel configurations. This shows the intention to develop the Ju 290C-1 as an interim reconnaissance aircraft until the arrival of the Ju 390. Note also the plan to incorporate a bomb 'gondola' in the D-1 and E-1.

Aircraft Establishment (RAE) out-station at Schleswig. McCarthy then ferried the Junkers from Lübeck to Wormingford in England on 2 July, and the following day it went on to the RAE at Farnborough. It later returned to Schleswig and then went to Copenhagen, returning to Schleswig on 10 July. It was coded 'AM 6' and went once more to Farnborough on 13 July. A week later, it was test-flown at the RAE, and again on 8 August. On 17 August, it was transferred to No. 6 MU at Brize Norton and remained there in storage until it was struck off charge on 14 August 1947.[8]

On 17 August 1945, Ju 290A-2 WK-Nr 110157 9V+BK of 2./FAGr 5 was flown by Squadron Leader McCarthy from Flensburg (to where the aircraft had last been flown by its Luftwaffe crew) to Schleswig. Subsequently, Squadron Leader H.J. King ferried it from Schleswig to Farnborough on 21 September, where it became coded 'AM 57'. It was not test-flown by the British, but it was included in the German Aircraft Exhibition held at Farnborough between 29 October and 9 November 1945. By December 1946, it had been relegated to the scrap area, and was finally broken up in 1950.[9]

APPENDICES

APPENDIX 1:
Ju 290A-2–A-7 TECHNICAL SPECIFICATIONS

	A-2	A-3	A-4	A-5	A-7	A-7 with 2 x Hs 293	A-7 with 3 x Hs 293	A-7 with 2 x Fritz X
Length (m)	28.68	28.68	28.68	28.68	29.15			
Height (m)	7.02	7.02	6.9	6.9	6.9			
Wingspan (m)	42.0	42.0	42.0	42.0	42.0			
Wing area (m2)	203.6	203.6	203.6	203.6	203.6			
Track span (m)	7.3	7.3	7.3	7.3	7.3			
Mainwheel tyre size (mm)	1320 x 480	1320 x 480	1320 x 480	1320 x 480	1320 x 480			
Tailwheel tyre size (mm)	875 x 320	875 x 320	875 x 320	875 x 320	875 x 320			
Engine type	BMW 801L	BMW 801L/D	BMW 801D-2	BMW 801D-2	BMW 801D-2			
Power output at take-off (PS)	1600	1600/1730	1730+70 kg	1730+70 kg	1730+70 kg			
Max. rating (PS)	1380	1380/1350	1350+62 kg	1350+ 62 kg	1350+62 kg			
Rated / pressurized height (m)	4600	4600/2000	2000	2000	2000			
Weight empty (kg)	c.14,225	c.14,225	c.14,225	c.14,225	c.14,225			
Structural weight equipped (kg)	c.20,860	c.20,860	c.20,860	24,085	24,085	24,780	24,780	24,780
Fuel (kg)	10200	10200	10200	14220	14220			
Oil/lubricant (kg)	550	550	550	795	795			
Ammunition (kg)	330	330	330	985	985			
Crew (kg)	9 (600)	9 (600)	(600)	(800–1000)	(1000)			
Armament A (Nose)	–	–	–	–	1 x MG 151			
B1 (Forward dorsal)	1 x HD 151	1 x HD 151	1 x FW 19	1 x HD 151	1 x HD 151			
B2 (Aft dorsal)	1 x HD 151	1 x FW 20	1 x FW 20	1 x HD 151	1 x HD 151			

	A-2	A-3	A-4	A-5	A-7	A-7 with 2 x Hs 293	A-7 with 3 x Hs 293	A-7 with 2 x Fritz X
C1 (Forward ventral)	1 x MG 151	1 x MG 151	1 x MG 151	1 x MG 151	1 x MG 151			
C2 (Aft ventral)	1 x MG 131	1 x MG 131	1 x MG 131	1 x MG 131	1 x MG 131			
S (Side)	2 x FL 131	2 x FL 131	2 x FL 131	2 x FL 131	2 x FL 131			
T (Tail)	1 x MG 151	1 x MG 151	1 x MG 151	1 x MG 151	1 x MG 151			
Guided bombs (kg)						1930	2895	3000
Misc. remaining weight (kg)	–	–	–	220 (inc. rubber dinghy etc.)	220 (inc. rubber dinghy etc.)			
Maximum weight at take-off (kg)	40500	40500	40500	41305	41305	c.45,000	c.45,000	c.45,000
Maximum speed (km/h)	–	–	–	409	403			
— at altitude (m)	–	–	–	2000	2000			
Maximum speed (km/h)	424	424	424	455	455	447	446	448
— at altitude (m)	5000	5000	5000	5800	5800			
Cruising speed (km/h)	c.356	c.356	c.356	318	318			
— at altitude (m)	c.4700	c.4700	c.4700	2000	2000			
Climbing time to 4,000 m (min)	c.31.5	c.31.5	c.31.5	21.5	21.5			
Service ceiling (m)	c.5550	c.5550	c.5550	8850	8850			
Max. range (km)	4000?	4000?	4000?	6760	6760	4600	4300	4280
Max. endurance (hr)	?	?	?	21.2	21.2			
Taxiing/ take-off distance (m)	780/1120	780/1120	780/1120	625/970	625/1210	625/1240	625/1240	625/1240

APPENDIX 2:
LIST OF KNOWN AIRCRAFT AND LOSSES (FAGr 5)

LIST OF KNOWN AIRCRAFT

Werknummer (Wk-Nr)	Variant	Factory Code	First Flight	Unit Code	Remarks
290110157	A-2	SB+QG	29.5.43	9V+BK	25.10.43 to Rechlin. First *Fernaufklärer*. First aircraft to 2./FAGr 5 as 9V+AC. At Schleswig May 1945. To UK as AM.57. Scrapped 1949.
290110158	A-2	SB+QH	7.6.43	9V+BC 9V+BK 9V+AH	From 1. (BC) to 2./FAGr 5 (BK). To KG 200. Total loss after hit by own Flak, near Oranienburg. Lost 22.04.45.
290110159	A-2	SB+QI	22.6.43	9V+CC 9V+CK	Shot down 20.11.43.
290110160	A-3	SB+QJ	18.7.43	9V+BH 9V+AK	To 1./FAGr 5 19.4.44. Probably destroyed in bombing raid, Rechlin-Roggentin 10.4.45.
290110161	A-3	PI+PO SB+QK	18.7.43	9V+DK	Crashed into mountains, Lesaca, Spain in bad weather 26.12.43.
290110162	A-3	PI+PP SB+QL(?)	10.8.43	9V+EK	15 per cent damaged at Neubiberg; technical fault. Surrendered unusable at Salzburg 30.4.45.
290110163	A-3	PI+PQ SB+QM	20.8.43	9V+AK 9V+CH 9V+IK	30 per cent damage in belly-landing at Achmer; engine failure. Passed to 2./FAGr 5. Assigned for a flight to Japan, but destroyed before being surrendered, 3.5.45.
290110164	A-3	PI+PR SB+QN(?)	22.8.43	9V+GK	Shot down over the Atlantic 26.5.44.
290110165	A-4	PI+PS	8.9.43	9V+BK 9V+DH	V7/A-4 prototype. Modified to A-7. With KdE. To KG 200 (A3+HB) 6.7.44. Surrendered 8.5.45. USAAF at Munich-Riem as FE3400. To USA, flight trials, exhibited and later scrapped.
290110166	A-3	PI+PT	15.9.43	9V+BK 9V+DH	20 per cent damage at Mont de Marsan 26.11.43; damage to undercarriage. To 1./FAGr 5. Later caught fire at Bourges during bombing raid.
290110167	A-4	PI+PU	28.9.43	9V+HK	Missing in southern sector of Eastern Front for 1./KG 200? 14.6.44.
290110168	A-4	PI+PV SB+QY	5.10.43	9V+FK	Crashed on take-off Mont de Marsan. Burned on ground 24.11.43.
290110169	A-4	PI+PW	13.10.43	9V+KK	Air-to-air refuelling trials at Dessau November 1943. Believed destroyed during attack on Finsterwalde, 11.4.44.
290110170	A-5	KR+LA	4.11.43	(KdE) 9V+DH	Intended as test-bed for jet engine trials (with KdE). To FAGr 5 22.11.43. Probably destroyed in bombing raid, Rechlin-Roggentin, 10.4.45.

Werknummer (Wk-Nr)	Variant	Factory Code	First Flight	Unit Code	Remarks
290110171	A-5	KR+LB	13.11.43	9V+CH	To FAGr 5 1.2.43. 31.12.43 damaged by bombs at Cognac. To KG 200 A3+AB. Surrendered to RAF May, Flensburg, 1945. Scrapped.
290110172	A-5	KR+LC	21.11.43?	9V+BH	Damaged 20 per cent on landing Bernburg, 18.8.44.
290110173	A-5	KR+LD	12.1.44	9V+CK	August 1943, suffered undercarriage damage. Destroyed in bombing raid, Neubiberg(?) 4.12.44.
290110174	A-5	KR+LE	10.12.43	DLH D-AITP, 'Sachsen' 9V+EH	September 1944 to DLH for conversion to civil operation. 27.12.44 (destroyed in air raid at Munich while with DLH)
290110175	A-5	KR+LF	24.12.43	9V+FH	Shot down over Atlantic, 16.2.44.
290110176	A-5	KR+LG		9V+GH, D-AITQ, DLH 'Preussen'	To DLH at Berlin-Tempelhof for conversion to civil operation. Damaged on landing in/or low-level attack, Munich, 7.4.45. Not repaired.
290110177	A-5	KR+LH	17.12.43	9V+DK	Shot down over Atlantic, 16.2.44.
290110178	A-5	KR+LI	8.2.44	9V+DK D-AITR, DLH 'Bayern'	September 1944 to DLH at Berlin-Tempelhof for conversion to civil operation. Damaged on landing 6.4.45. Barcelona with Spanish Air Force as 74+23. Scrapped 6.5.53.
290110179	A-5	KR+LJ	20.1.44	9V+FK	Shot down Atlantic, 19.2.44.
290110180	A-5	KR+LK	23.3.44	9V+KH	Probably destroyed in bombing raid, Rechlin, 10.4.45.
290110181	A-7	KR+LL	1.4.44	9V+GK	Assigned to 1./KG 200 July–August 1944. Destroyed at Dessau during raid, 16.8.44.
290110186	A-7	KR+LQ	11.3.44	9V+FH	Assigned to 1./KG 200. Returned to FAGr 5. Surrendered Flensburg, May 1945. 6.5.45, became RAF AM 6. Later scrapped.
290110187	A-7	KR+LR	22.4.44	9V+LK	Crashed into mountain at Posada de Llanes, Asturias, Spain, 31.5.45.
290110188	A-7	KR+LS	18.3.44	9V+FK	Missing from Atlantic, west of Portugal, 26.5.44.
290110189	A-7	KR+LT	7.4.44	9V+KK	Damaged (or destroyed?) in air raid, 30.9.44.
290110190	A-7	KR+LU	13.5.33	9V+MK	(With 1./KG 200 as A3+PB April 1944.) 20.2.45 landing accident at Hildesheim, 20 per cent damage. Later destroyed on ground in Allied attack.

Werknummer (Wk-Nr)	Variant	Factory Code	First Flight	Unit Code	Remarks
290110191	A-7	KR+LV	?	9V+AB	To FAGr 5, 2.5.44. Damaged during air raid, Brunntal, 10.9.44. Later blown up.
290110192	A-7	KR+LW	24.5.44	9V+HH	To FAGr 5 September 1944. Damaged during air raid at Munich, 24.3.45 (with *Fliegerstaffel des Führers* as transport for *Führer*).
290110193	A-7	KR+LX	20.5.44	9V+FK	Probably destroyed in bombing raid, Rechlin-Roggentin, 10.4.45.
290110194	A-7	KR+LY (?)	?	?	Destroyed at Dessau prior to maiden flight.
290110195	A-7	KR+LZ	14.6.44	9V+LK	Damaged during air raid, Brunntal, 11.9.44.
290110196	A-7	PJ(I)+PS KR+MU	8.7.44	9V+IH	Probably destroyed in bombing raid, Rechlin, 10.4.45.

Ju 290 LOSSES FAGr 5

Month	Due to enemy action	Due to accident	Total	Strength (inc. deliveries)
November 1943	1	1	2	9
December	1	1	2	10
February 1944	3	–	3	13
May	3	–	3	17
August	1	3	4	12
September	3	–	3	10
December	1	–	1	8
March 1945	–	1	1	8
April	6	2	8	0

APPENDIX 3: LIST OF OFFICERS

Previous units are given where known; ranks shown are the last known.

Gruppenkommandeur
Maj. Hermann Fischer (3.(F)/22, to FAGr 1)

Gruppenstab
Oblt. Herbert Abel (*Gruppen Adjutant*) (3.(F)/Aufkl.Gr.10)
Tech.Insp. Baerwald
Reg.Rat. Dr. Konrad Blank (Meteorologist)
Dr. Wilhelm Dünnweber (Meteorologist)
Oblt. Siegfried Frank (Signals Officer)
Stabs.Int. Heinrich
Oblt. Ludwig (Lutz?) Herlein (Pilot) (3.(F)/22)
Maj. Ernst Kloppenburg (*Gruppe* Navigation Officer)
Oblt. Hans Müller (*Gruppe* Technical Officer)
Flg.Ing. Unger
Hptm. Jochen Wanfried (Pilot)

Stabskompanie
Hptm. Oskar H. Schmidt (*Chef,* Pilot and Observer)
Hptm. Karl Nather (Photographic Officer)
Lt. Hans Wessel (Signals Officer) (3.(F)/Aufkl.Gr.10)

Medical
Dr. Oberarzt Rückstuhl (Achmer) (3.(F)/Aufkl.Gr.10)
Dr. Stabsarzt Willy Spiesmann
Dr. Oberarzt Krüger (from 28.6.44)

1./FAGr 5

Staffelkapitän
Maj. Josef Augustin

Oblt. Hans Ascheid (Observer) (3.(F)/Aufkl.Gr.10, det. to 1./KG 200)
Lt. Uwe Baumann (Signals Officer)
Oblt. Beuthel (Observer and Offz.z.b.V.)
Oblt. Paul Birnkraut (Pilot)
Lt. Horst Blum (Pilot)
Lt. Günther Dittrich (Pilot) (also 2./FAGr 5)

Lt. Eberhard Elfert (Pilot)
Oblt. Erich Grün (Observer) (3.(F)/Aufkl.Gr.10)
Oblt. Hans-Günther Hassold (Observer)
Lt. Hellmut Hetz (Pilot and Technical Officer, to FAGr 1 Ar 234)
Lt. Hans Koithka (Observer) (3.(F)/Aufkl.Gr.10)
Oblt. Günther Korn (Pilot and Technical Officer) (3.(F)/Aufkl.Gr.10)
Lt. Heinrich Morf (Observer)
Lt. Hellmut Nagel (Pilot) (3.(F)/Aufkl.Gr.10)
Lt. Kurt Nonnenburg (Pilot)
Lt. Albert Pape (Observer)
Hptm. Wille Pawlittke (Pilot)
Oblt. Adalbert Frhr. von Pechmann (Observer and Signals Officer)
Oblt. Hans Rehne (Observer)
Lt. Rolf Rodenburg (Pilot)
Hptm. Emil Sachtleben (Pilot) (det. to 1./KG 200)
Oblt. Heinz Schlichting (Observer – also with *Gruppenstab*)
Lt. Eduard Schmitt (Pilot) (to FAGr 1 Ar 234)
Hptm. Walter Schoof (Pilot) (3.(F)/Aufkl.Gr.10)
Hptm. Hubert Schreiner (Pilot) (KG 40)
Oblt. Horst Thede (Observer)
Lt. Augustin Thomas (Pilot)
Oblt. August Vaupel (Observer and Offz.z.b.V.) (3.(F)/Aufkl.Gr.10)
Oblt. Siegfried Wache (Pilot) (det to 1./KG 200)
Oblt. Herbert Wagner (Pilot – also with crew of *Gruppenkommandeur*)
(Tr.fl.st.5)

2./FAGr 5

Staffelkapitäne
Hptm. Karl-Friedrich Bergen (lost 16.2.44)
Hptm. Georg Eckl (from 20.2.44)

Lt. Wolfgang Adler (Pilot)
Lt. Dr. Heinz Arnold (Observer)
Lt. Hermann Barth (Observer)
Oblt. Kurt Baumgartner (Pilot)
Hptm. Heinz Braun (Pilot) (LTS 290, det. to 1./KG 200)
Oblt. Hans-Georg (Heinz) Bretnütz (Pilot)
Lt. Clement (Pilot)
Oblt. Herbert Daubenspeck (Navigation Specialist)

Oblt. Eberhardt
Lt. Heinz Ernst (Pilot)
Oblt. Horst Degenring (Observer)
Lt. Fliege (Pilot)
Lt. Hans-Roger Friedrich (Pilot) (LTS 290)
Lt. Martin Glöckelhofer (Observer)
? Gudde (Navigator)
Hptm. Hasenberg
Lt. Lothar Hecker (?)
Lt. Hertel (Pilot)
Lt. Hermann Kersting (Pilot) (LTS 290)
Lt. Klose (Pilot)
Hptm. Hanns Kohmann (Pilot) (LTS 290)
Oblt. Otto-Karl Kremser (Pilot) (KG 40)
St.Int. Albert Manthey
Lt. Hans Mahs (Pilot)
Hptm. Helmut Miersch (Pilot)
Maj. Kornelius (Konrad?) Mildenberger (Observer)
Oblt. Motzkus (Pilot)
Oblt. Hans Münsterer (Pilot)
Oblt. Oskar Nau (Observer)
Oblt. Werner Nedala (Pilot) (KG.r.z.b.V.102)
Oblt. Günther Pfeiffer (Pilot) (3.(F)/Aufkl.Gr.Ob.d.L.)
Lt. Gottfried Sachse (Pilot)
Oblt. Reinhard Sigel (Pilot)
Lt. Robert Stein (Observer)
Lt. Scherp (Pilot)
Oblt. Karl-Heinz Schmidt (Pilot)
Hptm. Richard Schmoll (Observer)
Oblt. Karl Schöneberger (Pilot)
Hptm. Ernst Treskatis (Observer)
Hptm. Vermehren (Pilot)

APPENDIX 4:
AIRCRAFT STRENGTH, JULY 1943 TO MARCH 1945

Total aircraft strength shown as at month's end.

1943	
July	2
August	5
September	6
October	9
November	9
December	10

1944	
January	12
February	13
March	13
April	14
May	17
June	17
July	17
August	12
September	10
October	11
November	11
December	8

1945	
January	8
February	8
March	8

APPENDIX 5:
NAVIGATIONAL METHODS EMPLOYED BY FAGr 5

Leutnant Wilhelm Koitka served as a navigator with 1./FAGr 5 based at Mont de Marsan. On 26 May 1944, while on a convoy reconnaissance mission on board Ju 290A-4 Wk-Nr 0164 9V+GK, he was shot down over the Atlantic by Sea Hurricanes of 835 NAS operating from HMS *Nairana*. Koitka survived and was taken to England, where, as per common practice with captured enemy airmen, he was interrogated by British Air Directorate of Intelligence (Section K).

Section K described Koitka as 'a man of considerable experience'. The following is an extract from ADI(K) Report No. 249/1944 which is based on Koitka's description of the navigational methods used by the crews of FAGr 5. This information would clearly have been of interest to Allied airmen flying long-range operations, particularly navigators.

Navigation

Methods employed

Navigation is normally by track plot and the air plot is only used when a D.R. [dead reckoning] position is doubtful or when the aircraft is being chased by fighters. Distance is reckoned in kilometres.

No standard navigational drill has been formulated in the *Gruppe*, however, and observers are free to take drifts, find winds or obtain fixes in their own good time. On returning from sorties, the observers' logbooks are analysed, although not marked or assessed in any way.

The observer of the 9V+GK, a man of considerable experience, described in some detail the methods of navigation in general use with FAG 5. These methods, including navigational aids used, are given in the following paragraphs.

Wind Finding

The usual method of wind finding employed by this observer was to take a quick drift on one-minute alterations of course 30° to port then 30° to starboard and to work out a three-drift wind on the *Knemeyer* (three-point calculator). In such cases it was not necessary to allow any additional flying time along the track flown. P/W [Prisoner of War] confessed however, that he often relied on wind estimation from wind lanes and the Beaufort scale, which in practice was accurate enough when helped from time to time with *Sonne* and astro fixes.

The W/T operator [Feldwebel Wilhelm Meyer], who was fairly knowledgeable on navigation, and himself sometimes took shots of the sun, said that the standard method of wind finding was by taking drifts on 60° and 120° alterations of course for two minutes with compensation for flying time.

The drift sight installed in the Ju 290 is a simple circular drift recorder built into the port side of the aircraft behind the observer's seat. In this instrument there are no cross-lines or height scale to enable the navigator to obtain the ground speed with the use of a stopwatch; there is no backward scanning mirror and tail drift cannot, therefore be obtained.

No drifts were taken at night, neither were flame floats carried for this purpose; astro and *Sonne* fixes were, however, considered sufficient means for keeping on track and finding ground speed.

Sonne

The present observer considered *Sonne* accurate out to 20° W. – as far as the aircraft of FAG 5 flew – except under certain circumstances which had to be watched carefully. These were when the mountains of Scotland interfered with the beam from *Sonne* 1 in Norway, and the mountains of North-West Spain obstructed the *Sonne* at Corunna in an area west of Portugal. P/W had heard that *Sonne* 6 in the Brest peninsula had been interfered with by the British.

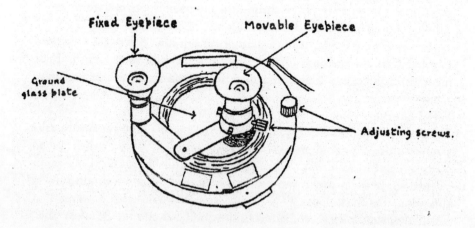

A sketch taken from the British Intelligence report, ADI(K) No. 249/1944 from June 1944, showing the *Astronomisches Rechen Gerät* (astro calculator) used by the crews of FAGr 5 to take a navigational fix from two stars when undertaking astro-navigation.

In general, an accuracy to within ten kilometres was accepted, provided the angle of intersection was not too acute, no mountains intervened, and atmospheric conditions were not too bad. A reliable fix was possible a long way out by obtaining a near right angle of intersection from *Sonne* 1 and the *Sonne* at Corunna.

Sonne beacons could also be D/F'd and this was occasionally done by observers who were in doubt of their position, particularly when approaching the French coast; a D/F plot gave the sector of the *Sonne* pattern in which the aircraft was flying, and thus a rough check on position.

Broadcasting stations at Lisbon, Bordeaux, Rennes and in Ireland were also used for obtaining bearings, but were not very reliable; P/W related that once a 90° error had been found when using Lisbon.

Astro-Navigation

When taking a shot the octant is usually held in the hand and the sight is taken through the clear vision panel of the astrodome, which can be fully revolved. In the Ju 290 there is also a means of hooking the octant onto the roof of the astrodome to ease the taking of a sight, but in practice this is not steady, in addition to which the varying heights of individuals make it impracticable.

The present observer was shown a British Mark IXA sextant and his comparison between the latter and the octant in use in FAG 5 is not without interest.

He considered the German octant to be lighter, tidier and more elegant looking, in addition to which there is no obstruction to prevent the left eye from viewing the star directly; he stated that the control nut of the octant is larger and easier to adjust finally than that of the sextant.

The automatic averaging of shots is possible for three different periods of 40, 80, or 120 seconds; P/W stated that he usually made use of the full two minutes.

The average time taken for working out a fix from two stars was estimated as being eight to ten minutes; the actual calculations could, however, be reduced to two minutes by using the ARG 1 (*Astronomisches Rechen Gerät* – astro calculator).

ARG 1

The present P/W was able to describe the operation of this instrument more fully than his predecessors; it is about 14 inches in diameter, and non-automatic. A ground glass plate is geared to the adjusting screw on the circumference of the ring, and extends under the latter so that its edge passes underneath the fixed eyepiece on the left, which contains a magnifying lens.

On the plate, which can be lighted from underneath for use at night, is a zenithal projection of the lines of latitude and longitude upon a plane surface. An hour-angle scale is marked along the lines of longitude from 0° on the left to 180° on the right and back to 360°, the hours being marked off at 15° intervals.

The declination is shown on a latitude scale, the lines curving outwards towards the Pole. This is marked from 0° at the centre to 90° at the Poles, but for purposes of reading off the declination the first 23 degrees are the ones used. The latitude is also marked on the circumference of the plate underneath the ring, but not on the same scale as that on the zenithal projection.

Any part of the plate can be viewed through the central eyepiece, which is on a movable arm. This eyepiece contains a graticule, a magnifying lens, and there is a screw for fine adjustment.

Operation:

1.　The latitude is set at the neutral position of 90° on the outer scale against the pointer underneath the fixed eyepiece. When in this position the North of the zenithal projection is at 12 o'clock.

2.　The declination and hour angle is obtained from tables, and the graticule of the movable eyepiece set over the intersecting point of those on the plate.

3.　The plate is then revolved by means of the control screw until the latitude of the observer is set against the pointer underneath the other (fixed) eyepiece.

4.　The new point beneath the movable eyepiece will now show the calculated altitude of the star for the position of the observer on the scale of the declination and the azimuth of the star on the hour-angle scale.

5.　The error is then noted between the calculated altitude and azimuth, and the shot altitude of the star. The result is a position line, which is then plotted on the chart.

The time taken for the calculation of each shot can with practice be reduced to two minutes. An apparent advantage of using the ARG 1 is that astro tables are eliminated and it is only necessary to carry an almanac.

S.D. Felkin
Wing Commander
ADI(K)
9 June 1944

ENDNOTES

AUTHOR'S NOTE

1   Conyers Nesbit, Roy, Elliott, Peter, Fowler, Simon and Goulter, Christina, *RAF Records in the PRO*, PRO Publications, London, 1994, pp. 63–64

CHAPTER ONE

1   UK National Archives, AIR 20/7705.

2   See Supf, Peter, *Das Buch der deutschen Fluggeschichte, Band 2*, Drei Brunnen Verlag, Stuttgart, 1958.

3   Padfield, Peter, *Dönitz: The Last Führer*, Harper & Row, New York, 1984, p. 28 *et passim*.

4   Terraine, John, *Business in Great Waters: The U-Boat Wars 1916–1945*, Leo Cooper, London, 1989, p. 194.

5   UK National Archives, AIR 20/7705.

6   Wadman, David, *Aufklärer*, Vol. I: *Luftwaffe Reconnaissance Aircraft and Units 1935–1941*, Classic Publications, Hersham, 2007, p. 71.

7   *Ibid.*, p. 71, and see also Gould, Winston A., *Luftwaffe Maritime Operations in World War II: Thought, Organization and Technology*, Air Command and Staff College, Air University, Maxwell AFB, 2005, p.13 and *Das Seewesen in der deutschen Luftwaffe 1933–1945* [website], <www.luftwaffe-zur-see.de/seeluft/seeluft.htm>, accessed November 2016.

8   Hessler, Günter, *The U-Boat War in the Atlantic 1939–1945*, Vol. I: *1939–1941*, Her Majesty's Stationery Office, London, 1989, p. 62.

9   Claasen, Adam R.A., *Hitler's Northern War: The Luftwaffe's Ill-Fated Campaign, 1940–1945*, University Press of Kansas, Lawrence, 2001, pp. 159–60.

10   UK National Archives, AIR 20/7705 and Thompson, Adam, with Wadman, David, *Seeflieger: Luftwaffe Maritime Aircraft and Units 1935–1945*, Classic Publications, Hersham, 2009, p. 15.

11   ADI(K) Report No. 377/1945.

12   Hessler 1989, Vol. I, p. 63.

13   *Ibid.*, p. 67.

14   *Ibid.*, p. 69.

15   UK National Archives, AIR 20/7705.

16   *Ibid.*

17   Gould 2005, p. 21.

18   Terraine 1989, p. 355.

19   UK National Archives, AIR 20/7700.

20   Hessler 1989, Vol. I, p. 80.

21   UK National Archives, AIR 20/7705.

22   *Ibid.*

23   UK National Archives, AIR 20/7700.

24   UK National Archives, AIR 20/7705.

25   *Ibid.*

26   *Ibid.*

27   UK National Archives, AIR 20/7700 and 7705.

28   Terraine 1989, p. 442, 450.

29   Claasen 2001, p. 208.

30   Mallmann Showell, Jak P., *Dönitz, U-boats, Convoys: The British Version of His Memoirs from the Admiralty's Secret Anti-Submarine Reports*, Frontline Books, Barnsley, 2013, p. 87.

31   Terraine 1989, p. 461.

32   Gannon, Michael, *Black May: The Epic Story of the Allies' Defeat of the German U-boats in May 1943*, Harper Collins, New York, 1998, p. 113.

33   *Ibid.*, p. 113.

34   UK National Archives, AIR 20/7700.

35   Cited in Roskill, Captain S.W., *The War at Sea 1939–1945,* Vol. II: *The Period of Balance*, The Naval & Military Press Ltd, Uckfield, 2004, p. 210.

36   *Ibid.*, p. 201.

37   *Ibid.*, p. 206.

38   Terraine 1989, p. 485.

39   *Ibid.*, p. 433.

40   *Ibid.*, p. 462.

41   Roskill cited in Terraine 1989, p. 514.

42   Roskill 2004, Vol. II, p. 218

43   Werner cited in Terraine 1989, p. 524.

44 UK National Archives, AIR 20/7700.

45 Blair, Clay, *Hitler's U-Boat War: The Hunted, 1942–1945*, Weidenfeld & Nicolson, London, 1999, p. 173.

46 Terraine 1989, p. 528.

47 Mallmann Showell, Jak P., *Fuehrer Conferences on Naval Affairs 1939–1945*, Greenhill Books, London, 1990, p. 311.

48 UK National Archives, AIR 20/7700.

49 Griehl, Manfred, *Luftwaffe over America: The Secret Plans to Bomb the United States in World War II*, Greenhill Books, 2005, p. 92.

50 Griehl, Manfred, '*Das "Bananaenflugzeug" – Die Entwicklungsgeschichte der Me 264 – Teil 1*', *Flugzeug*, February 1996.

51 Terraine 1989, p. 545.

52 Roskill 2004, Vol. II, p. 358.

53 UK National Archives, AIR 20/7705.

54 *Ibid.*

55 Terraine 1989, p. 566.

56 *Ibid.*, p. 582.

57 Hessler 1989, Vol. II, p. 86.

58 Terraine 1989, p. 466.

59 Churchill, Winston S., *The Second World War*, Volume V: *Closing the Ring*, Cassell & Co., London, 1952, p. 7.

60 Terraine 1989, p. 594.

61 Mallmann Showell 1990, p. 334.

62 Gould 2005, p. 36.

63 Kington, John A., and Selinger, Franz, *Wekusta: Luftwaffe Meteorological Reconnaissance Units and Operations 1938–1945*, Flight Recorder Publications, Ottringham, 2006, p. 175; Thompson 2009, p. 46; and *Seeaufklärungsgruppe* 129 [website], <www.ww2.dk/air/seefl/sagr129.htm>, accessed 2016.

64 Mallman Showell 1990, p. 339.

65 Gannon 1998, p. 59.

66 UK National Archives, AIR 20/7705.

67 Lewin, Ronald, *Ultra Goes to War*, Grafton, London, 1988, p. 220.

68 Terraine 1989, p. 640.

69 UK National Archives, AIR 20/7705.

70 Bennett, G.H., and Bennett, R., *Hitler's Admirals*, Naval Institute Press, Annapolis, 2004, p. 92.

71 UK National Archives, AIR 20/7701.

72 UK National Archives, AIR 20/7705.

73 *Ibid.*

74 *Ibid.*

75   Schmidt, Oskar H., *Fernaufklärungsgruppe 5 Atlantik: Eine Aufzeichnung von Oskar H. Schmidt*, private publication, Melle, May 1990, p. 1.

CHAPTER TWO

1   Mahncke, Alfred, *For Kaiser and Hitler: From Military Aviator to High Command: The Memoirs of Luftwaffe General Alfred Mahncke*, Tattered Flag Press, Pulborough, 2010, p. 128.

2   Vajda, Ferenc A., and Dancey, Peter, *German Aircraft Industry and Production 1933–1945*, Airlife, Shrewsbury, 1998, p. 14.

3   Homze, Edward L., *Arming the Luftwaffe*, University of Nebraska Press, Lincoln, 1996, p. 123.

4   Budrass, Lutz, *Flugzeugindustrie und Luftrüstung in Deutschland 1918–1945*, Droste Verlag, Düsseldorf, 1998, p. 388, 485.

5   Zindel, Ernst, *Die Geschichte und Entwicklung des Junkers-Flugzeugbaus von 1910 bis 1945 und bis zum endgültigen Ende 1970*, Deutsche Gesellschaft für Luft- und Raumfahrt, Köln, 1979, p. 88.

6   Kössler, Karl and Ott, Günther, *Die großen Dessauer: Junkers Ju 89, Ju 90, Ju 290, Ju 390 – Die Geschichte einer Flugzeugfamilie*, Aviatic Verlag, Planegg, 1993, p. 30.

7   Budrass 1998, p. 528.

8   Kössler and Ott 1993, p. 74.

9   *Ibid.*, pp. 73–75.

10   Hitchcock, Thomas H., *Junkers 290* (Monogram Close-Up 3), Monogram Aviation Publications, Boylston, 1975, p. 8.

11   Kay, Antony L., *Junkers Aircraft & Engines 1913–1945*, Putnam Aeronautical Books, London, 2004, p. 199.

12   Lerche, Hans-Werner, *Luftwaffe Test Pilot: Flying captured Allied Aircraft of World War 2*, Jane's, London, 1980, pp. 39–40.

13   Kössler and Ott 1993, pp. 151–55.

14   CSDIC (Air), CMF, Rep.No.A.579.

15   *Luftwaffe Officer Career Summaries by Henry L. deZeng IV and Douglas G. Stankey* [website], <www.ww2.dk/lwoffz.html>, accessed 1 April 2015. Hereafter referred to as *Luftwaffe Officer Career Summaries*.

16   Morzik, Generalmajor a.D. Fritz, *German Air Force Airlift Operations*, USAF Historical Division, Arno Press, New York, 1961, pp. 367–68.

17   Mallmann Showell 1990, p. 311.

18   Kössler and Ott 1993, p. 84.

19   *Ibid.*, p. 84.

20   UK National Archives, AIR 20/7701: AHB.6 Translation No.VII/35, 20.7.74.

21   Kössler and Ott 1993, p. 236, and Felkin, W/Cdr. S.D., ADI(K) Report No. 249/1944.

CHAPTER THREE

1   Citino, Robert M., *Death of the Wehrmacht: The German Campaigns of 1942*, University Press of Kansas, Lawrence, 2007, p. 252.

2   Wadman, David, Bradley, John and Ketley, Barry, *Aufklärer: Luftwaffe Reconnaissance Aircraft & Units 1935–1945*, Hikoki Publications, Aldershot, 1997, p. 10.

3   Schmidt 1990, p. 128.

4   Wadman, Vol. I, 2007, p. 29.

5   Wadman *et al.* 1997, p. 13.

6   Kay 2004, p. 176, and Filley, Brian, *Junkers Ju 88 in Action, Part 1*, Squadron/Signal Publications, Carrolton, 1988, p. 47.

7   Wadman, Vol. II, 2007, p. 21; and *The Luftwaffe, 1933–45* [website], <www.ww2.dk>, accessed November 2016.

8   *Luftwaffe Officer Career Summaries.*

9   *Ibid.*

10   Schmidt 1990, p. 2, 129; and *Luftwaffe Officer Career Summaries.*

11   Information via Mikael Olrog.

12   *The Luftwaffe, 1933–45* [website], <www.ww2.dk>, accessed November 2016; and *Luftwaffe Officer Career Summaries.*

13   *Luftwaffe Officer Career Summaries.*

14   Schmidt 1990, p. 9.

CHAPTER FOUR

1   UK National Archives, AIR 51/223, and *Luftwaffe Airfields 1935–1945 by Henry L. deZeng IV* [website], <www.ww2.dk/lwairfields.html>, accessed November 2016.

2   Schmidt 1990, p. 6; and Bundesarchiv-Militärarchiv RL 10/366.

3   Schmidt 1990, p. 10.

4   Kössler and Ott 1993, p. 181.

5   Schmidt 1990, p. 9.

6   Kössler and Ott 1993, p. 180, 230.

7   *Ibid.*, p. 240.

8   UK National Archives, AIR 20/7705.

9   Schmidt 1990, p. 9, 11.

10   Schmidt 1990, p. 8, 9, 12; and *Luftwaffe Officer Career Summaries.*

11   Neitzel, Sönke, *Der Einsatz der deutschen Luftwaffe über dem Atlantik und der Nordsee 1939–1945*, Bernard & Graefe Verlag, Bonn, 1995, p. 191.

12   Schmidt 1990, p. 12; Carlsen, Sven and Meyer, Michael, *Die Flugzeugführer-Ausbildung der Deutschen Luftwaffe 1935–1945*, Vol. II: *Fliegerwaffenschulen und Ergänzungsgruppen*, VDM Heinz Nickel Verlag, Zweibrücken, 2000, p. 512; ADI(K) No. 249/1944; Bundesarchiv-Militärarchiv RL 10/366.

13 Schmidt 1990, p. 12.

14 Kössler and Ott 1993, p. 240.

15 *Ibid.*, p. 182.

16 Schmidt 1990, p. 13.

17 *Ibid.*

18 Kössler and Ott 1993, p. 240.

19 Schmidt 1990, Anlage 4, 'Verlegungsbericht', p. 111.

CHAPTER FIVE

1 *War Diary of the German Naval Staff Operations Division, Part A, October 1943, Volume 50*, 30.10.43, available at *Archive.org* [website], <archive.org/details/wardiarygermann501943germ>, accessed November 2016. Hereafter referred to as *War Diary of the German Naval Staff Operations Division, Volume 50*.

2 Roskill 2004, Vol. III, p. 41.

3 UK National Archives, HW 13/37.

4 Blair 1999, pp. 429–30.

5 Poolman, Kenneth, *Focke-Wulf Condor: Scourge of the Atlantic*, Macdonald and Janes, London, 1978, p. 177; and UK National Archives, HW 13/37.

6 *War Diary of the German Naval Staff Operations Division, Part A, October 1943, Volume 50*, 30.10.43.

7 *War Diary of the German Naval Staff Operations Division, Part A, November 1943, Volume 51*, 9.11.43, available at *Archive.org* [website], <archive.org/details/wardiarygermann511943germ>, accessed November 2016. Hereafter referred to as *War Diary of the German Naval Staff Operations Division, Volume 51*.

8 Hessler 1989, Vol. III, p. 36.

9 Roskill 2004, Vol. III, p. 50.

10 Blair 1999, p. 439.

11 Terraine 1989, p. 641.

12 ADI(K) Report No. 249/1944.

13 UK National Archives AIR 51/216 and AIR 22/80.

14 Kössler and Ott 1993, p. 181.

15 UK National Archives AIR 20/7700.

16 *Flugzeugbestand und Bewegungsmeldungen II./KG 40* [website], <www.ww2.dk/oob/bestand/kampf/biikg40.html>, accessed November 2016. Data is for November 1943.

17 *Ibid.*

18 *Flugzeugbestand und Bewegungsmeldungen 1./SAGr.129* [website], <www.ww2.dk/oob/bestand/see/b1kfl129.html>, accessed November 2016.

19 *Flugzeugbestand und Bewegungsmeldungen I./ZG1* [website], <www.ww2.dk/oob/bestand/zerst/bizg1.html>, accessed November 2016; and Goss, Chris, *Bloody*

Biscay: *The History of V.Gruppe/Kampfgeschwader 40*, Crecy Publishing, 1997, p. 12.

20   *Flugzeugbestand und Bewegungsmeldungen 3.(F)/Aufklärungsgruppe 123* [website], <www.ww2.dk/oob/bestand/aufkl/b3ag123.html>, accessed November 2016.

21   *Flugzeugbestand und Bewegungsmeldungen 1./SAGr.128* [website], <www.ww2.dk/oob/bestand/see/b1kfl128.html >, accessed November 2016.

22   Neitzel 1995, p. 175.

23   ADI(K) Report No. 249/1944.

24   '*Fliegerführer Atlantik*': (G 351154/EFT/11/52/60): Allied translation of a 1943 German document (via Goss).

25   Hinsley, F.H., Thomas, E.S., Ransom, C.F.G. and Knight, R.C., *British Intelligence in the Second World War*, Vol. III, Part 1, HMSO, London, 1984, p. 227.

26   UK National Archives, HW 13/37.

27   ZIP/ZTPGU/19196, 13.11.43. (via Beale).

28   Schmidt 1990, p. 107.

29   *Ibid.*, p. 15.

30   Rohwer, Prof. Dr. Jürgen, and Hümmelchen, Gerhard, *Chronik des Seekrieges 1939–1945* [website] – *Zeittafel*, November 1943, Württembergische Landesbibliothek, Stuttgart 2007 <www.wlb-stuttgart.de/seekrieg/chronik.htm>, accessed November 2016, hereafter referred to as *Chronik des Seekrieges 1939–45*; and Hessler 1989, Vol. III, p. 36.

31   Hessler 1989, Vol. III, p. 38.

32   Roskill 2004, Vol. III, p. 50.

33   UK National Archives, HW 13/37: Zip No.992, 17.11.43; and *War Diary of the German Naval Staff Operations Division, Volume 51*, 15.11.43.

34   *Chronik des Seekrieges 1939–1945 – Zeittafel*, November 1943.

35   Poolman, Kenneth, *Escort Carrier 1941–1945*, Ian Allan, Shepperton, 1972, p. 107 and Roskill 2004, Vol. III, p. 50.

36   UK National Archives, HW 13/37: Zip No.992, 17.11.43.

37   Schmidt 1990, p. 15.

38   UK National Archives, HW 13/37: Zip No.993, 18.11.43.

39   UK National Archives, HW 13/37: Zip No.994, 19.11.43.

40   Blair 1999, p. 448.

41   Cremer, in Blair 1999, p. 449.

42   Roskill 2004, Vol. III, p. 50.

43   Blair 1999, p. 448.

44   UK National Archives, HW 13/37: Zip No.995, 20.11.43.

45   Blair 1999, p. 448.

46   *Ibid.*, p. 449.

47   UK National Archives, HW 13/37.11: Zip No.995, 20.11.43.

48 Green, William and Swanborough, Gordon, *RAF Bombers Part 2*, Jane's Publishing Co., London, 1981, pp. 66–67; and Mallmann Showell 2013, p. 166.

49 Blair 1999, p. 449.

50 Hessler 1989, Vol. III, p. 39.

51 Heiber, Helmut and Glantz, David, (Eds.), *Hitler and his Generals: Military Conferences 1942–1945*, Greenhill Books, London 2002, p. 300.

52 UK National Archives, HW 13/37: Zip No.996, 21.11.43.

53 Roskill 2004, Vol. III, p. 51; and Blair 1999, p. 450.

54 Blair 1999, p. 449.

55 UK National Archives, HW 13/37: Zip No.997, 22.11.43.

56 Goss 1997, p. 128; Goss, Chris, 'Wrong Place, Wrong Time' (article draft kindly provided by Chris Goss); Lfl.Kdò 3 Eins.Nr.8493/43 & Nr.8500/43 (via Goss).

57 Goss, 'Wrong Place, Wrong Time' (article draft).

58 UK National Archives, AIR 50/66.

59 UK National Archives, AIR 27/1045; and Sharp, C. Martin and Bowyer, Michael J.F., *Mosquito*, Faber, London, 1971, p. 346.

60 Goss 1997, p. 128, 233.

61 Letter from Rodriguez to Lopez, June 1944 (via Juan Carlos Salgado Rodríguez).

62 Information from Juan Carlos Salgado Rodríguez.

63 Schmidt 1990, p. 16.

64 Roskill, Vol. III, p. 52.

65 Blair 1999, p. 450.

66 *FdU/BdU War Log*, 16–30 November 1943 (*Kriegstagebücher* [*KTB*] & *Stehender Kriegsbefehl, Des Führers/Befehlshaber der Unterseeboote* [*FdU/BdU*]), available at U-boat Archive [website], <www.uboatarchive.net>, accessed November 2016. Hereafter referred to as *FdU/BdU War Diary*.

67 Hessler 1989, Vol. III, pp. 40–41.

68 UK National Archives, HW 13/37: Zip No.998, 23.11.43.

69 *SL/MKS Convoy Series* [website], <www.convoyweb.org.uk/sl2/index.html>, accessed November 2016.

70 Smith, J. Richard and Creek, Eddie J., *Heinkel He 177 Greif: Heinkel's Strategic Bomber*, Classic Publications, Hersham, 2008, p. 112; and Bollinger, Martin J., *Warriors and Wizards: The Development and Defeat of Radio-Controlled Glide-Bombs of the Third Reich*, Naval Institute Press, Annapolis, 2010, p. 77.

71 Schmidt 1990, p. 16.

72 Roskill, Vol. III, p. 53.

73 Schmidt 1990, p. 6.

74 *Ibid.*, p. 6, 107.

75 Neitzel, Sönke, 'Kriegsmarine and Luftwaffe Co-operation in the War against Britain, 1939–1945', *War in History*, Vol. 10, Number 4, October 2003, pp. 168–69.

76 US War Department, *Directory of German Radar Equipment*, TM E 11-219, 20 April 1945.

77 Schmidt 1990, pp. 6–7.

78 *Ibid.*, p. 17.

79 Kössler and Ott 1993, p. 182.

80 Schmidt 1990, p. 17; and Kössler and Ott 1993, p. 182, 243.

81 Schmidt 1990, p. 17; and Kössler and Ott 1993, p. 184, 243.

82 Schmidt 1990, p. 15.

83 *OS and OS/KMS Convoy Series* [website], <www.convoyweb.org.uk/oskms/index.html>, accessed November 2016.

84 UK National Archives, HW 13/37: Zip No.999, 24.11.43.

85 *U-boat.net* [website], <www.uboat.net>, accessed November 2016.

86 Roskill, Vol. III, p. 53.

87 UK National Archives, HW 13/37: Zip No.1000, 25.11.43; and Hessler 1989, Vol. III, p. 40.

88 UK National Archives, HW 13/37: Zip No.1003, 26.11.43.

89 Hessler 1989, Vol. III, p. 40.

90 Hinsley 1984, p. 227.

91 Poolman 1972, p. 108; Blair 1999, p. 452; and *U-boat.net* [website], <www.uboat.net>, accessed November 2016.

92 UK National Archives, HW 13/37: Zip No.1004, 29.11.43 and Zip No.1005, 30.11.43.

93 Blair 1999, p. 452.

94 *Ibid.*, p. 442.

95 UK National Archives, HW 13/37: Zip No.1010, 5.12.43.

96 *War Diary of the German Naval Staff Operations Division, Part A: December 1943, Volume 52*, 2.12.43, available at *Archive.org* [website], <archive.org/details/wardiarygermann521943germ>, accessed November 2016. Hereafter referred to as *War Diary of the German Naval Staff Operations Division, Volume 52*.

97 UK National Archives, HW 13/37: Zip No.1011, 6.12.43.

98 Blair 1999, p. 443.

99 UK National Archives, HW 13/37: Zip No.1012, 7.12.43.

100 *ONS Convoys* [website], <www.convoyweb.org.uk/ons/index.html>, accessed November 2016.

101 *War Diary of the German Naval Staff Operations Division, Volume 52*, 5.12.43.

102 *SL/MKS Convoys* [website], <www.convoyweb.org.uk/sl2/index.html>, accessed November 2016.

103 UK National Archives, HW 13/37: Zip No.1017, 12.12.43.

104 *War Diary of the German Naval Staff Operations Division, Volume 52*, 11.12.43.

105 *ONS Convoys* [website], <www.convoyweb.org.uk/ons/index.html>, accessed November 2016.

106 UK National Archives, HW 13/37: Zip No.1019, 14.12.43.

107 *War Diary of the German Naval Staff Operations Division, Volume 52*, 12.12.43.

108 *Ibid.;* 13.12.43.

109 UK National Archives, HW 13/37: Zip No.1020, 15.12.43.

110 UK National Archives, HW 13/37: Zip No.1021, 16.12.43.

111 UK National Archives, HW 13/37: Zip No.1022, 17.12.43.

CHAPTER SIX

1 Bundesarchiv-Militärarchiv RL 10/366.

2 Goss, Chris, *Sea Eagles*, Vol. II: *Luftwaffe Anti-Shipping Units 1942–45*, Classic Publications, Hersham, 2006, p. 147, 153; and Pocock, Rowland F., *German Guided Missiles*, Ian Allan, London, 1967, pp. 29–32, 43–44.

3 Pocock 1967, pp. 36–42.

4 Bollinger 2010, p. 18.

5 Bundesarchiv-Militärarchiv RL 10/366.

6 Kössler and Ott 1993, p. 240.

7 Schmidt 1990, p. 107.

8 *Ibid*, pp. 107–109.

9 UK National Archives, AIR 20/7705.

10 Kössler and Ott 1993, pp. 98–105.

11 Bundesarchiv-Militärarchiv RL 10/366.

12 Neitzel 1995, p. 185.

CHAPTER SEVEN

1 *U-boat.net* [website], <www.uboat.net>, accessed November 2016; and Blair 1999, p. 442.

2 Blair 1999, p. 443.

3 *War Diary of the German Naval Staff Operations Division, Volume 52*, 18.12.43.

4 Hessler 1989, Vol. III, p. 42.

5 Neitzel 1995, p. 179.

6 *War Diary of the German Naval Staff Operations Division, Part A: December 1943, Volume 52*, 20.12.43.

7 Mallmann Showell 1990, p. 373.

8 Schmidt 1990, p. 18.

9 Nagel, Hellmut, *Flugbuch September 1938–Juli 1959* (via Knirim).

10 *War Diary of the German Naval Staff Operations Division, Volume 52*, 21.12.43.

11 Schmidt 1990, p. 18.

12 Bollinger 2010, p. 85.

13   UK National Archives, HW 13/37: Zip No.1030, 25.12.43.

14   Bundesarchiv-Militärarchiv RL 10/366.

15   Schmidt 1990, p. 109.

16   *Operation Bernau* [website], <codenames.info/operation/bernau/>, accessed November 2016.

17   *War Diary of the German Naval Staff Operations Division, Volume 52*, 27.12.43.

18   Schmidt 1990, p. 18.

19   Neitzel 1995, p. 180; and *Operation Trave* [website], <codenames.info/operation/trave/>, accessed November 2016.

20   *War Diary of the German Naval Staff Operations Division, Part A: December 1943, Volume 52*, 26.12.43.

21   UK National Archives, HW 13/37: Zip No.1033, 28.12.43.

22   Kössler and Ott, p. 186; and Schmidt 1990, p. 18.

23   Schmidt 1990, p. 18 and Anlage 5, 'Herbert Littek, Feindflug: Suchen eines Geleitzuges u. Fühlungshalter' p. 116.

24   UK National Archives, HW 13/37: Zip No.1034, 29.12.43.

25   Roskill, Vol. III, p. 74.

26   Hinsley *et al.* 1984, p. 251.

27   Bollinger 2010, p. 87; and ('half-hearted') Roskill, Vol. III, p. 74; see also Smith and Creek, 2008, p. 113.

28   Blair 1999, p. 452.

29   *SL/MKS Convoys* [website], <www.convoyweb.org.uk/sl2/index.html>, accessed November 2016.

30   UK National Archives, HW 13/37: Zip No.1036, 31.12.43.

31   Blair 1999, p. 443.

32   Roskill, Vol. III, p. 54.

33   Blair 1999, p. 454.

34   Bennett and Bennett 2004, p. 178.

CHAPTER EIGHT

1   Freeman, Roger, *Mighty Eighth War Diary*, Jane's, London, 1981, p. 160.

2   *War Diary of the German Naval Staff Operations Division, Part A: January 1944, Volume 53*, 6.1.44, available at Archive.org [website], <archive.org/details/wardiarygerman531944germ>, accessed November 2016. Hereafter referred to as *War Diary of the German Naval Staff Operations Division, Volume 53*.

3   Nagel, *Flugbuch*, 7–8.1.44.

4   *War Diary of the German Naval Staff Operations Division, Volume 53*, 6.1.44.

5   *Ibid.*

6   UK National Archives, HW 13/38: Zip No.1044, 8.1.44.

7   *War Diary of the German Naval Staff Operations Division, Volume 53*, 6.1.44.

8   *Ibid.*, 7.1.44.

9   UK National Archives, HW 13/38: Zip No.1046, 10.1.44.

10   *SL and SL/MKS Convoy Series* [website], <www.convoyweb.org.uk/sl/index.html>, accessed November 2016.

11   Hessler 1989, Vol. III, p. 41.

12   UK National Archives, HW 13/38: Zip No.1047, 11.1.44.

13   Neitzel 1995, p. 185; and Hessler 1989, Vol. III, p. 41.

14   *War Diary of the German Naval Staff Operations Division, Volume 53*, 9.1.44.

15   Neitzel 1995, p. 185.

16   UK National Archives, HW 13/38: Zip No.1048, 12.1.44.

17   *FdU/BdU War Diary*, 1–15 January 1944.

18   *War Diary of the German Naval Staff Operations Division, Volume 53*, 10.1.44.

19   UK National Archives, HW 13/38: Zip No.1049, 13.1.44.

20   *Ibid.*

21   *FdU/BdU War Diary*, 1–15 January 1944.

22   UK National Archives, HW 13/38: Zip No.1050, 14.1.44.

23   Hessler 1989, Vol. III, p. 41.

24   Blair 1999, pp. 490–91.

25   *Ibid.*, p. 493.

26   Roskill, Vol. III, p. 248.

27   UK National Archives, HW 13/38: Zip No.1055, undated, for activity on 17.1.44.

28   *ON* Convoys [website], <www.convoyweb.org.uk/on/index.html>, accessed November 2016.

29   Nagel, *Flugbuch*, 18.1.44.

30   UK National Archives, HW 13/38: Zip No.1056, 18.1.44.

31   Nagel, *Flugbuch*, 18.1.44.

32   *War Diary of the German Naval Staff Operations Division, Volume 53*, 18.1.44.

33   UK National Archives, HW 13/38: Zip No.1057, 19.1.44.

34   Blair 1999, p. 493.

35   *War Diary of the German Naval Staff Operations Division, Volume 53*, 20.1.44.

36   UK National Archives, HW 13/38: Zip No.1058, 22.1.44.

37   Roskill 2004, Vol. III, p. 249.

38   *War Diary of the German Naval Staff Operations Division, Volume 53*, 21.1.44.

39   UK National Archives, HW 13/38: Zip No.1059, 23.1.44.

40   *Clydebuilt Wartime Convoys* [website], <www.clydesite.co.uk/clydebuilt/convoys/EMPIRE_TREASURE_977.html>, site unavailable, November 2016.

41   UK National Archives, HW 13/38: Zip No.1060, 24.1.44.

42   UK National Archives, HW 13/38: Zip No.1061, 25.1.44.

43   UK National Archives, HW 13/38: Zip No.1063, 27.1.44; and *War Diary of the German Naval Staff Operations Division, Volume 53*, 21.1.44.

44 UK National Archives, HW 13/38: Zip No.1064, 28.1.44.
45 Hessler 1989, Vol. III, p. 43.
46 *FdU/BdU War Diary*, 16–31 January 1944.
47 *Ibid.*
48 Roskill 2004, Vol. III, p. 249.
49 Poolman 1972, p. 115.
50 *FdU/BdU War Diary*, 1–15 March 1944.
51 Nagel, *Flugbuch*, 28.1.44.

CHAPTER NINE

1   Hooton, E.R., *Eagle in Flames: The Fall of the Luftwaffe*, Arms and Armour Press, London, 1997, p. 61.
2   Schmidt 1990, pp. 18–19.
3   Nagel, *Flugbuch*, 1.2.44.
4   UK National Archives, HW 13/38: Zip No.1073, 6.2.44.
5   Bollinger 2010, p. 117.
6   Schmidt 1990, Anlage 7, 'Einsatzbericht des Mj. Josef Augustin – Staffelkpt. 1.FAG5', pp. 119–20.
7   Kington and Selinger 2006, p. 175.
8   UK National Archives, HW 13/38: Zip No.1074, 7.2.44.
9   UK National Archives, HW 13/38: Zip No.1076, 9.2.44.
10 Roskill 2004, Vol. III, Map 17; and Poolman 1972, p. 116.
11 Nagel, *Flugbuch*.
12 Trenkle, Fritz, *Die deutschen Funk-Navigations- und Funk-Führungsverfahren bis 1945*, Motorbuch Verlag, Stuttgart, 1979, pp. 18–21; and Kössler and Ott 1993, p. 177.
13 Kössler and Ott 1993, p. 187.
14 ADI(K) Report No.249/1944.
15 *U-boat.net* [website], <www.uboat.net>, accessed November 2016; and Blair 1999, p. 497.
16 UK National Archives, HW 13/38: Zip No.1077, 10.2.44.
17 UK National Archives, HW 13/38: Zip No.1081, 14.2.44.
18 Schmidt 1990, Anlage 5, 'Herbert Littek, Feindflug: Suchen eines Geleitzuges u. Fühlungshalter' pp. 114–16.
19 Smith and Creek 2008, pp. 121–23; Bollinger 2010, p. 117; and Poolman 1972, p. 116.
20 UK National Archives, HW 13/38: Zip No.1081, 14.2.44.
21 UK National Archives, HW 13/38: Zip No.1083, 16.2.44.
22 Nagel, *Flugbuch*, 15.2.44.
23 Roskill 2004, Vol. III, p. 253.

24   UK National Archives, HW 13/38: Zip No.1084, 17.2.44.

25   Poolman 1972, p. 116.

26   Kington and Selinger 2006, p. 175.

27   UK National Archives, HW 13/38: Zip No.1085, 18.2.44.

28   Schmidt 1990, Anlage 6, 'Einsatzbericht des Mj. Augustin – Staffelkpt. 1.FAG5' pp. 117–18.

29   UK National Archives, HW 13/38: Zip No.1085, 18.2.44.

30   Kössler and Ott 1993, pp. 186–87.

31   *A History of HMS Biter* [website], <www.royalnavyresearcharchive.org.uk/ESCORT/BITER.htm>, accessed November 2016.

32   Information from Thomas, Andrew, *'Fatal Encounter' – 16 February 1944*, private draft.

33   UK National Archives, ADM 1/29518.

34   UK National Archives, HW 13/38: Zip No.1085, 18.2.44.

35   UK National Archives, ADM 1/29518.

36   Schmidt 1990, p. 20.

37   UK National Archives, AIR 27/1444.

38   UK National Archives, AIR 15/472.

39   UK National Archives, AIR 27/1444.

40   Air Ministry News Service, News Bulletin No.13, 28.2.44, and page from S/L Wright's logbook, both available at *Ju-290s shot down off Northern Ireland Feb. 1944* [website], <www.ww2talk.com/index.php?threads/ju-290s-shot-down-off-northern-ireland-feb-1944.14512/>, accessed November 2016.

41   UK National Archives, HW 13/38: Zip No.1085, 18.2.44.

42   Schmidt 1990, p. 20.

43   *Ibid.*

44   *Ibid.*, Anlage 6, 'Einsatzbericht des Mj. Augustin – Staffelkpt. 1.FAG5', pp. 117–18.

45   Nagel, *Flugbuch*, 16.2.44.

46   UK National Archives, HW 13/38: Zip No.1085, 18.2.44.

47   Schmidt 1990, Anlage 6, 'Einsatzbericht des Mj. Augustin – Staffelkpt. 1.FAG5', pp. 117–18.

48   *Convoy Web* [website], <www.convoyweb.org.uk>, accessed November 2016; and *Convoy ON 224* [website], <www.warsailors.com/convoys/on224.html>, accessed November 2016. See also Roskill 2004, Vol. III, Map 17.

49   UK National Archives, HW 13/38: Zip No.1086, 19.2.44.

50   *Ibid.*,

51   Hessler 1989, Vol. III, p. 44.

52   Blair 1999, p. 500.

53   Knirim, Konrad, '*Navigationsuhren für die deutsche Luftwaffe: Luft-Navigation im Zweiten Weltkrieg – Fern-Aufklärung im Atlantik: Ein Erfahrungsbericht von Hellmut Nagel*', *Klassik Uhren*, May 2004.

54   ADI(K) Report No. 249/1944.

55   Nagel, H., 'Astronomical navigation with precision watch and octant on a Ju 290 over the Atlantic Ocean', *Horological Journal*, January 2007, available at *Navigational timepieces of the Luftwaffe* [website], <www.knirim.de/rlmbhi.pdf>, accessed November 2016.

56   Roskill 2004, Vol. III, p. 252.

57   UK National Archives, AIR 50/66 and AIR 27/1046.

58   ADI(K) Report No. 249/1944.

59   Schmidt 1990, p. 20; and Kössler and Ott 1993, p. 244.

60   Blair 1999, pp. 500–01 and Hessler 1989, Vol. III, p. 56.

61   Hessler 1989, Vol. III, pp. 44–45.

62   Hessler 1989, Vol. III, p. 45; and *FdU/BdU* War Diary, 16–29 February 1944.

63   Schmidt 1990, p. 19.

64   *Ibid.*, p. 20.

65   *Ibid.*, p. 19.

66   Nagel, *Flugbuch*, 14.2.44.

67   Roskill 2004, Vol. III, p. 254.

68   Schmidt 1990, p. 23.

69   *Ibid.*, p. 22.

70   *Ibid.*, p. 23.

71   *Ibid.*

72   Neitzel 1995, p. 215, n. 240.

CHAPTER TEN

1   UK National Archives, HW 13/38: CX/MSS/OPD 1107, 11.3.44. and others.

2   UK National Archives, HW 13/38: CX/MSS/OPD 1102, 6.3.44 and CX/MSS/OPD 1120, 24.3.44.

3   UK National Archives, HW 13/39.

4   Freeman 1981, p. 194.

5   UK National Archives, HW 13/25 (via Thompson).

6   Schmidt 1990, p. 23.

7   Neitzel 1995, p. 215, n. 240.

8   UK National Archives, HW 13/25 (via Thompson).

9   UK National Archives, AIR 27/153.

10   UK National Archives, AIR 40/555.

11   Roskill 2004, Vol. III, p. 256, 258; and Blair 1999, p. 509.

12   UK National Archives, AIR 40/587.

13 Schmidt 1990, p. 25.

14 *Ibid.*, p. 25.

15 Kössler and Ott 1993, p. 186.

16 See, for example, *Flugzeugbestand der Fernaufklärungsgruppe 5* from Bundesarchiv-Militärarchiv RL2/1702 in Kössler and Ott 1993, p. 240.

17 ADI(K) Report No. 249/1944.

18 See variously Nagel, *Flugbuch*; and UK National Archives, HW 13/39: CX/MSS/OPD 1144, 17.4.44; 1147, 20.4.44 and 1156, 29.4.44.

19 Kössler and Ott 1993, p. 231.

20 Schmidt 1990, p. 26.

21 Schmidt 1990, p. 26; and Kössler and Ott 1993, p. 187.

22 Schmidt 1990, p. 27.

23 *Ibid.*, p. 28.

24 UK National Archives, HW 13/39: CX/MSS/OPD 1176, 19.5.44; 1177, 20.5.44; and 1178, 21.5.44.

25 Nagel, *Flugbuch*, 19.5.44.

26 *SL and SL/MKS Convoy Series* [website], <www.convoyweb.org.uk/sl/index.html>, accessed November 2016.

27 Poolman 1972, p. 141.

28 UK National Archives, HW 13/39: CX/MSS/OPD 1181, 24.5.44.

29 Barringer, E.E., *Alone on a Wide, Wide Sea: The Story of 835 Naval Air Squadron in the Second World War*, Leo Cooper, Barnsley, 1995, p. 98.

30 UK National Archives, HW 20/388.

31 UK National Archives, HW 13/39: CX/MSS/OPD 1182, 25.5.44.

32 UK National Archives, HW 20/388.

33 UK National Archives, HW 13/39: CX/MSS/OPD 1184, 27.5.44; and Barringer 1995, p. 102.

34 *The Story of 'Nicki': Sea-Hurricane IIc NF 672- (7K) of FAA 804 and 835 Squadrons, Royal Navy as seen by one of her pilots* [website], <web.archive.org/web/20030202224021/http:/www.navismagazine.com/demo/nicki/story_of_nicki.htm>, accessed November 2016. Hereafter referred to as *The Story of 'Nicki'.*

35 Kington and Selinger 2006, p. 60.

36 Barringer 1995, p. 97.

37 UK National Archives, HW 13/39: CX/MSS/OPD 1185, 28.5.44.

38 *The Story of 'Nicki'.*

39 Barringer 1995, p. 104.

40 Schmidt 1990, p. 28; and Kössler and Ott 1993, p. 244.

41 Kössler and Ott 1993, p. 187.

42 ADI(K) Report No. 249/1944.

43 Schmidt 1990, p. 29.

44   *Ibid.*, 'Einsatzbericht von Mj. J. Augustin, Staffelkapitän', *1./FAG 5* p. 125.

45   ADI(K) Reports Nos. 245/1944 and 249/1944.

46   ADI(K) Report No. 249/1944.

47   Barringer 1995, p. 104.

48   ADI(K) Report No. 245/1944.

49   Schmidt 1990, 'Einsatzbericht von Mj. J. Augustin, Staffelkapitän', *1./FAG 5*
      p. 125.

50   Barringer 1995, p. 105.

51   ADI(K) Report No. 245/1944.

52   Barringer 1995, p. 105.

53   UK National Archives, ADM 1/29782.

54   ADI(K) Report No. 249/1944.

55   Information via Juan Carlos Salgado Rodríguez.

56   UK National Archives, AIR 20/7708.

57   Schmidt 1990, p. 31.

58   *Ibid.*

59   *Ibid.*

CHAPTER ELEVEN

1   UK National Archives, HW 20/388.

2   Schmidt 1990, p. 32.

3   Nagel, *Flugbuch.*

4   UK National Archives, HW 13/39: CSS/MX/OPD 1194 6.6.44 and UK National
      Archives, HW 20/388.

5   UK National Archives, HW 13/39: CSS/MX/OPD 1195 7.6.44.

6   Kössler and Ott 1993, p. 187.

7   Schmidt 1990, p. 33.

8   UK National Archives, HW 13/39, 23.6.44.

9   Kössler and Ott 1993, p. 189; and Kington and Selinger 2006, p. 175.

10   Krause, Tilo and Fog Jensen, Jens, 'The Weather War: The German Operation
      '*Bassgeiger*' on Shannon Island 1943/44', Conference Paper from *Report from
      Workshop 2 at the National Museum, Copenhagen, 1 November 2011,*
      Nationalmuseet, 2012, p. 48.

11   *Ibid.*

12   Kington and Selinger 2006, p. 172.

13   Kössler and Ott 1993, p. 190.

14   Gilbert, Martin, *The Second World War*, Weidenfeld & Nicolson, London, 1989.

15   Schmidt 1990, p. 36.

16   *Ibid.*, pp. 34–37.

17   Kössler and Ott 1993, p. 244.

18 Schmidt 1990, pp. 37–38.

19 *Ibid.*, p. 39.

20 Nagel, *Flugbuch.*

21 Bennett and Bennett 2004, p. 178.

22 Schmidt 1990, p. 41.

23 UK National Archives, HW 13/39: CSS/MX/OPD 1222 4.7.44 and HW 28/388.

24 UK National Archives, HW 13/39.

25 *OKL, Der Chef des Luftwaffenführungsstabes*, Ia Nr. 4532/44, 9.7.44.

26 Schmidt 1990, p. 42.

27 *Ibid.*, p. 42.

28 Kington and Selinger 2006, p. 62.

29 *Ibid.*, p. 175, and see UK National Archives, HW 13/40: CSS/MX/OPD 1254 5.8.44.

30 Kington and Selinger 2006, p. 175.

31 UK National Archives, HW 28/388.

32 Schmidt 1990, Anlage 5, 'Herbert Littek, Feindflug: Suchen eines Geleitzuges u. Fühlungshalter', pp. 114–16.

33 Kington and Selinger 2006, p. 177.

34 UK National Archives, HW 13/40: CSS/MX/OPD 1258 9.8.44 and HW 20/388.

35 Schmidt 1990, p. 46.

36 *Ibid.*, pp. 46–47.

37 *Ibid.*

38 Forsyth, Robert and Creek, Eddie J., *Messerschmitt Me 264 Amerika Bomber: The Luftwaffe's Lost Transatlantic Bomber*, Classic Publications, Hersham, 2006, p. 114.

39 Kington and Selinger 2006, p. 177.

40 Nagel, *Flugbuch.*

41 Kössler and Ott 1993, p. 193.

42 Ultra, HP 156, 21.8.44.

43 Cited in Gould 2005, p. 11.

CHAPTER THIRTEEN

1 UK National Archives, HW 13/40: CSS/MX/OPD 1267 18.8.44.

2 Kössler and Ott 1993, p. 194.

3 Hellmut Hetz, private recollection to J. Richard Smith, December 1982.

4 Schmidt 1990, p. 54.

5 Nagel, *Flugbuch.*

6 Schmidt 1990, p. 54.

7 Hellmut Hetz, private recollection to J. Richard Smith, December 1982.

8 Schmidt 1990, p. 55. The rest of the chapter is based mainly on Oskar Schmidt's account of the journey through France.

CHAPTER FOURTEEN

1   Schmidt 1990, p. 71.

2   ADI(K) Report No. 398/1945; and Gellermann, Günther W., *Moskau ruft Heeresgruppe Mitte – Was nicht im Wehrmachtbericht stand – Die Einsätze des geheimen Kampfgeschwaders 200 im Zweiten Weltkrieg*, Bernard & Graefe Verlag, Koblenz, 1988, p. 33, 214.

3   ADI(K) Report No. 398/1945; and Gellermann 1988, p. 34.

4   Ultra XL 2423, 17.7.44 (via Wadman).

5   Schmidt 1990, Anlage 14, 'Zusammenarbeit der FAG.5 mit dem KG.200', pp. 136–39; and Kössler and Ott 1993, p. 209.

6   Stapfer, Hans-Heiri, *Strangers in a Strange Land*, Squadron/Signal Publications, Carrollton, 1988, p. 60.

7   Kössler and Ott 1993, p. 209.

8   Gellermann 1988, pp. 75–76.

9   Kössler and Ott 1993, p. 209.

10   Gellermann 1988, p. 76.

11   Lucas, James, *Kommando: German Special Forces of World War Two*, Arms and Armour Press, London, 1985, p. 194.

12   Kahn, David, *Hitler's Spies: German Military Intelligence in World War II*, Hodder and Stoughton, London, 1978, p. 286.

13   Gellermann 1988, p. 78.

14   *Ibid.*, p. 77.

15   Kössler and Ott 1993, p. 210.

16   Schmidt 1990, Anlage 12, 'Bericht von Hptm. Georg Eckl über das von ihm geführte Kommando (FAG 5) in Offingen und Einsatz im Rahmen des KG 200'.

17   Correspondence between J.R. Smith and Erich Sommer, 1997 (via Smith).

18   Messerschmitt A.G., Augsburg: *Erprobungsbericht Nr. 6 17.4.–17.5.44*.

19   UK National Archives, AIR 40/2168.

20   Griehl, '*Das "Bananaenflugzeug"*' [article], 1996.

21   Schmidt 1990, p. 72.

22   *Ibid.*, pp. 74-77.

23   Kössler and Ott 1993, p. 211.

24   Schmidt 1990, p. 127.

25   Kössler and Ott 1993, p. 195.

26   *Oberkommando der Luftwaffe, Chef des Generalstabes* (Air Force High Command, Chief of the General staff) Gen.Qu.2.Abt. (IIB) Az.11b16 Nr.14 549/44 g.Kdos. dated 27 November 1944.

27   *Aktenvermark* (memo) from the Chef TLR to Major Fischer, *Kommandeur* of FAG 5, dated 14 November 1944.

28   Chef TLR document 46782/44 g.kdos. (Transcript of a conference with the Reichsmarschall on 12 December 1944), dated 28 December 1944.

29   *General der Aufklärungsflieger Nr.338/45 geh, Abgrenzung der Aufgaben FAG 5 und Sonderkommando Nebel* (General of the Reconnaissance Nr.338/45 geh: Demarcation of the boundaries between FAG 5 and *Sonderkommando* Nebel), dated 16 January 1945.

30   *General der Aufklärungsflieger, Nr.338/45*, 16.1.45.

31   Smith, J. Richard and Creek, Eddie J., *Dornier Do 335 Pfeil: The Luftwaffe's Fastest Piston-Engine Fighter*, Classic Publications, Hersham, 2006, p. 98.

32   *OKL, Chef der TLR Nr. 46442/44, 4. Dez. 1944.*

33   *General der Aufklärungsflieger, Nr.338/45*, 16.1.45.

34   Schmidt 1990, p. 77.

35   War diary of the *TLR*, covering the period 8–14 January 1945.

36   *Ibid.*, covering the period 22–28 January 1945.

37   *Ibid.*, covering the period 16 March to 4 April 1945.

38   *Lw. Organisationsstab Genst.Gen. 2 Abt.*, 12.2.45.

39   Gellermann 1988, pp. 99–100; and Kössler and Ott 1993, p. 211.

40   Schmidt 1990, p. 78.

41   *Ibid.*

CHAPTER FIFTEEN

1   Smith, J. Richard and Creek, Eddie J., with Dachner, Hans-Georg, *Arado Ar 234 A*, Classic Publications, Hersham, 2006, p. 74.

2   Smith, J. Richard and and Creek, Eddie J., *Arado 234 Blitz*, Monogram Aviation Publications, Sturbridge, 1992, pp. 210–11.

3   Schmidt 1990, p. 80.

4   Hellmut Hetz, private recollection to J. Richard Smith, December 1982.

5   Schmidt 1990, p. 79.

6   *Ibid.*, p. 82.

7   *Ibid.*, p. 84.

8   *Fernaufklärungsgruppe 1* [website], <www.ww2.dk/air/recon/fagr1.htm>, accessed November 2016; see also Dierich, Wolfgang, *Die Verbände der Luftwaffe 1935– 1945*, Verlag Heinz Nickel, Zweibrücken, 1993; Rosch, Barry, *Luftwaffe Codes, Markings & Units 1939–1945*, Schiffer Publishing, Atglen, 1995; and Wadman *et al.* 1997.

9   Schmidt 1990, Anlage 15, 'Bericht Major Josef Augustin über Vorkommando der 1.FAG1 (vorher 1.FAG5) in Norwegen und anschliessender Gefangenschaft', p. 140.

10   *Ibid.*, p. 85.

11   UK National Archives, AIR 20/7708.

12 Schmidt 1990, p. 86.

13 *Ibid.*, Anlage 15, 'Bericht Major Josef Augustin über Vorkommando der 1.FAG1 (vorher 1.FAG5) in Norwegen und anschliessender Gefangenschaft', p. 140.

14 Hellmut Hetz, private recollection to J. Richard Smith, December 1982; and Hetz, *Flugbuch*, extracts 1944–1945.

15 UK National Archives, AIR 20/7708 and *OKL KTB*, 26.2.45.

16 *The Arado Ar 234 in Norway and Denmark: 1945* [website], <www.ghostbombers.com/recon/234/Denmark/norway4.html>, accessed November 2016. Hereafter referred to as *The Arado Ar 234 in Norway and Denmark: 1945*.

17 *Ibid.*

18 Blair 1999, pp. 666–68.

19 *The Arado Ar 234 in Norway and Denmark: 1945*.

20 Hellmut Hetz, private recollection to J. Richard Smith, December 1982.

21 *The Arado Ar 234 in Norway and Denmark: 1945*; and *Luftwaffenkommando West* Morning & Evening Situation Reports, Nr.0927/45, 24 March 1945 (AHB.6 translation).

22 Hessler 1989, p. 97.

23 Ruud, Frithjof, *Arado 234 B-2*, Profiles in Norway No. 5, Andebu, 2005, p. 7.

24 Hellmut Hetz, private recollection to J. Richard Smith, December 1982; and Hetz, *Flugbuch*.

25 UK National Archives, AIR 20/7708.

26 *OKL Fü.St.Nr.040/45*, 21.2.45. See also UK National Archives, DEFE5/BT8507, 27.3.45.

27 Schmidt 1990, p. 87.

28 *Studie: Kampf gegen die russische Rüstungsindustrie,* Ia.Nr.8865/43, 9 November 1943 (Intelligence Div. W.D.G.S., War Dept. Washington D.C., Special Document Section Report Number 125, 21 February 1947: Plan for an Attack on the Russian Armament Industry).

29 *OKL.Fü.St.Nr.18436/44*, 22.11.44.

30 *Kr-g.Kdos.Chefs.-m.Anschr.Uberm.*, 6.11.44 (via Kitchens).

31 UK National Archives, AIR 40/2423.

32 *Chef der Generalstabes d.Lw. Nr.10564/45*, 18.1.45 and *Chef der Generalstabes d.Lw. Nr.10552/45*, 23.1.45 (via Kitchens).

33 *OKL, Ia., Nr.10514/44*, 10.1.45.

34 Schmidt 1990, p. 88.

35 Kössler and Ott 1993, p. 197.

36 UK National Archives, DEFE5/BT8507.

37 Kössler and Ott 1993, p. 199.

38 *Ibid.*, p. 245

39 *OKL.Fü.St.Nr.10708/45*, 12.4.45.

40 *OKL.Fü.St.Nr.10709/45*, 12.4.45.

41 UK National Archives, AIR 40/2423.

42 Fleischer, Wolfgang, *German Air-Dropped Weapons to 1945*, Midland Publishing, Hinckley, 2004, pp. 117–18; and UK National Archives, AIR 40/2423.

43 Ultra decrypts KO1289 10.4.45 and KO756 11.4.45 (via Norton).

44 *Das Oberkommando der Luftwaffe Kriegstagbuch (1 Februar–7 April 1945) 6.4.45.* p. 4: NARS Microfilm T-321, Roll 10.

45 Schmidt 1990, Anlage 12, 'Bericht von Hptm. Georg Eckl über das von ihm geführte Kommando (FAG.5) in Offingen und Einsatz in Rahmen KG 200'.

46 *Ibid.*, p. 89.

47 *Ibid.*, p. 90.

48 *Ibid.*, p. 91.

49 *Ibid.*, p. 92.

50 Kössler and Ott 1993, p. 245.

51 Schmidt 1990, Anlage 13, 'Bericht nach den Angaben des Oberfeldwebels Kroll (Fl.-Schütze 1.FAG5) über den Abschuss einer Ju 290 durch wahrscheinlich eigene Flakabwehr'.

52 Kössler and Ott 1993, p. 199.

53 *Ghost Bombers* [website], <www.ghostbombers.com/recon/234/Denmark/norway3. html >, accessed November 2016.

CHAPTER SIXTEEN

1 Schmidt 1990, Anlage 12, 'Bericht von Hptm. Georg Eckl über das von ihm geführte Kommando (FAG.5) in Offingen und Einsatz in Rahmen KG 200'.

2 The material from this chapter is based on information contained in Schmidt's account unless otherwise noted.

3 Ruud 2005, p. 8.

4 *Ibid.*, pp. 8–15.

5 Butler, Phil, *War Prizes: An Illustrated Survey of German, Italian and Japanese Aircraft brought to Allied Countries During and After the Second World War*, Midland Counties Publications, Leicester, 1994, p. 109.

6 Ruud 2005, p. 17.

7 *Ibid.*

8 Butler 1994, p. 77.

9 *Ibid.*, p. 89.

BIBLIOGRAPHY
AND SOURCES

UNPUBLISHED AND MISCELLANEOUS SOURCES

Felkin, W/Cdr. S.D., ADI(K) Report No. 245/1944: *Ju 290 9V+GK, 26th May 1944*, 4 June 1944

—, ADI(K) Report No. 249/1944: *Atlantic Reconnaissance by the Ju.290s of F.A.G.5. Further Report on a Ju.290, the 9V+GK, of 1./F.A.G.5, shot down in the Atlantic on the evening of 26th May 1944*

—, ADI(K) Report No. 377/1945: *The Life and Work of Oberst Petersen*, 22 August 1945

—, ADI(K) Report No. 398/1945: *A Short History of KG 200*, 9 October 1945

'Fliegerführer Atlantik': (G 351154/EFT/11/52/60): Allied translation of a 1943 German document (via Goss)

Gould, Winston A., *Luftwaffe Maritime Operations in World War II: Thought, Organization and Technology*, Air Command and Staff College, Air University, Maxwell AFB, 2005

Krause, Tilo and Fog Jensen, Jens, 'The Weather War: The German Operation *'Bassgeiger'* on Shannon Island 1943/44', Conference Paper from *Report from Workshop 2 at the National Museum, Copenhagen, 1 November 2011*, Nationalmuseet, 2012, pp. 46–54

Luftflottenkommando 3, Nr.8493/43 Einzelmeldung Nr.1 vom 21 November 1943 / Nr.8500/43 Tagesergebnis vom 20 November 1943 (via Goss)

Nagel, Hellmut, *Flugbuch September 1938–Juli 1959* (via Knirim)

Office of Naval Intelligence, Washington D.C., 1949, *War Diary, German Naval Staff Operations Division, Part A*: Vols. 50–53, October 1943–January 1944 (translation of *Kriegstagebuch der Seekriegsleitung*) – see also Websites section below

OKL Documents:
    Der Chef des Luftwaffenführungsstabes, Ia Nr. 4532/44, 9.7.44
    Chef der TLR Nr.46442/44, 4.Dez.44

Gen der Aufklärungsflieger, Nr.338/45, 16.1.45

Lw. Organisationsstab Genst.Gen. 2 Abt., 12.2.45

OKL Fü.St.Nr.040/45, 21.2.45

OKL.Fü.St.Nr.18436/44, 22.11.44

Chef der Generalstabes d.Lw. Nr. 10564/45, 18.1.45 and Chef der Generalstabes d.Lw. Nr. 10552/45, 23.1.45

OKL, Ia., Nr.10514/44, 10.1.45

OKL.Fü.St.Nr.10708 & 709/45, 12.4.45

Schmidt, Oskar H., *Fernaufklärungsgruppe 5 Atlantik: Eine Aufzeichnung von Oskar H. Schmidt*, private publication/unpublished, Melle, May 1990

Thomas, Andrew, *'Fatal Encounter' – 16 February 1944*, private draft

US War Department, *Directory of German Radar Equipment*, TM E 11-219, 20 April 1945

Bundesarchiv-Militärarchiv, Freiburg im Breisgau:

RL10/366 Fischer, Hermann, *Erfahrungen aus dem Einsatz der F.A.G.5 vom 15.11.–15.12.43, Anlage zu 214/43*, 15.12.43

UK National Archives, Kew:

ADM 1/29518: *HMS Biter – Attacks on Enemy Aircraft, February 1944*

ADM 1/29782: *835 Squadron FAA attached to HMS Nairana: Defence of Convoy against enemy air attacks 26th May 1944*

AIR 15/472: *Coastal Command Review*, Vol. III, *January–December 1944*

AIR 20/7700: *The Role of the German Air Force in the Battle of the Atlantic*, January 1944

AIR 20/7701: *The Importance of Long Range Aerial Reconnaissance in Submarine Warfare*, 8.Abt. 5.4.44, AHB.6 Translation No.VII/35, 20.7.74

AIR 20/7705: *The Operational Use of the Luftwaffe in the War at Sea*, Translation No. VII/102, AHB.6 October 1950 (originally 8.Abt., January 1944)

AIR 20/7708: AHB 6 Translation No. VII/124 – *Extract from report of the Goering Conference on Aircraft Production Programme*, 23 May 1944

The Western Front 1–14 February 1945 and 15–28 February 1945: Daily Situation Reports issued by OKL Operations Staff Ia (Translation of *Das Oberkommando der Luftwaffe Kriegstagbuch (1 Februar–7 April 1945)* 15.2.45. p. 4: NARS Microfilm T-321, Roll 10)

AIR 22/80: *Atlantic Reconnaissance by the Ju 290's of F.A.G.5.*, Air Ministry: Periodical Returns, Intelligence Summaries and Bulletins, Weekly Intelligence Summaries 239–265, 1 April–30 September 1944

AIR 27/153: No 10 Squadron RAAF: Operations Record Book, January 1944–June 1945

AIR 27/1046: No. 157 Squadron, Operations Record Book, February 1944

AIR 27/1444: No. 235 Squadron, Operations Record Book, February 1944

AIR 40/555: Air Intelligence 3 (USA) US VIII Bomber Command: Operation 228: Brunswick Achmer and Diepholz aerodromes and Luftwaffe installations, 21 February 1944

AIR 40/587: Air Intelligence 3 (USA) US VIII Bomber Command: Operation 282: Luftwaffe aerodromes and aircraft factory Western and North-Western France, 27 March 1944

AIR 40/2168: AI2 (g) Reports 2375–3027: *German Aircraft – New and Projected Types*

AIR 40/2423: ADI(K) Report No. 358/1945 *Special GAF Operations planned for the Eastern Front*, 25 July 1945

AIR 50/66: Combat Reports, No. 157 Squadron

AIR 51/216: *Mediterranean Allied Air Forces, Intelligence Section, Target Analysis, Mont de Marsan, Op.No.Z 731, AM No. S 5681*, 12 September 1943

AIR 51/223: *Germany, Austria and Czechoslovakia: Achmer/Bramsche*, MAAF Intelligence Section, Target Files, December 1944

HW 13/25: *GAF Recce and bombing operations, Mar 19 1944–Mar 28 1945*

HW 13/37: *German Naval Air Activity*, Vol. XI: *Zip 977–1038, 1.10.43–31.12.43* (reports on GAF Sea Reconnaissance and Offensive Activity [Home Area and Atlantic])

HW 13/38: Vol. XII: *Zip 1039–1129, 1.1.44–31.3.44*

HW 13/39: Vol. XIII: *Zip 1130–1250, 1.4.44–31.7.44*

HW 13/40: Vol. XIV: *Zip 1251–1312, 1.8.44–1.10.44*

HW 13/69: *Reports on GAF Sea Reconnaissance and offensive operations, 21.2.44–6.6.44*

HW 20/388: *Signals containing information about GAF anti-invasion reconnaissance, issued by Hut 3 to DDI3, Air Ministry, and Allied Commands, Western Front, 23.5.44–8.3.45*

PUBLISHED SECONDARY SOURCES

Barringer, E.E., *Alone on a Wide, Wide Sea: The Story of 835 Naval Air Squadron in the Second World War*, Leo Cooper, Barnsley, 1995

Bennett, G.H. and Bennett, R., *Hitler's Admirals*, Naval Institute Press, Annapolis, 2004

Blair, Clay, *Hitler's U-Boat War: The Hunted, 1942–1945*, Weidenfeld & Nicolson, London, 1999

Bollinger, Martin J., *Warriors and Wizards: The Development and Defeat of Radio-Controlled Glide-Bombs of the Third Reich*, Naval Institute Press, Annapolis, 2010

Budrass, Lutz, *Flugzeugindustrie und Luftrüstung in Deutschland 1918–1945*, Droste Verlag, Düsseldorf, 1998

Butler, Phil, *War Prizes: An Illustrated Survey of German, Italian and Japanese Aircraft brought to Allied Countries During and After the Second World War*, Midland Counties Publications, Leicester, 1994

Carlsen, Sven and Meyer, Michael, *Die Flugzeugführer-Ausbildung der Deutschen Luftwaffe 1935–1945*, Volume II: *Fliegerwaffenschulen und Ergänzungsgruppen*, VDM Heinz Nickel Verlag, Zweibrücken, 2000

Churchill, Winston S., *The Second World War*, Volume V: *Closing the Ring*, Cassell & Co., London, 1952

Citino, Robert M., *Death of the Wehrmacht: The German Campaigns of 1942*, University Press of Kansas, Lawrence, 2007

Claasen, Adam R.A., *Hitler's Northern War: The Luftwaffe's Ill-Fated Campaign, 1940–1945*, University Press of Kansas, Lawrence, 2001

Filley, Brian, *Junkers Ju 88 in Action, Part 1*, Squadron/Signal Publications, Carrolton, 1988

Fleischer, Wolfgang, *German Air-Dropped Weapons to 1945*, Midland Publishing, Hinckley, 2004

Forsyth, Robert and Creek, Eddie J., *Messerschmitt Me 264 Amerika Bomber: The Luftwaffe's Lost Transatlantic Bomber*, Classic Publications, Hersham, 2006

——, *Junkers Ju 52: A History, 1930–1945*, Classic Publications, Manchester, 2014

Freeman, Roger, *Mighty Eighth War Diary*, Jane's, London, 1981

Gannon, Michael, *Black May: The Epic Story of the Allies' Defeat of the German U-boats in May 1943*, Harper Collins, New York, 1998

Gellermann, Günther W., *Moskau ruft Heeresgruppe Mitte – Was nicht im Wehrmachtbericht stand – Die Einsätze des geheimen Kampfgeschwaders 200 in Zweiten Weltkrieg*, Bernard & Graefe Verlag, Koblenz, 1988

Gilbert, Martin, *The Second World War*, Weidenfeld & Nicolson, London, 1989

Goss, Chris, *Bloody Biscay: The History of V.Gruppe/Kampfgeschwader 40*, Crecy Publishing, 1997

——, *Sea Eagles,* Vol. II: *Luftwaffe Anti-Shipping Units 1942–45*, Classic Publications, Hersham, 2006

Green, William and Swanborough, Gordon, *RAF Bombers Part 2*, Jane's Publishing Co., London, 1981

Griehl, Manfred, *Luftwaffe over America: The Secret Plans to Bomb the United States in World War II*, Greenhill Books, 2005

Heiber, Helmut and Glantz, David, (Eds.), *Hitler and his Generals: Military Conferences 1942–1945*, Greenhill Books, London 2002

Hessler, Günter, *The U-Boat War in the Atlantic 1939–1945*, 3 Vols, Her Majesty's Stationery Office, London, 1989

Hinsley, F.H., Thomas, E.S., Ransom, C.F.G. and Knight, R.C., *British Intelligence in the Second World War*, Vol. III, Part 1, HMSO, London, 1984

Hitchcock, Thomas H., *Junkers 290* (Monogram Close-Up 3), Monogram Aviation Publications, Boylston, 1975

Homze, Edward L., *Arming the Luftwaffe*, University of Nebraska Press, Lincoln, 1996

Hooton, E.R., *Eagle in Flames: The Fall of the Luftwaffe*, Arms and Armour Press, London, 1997

Kahn, David, *Hitler's Spies: German Military Intelligence in World War II*, Hodder and Stoughton, London, 1978

Kay, Antony L., *Junkers Aircraft & Engines 1913–1945*, Putnam Aeronautical Books, London, 2004

Kington, John A. and Selinger, Franz, *Wekusta: Luftwaffe Meteorological Reconnaissance Units and Operations 1938–1945*, Flight Recorder Publications, Ottringham, 2006

Kössler, Karl and Ott, Günther, *Die großen Dessauer: Junkers Ju 89, Ju 90, Ju 290, Ju 390 – Die Geschichte einer Flugzeugfamilie*, Aviatic Verlag, Planegg, 1993

Lerche, Hans-Werner, *Luftwaffe Test Pilot: Flying captured Allied Aircraft of World War 2*, Jane's, London, 1980

Lucas, James, *Kommando: German Special Forces of World War Two*, Arms and Armour Press, London, 1985

Mahncke, Alfred, *For Kaiser and Hitler: From Military Aviator to High Command: The Memoirs of Luftwaffe General Alfred Mahncke*, Tattered Flag Press, Pulborough, 2010

Mallmann Showell, Jak P., *Fuehrer Conferences on Naval Affairs 1939–1945*, Greenhill Books, London, 1990

——, *Dönitz, U-boats, Convoys: The British Version of His Memoirs from the Admiralty's Secret Anti-Submarine Reports*, Frontline Books, Barnsley, 2013

Morzik, Generalmajor a.D. Fritz, *German Air Force Airlift Operations*, USAF Historical Division, Arno Press, New York, 1961

Neitzel, Sönke, *Der Einsatz der deutschen Luftwaffe über dem Atlantik und der Nordsee 1939–1945*, Bernard & Graefe Verlag, Bonn, 1995

Padfield, Peter, *Dönitz: The Last Führer*, Harper & Row, New York, 1984

Pegg, Martin, *Transporter*, Vol. I: *Luftwaffe Transport Units 1939–1943*, Classic Publications, Hersham, 2006

——, *Transporter*, Vol. II: *Luftwaffe Transport Units 1943–1945*, Classic Publications, Hersham, 2006

Pocock, Rowland F., *German Guided Missiles*, Ian Allan, London, 1967

Poolman, Kenneth, *Escort Carrier 1941–1945*, Ian Allan, Shepperton, 1972

——, *Focke-Wulf Condor: Scourge of the Atlantic*, Macdonald and Janes, London, 1978

Roskill, Captain S.W., *The War at Sea 1939–1945*, Vol. II: *The Period of Balance*, The Naval & Military Press Ltd, Uckfield, 2004

——, *The War at Sea 1939–1945*, Vol. III: *The Offensive Part I: 1st June 1943–31st May 1944*, The Naval & Military Press Ltd, Uckfield, 2004

Ruud, Frithjof, *Arado 234 B-2*, Profiles in Norway No. 5, Andebu, 2005

Sharp, C. Martin and Bowyer, Michael J.F., *Mosquito*, Faber, London, 1971

Smith, J. Richard and Creek, Eddie J., *Arado 234 Blitz*, Monogram Aviation Publications, Sturbridge, 1992

——, *Dornier Do 335 Pfeil: The Luftwaffe's Fastest Piston-Engine Fighter*, Classic Publications, Hersham, 2006

——, *Heinkel He 177 Greif: Heinkel's Strategic Bomber*, Classic Publications, Hersham, 2008

Smith, J. Richard and Creek, Eddie J., with Dachner, Hans-Georg, *Arado Ar 234 A*, Classic Publications, Hersham, 2006

Smith, J. Richard, Creek, Eddie J., and Petrick, Peter, *On Special Missions: The Luftwaffe's Research and Experimental Squadrons 1923–1945*, Classic Publications, Hersham, 2003

Stapfer, Hans-Heiri, *Strangers in a Strange Land*, Squadron/Signal Publications, Carrollton, 1988

Terraine, John, *Business in Great Waters: The U-Boat Wars 1916–1945*, Leo Cooper, London, 1989

Thomas, Andrew, ACE 57: *Hurricane Aces 1941–45*, Osprey Publishing, Oxford, 2003

Thompson, Adam, with Wadman, David, *Seeflieger: Luftwaffe Maritime Aircraft and Units 1935–1945*, Classic Publications, Hersham, 2009

Trenkle, Fritz, *Die deutschen Funk-Navigations- und Funk-Führungsverfahren bis 1945*, Motorbuch Verlag, Stuttgart, 1979

Vajda, Ferenc A. and Dancey, Peter, *German Aircraft Industry and Production 1933–1945*, Airlife, Shrewsbury, 1998

Wadman, David, *Aufklärer*, Vol. I: *Luftwaffe Reconnaissance Aircraft and Units 1935–1941*, Classic Publications, Hersham, 2007

——, *Aufklärer*, Vol. II: *Luftwaffe Reconnaissance Aircraft and Units 1942–1945*, Classic Publications, Hersham, 2007

Wadman, David, Bradley, John and Ketley, Barry, *Aufklärer: Luftwaffe Reconnaissance Aircraft & Units 1935–1945*, Hikoki Publications, Aldershot, 1997

Wagner, Wolfgang, *Hugo Junkers – Pionier der Luftfahrt – seine Flugzeuge*, Bernard & Graefe, Bonn, 1996

Zindel, Ernst, *Die Geschichte und Entwicklung des Junkers-Flugzeugbaus von 1910 bis 1945 und bis zum endgültigen Ende 1970*, Deutsche Gesellschaft für Luft- und Raumfahrt, Köln, 1979

ARTICLES

Goss, Chris, 'Wrong Place, Wrong Time' (article draft kindly provided by Chris Goss)

Griehl, Manfred, '*Das "Bananaenflugzeug" – Die Entwicklungsgeschichte der Me 264 – Teil I*', *Flugzeug*, February 1996

Knirim, Konrad, '*Navigationsuhren für die deutsche Luftwaffe: Luft-Navigation im Zweiten Weltkrieg – Fern-Aufklärung im Atlantik: Ein Erfahrungsbericht von Hellmut Nagel*', *Klassik Uhren*, May 2004

Nagel, H., 'Astronomical navigation with precision watch and octant on a Ju 290 over the Atlantic Ocean', *Horological Journal*, January 2007, available at *Navigational timepieces of the Luftwaffe* [website], <www.knirim.de/rlmbhi.pdf>, accessed November 2016

Neitzel, Sönke, 'Kriegsmarine and Luftwaffe Co-operation in the War against Britain, 1939–1945', *War in History*, Vol. 10, Number 4, October 2003

Overy, R.J., 'From "Uralbomber" to "Amerikabomber": the Luftwaffe and Strategic Bombing', *The Journal of Strategic Studies*, 1(2), September 1978

WEBSITES

835 Squadron, <www.fleetairarmarchive.net/squadrons/835.html>, accessed November 2016

A History of HMS Biter, <www.royalnavyresearcharchive.org.uk/ESCORT/BITER.htm>, accessed November 2016

Chronik des Seekrieges, 1939–1945, by Prof. Dr. Jürgen Rohwer and Gerhard Hümmelchen, Württembergische Landesbibliothek, Stuttgart 2007 <www.wlb-stuttgart.de/seekrieg/chronik.htm>, accessed November 2016

BIBLIOGRAPHY AND SOURCES

Clydebuilt Wartime Convoys, <www.clydesite.co.uk/clydebuilt/convoys/html>, site currently unavailable, November 2016

Codenames: Operations of World War 2, <codenames.info>, accessed November 2016

Convoy Web, <www.convoyweb.org.uk>, accessed November 2016

Das Seewesen in der deutschen Luftwaffe 1933–1945, <luftwaffe-zur-see.de>, accessed November 2016

Flugzeugbestand und Bewegungsmeldungen 3.(F)/Aufklärungsgruppe 123, <www.ww2.dk/oob/bestand/aufkl/b3ag123.html>, accessed November 2016

Flugzeugbestand und Bewegungsmeldungen 1./SAGr.129, <www.ww2.dk/oob/bestand/see/b1kfl129.html>, accessed November 2016

Flugzeugbestand und Bewegungsmeldungen I./ZG1, <www.ww2.dk/oob/bestand/zerst/bizg1.html>, accessed November 2016

Flugzeugbestand und Bewegungsmeldungen II./KG 40, <www.ww2.dk/oob/bestand/kampf/biikg40.html>, accessed November 2016

Ghost Bombers, <www.ghostbombers.com/recon/234/Denmark/norway3.html >, accessed November 2016

HMS Nairana, <www.fleetairarmarchive.net/Ships/NAIRANA.html>, accessed November 2016

Info for LUMA, <www.gyges.dk/LUMA%20Guide%20v2007%2005.pdf>, accessed December 2016

Ju-290s shot down off Northern Ireland Feb. 1944, <www.ww2talk.com/index.php?threads/ju-290s-shot-down-off-northern-ireland-feb-1944.14512/>, accessed November 2016

Lexikon der Wehrmacht, <www.lexikon-der-wehrmacht.de>, accessed November 2016

Luftwaffe Airfields 1935–1945 by Henry L. deZeng IV, <www.ww2.dk/lwairfields.html>, accessed November 2016

Luftwaffe Officer Career Summaries by Henry L. deZeng IV and Douglas G. Stankey, <www.ww2.dk/lwoffz.html>, accessed 1 April 2015

Military Timepieces/Militäruhren, <www.knirim.de>, accessed November 2016

The Arado Ar 234 in Norway and Denmark: 1945, <www.ghostbombers.com/recon/234/Denmark/norway4.html>, accessed November 2016

The Hugo Junkers Homepage, <hugojunkers.pytalhost.com/ju_home.htm>, accessed November 2016

The Luftwaffe, 1933–45, <www.ww2.dk>, accessed November 2016

The Luftwaffe Map Reference System (Gradnetzmeldeverfahren) by Andreas Brekken, <www.stormbirds.com/eagles/research/gradnetz/gradnetz.html>, accessed December 2016

The Story of 'Nicki': Sea-Hurricane IIc NF 672- (7K) of FAA 804 and 835 Squadrons, Royal Navy as seen by one of her pilots, <web.archive.org/web/20030202224021/http:/www.navismagazine.com/demo/nicki/story_of_nicki.htm>, accessed November 2016

U-boat Archive, (*Kriegstagebücher [KTB] & Stehender Kriegsbefehl, Des Führers/Befehlshaber der Unterseeboote [FdU/BdU]* – War Diary and War Standing Orders of Commander in Chief, Submarines), <www.uboatarchive.net>, accessed November 2016

U-boat.net, <www.uboat.net>, accessed November 2016

War Diary of the German Naval Staff Operations Division, Part A:

October 1943, Volume 50, available at *Archive.org*, <archive.org/details/wardiarygermann501943germ>, accessed November 2016

November 1943, Volume 51, available at *Archive.org*, <archive.org/details/wardiarygermann511943germ>, accessed November 2016

December 1943, Volume 52, available at *Archive.org*, <archive.org/details/wardiarygermann521943germ>, accessed November 2016

January 1944, Volume 53, available at *Archive.org*, <archive.org/details/wardiarygermann531944germ>, accessed November 2016

Warsailors.com, <www.warsailors.com>, accessed November 2016

INDEX

Note: page numbers in **bold** refer to maps and illustrations.